INTRODUCTION TO SPORT PSYCHOLOGY: TRAINING, COMPETITION AND COPING

Sports and Athletics Preparation, Performance, and Psychology

Additional books in this series can be found on Nova's website under the Series tab.

Additional E-books in this series can be found on Nova's website under the E-books tab.

INTRODUCTION TO SPORT PSYCHOLOGY: TRAINING, COMPETITION AND COPING

ROBERT SCHINKE

EDITOR

Nova Science Publishers, Inc.

New York

LIBRARY OF CONGRESS CATALOGING-IN-PUBLICATION DATA

Introduction to sport psychology : training, competition and coping /
editors, Robert Schinke.
p. cm.
Includes index.
ISBN 978-1-61761-973-1 (hardcover)
1. Sports--Psychological aspects. I. Schinke, Robert, 1966-
GV706.4.I594 2010
796.01--dc22
2010037355

Published by Nova Science Publishers, Inc. † New York

CONTENTS

PREFACE

On behalf of Athletic Insight, the journal that made this book possible, welcome to the "Sport Psychology: Training, Competition and Coping". Following the release of "Contemporary Sport Psychology" (2010), where revised versions of earlier featured materials from Athletic Insight were printed, the present book is built from the most recent contributions to Athletic Insight, accepted in 2009. Within the present compilation you will find an international listing of contributors. Authors have contributed to this compilation from the United States, Canada, Switzerland, Finland, Sweden, Israel, Japan and Australia.

The structure for this book is comprised of four sections. Section one includes three invited papers that are not found in the 2009 installment of Athletic Insight. The first paper is guest authored by Dr. Frank Gardner (Kean University) and Dr. Zella Moore from Manhattan College. Frank is among the premiere applied sport psychologists in professional ice-hockey, having worked with NHL Stanley Cup winning teams. Zella is an elite sport psychologist as well with elite amateur and professional athletes and teams. Frank and Zella have been asked to speak about clinical practice within their submission, and they do so with a paper titled "Challenges and Opportunities in the Assimilation and Delivery of Acceptance-based Behavioral Interventions". Dr. Kerry McGannon presently works at Laurentian University as an exercise and health psychology researcher. Kerry is also in my view, among the research elite among those who employ qualitative methods in sport and exercise. Within her submission, Kerry combines auto-ethnography and creative non-fiction to produce a self-reflexive story about exercise self-identity and embodied running. Jack Watson and his colleagues have written about the ethical concerns that surround internet page use in sport and exercise psychology. Jack is among the most prolific researchers in topic matter pertaining to the intersection of ethics and our field. Thereafter, we follow with sections that reflect the consecutive released Athletic installments from 2009.

Section Two features six submissions found in the Spring 2009 installment. The first contribution is from Mark Aoyagi, Kevin Burke and their colleagues. Their paper is titled "The Associations of Competitive Trait Anxiety andPersonal Control with Burnout in Sport". Next, Anthony A. Volk and Larissa Lagzdins investigate "Bullying and Victimization among Adolescent Girl Athletes". Third, Gregory Wilson and Mary Pritchard examine "The Relationship between Coping Styles and Drinking Behaviors in Teenage Athletes". Fourth, Linda Keeler, Edward Etzel and Lindsey Blom provide an "Initial Examination of a Brief Assessment of Recovery and Stress (BARS)". Fifth, Mark Aoyagi and Richard Cox investigate "The Effects of Scholarship Status on Intrinsic Motivation". To close the section,

Martin Camiré, Penny Werthner, and Pierre Trudel write about "Mission statements in sport and their ethical messages.

Section Three features five submissions found in the Summer 2009 installment. First, Julia Schüler, Sibylle Brunner and Marianne Steiner investigated "Different Effects of Activity and Purpose-related Incentives on Commitment and Well-being in the Domain of Sports". Second, Esa Rovio, Jari Eskola, Daniel Gould and Taru Lintunen authored a paper titled "Linking Theory to Practice – Lessons Learned in Setting Specific Goals in a Junior Ice Hockey Team". Third, Brandonn Harris and Meredith Smith submitted "The Influence of Motivational Climate and Goal Orientation on Burnout: An Exploratory Analysis Among Division I Collegiate Student-Athletes". Fourth, Erwin Apitzsch examined "Coaches' and Elite Team Players' Perception and Experiences of Collective Collapse". Fifth to the installment, Samuel J. Zizzi, Lindsey C. Blom, Jack C. Watson II, V. Paul Downey, John Geer authored a paper titled "Establishing a Hierarchy of Psychological Skills: Coaches', Athletic Trainers', and Psychologists' Uses and Perceptions of Psychological Skills Training".

Section Four features The Autumn/Winter releases denoted as Installment Three. Featured within the section is a special edition culturally safe sport psychology practice. Cultural sport psychology (CSP) has quickly become an important mandate to the field of sport and exercise psychology. The first ever compilation on the topic was provided through Athletic Insight in 2005. In the Autumn of 2009 the International Journal of Sporty and Exercise Psychology also reflected an updated compilation on culturally reflexive methods for our domain. Complimenting IJSEP, Athletic Insight has just released a special edition pertaining to culturally reflexive practice in the filed. As part of the submission, contributions were authors by Tatiana Ryba (Finland), Ronnie Lidor and Boris Blumenstein (Israel), Yoichi Kozuma (Japan), Amma Campbell and Christopher Sonn (Australia), and Gershon Tenenbaum (originally from Israel, located to Florida State University). The submissions from Ryba and Tenenbaum feature a conceptual submission and commentary to frame the installment. The submissions from Israel, Japan and Australia provide the reader with a glimpse into cultural challenges such as inter-cultural communication, work with oppressed populations, and in the case of Yoichi Kozuma, practices that have a Japanese flavor.

In summary, it is my hope that you enjoy the well written and conceived contributions found in this book. Given the breadth of topic matter, this book might be used as a sport psychology textbook for under-graduate and graduate students, though also as reference materials for faculty. It is my hope that you enjoy "Introduction to Sport Psychology: Training, Competition and Coping". Inclosing, I would also like to thank Athletic Insight's Associate Editors, who are also wonderful scholars and good friends of the journal. Thank you Mary Pritchard (Boise State University), Sandy Kimbrough (Texas A&M University) and our recent addition Jack Watson III (West Virginia University) for your commitment to Athletic Insight.

Robert J. Schinke, PhD, CSPA
Editor and Co-proprietor of Athletic Insight

In: Introduction to Sport Psychology
Editor: Robert Schinke

ISBN: 978-1-61761-973-1
© 2011 Nova Science Publishers, Inc.

BULLYING AND VICTIMIZATION AMONG ADOLESCENT GIRL ATHLETES

Anthony A. Volk[*] and Larissa Lagzdins

Department of Child and Youth Studies, BrockUniversity,
St. Catherines, Ontario, Canada

ABSTRACT

The goal of the present study was to examine the prevalence of bullying and victimization in adolescent girl athletes. The participants in this study were 69 girls of ages 12-15 who were members of off-school competitive athletic clubs. Participants completed a series of written questionnaires detailing their athletic participation, aspects of their sport and school, and their participation as a bully or victim within their sport and school. Prevalence rates of bullying and victimization at school were two to three times higher for the female athletes when compared to average prevalence rates of a separate national study of female bullying. Bullying and victimization were more prevalent at school than at sports. We suggest that "girl culture", learned aggression, and/or withdrawal from school may cause the high prevalence rates observed among the adolescent girl athletes in this study.

BULLYING AND VICTIMIZATION AMONG ADOLESCENT GIRL ATHLETES

Women and girls are increasingly competing in more diverse, and more competitive, sports (e.g.,Messner, 2002; Theberge, 1997). Generally speaking, competitive sports are depicted as a positive environment for youth, teaching them beneficial mental, physical, and social skills that translate to other life situations (Leysk & Kornspan, 2000; Rees, Howell, & Miracle, 1990; Steiner, McQuivey, Pavelski, & Kraemer, 2000). Research shows that many athletes form friendships within the bonds of teams, where the athletes work towards common goals and train for success (Miller & Kerr, 2002; Turman, 2003). Unfortunately, competitive sports may also be a negative environment that promotes conflict, stress, and concerns about body image (Evans, 2006; Kavussanu, Seal, & Phillips, 2006). An extreme example of this is hazing, which is a *potentially* dangerous behavior practiced by an estimated 17% of both boy and girl adolescent athletes (Gershel, Katz-Sidlow, Small, & Zandieh, 2003). One might therefore legitimately wonder whether participation in sports is beneficial, or harmful, to

* Department of Child and Youth Studies, Brock University, 500 Glenridge Avenue, St. Catherines, Ontario, Canada, L2S 3A1, tvolk@brocku.ca, phone: 905-688-5550 (ext. 5368), fax: 905-641-2509

adolescent athletes' peer and friend relationships. The goal of the current study is to determine whether sports participation influences one aspect of adolescent peer and friend relationships among teenage girl athletes: bullying and victimization.

BULLYING

Bullying can be defined as a relationship problem characterized by an imbalance of power whereby a more powerful individual repeatedly causes harm to a weaker individual (Craig & Pepler, 2003). Victimization is defined as the converse of bullying. While bullying is more prevalent amongst boys, up to one third of girls are bullies and/or victims (Simmons, 2002). In schools, girl bullying and victimization peaks at the ages of 13-14 (Bright, 2005; Volk, Craig, Boyce, & King, 2006). Numerous studies show that bullying and victimization are correlated with a host of negative outcomes, ranging from physical and mental health problems, to engaging in risky behaviors such as drug use and crime (Austin & Joseph, 1996; Berthold & Hoover, 2000; Borg, 1999; Craig, 1998; Marini, Dane, Bosacki, & YLC-CURA, 2006; Volk et al. 2006; Whitney & Smith, 1993; Wild, Fisher, Bhana, & Lombard, 2004). Bullying and victimization therefore represent significant problems for many adolescent girls.

AGGRESSION AND SPORTS

Research on bullying and victimization among athletes primarily focuses on boys and college athletes. Some research suggests that athletes are taught that aggression is a suitable tool for conflict resolution (Rowe, 1998). Bredemeier and Shields (1986) report that contact-sport athletes considered aggression to be an important component of competitive sports. Indeed, a focus on performance/competition (versus mastery/fun) is associated with increased antisocial, and less prosocial, behaviors and morals in boys' sports (Kavussanu et al., 2006; Keating, 1964). Other studies note that intimidation and violence are used as social tools in adolescent boys' athletics (Parker, 1996; Shields, 1999). Endresen and Olweus (2005) report that adolescent boys in "power" (highly masculinized, aggressive) sports tend to act more aggressively inside and outside of the sporting context. In one of the few studies focusing on aggression among adolescent girl athletes, teenage girl soccer teams' general pro-aggression attitudes are the best predictor of individuals' aggression (Stephens & Bredemeier, 1996). Studies of male and female college athletes demonstrate links in both sexes between internal sports aggression and external aggressive behavior (Keeler, 2007; Nixon, 1997). Although sports aggression may not necessarily directly translate into bullying and/or victimization, evidence suggests that increased general aggression is frequently related to increased rates of bullying and victimization (NIHCD, 2004; Olweus, 1992). Adolescents who engage in high levels of aggression in one social context are likely to use aggression in other social situations (Moffit, Caspi, Harrington, & Milne, 2002).

Victimization is the flip side of aggression, and bullying in particular. With respect to athletics, hazing clearly represents a form of sports victimization, particularly if it persists over time (Gershel et al., 2003). Given the link between hazing and athletics, adolescent athletes may face an increased risk of victimization. In contrast, Wild and colleagues (2004) show that low sports self-esteem (i.e., perceived competence) is positively correlated with victimization in adolescent girls. This suggests that sports participation may protect girls from victimization.

GIRL CULTURE

The link between aggression and some male sports leads to the question of feminine cultural ideals and sports participation. Merten (1997) suggests that the feminine ideal for aggression differs from the masculine, physical ideal often associated with sports. Evidence suggests that some girls turn away from sports participation because of the conflicting demands of sporting aggression versus accepted feminine norms of behavior (Guillet, Sarrazin, & Fontayne, 2000). Adolescent girls playing recreational softball are sometimes encouraged to abandon their feminine attitudes towards pain through coaches' taunting and ignoring of players' complaints (Malcolm, 2006). This suggests that compared to non-athletes, adolescent girl athletes may have a more masculine view of competition, aggression, pain, bullying, and/or victimization.

If adolescent girl athletes embrace more masculinized behavior, research suggests that they will be more supportive of, and involved with, bullying and victimization than average adolescent girls (Young & Sweeting, 2004). The same study found that for both boys and girls, a masculine gender role is related to increased bullying; however, amongst girls, a masculine gender identity is also related to increased victimization. The latter finding suggests that a masculine gender role renders girls vulnerable to peer victimization, perhaps their masculinized gender role creates social conflicts with girls who adopt more typical feminine gender roles.

Presenting further evidence for a lack of traditional girl-girl support, a study of Toronto adolescents by Zucker and colleagues found that girls expressed a preference for feminine versus masculine friends, suggesting that more masculine girls may face a greater risk of same-sex alienation (Zucker, Wilson-Smith, Kurita, & Stern, 1995). This appears to be true for adults, with masculine women preferring men as friends and reporting lower-quality friendships than feminine women who prefer women as friends and report higher-quality friendships (Reeder, 2003). Furthermore,gender-mixed or gender-confused adolescents often have significantly lower social competence (including sports participation) than average adolescents (Cohen-Kettenis, Owen, Kaijser, Bradley, & Zucker, 2003). Sexual behaviors and orientations are also known to be vehicles for both bullying and victimization in adolescent boys and girls (McMaster, Connolly, Pepler, & Craig, 2002). Thus, masculine adolescent girls may have deficits in forming female friendships, close friendships, and have lower a social competency that may expose them to increased levels of gender-related forms of bullying and victimization. These problems with relationships may also result in masculine adolescent girls feeling isolated and alienated from their peers.

SCHOOL ALIENATION

Adolescents who feel socially alienated at school may generalize that emotion towards feeling generally alienated from school. School alienation is an important risk factor for adolescent mental health (Brofenbrenner, 1986). Research has shown that an increased sense of school alienation is associated with an increase in bullying behavior (Natvig, Albrektsen, & Qvarnstrom, 2001a; Volk et al., 2006). School alienation can also be a potent predictor of victimization (Natvig, Albrekston, & Qvarnstrom, 2001b; Schreck, Miller, & Gibson, 2003; Volk et al., 2006). Adolescent girl athletes may face a double-risk for school alienation. First, gender is associated with increased school alienation, with boys typically (Brown, Higgins, Pierce, Hong, & Thoma, 2003), but not always (Calabrese & Seldin, 1987), showing higher levels of school alienation than girls. This could mean that by adopting a masculinized gender, girls face a boy-like increase in their risk of school alienation. Second, some college athletes report that the demands of their sport leads to increased isolation from the school community (Adler & Adler, 1985). In this regard, the time demands of the sport remove opportunities for engaging in non-sport social relationships and social-skills building. Therefore, if adolescent girl athletes experience increased school alienation due to their non-traditional gender roles and the demands of their sport, this may place them at increased risk for both school bullying and school aggression.

To summarize, there appear to be links between athletic participation and bullying or victimization. Some studies suggest that athletes (particularly male, contact, and/or team athletes) may be encouraged to be overtly aggressive and competitive. This may contrast with typical norms associated with feminine culture (e.g., passive body image - Evans, 2006; low levels of overt aggression - Guillet et al., 2000; Volk et al., 2006), causing female athletes to become more male-like by increasing their aggression (bullying) at the same time as they become more vulnerable to aggression by removing traditional female social support. Furthermore, female athletes may have higher levels of school alienation that further reduce their social opportunities and increase their risk of both bullying and victimization at school. To date, no study has explored any of these potential associations between competitive athletics and adolescent girls' bullying behavior.

CURRENT STUDY

In the current study we conducted a preliminary examination of bullying and victimization prevalence rates among a sample of 12-15 year old girls engaged in extra-curricular sports. Given the novelty of the area of study, the current study was necessarily exploratory. We had three primary goals: (a) to determine the prevalence rates of bullying and victimization for adolescent girl athletes, (b) to examine differences between school and sports bullying and victimization, and (c) to explore related factors that could influence bullying and victimization in our sample.

We chose to explore the prevalence rates of bullying and victimization because they are simply unknown for this population at this point in time. As we did not have a matched control group in this study, we used a large (approximately 6,000 girls) sample of Canadian bullying and victimization rates for girls of the same age collected by the World Health Organization as our comparison (Volk et al., 2006). Given that aggressive behavior may be more common among athletes (Rowe, 1998), we predicted higher-than-average bullying prevalence rates in our sample (specifically, higher than the average rates found in Volk et al., 2006). Due to their higher levels of aggression, we also predicted that there would be a concurrent higher prevalence of victimization to match the higher rates of bullying.

We also expected differences between the prevalence rates of bullying and victimization of athletes within sports and within school. The two environments are substantially different from each other. It may be that the increased competitiveness and aggression associated with sports participation (Endreson & Olweus, 2005; Shields, 1999) leads to greater prevalence rates of bullying and victimization in sports than at school. However, in school, more traditionally feminine forms of aggression may dominate (Merten, 1997), so increased sports aggression may not be relevant. Moreover, female athletes may face problems with alienation at school that are not present in their sport that increase their risk of bullying and victimization at school. Indeed, their chosen sport may serve as both the cause of, and the refuge from, this school alienation. Previous research (Marini et al., 2006; Volk et al., 2006; Volk, Dane, & Marini, in press) has shown that different kinds of bullying and victimization can be associated with different risk factors. Therefore, we chose to look at global levels of bullying and victimization in sports and schools, as well as six different sub-types of bullying and victimization: ethnic (racial/religious/regional insults), verbal (cursing, yelling), physical (hitting, kicking), threat (threatening to commit any type of harm), rumor (spreading mean rumors), and sexual (making inappropriate sexual comments or advances). One might well expect differences in the sub-types of bullying employed in the different environments (e.g., greater physical aggression in sports than in school).

Because bullying and victimization are related to a variety of ecological and social variables (Marini et al., 2006), we also examined several other factors related to adolescent bullying and victimization: demographics, parents' and coaches' motivations, training together versus competing together, school enjoyment, school performance, and popularity. These factors are each related to athletic performance (Bowker & Bauhaus, 2007; Miller & Kerr, 2002; Turman, 2003) and/or bullying and victimization (Prinstein & Cillessen, 2003; Vaillaincourt & Hymel, 2006; Volk et al., 2006; Wild et al., 2004). We expected positive parental and coach motivation to reduce bullying and victimization in sports. We expected low SES to be negatively related to bullying and victimization in both sports and school. Finally, we expected school enjoyment, achievement, and popularity to be negatively correlated with bullying and victimization in schools.

METHOD

All of the materials and procedures were approved by the Brock University Research Ethics Committee.

Participants

The participants in this study were 69 adolescent girls between the ages of 12-15 ($M = 13.3$, $SD = 1.6$). These participants were primarily white (90%, 5% Chinese, 5% African Canadian), middle class (80% estimate parental salaries of $40-80,000), Canadian citizens (92% born in Canada, 6% in Asia, 2% in Africa). All of these girls were members of various external (i.e., not related to school) competitive athletic clubs in the Niagara Region. The primary type of sport for which each participant was identified varied among athletes, and included: baseball (2), basketball (1), boxing (1), cross-country running (2), figure skating

(5), gymnastics (7), hockey (23), horseback riding (1), orienteering (11), rowing (11), and soccer (5). A majority of the athletes (52%) participated in at least two different sports throughout the year, and the average length of primary sport participation was over five years ($M = 5.7$, $SD = 3.2$). Most of the athletes (91%) saw their teammates outside of sports least once a month, and over 55% saw their teammates at least once a week outside of the athletic club. Over 80% of the girls we contacted in the various athletic clubs agreed to participate and returned completed forms. The remaining 20% were primarily absent when we visited, so we do not believe there are any problems with representation beyond attendance.

Measures

Participants were asked to fill out a 12-page, four-section self-report questionnaire.

Section 1. The first section of the questionnaire involved demographic information such as age, ethnicity, religion, and family socioeconomic status.

Section 2. The second section asked about social relationships in school, including number of friends, length of best friendships, and whether boys or girls where their primary source of friends. They also completed Likert-like (*1Low* to *5High*) self-reports of: relative school grades, whether they enjoyed school, whether school was a positive environment for them, and how popular they were at school. Participants were also asked how often in the last school term they had participated as a bully or victim of racial/ethnic, verbal, physical, threatening, negative rumoring, or sexual bullying at school. Each form of bullying and victimization had its own question. For example, to measure negative rumouring bullying, participants were asked, "In school, how often have you spread rumours or mean lies about someone much weaker or less popular this term?" To measure negative rumouring victimization participants were asked, "In school, how often has someone much stronger or more popular spread rumors or mean lies about you this term?" Participants answered on a one to four point scale of: *that hasn't happened (1); once or twice (2); once a month (3); once a week (4).* This questionnaire was based on the bullying and victimization questioned used in Volk et al.'s Canadian comparison study (2006). We changed removed Volk et al.'s frequency of "More than once a week" to "Once a month" to balance the frequencies across a broader range of times. Otherwise, the questions (particularly the behavioral content) were identical. Volk et al's questions were developed by the World Health Organization as standardized measures of bullying and victimization (Currie, 1998). The questions used in our study were also very similar to those used by Marini et al (2006) in a large (5,000+) study of teenage bullying in Southern Ontario (the same geographical area as the current study).

Besides the individual subtype frequencies, we also computed a total bullying score and a total victimization score. Each score was the sum of all of the individual subtype frequencies. For the total bullying score $\alpha = .75$, while for the total victimization score $\alpha = .82$.

Section 3. In the third section, participants were asked about their primary sport, their time with that sport, the number of sports they participated in, what they enjoyed about the sport, and how often they saw team mates outside of the sport. The third questionnaire repeated the school bully and victim questions from the second questionnaire translated into the context of their primary sport (e.g., "In your sport or club, how often has someone much stronger or more popular made fun of you because of your race or religion during the last school semester?"). As with the school bullying and victimization questions, we again computed total bullying and victimization scores. This was the sum of all of the individual subtype frequencies. For the total bullying score $\alpha = .62$, while for the total victimization score $\alpha = .61$. Finally, the third questionnaire asked participants to rate how much their parents, and their coaches, encouraged them to win, and to play fair (on Likert-scales of *1=Not At All* to *5=Always*).

Section 4. In the fourth section (used in a concurrent Honours thesis studying parental support and self-esteem), participants were asked to rate the degree of maternal and paternal support in their lives, and to fill out a self-esteem measure. This last section was not analyzed for this paper. The order of presentation of the four sections was randomized between participants. No order effects were observed in the presentation of the different questionnaires.

PROCEDURE

Data collection took place during the 2006-07 academic year. Local sporting organizations and coaches were contacted through existing connections with the researchers and through email solicitations. Coaches were briefed on the general goals of the study and asked to provide written consent to approach their participants. Researchers then visited participating athletic clubs to answer any questions and hand out the surveys.

During this visit, the participants were given a verbal briefing on the general study goals and procedures as well as given a chance to ask questions about the methods. To reduce participant bias relating to the potentially sensitive issue of bullying, the girls were told it was a study of school and sports relationships. Participating girls brought home a large envelope with two smaller envelopes. The first envelope contained a parental letter of information and assent that was signed and sealed. The girls opened the second envelope, read a participant letter of assent, filled out their own assent form, and then completed the questionnaires in private, at a time of their choosing. Both parental consent and participant assent was required. Parents were asked to not discuss the study in order to avoid biasing the girls' answers. Due to the anonymous nature of participant responses, participants were protected from any personal liability associated with their answers. Participation was voluntary and there was no penalty for withdrawing from the study.

At a predetermined date, the participants returned their questionnaires, along with the consent and assent forms, and received a verbal debriefing in person. After this debriefing period (where participants could ask any remaining questions), participants were asked to complete a second assent form because they initially received an incomplete briefing (again, to avoid participant bias). The participants then received $5 as a thank you for their participation.

RESULTS

Bullying and Victimization Prevalence

Given the similarity of the questions asked in the two studies, we statistically compared the prevalence rates of bullying and the prevalence rates of victimization in this preliminary study to the prevalence rates found for girls in the aforementioned Canadian study (Volk et al., 2006). In the first comparison, we looked at the frequency of low-level (at least once a semester) bullying and victimization (see Figure 1). We found that the girls in our study reported significantly higher participation rates as bullies and victims in school as compared to either in sports ($\chi^2(1, N = 5,881) = 46.1, p < .01$; $\chi^2(1\ N = 5,881) = 33.5, p< .01$) or to the Canadian data ($\chi^2(1, N = 5,881) = 35.8, p < .01$; $\chi^2(1\ N = 5,881) = 62.1, p< .01$). There were no significant differences between the prevalence rates within sports and the Canadian averages (bullying - $\chi^2(1, N = 5,881) = .40$; victimization - $\chi^2(1\ N = 5,881) = 2.99$).

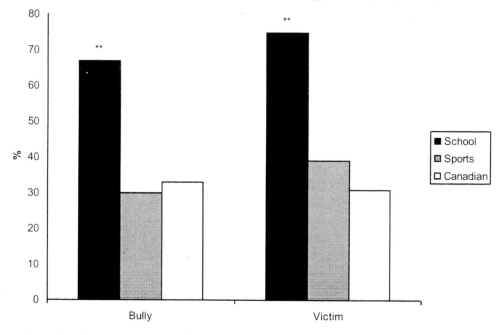

Note. **$p< .01$ with respect to both other groups.

Figure 1. Low frequency (at least once a semester) prevalence in sports (N = 69), schools (N = 69), and a separate Canadian sample (N = 5,812).

In the second comparison, we looked at the frequency of high-level (at least once a week/at least once a week-more than once a week in Volk et al., 2006) bullying and high-level victimization (see Figure 2). Although the cell sizes and expected frequencies were relatively small, they did not violate conservative, conventional minimums (Fienberg, 1979; Howell, 2002). There was a significant difference between the prevalence rates for school and the prevalence rates for both high-level sports victimization ($\chi^2(1, N = 5,881) = 22.3, p < .01$) and the high-level Canadian averages ($\chi^2(1, n = 5,881)= 48.1, p < .01$; $\chi^2(1\ N = 5,881) = 48.2, p< .01$). There was no significant difference between the prevalence of high-level school and sports bullying ($\chi^2(1\ N = 5,881) = .60.$). Although there was no significant difference between the prevalence of high-level sports and Canadian average victimization ($\chi^2(1\ N = 5,881) = 1.60$), high-level sports bullying was significantly more prevalent in the current study than in the Canadian average ($\chi^2(1, N = 5,881) = 16.5, p < .01$).

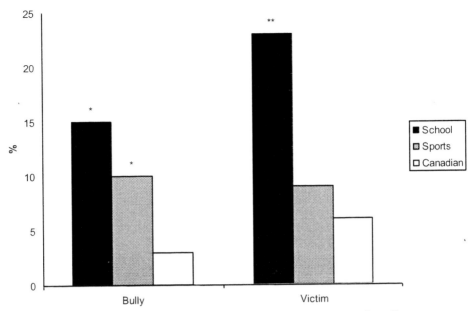

Note. **$p < .01$ with respect to both other groups. *$p < .01$ with respect to Canadian average.

Figure 2. High frequency (at least once a week) prevalence in sports (N = 69), schools (N = 69), and a separate Canadian sample (N = 5,812).

SPORTS VERSUS SCHOOL BULLYING AND VICTIMIZATION

To compute the total score for bullying and victimization in sports and school, we added the Likert scores for each of bullying and victimization to create a total measure for each particular environment. This total score encompassed both the number of different types of bullying/victimization (e.g., physical, verbal, etc.) as well as the total frequency of each type. A paired t-test showed that the average bullying score in sports ($M = .91$, $SD = 1.93$) was significantly smaller than the average bullying score in school ($M = 1.46$, $SD = 1.41$; $t(67) = -2.32$, $p < .05$, $d = -.35$). The average total victimization score in sports ($M = 1.22$, $SD = 2.28$) was also significantly smaller than the average total victimization score in school ($M = 3.25$, $SD = 4.14$; $t(67) = -3.93$, $p < .01$, $d = -.61$). We used a series of paired-samples t-tests without correcting for multiple comparisons to compare the different types of bullying and victimization at sports and school. This liberal statistical decision is suggested by Bender and Lange (2001) when conducting exploratory (vs. confirmatory) analyses. Participants reported significantly higher levels of verbal ($t(67) = 3.95$, $p < .01$, $d = .62$) and threat ($t(67) = 2.41$, $p < .05$, $d = .25$) bullying at school than at sports (see Figure 3). Participants also reported significantly higher levels of ethnic ($t(67) = 2.92$, $p < .01$, $d = .48$), verbal ($t(67) = 3.57$, $p < .01$, $d = .56$), rumor ($t(67) = 4.93$, $p < .01$, $d = .82$), and sexual victimization ($t(67) = 3.23$, $p < .01$, $d = .43$) at school as compared to sports (see Figure 4).

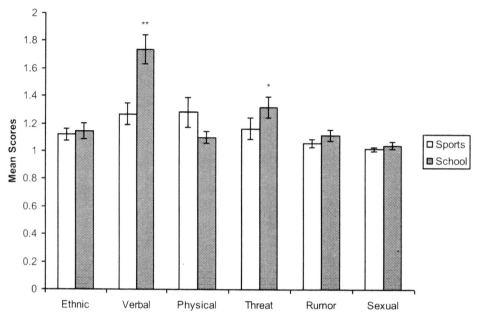

Note. **p< .01. *p< .05.

Figure 3. Average bullying subtype scores amongst adolescent girl athletes (N = 69) in sports vs. schools.

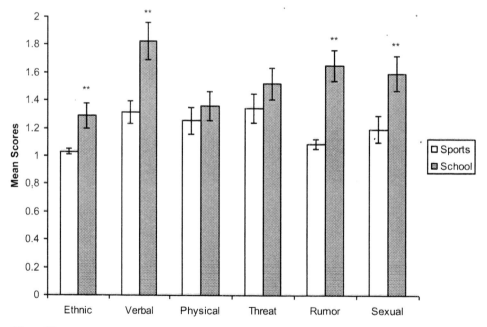

Note. **p< .01.

Figure 4. Average victimization subtype scores amongst adolescent girl athletes (N = 69) in sports vs. schools.

TEAM, INDIVIDUAL, AND SCHOOL VARIABLES

We analyzed the relationship between sports and school bullying and victimization using a series of correlations ($n = 67$). There were no significant relationships between bullying and victimization scores and whether individuals competed as a team versus as individuals (see Table 1). The degree to which coaches encouraged their players to win, or to play fair, were not significantly related to levels of bullying and victimization. Nor was the degree to which parents encouraged their daughter to win or play fair. Participant age, grade, country of birth, ethnicity, race, and relative SES were not significantly related to sports or school bullying and victimization. Using Spearman's rho, non-Christian religion was positively associated with school victimization ($r_s(67) = .25$, $p < .05$), and having boys as your primary friends was significantly correlated with total sports bullying ($r_s(67) = .24$, $p = .05$). The correlations between the different forms of bullying and victimization at sports and school are presented with various school-related items in Table 2. School grades were significantly and negatively correlated with higher levels of sports and school bullying and victimization. There were significant negative relationships between school enjoyment and school bullying and victimization, and a large significant negative relationship between whether school was a positive environment and school victimization. Being popular at school was positively and significantly correlated with sports bullying.

Table 1. Non-Significant Correlations between Adolescent Girl Athletes' School and Sports Bullying/Victimization Scores and Coaching, Parenting, and Demographic Variables (n = 67)

	Sports Bullying	Sports Victimization	School Bullying	School Victimization
Win As A Team or Individually	0.05	0.19	0.12	-0.06
Coach Encourages Fairness	0.01	-0.02	0.03	0.10
Coach Encourages Winning	0.14	0.19	0.07	0.17
Parents Encourages Fairness	-0.21	-0.22	-0.16	-0.18
Parents Encourages Winning	-0.13	-0.01	-0.02	-0.13
Age	0.16	0.05	0.03	-0.20
Grade	0.10	-0.01	0.08	-.292(*)
Country	-0.07	0.15	0.06	-0.05
Ethnicity	0.12	-0.06	0.02	-0.05

Table 1 – (Continued)

Race	0.13	-0.10	-0.06	-0.10
SES	0.20	0.21	-0.03	-0.23

Note. p for all correlations> .05.

Table 2. Correlations between Adolescent Girl Athletes' School and Sports Bullying/Victimization Scores and Their School Environments (n = 67)

	2	3	4	5	6	7	8
1 School Bullying	.249*	.412**	.468**	-.381**	-.265*	-.069	.121
2 School Victimization	-	.078	.240*	-.322**	-.341**	-.451**	-.077
3 Sports Bullying		-	.599**	-.280*	.015	.125	.258*
4 Sports Victimization			-	-.296*	-.046	.018	.204
5 I Get Good Grades				-	.368**	.239*	-.061
6 I Enjoy School					-	.517**	.303*
7 School Is A Positive Environment For Me						-	.431*
8 I Am Popular At School							-

Note. *p < .05. **p < .01.

DISCUSSION

The current study was an exploration of bullying and victimization among Canadian adolescent girls engaged in competitive extracurricular sports. We were able to meet the three initial goals of: 1) determining the prevalence rate of bullying and victimization, 2) examining differences between school and sports bullying and victimization, and 3) examining some of the factors that may be related to these differences. Perhaps the most significant finding of our study is the extremely high prevalence of bullying and victimization these girls experienced at school compared to Canadian averages. This finding was striking, both statistically and practically. The prevalence rates were double the average for low-level bullying and victimization, and triple the average for high-level bullying and victimization! If true for all female adolescent athletes (see *Limitations* below), these rates represent an astonishing increase in the likelihood that female adolescent athletes will be a bully or a victim at school. Given the exploratory nature of the current study, it is difficult to provide an exact answer for these extremely high school prevalence rates. Nevertheless, we offer three separate, but not necessarily independent, hypotheses: athletic aggressiveness, girl culture, and school alienation.

ATHLETIC AGGRESSIVENESS

Our first hypothesis is that girls who participate in competitive sports would be more competitive and aggressive than average girls. This aggression may lead them to engage in more bullying behavior. As discussed in our introduction, there is evidence that some athletes display more aggression outside of sport settings (Enderson & Olweus, 2004; Keeler, 2007; Nixon, 1997). Amongst the girls in our sample, there was a strong positive correlation between bullying in sports and bullying in school, suggesting that there is indeed some cross-over of aggression between the two domains. However, higher aggression might explain an increase in bullying, but it does not explain the increase in victimization unless the increase in victimization is solely due to "reactive" aggression (Hara, 2002). "Reactive" aggression is a specific form of aggression whereby normally passive individuals respond aggressively (reactively) to social threats (Marini et al., 2006). This reactive aggression can in turn render the individual vulnerable to further aggression and victimization (Hara). It differs from proactive aggression, which is used instrumentally to obtain a specific goal (e.g., issue a threat to get an object versus responding aggressively to said threat). Given that reactive aggression is less frequent amongst bullies than bully-victims (Marini et al.), we do not believe that increased aggression is the sole explanation for the increased prevalence rates found in our study.

GIRL CULTURE

Our second hypothesis is that girls who participate in competitive extracurricular sports are acting contrary to general feminine ideals or "girl culture" (Goldberger & Chandler, 1991; Guillet et al., 2000; Simmons, 2002), and may therefore have problems fitting in with traditional girl culture. We know from our data that girls who deviated from the religious norm (Christianity) were significantly more likely to be victims at school. This suggests a link between atypical cultural behavior and increased victimization amongst the girls in our sample. Also, girls who reported having more boys as friends reported higher levels of bullying in sports, suggesting another link between gender culture and aggression. Evidence against this hypothesis is that there were no significant correlations between bullying and victimization and perceived popularity, number of good friends, or duration of school attendance. Indeed, sports bullying was significantly and positively correlated with school popularity. This reinforces previous data showing that bullies, contrary to popular stereotypes, often show above-average popularity (Hawley, 2003). Furthermore, not fitting in with girl culture in school may explain why female athletes are targeted as victims, but it does not explain as well why they are more likely to act as bullies in the same environment.

SCHOOL ALIENATION

The girls in our study all competed in sports outside of the school setting (versus in school varsity settings). Our third hypothesis is that this increased engagement in external, competitive sports is accompanied by a reciprocal decreased engagement with school. Thus, girl athletes feel less pressure to conform to socially acceptable school behaviors and therefore they engage in more school bullying and/or present themselves as greater targets to school bullies. The advantage of this hypothesis over the previous two is that it explains the increase in both bullying and victimization prevalence rates. This hypothesis is supported by the significant negative correlations between levels of school bullying and victimization, and self-reported school grades and enjoyment. Lower school grades and lower school enjoyment could represent the hypothesized disengagement from school. School victims also reported that the school environment was significantly less positive for them, which further suggests school disengagement.

While this third hypothesis seems to fit our data, it too, has problems. The correlational nature of this study makes it impossible to conclude whether poor grades and school enjoyment lead to bullying and victimization, or the reverse, or both. Furthermore, does the increase in school bullying and victimization cause students to disengage from school and engage in sports, or does increased sports engagement cause social problems at school? We are unable to answer these causal questions without further experimental or longitudinal data. In any case, while our data most strongly supports the third hypothesis, we cannot rule out possible contributions from the previous two hypotheses. Indeed, it may be that all three are true to some degree. Girl athletes could distance themselves from girl culture, increasing their risk of being victimized, while their aggressiveness increases their risk of acting as bullies, and their overall engagement with school norms declines as they engage in more sports and more bullying and/or victimization. This fits with research showing that gender atypical girls (i.e., masculinized girls) are more likely to be both bullies and victims (Young & Sweeting, 2004).

SUBTYPES OF BULLYING AND VICTIMIZATION

In addition to overall differences with the Canadian average, there were also differences between the subtypes of bullying and victimization between sports and school. For bullying, verbal and threat bullying were more prevalent in school than in sports. This is especially surprising given the competitive, sometimes aggressive nature of sports (Rowe, 1998). These results suggest that the girls are capable of interacting with other girls in stressful sporting situations without resorting to bullying behavior.

Levels of ethnic, verbal, rumor, and sexual victimization were significantly higher in school than in sports. It may simply be that victimization is generally higher in school, but physical and threat victimization are equally common in sports as a result of their physical and competitive nature. It may also be that a group of girls with shared interests, and common goals, engage in less bullying. These shared values and interests may result in less social conflict amongst girls within a sporting organization than amongst the more heterogeneous school populations.

But if this is the case, why are there not equal drops in the level of self-reported bullying for the same subtypes? This difference between the sport bullying and sport victimization sub-types is somewhat puzzling. Why are there larger differences between sports-school victimization than for sports-school bullying? A clue could be the relatively high prevalence of high-level bullying in sports (see Figure 2). It may be that in sports, high-level bullying persists because of aggressive athletic competition. Girls might under-report this high-level sports victimization to preserve team spirit and/or because the victimization is perceived as regular sports aggression rather than bullying.

Another explanation is that some of the sports bullying behaviors reported in our sample are directed towards girls outside of one's own team, and therefore the accompanying higher levels of victimization were not captured in our samples. That is, girls may have reported victimizing someone on another team, but not being victimized by someone on another team. Our questions did not distinguish between within-team and between-team bullying and victimization. If the most active sports bullies primarily targeted girls from other teams, those victim's responses were not likely to be included in our data, and could account for the discrepancy between the self-reported levels of bullying and victimization in sports.

LIMITATIONS

One possible explanation for our results is that the average Canadian prevalence rates were too low. The average prevalence rates used in Volk et al. (2006) are similar to, or higher than, prevalence rates reported in another large Canadian study that sampled from the same geographical area as the current study (Marini et al., 2006). Volk et al.'s averages are also similar to numerous other large, non-Canadian samples (e.g., Austin & Joseph, 1996; Berthold & Hoover, 2000; Borg, 1999; Whitney & Smith, 1993; Wild et al., 2004). Thus, it is very unlikely the average prevalence rates used as a comparison were too low. Although it might not be ideal to use an external comparison group, the similarity of our questions lends construct validity to our bullying and victimization measures when they are compared to other popular measures of bullying. Another methodological possibility is that our questions in this study solicited an above-average number of positive responses. The fact that sports and school bullying and victimization prevalence rates were significantly different from each other suggests that our questions did not simply lead to prevalence inflation. A third possibility is participant biases or errors in recall given the anonymous, self-report nature of this study. However, there is evidence that self-report data on bullying are reliable (Pellegrini & Bartini, 2000; Solberg & Olweus, 2003), so we have no specific reason to believe that this is not also the case for our data. Thus, we believe our data are reliable.

A more serious limitation is the nature of the current sample. We recruited a medium-sized group of local, predominantly Caucasian, middle-class adolescent girls to participate in the study. This group may not generalize to adolescent girl athletes in different populations, or from different ethnic or SES groups. Indeed, the narrow range of SES in this study may be why we failed to find any significant relationship between SES and bullying. Another sampling issue is that we lacked a non-sporting control group. This would allow for a comparison using the same questions and methods instead of relying on prevalence rates in the literature. This would help answer some of the questions pertaining to generalization and methodology. In our defense, the construct validity of our measure gives us reasonable confidence regarding the validity of our results and this study was exploratory, not confirmatory, in nature. That said, future confirmatory studies should aim at increasing the size and diversity of the sample as well as adding a control group for direct comparison in order to address the sampling limitations of the current study. It might also be interesting to recruit male participants to examine whether the same issues are present in adolescent boy athletes.

Finally, the current study was cross-sectional. A longitudinal study might allow us to explore the relationships between athletic participation and bullying and victimization as they develop amongst individuals. Adolescence is a dynamic period of development, and we would not expect any social relationship to remain static over time. It might also assist us in making stronger causal statements.

CONCLUSION

Personal and social development is supposed to be an important goal of athletic participation. Ironically, we report that girl athletes reported a shocking two- to threefold difference in school bullying and victimization prevalence compared to the Canadian average for girls their age! Girl culture, increased aggression, and school disengagement may all play a role in explaining why there is such a dramatic difference in the prevalence rates of school bullying and victimization for these girls. Compared to schools, sports seem to be a relatively safe haven for these girls. Both bullies and victims reported a greater disengagement from school. Although we explored several external factors in thus study, a much broader and deeper exploration combined with longitudinal and/or experimental research is necessary to help clarify some of the causal issues raised in this study. The relatively small sample size, correlational nature, and lack of an internal control group are part of the exploratory nature of this study, but their attendant limitations should be recognized. Clearly though, our data suggest a potential risk of increased school bullying and victimization amongst girls who participate in competitive athletics. Given the goals of sports participation, and the welfare of the girls involved, we believe our results highlight the urgent need for further attention and investigation of this topic.

REFERENCES

Adler, P., & Adler, P. A. (1985). From idealism to pragmatic detachment: The academic performance of college athletes. *Sociology of Education, 58, 241-250.*

Austin, S., & Joseph, S. (1996). Assessment of bully-victim problems in 8 to 11 year-olds. *British Journal of Educational Psychology, 66,* 447-456.

Bender, R., & Lange, S. (2001). Adjusting for multiple testing - When and how? *Journal of Clinical Epidemiology, 54,* 343-349.

Berthold, K. A., & Hoover, J. H. (2000). Correlates of bullying and victimization among intermediate students in the Midwestern USA. *School Psychology International, 21,* 65-78.

Borg, M. (1999). The extent and nature of bullying among primary and secondary school children. *Education Research, 41,* 137-53.

Bowker, A., & Bauhaus, S. (2007). *The role of parental and peer relationships in girls' sports experiences: A look into the world of girls' hockey.* Poster presented at the Canadian Psychological Association Conference, Ottawa, Canada.

Bredemeier, B. J., & Shields, D. L. (1986). Athletic aggression: An issue of contextual morality. *Sociology of Sport Journal, 3,* 15-28.

Bright, R. (2005). It's just a grade 8 girl thing: Aggression in teenage girls. *Gender and Education, 17*, 93-101.

Brofenbrenner, U. (1986). Alienation and the four worlds of childhood. *Phi Delta Kappan, 59*, 436-436.

Brown, M. R., Higgins, K., Pierce, T., Hong, E., & Thoma, C. (2003). Secondary students' perceptions of school life with regards to alienation: The effects of disability, gender, and race. *Learning Disability Quarterly, 26*, 227-238.

Calabrese, R.L., & Seldin, C.A. (1987). A contextual analysis of alienation among school constituencies. *Urban Education, 22*, 227-237.

Cohen-Kettenis, P. T., Owen, A., Kaijser, V. G., Bradley, S. J., & Zucker, K. J. (2003). Demographic characteristics, social competence, and behavior problems in children with Gender Identity Disorder: A cross-national, cross-clinic comparative analysis. *Journal of Abnormal Child Psychology, 31*, 41-53.

Craig, W. M. (1998). The relationship among bullying, victimization, depression, anxiety, and aggression in elementary school children. *Personality and Individual Differences, 24,* 123-130.

Craig, W. M., & Pepler, D. J. (2003). Identifying and targeting risk for involvement in bullying and victimization. *Canadian Journal of Psychiatry, 48*, 577-582.

Currie, C. (1998). Health behavior in school-aged children: Research protocol for the 1997-98 survey. *WHO Coordinating Center for the Study of Health Behavior in School-Aged Children*. Edinburgh, Scotland.

Endressen, I., & Olweus, D. (2005). Participation in power sports and antisocial involvement in preadolescent and adolescent boys. *Journal of Child Psychology and Psychiatry, 46*, 468-478.

Evans, B. (2006). 'I'd feel ashamed': Girls bodies and sports participation. *Gender, Place, and Culture, 13*, 547-561.

Fienberg, S. E. (1979). The use of Chi-squared statistics for categorical data problems. *Journal of the Royal Statistical Society, Series B, 41*, 54-64.

Gershel, J. C., Katz-Sidlow, R. J., Small, E., & Zandieh, S. (2003). Hazing of suburban middle high school and high school athletes. *Journal of Adolescent Health, 32*, 333-335.

Goldberger, A., & Chandler, T. (1991). Sport participation among adolescent girls: role conflict or multiple roles? *Sex roles.25*, 213-234.

Guillet, E., Sarrazin, P., & Fontayne, P. (2000). "If it contradicts my gender role, I'll stop": Introducing survival analysis to study the effects of gender typing on the time of withdrawal from sport practice: A 3-year study. *European Review of Applied Psychology, 50*, 417-421.

Hara, H. (2002). Justifications for bullying among Japanese schoolchildren. *Asian Journal of Social Psychology, 5*, 197-204.

Hawley, P. H. (2003). Prosocial and coercive configurations of resource control in early adolescence: A case for the well adapted Machiavellian. *Merrill-Palmer Quarterly, 49*, 279-309.

Howell, D. C. (2002). *Statistical methods for psychology*. Toronto: Thomson Learning.Kavussanu, M., Seal, A. R., & Phillips, D. R. (2006). Observed prosocial and antisocial behaviours in male soccer teams: Age differences across adolescence and the role of motivational variables. *Journal of Applied Sport Psychology, 18*, 324-344.

Keating, J. (1964). Sportsmanship as a moral category. *Ethics, 75*(1), 25-35.

Keeler, L. A. (2007). The differences in sport aggression, life aggression, and life assertion among adult male and female collusion, contact, and non-contact sport athletes. *Journal of Sport Behavior, 30*, 57-76.

Lesyk, J. J., & Kornspan, A. S. (2000). Coaches' expectations and beliefs regarding benefits of youth sport participation. *Journal of Perceptual and Motor Skills, 90*, 399-402.

Malcolm, N. L. (2006). "Shaking it off" and "Toughing it out" – Socialization to pain and injury in girls' softball. *Journal of Comparative Ethnography, 35*, 495-525.

Marini, Z.A., Dane, A.V., Bosacki, S.L., & YLC-CURA. (2006). Direct and indirect bully-victims: Differential psychosocial risk factors associated with adolescents involved in bullying and victimization. *Aggressive Behavior, 32*, 1-19.

McMaster, L., Connolly, J., Pepler, D., & Craig, W. (2002). Peer to peer sexual harassment in early adolescence: A developmental perspective. *Developmental Psychopathology, 14*, 91-105.

Messner, M. A. (2002). *Taking the field: Women, men, and sports.* Chicago: University of Minnesota Press.

Merten, D. E. (1997). The meaning of meanness: Popularity, competition, and conflict among junior high school girls. *Sociology of Education, 70*, 175-191.

Miller, P., & Kerr, G. (2002). The athletic, academic and social experiences of intercollegiate student – athletes. *Journal of Sport BehaviourB, 25*, 346- 364.

Moffit, T. E., Caspi, A., Harrington, H., & Milne, B. J. (2002). Males on the life-course-persistent and adolescence-limited antisocial pathways: Follow –up at age 26 years. *Development and Psychopathology, 14*, 179-207.

NIHCD Early Child Care Research Network. (2004). Trajectories of physical aggression from toddlerhood to middle childhood. *Monographs of the Society for Research in Child Development, 69*, 1-129.

Natvig, G. K., Albrekston, G., & Qvarnstrom, U. (2001a). School-related stress experience as a risk factor for bullying behaviour. *Journal of Youth and Adolescence, 30*, 561-575.

Natvig, G. K., Albrekston, G., & Qvarnstrom, U. (2001b). Psychosomatic symptoms among victims of school bullying. *Journal of Health Psychology, 6*, 365-377.

Nixon II, H. L. (1997). Gender, sport, and aggressive behavior outside sport. *Journal of Sport & Social Issues, 21*, 379-391.

Olweus, D. (1992). Bullying among school-children: Intervention and prevention. In: R. Peters, R. McMahon, & V. Quinsey (Eds.). *Aggression and violencethroughout the lifespan* (pp. 100-125). London: Sage.

Parker, A. (1996). The construction of masculinity within boys' physical education. *Gender and Education. 8*, 141-158.

Pellegrini, A.D., & Bartini, M. (2000). An empirical comparison of methods of sample aggression and victimization in school settings. *Journal of Educational Psychology, 92*, 360-366.

Prinstein, M. J., & Cillessen, A. H. N. (2003). Forms and functions of adolescent peer aggression associated with high levels of peer status. *Merrill-Palmer Quarterly, 49*, 310-342.

Reeder, H. (2003). The effect of gender role orientation on same- and cross-sex friendship formation. *Sex Roles, 49*, 143-153.

Rees, C., Howell, F., & Miracle, A. (1990). Do high school sports build character? A quasi-experiment on a national sample. *The Social Science Journal, 27*, 303-315.

Rowe, C. J. (1998). Aggression and violence in sports. *Psychiatric Annals, 27*, 303-315.

Schreck, C. J., Miller, J. M., & Gibson, C. L. (2003). Trouble in the school yard: A study of risk factors of victimization at school. *Crime & Delinquency, 49*, 460-484.

Shields, E. (1999). Intimidation and violence by males in high school athletics. *Adolescence. 34*, 503-521.

Simmons, R. (2002). *Odd girl out: The hidden culture of aggression in girls.* New York: Harcourt Press.

Solberg, M. E., & Olweus, D. (2003). Prevalence and estimation of school bullying with the Olweus Bully/Victim Questionnaire. *Aggressive Behavior, 29*, 239-268.

Steiner, H., McQuivey, R.W., Pavelski, R.,& Kraemer, H. (2000).Adolescents and sports: Risk or benefit? *Journal of Clinical Pediatrics, 39*, 161-166.

Stephens, D., E., & Bredemeier, B. J. L. (1996). Moral atmosphere and judgments about aggression in girls' soccer: Relationships among moral and motivational variables. *Journal of Sport Exercise Psychology, 18*, 158-173.

Theberge, N. (1999). "It's part of the game": Physicality and the production of gender in women's hockey. *Gender and Society, 11*, 69-87.

Turman, P. (2003). Coaches and cohesion: The impact of coaching techniques on team cohesion in the small group sport setting. *Journal of Sport Behaviour, 26*, 86- 103.

Volk, A., Craig, W., Boyce, W., & King, M. (2006). Adolescent risk correlates of bullying and different types of victimization. *International Journal of Adolescent Medicine and Health.18(4)*, 375-386.

Volk, A.A., Dane, A.V., & Marini, Z.A. (*in press.*). Parent-focused interventions for the prevention of bullying: Accommodating children with difficulties regulating emotions. D. Pepler and W. Craig (Eds.). *Rise Up for Respectful Relationships. PREVNet Series (Volume 2).*

Whitney, I., & Smith, P.K. (1993). A survey of the nature and extent of bullying in junior/middle and secondary schools. *Educational Research, 35*, 3-25.

Wild, L., Flisher, A., Bhana, A., & Lombard, C. (2004). Associations among adolescent risk behaviours and self esteem in six domains. *Journal of Child Psychology and Psychiatry. 45*, 1454-1467.

Young, R., & Sweeting, H. (2004). Adolescent bullying, relationships, psychological well-being, and gender-atypical behavior: A gender diagnosticity approach. *Sex Roles, 50*, 525-537.

Zucker, K. J., Wilson-Smith, D. N., Kurita, J. A., & Stern, A. (1995). Children's appraisals of sex-typed behavior in their peers. *Sex Roles, 33*, 703- 725.

In: Introduction to Sport Psychology
Editor: Robert Schinke

ISBN: 978-1-61761-973-1
© 2011 Nova Science Publishers, Inc.

LINKING THEORY TO PRACTICE – LESSONS LEARNED IN SETTING SPECIFIC GOALS IN A JUNIOR ICE HOCKEY TEAM

Esa Rovio[a*], *Jari Eskola*[†b], *Daniel Gould*[‡c] *and Taru Lintunen*[#d]

[a] LIKESResearchCenter for Sport and Health Sciences, Jyväskylä, Finland
[b] Department of Education, University of Tampere, Tampere, Finland
[c] The Institute for the Study of Youth Sports, Michigan State University, Michigan, USA
[d] Deparment of Sport Sciences, University of Jyväskylä, Jyväskylä, Finland

ABSTRACT

The purpose of this qualitative case and action research study was to describe and evaluate the implementation of a one-season-long goal setting program in an ice hockey team in Finland. The aim of the study was to explore the process of setting specific and quantitatively measurable goals in team sports. The data were derived from field observations and interviews. It was found that setting specific and quantitatively measurable goals in a team, proposed by the goal setting theory, was difficult in practice. Setting specific and measurable goals, and goals concerning the core areas of team and individual performance would have led to multiple goals and consequently to an uncontrollable situation. It is therefore suggested that setting general and unspecific goals, which enable the development of technical, tactical and phycical ice-hockey skills would be beneficial.

[*] Correspondence: Esa Rovio, researcher, group dynamics and goal setting; LIKESResearchCenter for Sport and Health Sciences; Postal address: Rautpohjankatu 8a, FIN-40700 Jyväskylä, Finland; Tel + 358 50 4011951, Fax + 358 14 260 1571; E-mail: esa.rovio@likes.fi

[†] Jari Eskola, lecturer, qualitative research methods; Department of Education, University of Tampere, Tampere, Finland; Postal address: FIN-33014 Tampere, Finland; Tel + 358 3 551 6088, Fax + 358 3 3551 7502; E-mail: jari.eskola@uta.fi

[‡] Daniel Gould, professor, applied sport psychology; The Institute for the Study of Youth Sports, Michigan State University, Michigan, USA; Tel 517 432-0175, Fax 517 353-5363; 210 IM Sports Circle Building, MichiganStateUniversity, East Lansing, MI48824, USA; E-mail: drgould@msu.edu

[#] Taru Lintunen, professor, sport and exercise psychology; Department of Sport Sciences, P.O. Box 3 (Viv), FIN-40014 University of Jyväskylä, Finland; Tel +358 14 260 2113, Fax +358 14 260 4600; E-mail: taru.lintunen@sport.jyu.fi

INTRODUCTION

Goal setting is one of the most popular motivational techniques for enhancing performance and productivity in business, education, and sport. Most of the current research on goal setting can be traced back to Locke (1968), including both the basic premise that conscious goals and intentions govern an individual's action and the principles of initiating goal setting. Subsequent refinements (Locke & Latham, 1990), based on a detailed and systematic program of empirical testing and theoretical reasoning, have made this research domain one of the most active in behavioural science.

More systematic testing of the goal setting theory in sport started after the mid-1980s when Locke and Latham (1985) maintained that the effects of goal setting should be generalisable to sports, which share many contextual similarities with organizational settings. Locke and Latham proposed 10 hypotheses based on the findings in the organizational literature. After this challenge to sport researchers, the number of goal setting studies in sport increased steadily.

Both in organizations and in sport settings, three basic assumptions of the theory of goal setting have mainly been tested including specificity, effectiveness, and difficulty. Several reviews and meta-analyses have supported the fact that goal setting is an effective performance enhancement strategy, and that the goals set should be specific, measurable, and moderately difficult (e.g., Burton, Naylor, & Holliday, 2001; Chidester & Grigsby, 1984; Hall & Kerr, 2001; Kyllo & Landers, 1995; Locke & Latham, 1990; Mento, Steel, & Karren, 1987; Tubbs, 1991; Weinberg, 1994; Wood, Mento, & Locke, 1987). However, thesebasic assumptions of goal setting theory (i.e. goal specificity, effectiveness, and difficulty) have been less consistently applied in sport and physical exercise context compared to industry and organizations (Burton et al., 2001; Hall & Kerr, 2001; Kyllo & Landers, 1995).

In this study the premise of goal specificity is evaluated. According to the goal setting theory (Locke & Latham, 1985, 1990), specific goals have superior effects on performance compared to general or do-your-best goals or no goals. Reviews and meta-analyses clearly indicate that goals should be specific (Chidester & Grigsby, 1984; Latham & Lee, 1986; Locke & Latham, 1990; Locke, Shaw, Saari, & Latham, 1981; Mento et al., 1987; Tubbs, 1991).

Numerous studies on sports have concluded that setting specific goals has superior effects on performance over setting no goals, general goals, or vague goals (e.g., Bar-Eli, Tenenbaum, Pie, Btesh, & Almog, 1997; Barnett & Stanicek, 1979; Boyce, 1990; 1992a; 1992b; Erbaugh & Barnett, 1986; Hall & Byrne, 1988; Hall, Weinberg, & Jackson, 1987). However, many studies have failed to support this basic assumption made by Locke and Latham (e.g., Anshel, Weinberg, & Jackson, 1992; Bar-Eli, Levy-Kolker, Tenenbaum, & Weinberg, 1993; Boyce, 1994; Miller & McAuley, 1987; Weinberg, Bruya, Garland, & Jackson, 1990; Weinberg, Bruya, & Jackson, 1985; Weinberg, Bruya, Jackson, &Garland, 1987; Weinberg, Fowler, Jackson, Bagnall, & Bruya, 1991). In a more recent review (Burton et al., 2001) it was found that in15 out of 25 studies athletes who set specific goals performed significantly better than those who set general, do-your-best goals or no goals.

Such inconsistent findings have given rise to a lively debate among researchers (Hall, Byrne 1988; Burton 1992, 1993; Locke 1991, 1994; Weinberg & Weigand 1993, 1996). In this debate five key methodological issues have been highlighted: (1) participant motivation,

(2) goal setting in do-your-best conditions, (3) feedback in do-your-best conditions, (4) personal goals and (5) goal difficulty. The debate does not seem to be lessening (Burton et al., 2001; Hall & Kerr 2001). Burton (1993; Burton et al., 2001) has suggested five plausible explanations for the inconsistency of the results of goal setting studies in sport: (1) small sample sizes, (2) athletes operating closer to their performance potential, (3) task complexity, (4) individual differences, and (5) failure to employ appropriate goal implementation strategies. The debate itself has not generated clear answers.

Despite disagreement, however, scholars (Burton et al., 2001; Hardy, Jones, & Gould, 1997, 39; Widmeyer & Ducharme, 1997) are unanimous about the need for longitudinal studies on the goal setting process. Reviews (Burton et al., 2001; Hall & Kerr, 2001) have evaluated the results of previous studies (e.g., goal specificity, difficulty, proximity), but not their specific particularities. A focus on the questions of *who* have been studied and *how* would give a clearer picture of both what has been studied previously and what remains to be studied in the future. The review by Rovio (2002) examined 81 goal setting studies in the field of physical activity and sports. Surprisingly, few studies (16 %) were found on goal setting in competitive sports. A notable proportion (70%) of the studies investigated students or people who engaged in any kind of sport only occasionally. Nearly half (46%) of the studies did not involve any kind of goal program, and most (70%) of those with programs did not deal with competing athletes. The studies with goal programs were short-term; nearly half (45%) lasted only five weeks or less. The overwhelming majority (85 %) of the studies were based on a quantitative pre-post design. Very few goal program studies described the events that took place between the tests. However, a process-oriented analysis might reveal important contextual features of goal setting. In only a few studies did the researcher describe the process that took place during the intervention between the pre and post tests (Burton, 1989; Daw & Burton, 1994; Evans, Hardy, & Fleming, 2000).

Much research to date has been concerned with setting goals on an individual level in individual sports. It is in only a few studies that goals have been set in team sports, and for only few tasks (Anderson, Crowell, Doman, & Howard, 1988; Lerner, Ostrow, Yura, & Etzel, 1996; Shoenfelt, 1996; Swain & Jones, 1995; Weinberg, Stitcher, & Richardson, 1994). It is interesting that in the context of competitive team sports, no goal setting studies have been conducted in which goals have been set for both team and individual players. Moreover, the assumption of goal specificity has been studied in individual sports only. Conducting qualitative longitudinal studies describing the goal setting process among competitive athletes in team sports is therefore warranted.

The present study is a qualitative case and action study. The aim was to describe and evaluate the implementation over one season of a goal setting program for an ice hockey team. More specifically, the aim was to study the setting of specific and quantitatively measurable goals in team sports at both the individual and team levels.

METHOD

Participants

The participants were members of a junior-league ice hockey team, consisting of three coaches and 22 players 15–16 years of age. The main informant, the head coach, had eleven years of experience coaching at the junior and elite levels. On average, the players had been playing ice hockey for nine years. The club team played at the highest level in the national league. During the competitive season, the team practised four or five times and had one or two games a week. Practice often included both on and off-ice training. In addition, the team gathered two or three times a week to discuss performance. As many as nine of the players also played for the national team during the season. All this indicates that the involvement of the participants in ice hockey was both intensive and purposeful. The principal researcher served as a consultant to the head coach and to the team on the issue of goal setting and performance enhancement. The principal research also held 25 years of experience in team sports as a junior and professional player and a doctoral-level education in sport and exercise psychology.

Design

The present study is a qualitative case study as well as an example of action research. It can be regarded as an intrinsic case study, as it aims at illustrating and understanding a particular issue, the detailed structures of specific events and a specific group of people in a natural situation (Dobson, 2001; Stake, 2005). In addition, this is also an instrumental case study, as it aims at the refinement of theory. Specifically, the perceptions of the principal researcher and the head coach involved in the goal-setting process in an ice hockey team constitute the case. The action research nature of the study is expressed in the aim of studying social systems and attempting to bridge the gap between theory and practice on the one hand and between the researcher and the target group on the other (Kemmis & McTaggart, 2005). As action research, the study proceeds via a continuous process of consideration, discussion, and negotiation from plan to action, all of which are minutely observed and then changed on the basis of the experience gained. In an action research study, during the implementation phase, the researchers are constantly focusing their observations (and reformulating the research questions). In the present study the initial target of the observations was both the players and the head coach. In the field work period during the ice hockey season, researchers noticed, that the most important actor in the goal setting program was the head coach. He had status to make decisions of this kind. Consequently, this study tells a story of about collaboration in goal setting between the head coach and the sport psychology consultant. The focus of the study is on the discussions held between the head coach and the consultant. However, the results of the goal setting program can also be seen on the level of the players. Therefore, to some extent data on observations of, discussions with and comments made by the players are also included.

The study is also situation-specific. The aim of the study and development of the theory are influenced by the perspective of the head coach. This study is also based on a thorough knowledge of the relevant theory. In this study the cyclic nature of action research (planning, acting, observing and reflecting) is manifested by investigation of the process of goal setting, firstly, in the processes of setting specific and measurable goals, secondly, in setting unspecific and holistic goals, and, thirdly, in evaluating and guiding action towards these goals.

The TeamBuilding Intervention Program

The present study is part of a larger team-building intervention program which aimed at creating a team that performs its tasks well and which is at the same time cohesive. The main methods used were group and individual goal setting. The program was implemented during the course of one ice hockey season.

Early in May the players set common team goals and individual personal goals on the basis of the discussions chaired by the head coach. Both the coaches and the players evaluated the accomplishment of the common goals in August, November, and January. Players' individual goals were evaluated in four small groups according to their ice hockey lines in August, October, December, and February. The ice hockey seasonended in April.

During the season 15 gatherings were held which, besides the coaches, were attended by the whole team and another 27 were held which were attended by players according to their ice hockey lines. During these meetings, early in the season, common team and individual goals were set. As the season proceeded, goal-directed actions were evaluated and feedback about the goals was given. The principal researcher was also present at the team training camp during the summer training season, and went to see most of the team's home matches. In addition, the head coach and the principal researcher had 78 telephone conversations or face-to-face meetings together. Two assistant coaches also attended some of these meetings. In these meetings the implementation of the program in terms of the goal setting principles was adopted, evaluation, feedback, and the performance level of the team and of individual players were discussed, and the team or line meetings were planned. Time was also allocated at these meetings for the researcher to make observations and give feedback to the head coach.

The intervention program was planned according to principles of goal setting used in earlier studies (e.g., Carron & Hausenblas, 1998; Hardy, et al., 1997; Widmeyer & Ducharme, 1997). The basic principles of the goal-setting program were: set difficult compared to easy or "do you best" goals; set specific and measurable compared to vague, general, "do your best" goals; set long-term outcome goals and then short-term performance and process goals; set individual and group goals; and , finally, involve all the members of the team in establishing and monitoring progress toward the agreed goals.

In individual goal setting, the method of performance profiling (e.g., Butler & Hardy, 1992; Dale & Wrisberg, 1996) was used. Using this method, each player assessed performance in relation to the technical, tactical and physical qualities needed in ice hockey. The profiles obtained in this way enabled assessment of the strengths and weaknesses experienced by the players, but also enabled identification of possible differences in viewpoints between the players and the coaches.

Data Gathering

The data were collected during the course of one ice hockey season starting at the end of April and ending in the April of the following year. The data were derived from continuous observations and a diary based on those observations, and interviews with the head coach. The principal researcher kept a diary of all the team's events and contacts with the team. The 105 single-spaced diary pages produced by the principal researcher included descriptions of the implementation of the goal-setting program, the actions of the team, summaries of discussions with team members and other researchers, opinions, assumptions, suggestions and preliminary interpretations, theoretical considerations and feelings and emotions. The video-recorded interviews with the head coach dealt with the implementation of the goal-setting program. Recordings of the interviews were transcribed verbatim (15 single-spaced pages).

Data Analysis

Abductive content analytical procedures were used (Magnani, 2001). Through abductive logic analysts explore the social and natural world through practical engagement with it, derive working models and provisional understandings, and use such emergent ideas to guide further empirical explorations. It represents a compromise between purely deductive logic and inductive logic (Atkinson & Delamont, 2005). During the planning and implementation phases, the programme was guided deductively by knowledge about goal setting theory. During the implementation of the goal setting program the description, classification, analysis and interpretation of the data proceeded in succession. The data were analysed inductively by extracting themes that illuminated the research aim. The aim was to find and name the central features and to construct a detailed picture of the target group and the events of the season. Another aim was to find regularities or similarities and to interpret the data. Further development of the theory was based on the empirical findings and is the outcome of a dialogue between data and theory in an abductive way.

As early as during the implementation phase at the start of the ice hockey season, four main themes emerged as important: the excessive number of goals, the difficulty of organizing goal setting because of the multiplicity of goals, the existence of unspecific goals, and the implementation of a goal-setting program using unspecific goals. In order to gain a better understanding of these four themes, the researcher refined his focus on the data. In the first phase, the analysis of the themes was continued by reading through the research diary several times and underlining the central issues and making notes. The interviews with the head coach was then analysed. In the first round, different themes and their times of occurrence in the videotape were marked. In the second round, accurate notes were made. In the third round, the findings surrounding the four central themes were written down. An analysis of the diary and of the interviews with the head coach verified the perceptions made during the period in the field. In the next phase all the findings were put in chronological order. In the third phase, during the process of analysing and writing the report, the researchers continuously scrutinized the theoretical literature and the earlier studies. The outcome of this process was a coherent, chronological story. The impact of the narrative analytical method (e.g., Polkinghorne, 1995) can be seen in the analysis and reporting of the present study: The results are presented in a form resembling a story, a common practice in action research (Greenwood & Levin, 1998, p. 123; Winter, 2002) and case study (Stake, 2005).

Trustworthiness

The central feature of an action research based on a case study compared to other qualitative research methods, for example the single-time interview, is the temporal data gathering and the use of several data gathering methods during the implementation or field phase. The second feature is the small number of findings. The researchers do not have a large amount of data concerning the central results. A key result may be based on only one observation (for example, in the present study the difficulty of setting specific and measurable goals), which will open a chain of other observations, which then confirm the result.

An action research study has specific validity criteria (seeHeikkinen, Huttunen, & Syrjälä, 2007). In the present study, historical continuity, communicative validity, the critical friend procedure, and the principles of workability and dialectics were used. First, according to the principle of historical continuity the research report can be presented in the form of a coherent, chronological story. Thus, the use of the narrative method in reporting the observations is not a writing style. The long-term process and the fact that the findings form a continuum, a story, is a way to validate the results. The reader of the story can follow the advance of the deductions of the researchers. The researchers narrate how their understanding of the phenomenon has been enhanced. In the present study, to confirm the critical points of implementing goal setting are described the communicative validity of the study (Kelchtermans, 1994). The head coach read the story forming the results. He agreed that the goal setting process progressed as described in the results section. Further, a critical friend procedure was used. This involved the last author asking questions in order to promote reflection and to propose alternative explanations of the data (Marshall & Rossman, 2006).

At the end of the process, the increase in the understanding achieved leads to a new useful and workable practise. This principle of workability is the fourth way to validate an action research study. In the present study the single observations form a continuum. During a lengthy process the functionality of previously arrived at solutions are tested in practice. If these solutions are not productive, this affects the future implementation of the program. In the present study the principle of workability is the better performance of the team and the players, but also a better understanding of goal setting on the team level. Finally, the reader evaluates, whether understanding has increased and whether workable solutions have been developed.

A fifth way to validate an action research study is by applying the principle of dialectics. Better understanding of the action is constructed as an interactive outcome of thesis and antithesis. An action research study is a story of the authentic speeches and multiple voices of the thoughts of the researcher and the participants in the field. Other findings of the phenomenon or references of the other researchers will also be added to this story. In the present study, for example, the researchers ended up with an observation contrary to what they had anticipated and set general goals instead of specific goals as recommended by the goal setting theory. This solution made possible to develop central areas of individual and team performance.

RESULTS

Setting Group and Individual Goals

The need of the coaches was to set goals that would promote the central aspects of performance both on the team (task and atmosphere) and on the individual (technical, tactical and physical) level. The aim of the researcher was to set specific and measurable goals. Hence, the composite aim was to set as many specific and measurable goals as would cover the central areas of performance.

The team's outcome goal, winning the national championship, was set for the following season, whereas the players' personal outcome goals extended as far ahead as ten years. They included ensuring a place in the team and succeeding in their respective junior age groups, national team, national league, and high-level leagues abroad.

The outcome goals were divided into smaller concrete goals that could be controlled by the athletes themselves. The players were asked to think about actions and strategies that would help them to attain the outcome goal of the team. The most commonly mentioned objectives were "creating a good team spirit", "hard training" and "having a tough attitude". The players were then asked to think about what actions would best lead to achieving these contributory goals. A total of 16 final team goals were expressed; for example, task related goals like "sticking to timetables", "preparing for training and matches", "testing one's limits", and goals related to the team's atmosphere like "equality", "an appropriate sense of humour; not embarrassing or ridiculing others", "encouragement" and "support".

On the basis of a performance profiling meter filled out by the players, four to eight individual goals were set for the following season. Typical goals were to develop "shooting", "stick handling", "skating" (technical), "carrying the puck", "blue-line play", "breakout play", "one-on-one situations" (tactical), "speed" and "strength" (physical).

Observation 1. Setting Specific and Measurable

Goals in a Team Sport is Difficult

The researcher realized that the team goals and personal goals set by players and contributing to the outcome goal were not specific enough to be quantitatively measurable in performance. Consequently, the researcher gave advice to the coach to make the goals more specific and measurable. However, after trying to set more specific and measurable goals the head coach concluded that setting such goals was difficult, because it took too much time and was impractical. If, for example, "encouraging the other players", one of the 16 team goals, had been shaped into a goal according to the guidelines presented in the sports psychology literature (Weinberg & Gould, 2003; Winter, 1995), it would have been necessary to make it more specific by further conceptualizing it. For example, the players might be asked to consider even more carefully what kind of encouragement would have to be improved, in what kind of situation, and by whom. After this, the different forms of encouragement would have to be quantified. The final goal would be to increase the amount of different forms of encouragement, for example, by a certain percentage each month. Alternatively, the goals could be formed by setting interim goals. For example, a 5% increase in the amount of encouragement would be pursued each month. This would be a specific and quantifiable goal, since its realization could be assessed by observing the actions of the coach and the players.

Operating this model would have led to an uncontrollable situation. If each of the 146 unspecific personal (on average 6.65 goals per player) and 17 team goals had been shaped into measurable goals as described above, the number of goals would have increased many times over. Setting the goals out on paper might have been possible, but assessing their realization and observing the players' behavior would have been impossible. Consequently, increasing the number of goals by making them more specific was out of the question.

The problem described above could have been solved by specifying goals and reducing their number. For example, "improving breakout play", an unspecified goal typical of the individual players in this team, could have been divided into sub-goals, such as improving short and long breakout passes, improving breakouts from the defensive, middle, and offensive zone, improving breakout in different playing strategies etc. This could have been done for each of the unspecific goals. In order to avoid chaos, three to five of the specific goals thus set would have been chosen. These would have been further "quantified" into the form of a goal: "I'm going to improve the accuracy of long breakout passes by 15% over the next three months". Had there been only a few specific goals of this kind, the players would probably have progressed towards their achievement.

Because of the desire and need of the coaches to develop all of the technical, tactical and physical areas of performance equally and holistically, specifying and reducing the number of goals was not possible. "It is important to assess performance holistically with the player, and to discuss the key points that make up his performance." (Interview with the head coach)

Setting only a few goals would not have taken into consideration every crucial aspect of the functioning of the team and the players. Thus the coach was not motivated to reduce the number of goals. It may be that coaches and athletes do not usually set specific and measurable goals, because specific goals do not aim at improving performance as a whole, but only a small component of it.

The conclusion that setting specific and measurable goals was not practical was formed after a process lasting three months, i.e., from the middle of May to early August. At first the cooperation between the researcher and the head coach worked well. Later the head coach began to have doubts about the practical value of the program because of too many goals. When the researcher noticed the coach's doubts, he tried to get the coach to become more committed to the goal setting program. For example, he gave the coach a paper laying out the goal setting principles and went through it several timeswith him. The coach still found it difficult to implement the program. A significant positive turn, however, was an open discussion about the problems encountered in goal setting.

> I had to ask the head coach about the drawbacks of the goal-setting program. If necessary, the goals would have to be changed or specified in the right direction. Goals have to be a part of daily practice. I believe in the message and idea of the program. It is good, but it has to be taken up more actively in practice. (Research diary)

The main finding was that specific goals can be overwhelming and coaches may have concerns about specific goals for practical reasons. However, we found a possible solution to the problem - setting general and unspecific goals.

Observation 2. Setting General and Unspecific Goals

The solution found in the discussion and presented in this study – setting general and unspecific goals– made it possible to develop all aspects of performance in a holistic way, as demanded by the head coach. Assessing the goals, and guiding action towards them was possible by utilizing the images that arose from the games and training. In setting and assessing the goals of the team and the individual players, it was essential to take into consideration the sport experience of the coaches and the players, and the images of performance they had developed during their sports career.

As the season advanced, there were team and line meetings where the coaches tried to present to the players as clear an image of the players' performance goals as possible. The coaches went into the player's goals in detail. For example, they sought to concretize a player's role on the ice for him.

> First, the players used their own written goals to consider their offensive and defensive roles. Each of the players introduced his view to his line and to the coaches. The introduction was followed by feedback from the coaches. In his feedback, the head coach tried his best to concretize each player's strengths for him: the kind of performance that would best make the player stand out in his line. By doing this he was trying to utilize the players' performance images. (Research diary)
>
> The head coach was going through Ryan's role. They were having a dialogue about Ryan's skills. The head coach created and expressed images of Ryan's strengths in relation to performance: "You have a strong skills element. You do pirouettes, stop and spin, just like Saku Koivu [an image of a fast and agile player]". Ryan's style gained approval and encouragement. It is hardly a coincidence that Ryan's father came to praise the head coach after the weekend game. (Research diary)

Video-recording was an excellent aid in strengthening the players' performance images. The number of video meetings increased steadily over the fall. Towards the end of the program, the coaches began to use video-recording as a tool for rating and guiding performance, even in game meetings and training. Videotaping helped players to assess their performance. The focus of the dialogue was on resources and means instead of hindrances and limitations. Goals are better achieved when set in a positive way and the athlete's attention is focused on what he is trying to achieve instead of on what he should try to avoid.

> The head coach gave the players images of good counter-rush play on the basis of last weekend's men's league game. He thought the team had performed excellently in this week's training. (Research diary)
>
> Looking for opportunities and giving them to players by considering what has to be done in the future is very important. Hence, we're seeking positive images of performance. We don't talk about problems anymore, just opportunities and solutions. (Interview with the head coach)

We (the researchers) perceived that for a person who does not know a sport very well – as is often the case with a researcher – the goals set by the coach and the athlete may seem unspecific and general, but for an experienced athlete they may be very specific. Although the image of a goal might be unclear to the researchers, the athlete knew exactly what he must do to achieve it. By the end of the season the goals were so over-learned that the coaches and the players actively and autonomously discussed the goals before a game, during breaks in a game and during a game. Players concentrated well on their own tasks and goals.

> Before and during the game the head coach discussed the players' goals in detail. Moreover, during breaks he focused the attention of the players on the task. They won 5 - 3, even though the opponent upped twice. The coach saw that goal-directed feedback was essential for the outcome of the game. (Research diary)

The players' ability to assess their own performance advanced during the season. Team performance improved as well. The team passed the preliminary level, interim level and advanced to the play-off games, did not make the final, but won the bronze medal. In addition, the players were asked to rate on a scale of 1 to 10 the achievement of both the team and their individual goals. The results revealed that the team achieved its common goals (a rise was from 6.7 pre-evaluation to 8.2 post evaluation) and the players their individual goals (rise from 5.7. to 6.8.). The qualitative observations are also in line with this quantitative data. According to the head coach, the team also got close to its optimal level of performance at the end of the season.

> Researcher: How would you describe a team's optimal performance?
> Head coach: Tuning a team to its optimal performance is like having to hit the center line when landing a plane on a runway. You have to hit precisely that line – landing on the runway isn't enough. First, the optimal performance of a team requires a good tactical game plan. It is a tactical mental image indicating group efficacy. It tells how the game will end. Second, you need the right emotional state for the game. Third, you have to be able to shut out external factors, such as the pressure to win, which often originates in the audience. These things depend on each other.
> Researcher: How is it possible to know when a team is in an optimal state?
> Head coach: When a coach knows his players, he can see it in their behavior. A peak performer focuses on his performance and things that are relevant to it. The player assumes responsibility. When he's on the ice he's not afraid of mistakes and trying to avoid them.
> Researcher: Did the group achieve such a state?
> Head coach: Yes, in several play-off games. (Interview with the head coach)

DISCUSSION

The aim of the present case and action research study was to describe and evaluate the implementation of a one-season-long goal setting program in an ice hockey team. More specifically, the research question was to study the setting of specific and quantitatively measurable goals in a team sport.

The researchers aimed at setting specific and measurable personal and team goals together with the coaches and players. It was found that setting such specific and quantitatively measurable goals for a team, as recommended in theory, was difficult in practice. Setting as many specific and measurable goals as needed to cover team (task and atmosphere) and individual (technical, tactical and physical) performance holistically would have led to an overwhelming multiplicity of goals. The obstacle to setting specific goals arose from the practical concerns of the head coach who felt that it was impossible to implement the theoretical principles proposed by the principal researcher. The alternative – reducing the number of goals to a few specific ones – did not motivate the coaches. A small number of specific goals would not have taken into account every crucial aspect of the functioning of the team and the players.

The solution developed in the present study was to set general and unspecific but holistic goals, such as "improving a move", "carrying the puck", "acceleration", or "playing to the end". It has been noted that coaches and athletes favour general and unspecific goals (Brawley, Carron, & Widmeyer, 1992). When they studied the specificity and clarity of athletes' goals in several team sports (13 teams, 154 athletes), Brawley et al., 1992 observed that 71% of the goals were general in nature, and only 29% were specific. The reason for this may be that coaches and players seek to develop all different aspects of performance holistically. If an attempt is made to set specific goals that constitute small measurable parts of the overall team's or player's performance, the most important aspect – development of the performance of the team and of the individual athlete – may suffer. In a situation like this it is not surprising that athletes are not motivated to work towards such goals. Weak commitment to goals has been suggested as one reason why specific goals have not fared better than general ones in team coaching (Hall & Kerr, 2001).

We found that setting specific and measurable goals was not even necessary. Setting general and unspecific goals, evaluating these goals, and guiding action towards them was possible through utilizing the performance images that had arisen from the games and training. Although such goals may be unclear to the researcher, the athletes may know exactly what they must do to achieve them. Brawley et al. (1992 pp. 331-332) expressed similar ideas. They found that "although athletes were unable to describe their goals well, they did perceive the goals to be quite clear. The average clarity for group goals was 7 on a 9-point scale". In spite of the unspecificity of goals, the athletes seemed to have a clear idea of what they were and what it would take to achieve them. Brawley et al. (1992) suggested that the crude and elementary goal-setting programs used by coaches might prove the best. Having a clear idea of what it takes to achieve an unspecific and general goal could be another reason why in so many studies general goals have proven to be better than specific ones (Hall & Kerr, 2001).

Specific and measurable goals work well in individual sports (e.g., Burton et al. 2001; Hall & Kerr, 2001). However, as the number of individuals in a team sport increases, coordinating the team's actions such as setting goals or evaluating performance is more complicated. Klein and Mulvey (1995) suggest that generalizing the results of studies on individual sports to team sports is not always possible. Research on goal setting in team sports is scarce and goal-setting instructions for team sports are derived mainly from individual sports. In an individual sport which requires, for example, endurance and strength, it is easier to measure the level of performance than in a team sport. The result of a physiological measurement is often valid: a good result often translates into a good result in a competition. The physiological characteristics of players can also be measured in team sports, but the results are not necessarily reflected as directly in performance. The performance of the individual in a sports team (as in an individual sport) is not only the sum of complex technical, tactical, physiological and psychological elements, but the cooperation of the team members also has an impact on the outcome. Thus it is easier to set measurable goals in individual sports than in team sports.

Most of the existing goal-setting studies have been conducted as laboratory studies or simulations using students as subjects. Typically, the goals studied have been assigned rather than self-set, have dealt with simple tasks and been performed independently or over short time periods. In the present study it was found that authentic team sport settings are different from laboratory settings. This result may explain the findings which contradict the basic assumptions of goal specificity. Setting specific and measurable goals in team sports is difficult.

Players' shared goals such as "equality", "sacrificing oneself" and "encouraging the other players", and their individual goals such as "playing one-on-one", "stick handling" and "assists" were not directly measurable in an objective and quantitative way. Consequently, new methods of assessment and feedback need to be developed. A few studies have investigated the connection between the effect of feedback and goal achievement. The effect of feedback on goal setting has been found to be positive (Goudas, Minardou, & Kotis, 2000; Hall et al., 1987; Shoenfelt, 1996; Tzetzis, Kioumourtzoglou, & Mavromatis, 1997), and feedback is seen as a central component of a goal program (Burton et al., 2001; Hall & Kerr, 2001). What kind of feedback is the best, or how feedback should be used in a goal setting program has not been assessed. However, some suggestions on assessment and feedback can be made on the basis of this study. At the beginning of the season concretizing the players' goals was attempted with numerical methods of assessment. However, the images of performance inspired by the training and the games were seen as a better alternative to "paper and pencil" assessment. The images of performance were guided by focusing the player's attention on what he was trying to achieve. Video-recording games turned out to be an excellent aid in guiding the players' images, and it enabled assessment of whether the image of achieving goals in training was verified on tape. Using videos and images of performance might be a good solution in giving holistic feedback. Videos and simulations have also been used to develop the cognitive skills of players (Starkes, 2001; Williams & Grant, 1999).

A limitation of this study is that the results are based on only one team and mainly on the perceptions of the principal researcher and the head coach. The researchers did not have a large amount of data or statistics, but they approached their research phenomena from a new perspective. Although the number of findings is small, the authenticity of the case (Winter, 2002), the long-term process and the fact that the findings form a continuum, a story, helps to validate them. During the year-long program, the observations made early in the season were verified. The difficulties experienced in setting specific and measurable goals led to the setting of unspecific holistic goals and utilizing images of performance in controlling the goal-setting process. This may have led to better achievement of the team's dual goal, i.e. group performance and cohesion, as the season proceeded. These findings are supported by the different data gathering methods used: field observations, research diary, and interviews with the head coach. In this qualitative action research and case study it was possible to obtain knowledge about the process of coaching over the course of time. A pre - post design with only a few measurement points would not have had this advantage.

The present results can not be generalized to all team sports in all situations. For example we do not know whether the results can be generalized to a team sport that relies heavily on individual performance such as baseball. However, we believe that in different contexts (sport, work organization, school), groups can encounter similar problems in implementing both individual and group goal-setting programs. The findings of the present study can be of value to coaches, athletes and sport psychology practitioners. If the goal set is not specific and measurable, coaches should ensure that the performance image of the player concerning the goal is clear. Athletes in a team should be required to can improve their strengths by setting individual goals, and in this way find an appropriate role inside the team. For sport psychology practitioners, it is necessary to be aware that development is possible only from the perspective of the target group. Because this study was implemented in only one team, it would be beneficial to replicate it in other teams and with other team sports in order to confirm the merits of the approach. Instead of testing the general principles of a goal-setting method, such as specificity and difficulty, the researcher, or better yet, the participating coaches, should construct a theory using athlete-based and phenomenon-based long-term programs that extend over several seasons.

In this study the lesson learned was that setting specific and measurable goals in a team sport context is difficult. Specific goals may be overwhelming and coaches may have concerns about these goals. It was also found that setting specific goals may not even be necessary. Setting general and unspecific but holistic goals is suggested as an alternative for team sports.

REFERENCES

Anderson, C. D., Crowell, C. R., Doman, M., & Howard, G. S. (1988). Performance posting, goal setting, and activity-contingent praise as applied to a university hockey team. *Journal of Applied Psychology, 73*, 87-95.

Anshel, M. H., Weinberg, R., & Jackson, A. (1992). The effect of goal difficulty and task complexity on intrinsic motivation and motor performance. *Journal of Sport Behavior, 15*, 159-176.

Atkinson, P., & Delamont, S. 2005. Analytic perspectives. In N. K. Denzin & Y. S. Lincoln (Eds.), *The Sage Handbook of Qualitative Research* (3rd ed., pp. 821-840). London: Sage.

Bar-Eli, M., Levy-Kolker, N., Tenenbaum, G., & Weinberg, R.S. (1993). Effect of goal difficulty on performance of aerobic, anaerobic and power tasks in laboratory and field settings. *Journal of Sport Behavior, 16*, 17-32.

Bar-Eli, M., Tenenbaum, G., Pie, J.S., Btesh, Y., & Almog, A. (1997). Effect of goal difficulty, goal specificity and duration of practice time intervals on muscular endurance performance. *Journal of Sports Sciences, 15*, 125-135.

Barnett, M. L., & Stanicek, J. A. (1979). Effects of goal-setting on achievement in archery. *Research Quarterly, 50*, 328-332.

Boyce, B. A. (1990). The effect of instructor-set goals upon skill acquisition and retention of a selected shooting task. *Journal of Teaching in Physical Education, 9*, 115-122.

Boyce, B. A. (1992a). Effects of assigned versus participant-set goals on skill acquisition and retention of a selected shooting task. *Journal of Teaching in Physical Education, 11*, 220-234.

Boyce, B. A. (1992b). The effects of goal proximity on skill acquisition and retention of a shooting task in a field-based setting. *Journal of Sport and Exercise Psychology, 14*, 298-308.

Boyce, B. A. (1994). The effects of goal setting on performance and spontaneous goal-setting behavior of experienced pistol shooters. *The Sport Psychologist, 8*, 87-93.

Brawley, L. R., Carron, A. V., & Widmeyer, W. N. (1992). The nature of group goals in sport teams: A phenomenological analysis. *The Sport Psychologist, 6*, 323-333.

Burton, D. (1989). The impact of goal specificity and task complexity on basketball skill development. *The Sport Psychologist, 3*, 35-47.

Burton, D. (1992). The Jekyll/Hyde nature of goals: Reconceptualising goal setting in sport. In T. Thorn (Eds.) *Advances in Sport Psychology* (pp. 267-297). Champaign, IL: Human Kinetics.

Burton, D. (1993). Goal setting in sport. In R. N. Singer., M. Murphey., & L. K. Tennant (Eds.) *Handbook of research on sport psychology*(pp. 467-491). New York: Macmillan.

Burton, D., Naylor, S., & Holliday, B. (2001). Goal setting in sport: Investigating the goal effectiveness paradox. In R. N. Singer, H. A. Hausenblas, & C. M. Janelle (Eds.) *Handbook of sport psychology* (2nd ed., pp. 497-528). New York: John Wiley & Sons.

Butler, R. J., & Hardy, L. (1992). The performance profile: Theory and application. *The Sport Psychologist, 6*, 253-264.

Carron A., & Hausenblas, H. (1998) *Group dynamics in sport* (2nd ed.). London, Ontario: Fitness Information Technology.

Chidester, J. S., & Grigsby, W. C. (1984). A meta-analysis of the goal setting performance literature. In J. A. Pearce, & R. B. Robinson (Eds.) *Proceedings of the 44th annual meeting of the academy of management*(pp. 202-206). Ada, OH: Academy of Management.

Dale, G. A., & Wrisberg, C. A. (1996). The use of a performance profiling technique in a team setting: Getting the athletes and coach on the "same page". *The Sport Psychologist, 10*, 261-277.

Daw J., & Burton, D. (1994). Evaluation of a comprehensive psychological skills training program for collegiate tennis players. *The Sport Psychologist, 8*, 37-57.

Dobson, P. J. (2001). Longitudinal case research: a critical realistic perspective. *Systemic Practise and Action Research, 14*, 283-296.

Erbaugh, S. J., & Barnett, M. L. (1986). Effects of modeling and goal-setting on the jumping performance of primary-grade children. *Perceptual and Motor Skills, 63*, 1287-1293.

Evans, L., Hardy, L., & Fleming, S. (2000). Intervention strategies with injured athletes: an action research study. *The Sport Psychologist, 14;* 188-206.

Goudas, M., Minardou, K., & Kotis, I. (2000). Feedback regarding goal achievement and intrinsic motivation. *Perceptual and Motor Skills, 90*, 810-812.

Greenwood, D. J., & Levin, M. (1998). Introduction to action research. Social research for social change. Thousands Oaks: Sage.

Hall, H. K., & Byrne, A. T. J. (1988). Goal setting in sport: Clarifying recent anomalies. *Journal of Sport and Exercise Psychology, 10*, 184-198.

Hall, H. K., & Kerr, A. W. (2001). Goal setting in sport and physical activity: Tracing empirical developments and establishing conceptual direction. In G. C. Roberts (Eds.) *Advances in motivation in sport and exercise*(pp.183-233). Champaign, IL: Human Kinetics.

Hall, H. K., Weinberg, R. S., & Jackson, A. (1987). Effects of goal specificity, goal difficulty, and information feedback on endurance performance. *Journal of Sport Psychology, 9*, 43-54.

Hardy, L., Jones, G., & Gould, D. (1997). *Understanding psychological preparation for sport*. Chichester, England: John Wiley & Sons.

Heikkinen, H. L. T., Huttunen, R., & Syrjälä, L. (2007). Action research as narrative: Five principles for validation. *Educational Action Research, 15*, 5–19.

Kelchtermans, G. 1994. Biographical methods in the study of teachers' professional development. In I. Carlgren, G. Handal., & S. Vaage (Eds.) *Teachers' mind and actions: Research on teachers' thinking and practice* (pp. 93-108). London: Falmer.

Kemmis, S., & McTaggart, R. (2005). Participatory action research: communicative action and the public sphere. In N. K. Denzin., & Y. S. Lincoln (Eds.) *The Sage handbook of qualitative research*(3rd ed., pp. 559-603). Thousand Oaks: Sage.

Klein, H, J., & Mulvey, P, W. (1995). Two investigations of the relationship among group goals, goal commitment, cohesion, and performance. *Organizational Behavior and Human Decision Processes, 61*, 44-53.

Kyllo, B. L., & Landers, D. M. (1995). Goal setting in sport and exercise: A research synthesis to resolve the controversy. *Journal of Sport and Exercise Psychology, 17*, 117-137.

Latham, G. P. & Lee, T. W. (1986). Goal setting. In E. A. Locke. (Eds.) *Generalizing from laboratory to field settings: Research findings from industrial-organizational psychology. Organizational behavior, and human resource management* (pp. 101-107). Lexington, MA: Heath.

Lerner, B. S., Ostrow, A. C., Yura, M. T., & Etzel, E. F. (1996). The effects of goal-setting and imagery training programs on the free-throw performance of female collegiate basketball players. *The Sport Psychologist, 10*, 382-397.

Locke, E. A. (1968). Toward a theory of task motivation incentives. *Organizational Behavior and Human Performance, 3*, 157-189.

Locke, E. A. (1991). Problems with goal setting research in sports-and their solution. *Journal of Sport and Exercise Psychology, 13*, 311-316.

Locke, E. A. (1994). Comments on Weinberg and Weigand. *Journal of Sport and Exercise Psychology, 16*, 212-215.

Locke, E. A., & Latham, G. P. (1985). The application of goal setting to sports. *Journal of Sport Psychology, 7*, 205-222.

Locke, E. A., & Latham, G. P. (1990). *A Theory of of goal setting and task performance.* Englewood Cliffs, NJ: Perntice- Hall.

Locke, E. A., Shaw, K. N., Saari, L. M., & Latham, G. P. (1981). Goal setting and task performance. *Psychological Bulletin, 90*, 125-152.

Magnani, L. (2001). *Abduction, reason, and science: Processes of discovery and explanation.* New York: Kluwer/Plenum.

Marshall, C., & Rossman, G. B. (2006). Designing qualitative research. 4th ed. Thousand Oakes, CA: Sage.

Mento, A. J., Steel, R. P., & Karren, R. J. (1987). A meta-analytic study of the effects of goal setting on task performance: 1966-1984. *Organizational Behavior and Human Decision Processes, 39*, 52-83.

Miller, J. T., & McAuley, E. (1987). Effects of a goal-setting training program on basketball free-throw self-efficacy and performance. *The Sport Psychologist, 1*, 103-113.

Polkinghorne, D. (1995). Narrative cofiguration in qualitative analysis. In J. A. Hatch. & R. Wisniewski (Eds.) *Life history and narrative* (pp. 5-23). London: Falmer.

Rovio, E. (2002). *Joukkueellinen yksilöitä. Toimintatutkimus psyykkisen valmennuksen ohjelman suunnittelusta, toteuttamisesta ja arvioinnista poikien jääkiekkojoukkueessa [A team of individuals. Planning, implementing and evaluating a program of psychological skills for coaching with a boys' ice hockey team. An action research].* Dissertation, Jyväskylä: LIKES Research Center for Sport and Health Sciences.

Shoenfelt, E.L. (1996). Goal setting and feedback as a posttraining strategy to increase the transfer of training. *Perceptual and Motor Skills, 83*, 176-178.

Stake, R. E. (2005). Qualitative case studies. In N. K. Denzin., & Y. S. Lincoln (Eds.) *The sage handbook of qualitative research*(3rd ed., pp. 443-466). Thousand Oaks: Sage.

Starkes, J. (2001). The road to expertise: Can we shorten the journey and lengthen the stay? In A. Papaioannou, G. Marios, & Y. Theodorakis (Eds.) *In Proceedings In the dawn of the new milllennium 10th World Congress of Sport Psychology* (pp. 198-205). Volume 2. Thessaloniki: Christodoulidis Publications.

Swain, A., & Jones, G. (1995). Effects of goal-setting interventions on selected basketball skills: A single-subject design. *Research Quarterly for Exercise and Sport, 66*, 51-63.

Tubbs, M. E. (1991). Goal-setting: A meta-analytic examination of the empirical evidence. *Journal of Applied Psychology, 71*, 474-483.

Tzetzis, G., Kioumourtzoglou, E., & Mavromatis, G. (1997). Goal setting and feedback for the development of instructional strategies. *Perceptual and Motor Skills, 84*, 1411-1427.

Weinberg RS. (1994). Goal setting and performance in sport and exercise settings: A synthesis and critique. *Medicine and Science in Sports and Exercise, 26*, 469-477.

Weinberg, R., Bruya, L., & Jackson, A. (1985). The effects of goal proximity and goal specificity on endurance performance. *Journal of Sport Psychology, 7*, 296-305.

Weinberg, R., Bruya, L., Garland, H., & Jackson, A. (1990). Effect of goal difficulty and positive reinforcement on endurance performance. *Journal of Sport and Exercise Psychology, 12*, 144-156.

Weinberg, R., Bruya, L., Jackson, A., & Garland, H. (1987). Goal difficulty and endurance performance: A challenge to the goal attainability assumption. *Journal of Sport Behavior, 10*, 82-92.

Weinberg, R., Fowler, C., Jackson, A., Bagnall, J., & Bruya, L. (1991). Effect of goal difficulty on motor performance: A replication across tasks and subjects. *Journal of Sport and Exercise Psychology, 13*, 160-173.

Weinberg, R. S., & Gould, D. (2003). Foundations of sport and exercise psychology (3rd ed.). Champaign, IL: Human Kinetics.

Weinberg, R., Stitcher, T., & Richardson, P. (1994). Effects of a seasonal goal-setting program on lacrosse performance. *The Sport Psychologist, 8*, 166-175.

Weinberg R. S., & Weigand, D. A. (1993). Goal setting in sport and exercise: A reaction to Locke. *Journal of Sport and Exercise Psychology, 15*, 88-96.

Weinberg R. S., & Weigand, D. A. (1996). Let the discussions continue: A reaction to Locke's comments on Weinberg and Weigand. *Journal of Sport and Exercise Psychology, 18*, 89-93.

Widmeyer, N. W., & Ducharme, K. (1997). Team building through team goal setting. *Journal of Applied Sport Psychology, Special issue: Team building, 9*, 97-113.

Williams, A. M., & Grant, A. (1999). Training perceptual skill in sport. *International Journal of Sport Psychology, 30*, 194-220.

Winter, G. (1995). Goal setting. In T. Morris, & J. Summers (Eds.) *Sport psychology, theory, applications and issues*(pp. 258-270). Singapore: John Wiley & Sons.

Winter, R. (2002). Truth or fiction: problems of validity and authenticity in narratives of action research. *Educational Action Research, 10*, 143-154.

Wood, R. E. Mento, A. J., & Locke, E. A. (1987). Task complexity as a moderator of goal effects: A meta-analysis. *Journal of Applied Psychology, 72*, 416-425.

In: Introduction to Sport Psychology
Editor: Robert Schinke

ISBN: 978-1-61761-973-1
© 2011 Nova Science Publishers, Inc.

THE RELATIONSHIP BETWEEN COPING STYLES AND DRINKING BEHAVIORS IN TEENAGE ATHLETES

Gregory S. Wilson*[a] and Mary E. Pritchard[b]

[a]University of Evansville, Evansville, Indiana, U.S.A.
[b]BoiseStateUniversity, Boise, Indiana, U.S.A.

ABSTRACT

Alcohol is the most widely used drug among athletes and its misuse with this population is well documented (O'Brien & Lyons, 2000). However, underlying emotional causes for its misuse have not been identified, nor has the interaction of gender and athletic status been examined. We hypothesized that coping styles used by athletes would relate to their drinking behaviors and this pattern would differ based on gender and athletic status. Female non-athletes consumed the least amount of alcohol and male non-athletes were the least likely to become intoxicated, whereas male athletes drank the greatest amount and were the most likely to become intoxicated. Drinking to cope had the highest correlation to drinking behaviors, but there were differences in the relation between coping tactics and drinking behaviors dependent upon gender and athletic status.

THE RELATIONSHIP BETWEEN COPING STYLES AND DRINKING BEHAVIORS IN TEENAGE ATHLETES

Alcohol is considered the most widely used drug among athletes (O'Brien & Lyons, 2000), and its misuse by athletes is well documented (Hildebrand, Johnson, & Bogle, 2001; Jerry-Szpak & Brown, 1994; O'Brien & Lyons; Watson, 2002). Although the dangers of alcohol abuse are known, reasons for the high level of use by athletes are less understood. Research indicates that athletes begin drinking at an earlier age, and drink in greater amounts than non-athletes. Hildebrand et al. found that college students, who were either current athletes or former high school athletes, began drinking at an earlier age, consumed more alcohol more often, and engaged in binge drinking and other risk taking behaviors more frequently than did college students who had never been athletes. Moreover, the Centers for Disease Control and Prevention (1998) reported that 91% of college athletes and 90% of high school athletes first began drinking before entering college.

* Contact Information: Gregory S. Wilson, P.E.D., FACSM, Associate Professor & Chair, Department of Exercise and Sport Science, Graves Hall, University of Evansville, Evansville, IN 47722, Tel: (812) 488-2847, Fax: (812) 488-2087, Email: gw3@evansvill.edu Boise State University

This problem is compounded by the fact that illicit alcohol use by teenagers is wide spread. This is perhaps not surprising given that The National Center on Addiction and Substance Abuse (CASA, 2007) found over44% of middle school and 80% of high schoolstudents have personally witnessed drug dealing, possession, and use at school. In addition, students are becoming used to seeing their peers high onalcohol, prescription drugs, or illegal drugs. While Johnston, O'Malley, and Bachman(1993) found that 90% of students had tried alcohol by the twelfth grade (see also Johnston, O'Malley, Bachman,& Schulenberg, 2007), the percentage of teens who are drinking to get drunk continues to rise with nearly 20% of 8th-graders and over 40% of 10th-graders drinking enough to be considered drunk at least once (Johnston et al., 2007). In addition, nearly 40% of 9th graders have had alcohol in the past months (Centers for Disease Control and Prevention, 2006) and nearly 20% of 9th-graders report binge drinking in the past month (Wagenaar, Harwood, &Bernat, 2002). Adding to this problem is the fact that the majority of students who have misused alcohol by this time have also engaged in high risk drinking behaviors or use of illegal drugs (CASA, 2007; Ellickson, McGuigan, Adams, Bell, & Hays, 1996). Importantly, a recurrent finding from these studies is that teenage males drink alcohol more frequently and in greater quantities than do teenage females(Barnes, Welte, & Dintcheff, 1993; Chen, Dufour, & Yi,2004/2005; Huselid & Cooper, 1992; but see Ellickson et al. for conflicting results), and that in particular teenage and collegiate male athletes drink in greater quantities and with greater frequency than do non-athletes (Hildebrand et al., 2001; Jerry-Szpak & Brown, 1994; Turrisi, Mastroleo, Mallett, Larimer, & Kilmer, 2007).

Unfortunately, reasons for such differences in teenage athletes and non-athletes are not fully understood. However, one study has been suggested (Wilson, Pritchard & Schaffer, 2004) that utilization of poor coping mechanisms may lead some groups of individuals to participate in higher levels of alcohol usage.

For example, coping is a response to stress by which a person deals with stressors and the negative responses that accompany them (Lazarus & Folkman, 1984). Unfortunately, because of increases in teenage substance abuse, it has been suggested that today's teenager faces increasing levels of stress while manifesting an inability to cope with these demands (Anda & Bradley, 1997). Thus, current research is placing more emphasis on identifying successful coping tactics used by teenagers in stressful situations. Researchers typically discuss three types of coping styles: problem-focused coping (addressing the stressor directly), emotion-focused coping (addressing the affective consequences of the stressor), and avoidant coping (denial of the problem) (Billings & Moos, 1981). Within each of these coping styles, there are a variety of coping tactics. For example, problem-focused coping includes tactics such as coming up with a strategy, concentrating on fixing the problem, and getting advice. Emotion-focused tactics include getting emotional support, venting, and making fun of the situation. Avoidant tactics include using alcohol to feel better, denying the problem, and giving up (Billings & Moos).

There is substantial agreement that the way in which an individual copes with stressrelates to not only mental health, but also physical well-being(Bonica & Daniel, 2003).In general, studies have found that male adolescents and college students use more problem-focused and avoidant coping, whereas females use more emotion-focused (Bird & Harris, 1990; Cauce et al., 2000; Dwyer & Cummings (2001); Piko, 2001; Rao, Moudad, & Subbakrishna, 2000; Schaffer & Pritchard, 2003).Research suggests that the reason for many of these gender differences in stress levels and health may involve differences in coping styles between adolescents and young adults (Dwyer & Cummings, 2001; Sheu & Sedlacek, 2004).

Less is known about the influence of athletic status on coping strategies. Wilson et al. (2004) foundthat correlations between alcohol behaviors and coping tactics varied by both gender and athletic status in college students (athlete v. non-athlete). Specifically, the most significant predictor for drinking in collegiate female athletes was the use of alcohol as a coping mechanism, whereas other coping tactics were relatedto male collegiate athletes' alcohol consumption (e.g., "getting advice from others," not "praying or meditating").

Although previous studies of teenagers have found that stress and coping play a role in teenage consumption of alcohol (Wills, Sandy, Yaeger, Cleary, & Shinar, 2001; Wills, Vaccaro, & Benson, 1995), previous studies have not examined the impact of coping on alcohol use in male and female teenage athletes. Although a significant proportion of teenagers in the United States misuse alcohol (Ellickson et al., 1996; Johnston et al., 2007), the student-athlete is at a potentially greater risk as a result of the stress and pressure often associated with the dual demands of academics and athletics (Watson, 2002). However, it is currently unknown whether differences in gender and coping tactics do in fact relate to the use of alcohol among high school athletes as compared to their non-athlete counterparts. This issue is of importance because if coping tactics relate to the use of alcohol among high school athletes (particularly male athletes), then alcohol prevention programs employed with high school athletes need to take into account the unique pressures faced by athletes and how they cope with these stressors(Wilson et al.,2004).

The purpose of this study was to determine whether differences in coping tactics used by male and female athletes and non-athletes relate to rates and frequency of alcohol consumption in teenagers. It was hypothesized that both coping tactics and athletic status (athlete v. non-athlete) would relate to the use and frequency of alcohol consumptionby male and female teenagers. Similar to previous research (Barnes et al., 1993; Chen et al.,2004/2005; Huselid & Cooper, 1992), we predicted that males drink more than females and athletes drink more than non-athletes (Hildebrand et al., 2001; Jerry-Szpak & Brown, 1994; Turrisi et al. 2007), especially male athletes.In addition, similar to Wilson et al. (2004), we predicted that drinking to cope would relate to alcohol use for all groups, but that the relation between other types of coping and alcohol use would vary by gender and athletic status (athlete v. non-athlete). However, because research investigating this topic is scant (especially in teenagers), no specific predictions were made for this hypothesis.

METHOD

Participants

The participants (n=453) were female and male middle school and high school students recruited from a variety of summer youth sports camps (e.g., cheerleading, band, track, baseball), local schools, and churches. Specifically, three hundred fifty six of the participants were recruited from the local summer sports camps sponsored by a Midwestern university; eighty came from local churches, and seventeen came from a local school. If students indicated on their survey that they participated in a sport (e.g., on a school team, part of a non-school league, etc.), they were considered an athlete. Based on this, participants were grouped as female athletes (n=146) and non-athletes (n=112) or male athletes (n=109) and non-athletes (n=86). All participants involved in the summer sports camps, school class, and church activities were invited to participate. The survey was administered in a closed classroom, with distractions minimized, and participants were given as much time as needed to complete the survey. As surveys were administered to these groups as an activity, a high percentage of those participants who were approached completed the survey (approximately 90%).

The participantsranged in age from 14 to 19, with a mean age of 15.35 (SD=1.17). Approximately 90 percent of participants were Caucasian, with Latino, African-American, Asian-American, and 'other' representing very small percentages of the overall sample.Informed consent was given by each participant and her/his parent/guardian prior to survey administration. All participants were assured that their responses would be confidential. The Subcommittee for the Protection of Research Subjects approved procedures for this investigation.

MEASURES

Coping tactics. Coping tactics were measured with a modified version of the Brief COPE (Carver, 1997). The Brief COPE is a Likert-type questionnaire that contains 14 tactics (e.g., "I would use alcohol or other drugs to make myself feel better,""I would get emotional support (comfort & understanding) from others,""I would give up trying to deal with it," etc.). Students responded to how they would deal with a stressful event on a four-point scale ranging from one (*I wouldn't do this at all*) to four (*I would do this a lot*). This measure has been tested on a variety of populations (Pritchard & McIntosh, 2003), and the measure has been validated and shown to be reliable (Carver 1997; Perczek, Carver, Price, & Pozo-Kaderman, 2000). In addition, the longer version has been tested and found to be reliable and valid in adolescent populations (Phelps & Jarvis, 1994), and, it has been used successfully with athletes (Baltzell, 1999; Wilson et al., 2004).

Alcohol behaviors. Alcohol use was assessed with three items from Cooper et al. (1992). In response to each question, participants were asked to indicate the frequency of drinking ("How often do you drink?" *0=never/rarely, 1=once a month, 2=once a week, 3 = 2-3 times a week, 4=daily or almost daily*), the frequency of drinking until intoxication("How often do you drink until intoxication?" *0=never/rarely, 1=once a month, 2=once a week, 3 = 2-3 times a week, 4=daily or almost daily*), and how much they drink per drinking occasion ("What is your usual quantity of alcohol consumed per drinking occasion (i.e. number of drinks)? One drink = 12 ounces of beer, 4 ounces wine, 1 ounce spirits").

RESULTS

Drinking Behaviors

The purpose of this study was to determine whether differences in coping tactics used by male and female athletes and non-athletes relate to rates and frequency of alcohol consumption in teenagers. The drinking behaviors of teenage male and female athletes and non-athletes were first compared. A two by two Analysis of variance (ANOVA) was run comparing gender to athletes versus non-athletes, with students initially asked to report how often they drank alcohol. These results revealed that there were no gender differences how often teens drank alcohol, $F (1, 416) = 3.43$. However, athletes ($M = .39$, $SD = .78$) drank significantly more often than did non-athletes ($M = .22$, $SD = .69$), $F (1, 416) = 5.67$, $p < .05$. Finally, there was no interaction between gender and athletic status, $F (1, 416) < 1$. In comparisons of the amount of alcohol consumed, a 2 (gender) x 2 (athlete v. non-athlete) ANOVA was performed. Results indicated that males reported that they drank higher quantities of alcohol per drinking occasion ($M = 1.59$ drinks, $SD = 3.97$) than did females ($M = .52$ drinks, $SD = 1.55$), $F (1, 416) = 12.07$, $p < .001$. Athletes also reported drinking more alcohol per drinking occasion ($M = 1.34$ drinks, $SD = 3.52$) than did non-athletes ($M = .46$ drinks, $SD = 1.48$), $F (1, 416) = 12.91$, $p < .001$. There was an interaction between gender and athletic status, $F (1, 416) = 5.68$, $p < .05$, with female non-athletes drinking the least alcohol per drinking occasion ($M = .33$ drinks, $SD = 1.40$) and male athletes drinking the most alcohol ($M = 2.30$ drinks, $SD = 4.95$).

Finally, a two x two ANOVA comparing gender to athletes versus non-athletes showed that teenagers reported rarely drinking until intoxicated, and there were no gender differences in frequency of intoxication, $F (1, 417) = 3.38$. However, athletes reported that they drank until intoxication more frequently ($M = .25$, $SD = .72$) than did non-athletes ($M = .08$ $SD = .41$), $F (1, 417) = 11.59$, $p < .001$. Finally, there was an interaction between gender and athletic status, $F (1, 417) = 4.73$, $p < .05$, with male non-athletes being the least likely to drink until intoxicated ($M = .08$, $SD = .46$) and male athletes being the most likely to drink until intoxicated ($M = .40$, $SD = .93$).

DRINKING BEHAVIORS IN RELATION TO COPING

Although teenagers were not drinking excessively, there were significant differences between males and females and between athletes and non-athletes. One possible reason for differences in alcohol behavior might be the students' use of coping tactics. Because some students drink to cope and others cope in different ways, we thought it important to examine the relationship between coping tactics and drinking behaviors. Because we found several interactions between gender and athletic status on drinking behaviors for some of the variables, it was important to examine the coping tactics based on gender and athletic status.

The relationship between quantity of alcohol consumed and coping tactics is displayed in Table 1. Using alcohol as "a way to feel better" was significantly related to quantity of alcohol consumption for all students. Other than this finding, the relationship between coping and quantity of alcohol consumed varied based on both gender and athletic status. For example, "turning to work or other activities" related positively to alcohol quantity only in female athletes, but "giving up" related to quantity only in male athletes.

Table 1.The Relationship between Quantity of Alcohol Consumed per Drinking Occasion and Coping Tactics

	FA	FNA	MA	MNA
Turn to work or activities	.20*	-.11	-.07	-.07
Concentrate on fixing it	.05	-.25*	-.05	.02
Use alcohol to feel better	.37***	.24*	.36***	.44***
Get emotional support	-.03	-.13	.08	.30**
Give up	.07	-.05	.27**	.01
Vent	.08	.24*	.07	.22
Criticize self	-.04	.06	.04	.28*
Find comfort in religion	-.17*	-.14	.02	.11
Make fun of situation	.18*	-.07	.01	.18

Note: FA=Female athlete, FNA=Female Non-athlete, MA=Male athlete, MNA=Male Non-athlete
*p < .05, **p < .01, ***p < .001 Coping tactics were rated on a 4-point scale (1=I wouldn't do this at all, 4=I would do this a lot), and alcohol consumption was measured in number of drinks per drinking occasion.

Table 2 displays the correlations between the frequency of alcohol consumption and coping tactics. Once again, using alcohol as a way to "feel better" was the only coping tactic significantly related to frequency of alcohol consumption for all students. Other strategies seemed to vary by gender and athletic status. For example, "concentrating on fixing the problem" was negatively related to frequency of consumption only in female non-athletes, whereas "venting" and "self-criticism" were only related to frequency of consumption in male non-athletes.

Table 2. The Relationship between Frequency of Alcohol Consumption and Coping Tactics

	FA	FNA	MA	MNA
Concentrate on fixing it	-.01	-.26*	-.06	-.12
Use alcohol to feel better	.38***	.54***	.44***	.65**
Get emotional support	.09	-.18	.01	.31**
Give up	-.06	-.10	.24*	.01
Vent	.03	.19	.05	.37***
Criticize self	.09	.01	.10	.26*

Note: FA=Female athlete, FNA=Female Non-athlete, MA=Male athlete, MNA=Male Non-athlete
*p < .05, **p < .01, ***p ≤ .001. Coping tactics were rated on a 4-point scale (1=I wouldn't do this at all, 4=I would do this a lot), and frequency of alcohol consumption was measured on the following scale: 0=never/rarely, 1=once a month, 2=once a week, 3 = 2-3 times a week, 4=daily or almost daily.

Table 3.The Relationship between Frequency of Alcohol Intoxication and Coping Tactics

	FA	FNA	MA	MNA
Use alcohol to feel better	.34***	.60***	.47***	.43***
Give up	-.07	-.12	.28**	.22
Vent	.04	.22*	.07	.18
See it more positively	-.01	-.23*	-.06	.12
Get support	.09	-.10	-.01	.31**
Criticize self	-.10	.06	.14	.33**
Come up with a strategy	-.03	-.22*	-.01	.20

Note: FA=Female athlete, FNA=Female Non-athlete, MA=Male athlete, MNA=Male Non-athlete
*$p < .05$, **$p < .01$, ***$p < .001$. Coping tactics were rated on a 4-point scale (1=I wouldn't do this at all, 4=I would do this a lot), and frequency of alcohol intoxication was measured on the following scale: 0=never/rarely, 1=once a month, 2=once a week, 3 = 2-3 times a week, 4=daily or almost daily.

The relationship between frequency of alcohol intoxication and coping tactics is displayed in Table 3. All groups again showed strong relationships between frequency of intoxication and using alcohol "to feel better." However, other patterns differed. For example, for female non-athletes, intoxication related to "venting," not "seeing things more positively," and failing to "come up with a strategy about what to do," whereas for male non-athletes, intoxication related to not "getting support from others" and "self-criticism."

For the instances where the pattern of correlations differed for the four groups, we thought it was important to determine whether these were significant differences. A Fisher's RHO was run to determine the correlation.In Table 1, the correlation between quantity of alcohol consumed and coping by "turning to work or activities" differed significantly for female athletes and female non-athletes (Fisher's r to $z = 2.48$), female athletes and male athletes (Fisher's r to $z = 2.17$) and female athletes and male non-athletes (Fisher's r to $z = 1.98$). The correlation between quantity of alcohol consumed and coping by "concentrating on fixing the problem" differed significantly for female athletes and female non-athletes (Fisher's r to $z = 2.42$) and female non-athletes and male non-athletes (Fisher's r to $z = 1.89$).The correlation between quantity of alcohol consumed and coping by "getting emotional support" differed significantly for female athletes and male non-athletes (Fisher's r to $z = -2.50$), and female non-athletes and male non-athletes (Fisher's r to $z = -3.32$).The correlation between quantity of alcohol consumed and coping by "giving up" differed significantly for female non-athletes and male athletes (Fisher's r to $z = -2.44$) and male athletes and male non-athletes (Fisher's r to $z = 1.79$). The correlation between quantity of alcohol consumed and coping by "criticizing oneself" differed significantly for female athletes and male non-athletes (Fisher's r to $z = -2.38$) and for male athletes and male non-athletes (Fisher's r to $z = -1.71$).Finally, the correlation between quantity of alcohol consumed and coping by "making fun of the situation" differed significantly for female athletes and female non-athletes (Fisher's r to z = 2.00).

For Table 2, the correlation between frequency of alcohol consumed and coping by concentrating on fixing the problem differed significantly for female athletes and female non-athletes (Fisher's r to z = 2.03).The correlation between frequency of alcohol consumed and coping by "using alcohol to feel better" differed significantly for female athletes and male non-athletes (Fisher's r to z = 2.72) and for male athletes and male non-athletes (Fisher's r to z = -2.09). The correlation between frequency of alcohol consumed and coping by "getting emotional support" differed significantly for female non-athletes and male non-athletes (Fisher's r to z = -3.47) and for male athletes and male non-athletes (Fisher's r to z = -2.14).The correlation between frequency of alcohol consumed and coping by "giving up" differed significantly for female athletes and male athletes (Fisher's r to z = -2.42) and for female non-athletes and male athletes (Fisher's r to z = -2.57).The correlation between frequency of alcohol consumed and coping by "venting" differed significantly for female athletes and male non-athletes (Fisher's r to z = -2.59), and male non-athletes and male athletes (Fisher's r to z = 2.33). Finally, the correlation between frequency of alcohol consumed and coping by "criticizing oneself" differed significantly for female non-athletes and male non-athletes (Fisher's r to z = 1.77).

For Table 3, the correlation between frequency of alcohol intoxication and coping by "using alcohol to feel better" differed significantly for female athletes and female non-athletes (Fisher's r to z = 2.69).The correlation between frequency of alcohol intoxication and coping by "giving up" differed significantly for female athletes and male athletes (Fisher's r to z = 2.84), and for female non-athletes and male athletes (Fisher's r to z = 3.04).The correlation between frequency of alcohol intoxication and coping by "seeing it more positively" differed significantly for female non-athletes and male non-athletes (Fisher's r to z = -2.41). The correlation between frequency of alcohol intoxication and coping by "getting emotional support" differed significantly for female non-athletes and male non-athletes (Fisher's r to z = 2.83) and for male athletes and male non-athletes (Fisher's r to z = -2.21). Finally, the correlation between frequency of alcohol intoxication and coping by "criticizing oneself" differed significantly for female athletes and male non-athletes (Fisher's r to z = 3.12) and for female non-athletes and male athletes (Fisher's r to z = 1.86).

m coping styles and gender influence alcohol use by teenage athletes. Although none of the teenagers drank excessively, similar to previous studies, we found that adolescent malesconsumed more alcohol than did adolescent females (Barnes et al., 1993; Huselid & Cooper, 1992; Jerry-Szpak & Brown, 1994) and that teenage athletes drank more than did their non-athletic counterparts (Hildebrand et al., 2001; Jerry-Szpak & Brown, 1994; Turrisi et al., 2007).

Similar to Wilson et al. (2004) findings in college students, this study found that the interaction between gender and athletic status influenced teenage alcohol behaviors. Specifically, the female non-athletes in this study consumed the least amount of alcohol, whereas male athletes drank the greatest amount, which replicates findings from college age populations (Wilson et al.).In addition, male non-athletes were the least likely to become intoxicated, whereas male athletes were the most likely to become intoxicated. This last finding is especially surprising given that males typically are found to drink to intoxication more often than females(Barnes et al., 1993; Huselid & Cooper, 1992). This may partly be due to the demographics of the present study. Nearly half of the male non-athletes (n=37) were recruited from church-affiliated youth groups, and it could be hypothesized that drinking behavior would be somewhat modified by this association.

A major challenge in alcohol programs and research is why such differences in alcohol consumption exist between athletes and non-athletes and between males and females. For example, college athletes (especially male athletes) are more likely to report that their peers frequently getdrunk and approve of binge drinking (Martens, Dams-O'Connor, & Duffy-Paiement, 2006; Turrisi et al., 2007). Athletes may also have more exposure to environmental and cultural factors conducive to drinking (e.g. ,having more drinking going on, having more alcohol available, and having more drinks given to them without asking hazing, etc; Martens, Dams-O'Connor, & Beck, 2006; Turrisi et al.). In addition, college athletes tend to place more emphasis on drinking to cope (especially with sport-related stresses) than do non-athletes (O'Brien, Ali, Cotter, O'Shea, & Stannard, 2007). Although a myriad of mechanisms have been offered to explain this occurrence, results from this study suggest that coping tactics correlated with drinking behaviors, and that these tactics varied by both gender and athletic status. Unlike previous studies that had reported gender differences in coping (e.g., Piko, 2001, Schaeffer & Pritchard, 2003), for the participants in this study, the most significant predictor for drinking behaviors in all teenage subgroups was drinking to cope. For all sub-groups, the use of alcohol as "a way to feel better" was significantly related to the quantity of alcohol consumed, the frequency of alcohol consumption, and the frequency of intoxication.

However, there were also some noticeable differences in how coping tactics related to alcohol use among the groups (although none specifically seemed to relate to either gender or athletic status). For example, "concentrating on fixing the problem" was significantly inversely related to alcohol behaviors only for female non-athletes, whereas "venting" was significantly positively related to alcohol behaviors in that subgroup. "Getting emotional support" and "criticizing oneself" were significantly positively related to alcohol behaviors only for male non-athletes, whereas "giving up" was significantly positively related to alcohol behaviors only for male athletes. Future studies should examine why these coping patterns differ in their predictive values for male and female athletes and non-athletes.

Regardless, a major question concerning the use of alcohol by athletes is the etiology of this behavior. For instance, does participation in sport promote the use of alcohol, or are specific personality characteristics associated with athletes similar to those traits found in individuals likely to engage high-risk behaviors (Hildebrand et al., 2001)? Although several correlational studies have examined factors mitigating athlete alcohol consumption as suggested above (e.g., Martens, Dams-O'Connor, & Beck, 2006; Martens, Dams-O'Connor, & Duffy-Paiement, 2006; O'Brien et al., 2007; Turrisi et al., 2007), no longitudinal studies have examined this topic. Although further research needs to examine these questions, results from this study provide partial answers in that differences exist in coping styles employed by male and female athletes and non-athletes, and that these styles are related to alcohol use.

LIMITATIONS

One limitation of this study was that it was conducted over a portion of the summer when none of the athletes were currently in their competitive seasons. However, some evidence suggests that being "out of season" may influence alcohol behavior. As a result, it is not known whether coping and drinking behaviors are influenced by the athlete's competitive sport season. Future investigations should examine the effect the competitive sport season may have on these variables. In addition, many of the non-athletes (especially male non-athletes) were recruited from churches. Non-athletic participants recruited from non-religious organizations might exhibit different patterns of alcohol usage.

CONCLUSION AND SUGGESTIONS FOR PRACTICE

In conclusion, although none of the teenagers drank excessively (e.g, binge drinking – drinking 5 or more drinks in one sitting), results from this study found significant differences in alcohol consumption related to coping styles in male and female athletes and non-athletes. With increasing attention being given to the specific needs of athletes in terms of substance abuse prevention programs, these findings suggest that gender and coping-related differences are of the utmost importance in the planning and implementation of intervention programs.

Many current prevention programs are designed as a "one size fits all" approach, often addressing only socially oriented variables, such as peer pressure to drink. However, individual coping tacticsemployed by male and female athletesneed to be considered when designing future prevention or intervention programs by practitioners in sport psychology.

Thus, middle school and high school coaches or sport psychology practitioners may wish to investigate how environmental, peer, or parental factors may influence drinking behaviors in their athletes. Schools could then design intervention programs accordingly. In addition, Turrisi et al. (2007) found that parental communication is a key factor mediating athlete drinking behaviors. Thus, sport psychology practitioners and coaches should involve parents in their efforts to reduce or prevent teenage athlete drinking.

REFERENCES

Anda, D., & Bradley, M. (1997). A study of stress, stressors, and coping strategies among middle school adolescents. *Social Work in Education, 19,* 87-99.

Baltzell, A. (1999). Psychological factors and resources related to rowers' coping in elite competition. Eugene, OR : Microform Publications, University of Oregon. http://kinpubs.uoregon.edu/

Barnes, G. M., Welte, J. W. &Dintcheff, B. A. (1993). Decline in alcohol use among 12th grade students in New York State, 1983-1990.Alcoholism: *Clinical and Experimental Research,17,* 797-801.

Billings, A. C., & Moos, R. H. (1981). The role of coping responses and social resources in attenuating the stress of life events. *Journal of Behavioral Medicine,4,* 139-157.

Bird, G. W., & Harris, R. L. (1990). A comparison of role strain and coping strategies by gender and family structure among early adolescents. *Journal of Early Adolescence, 10,* 141-158.

Bonica, C., & Daniel, J. H. (2003). Helping adolescents cope with stress during stressful times. *Current Opinion in Pediatrics, 15,* 385-390.

Carver, C.S. (1997). You want to measure coping, but your protocol's too long: Consider the brief COPE. *International Journal of Behavioral Medicine,4,* 92-100.

Cauce, A. M., Paradise, M., Ginzler, J. A., Embry, L., Morgan, C. J., Lohr, Y. & Theofolis, J. (2000). The characteristics and mental health of homeless adolescents: Age and gender differences. *Journal of Emotional and Behavioral Disorders,8,* 230–239.

Centers for Disease Control and Prevention (1998). *CDC Surveillance Summaries, Morbidity and Mortality Weekly Report, 47,* (No.SS-3).

Centers for Disease Control and Prevention. (2006). Youth Risk Behavior Surveillance United States, 2005. *Morbidity and Mortality Weekly Report:* CDC Surveillance Summaries 55(SS-5):1-108.

Chen, C.M., Dufour, M.C.,& Yi, H Y. (2004/2005). Alcohol consumption among young adults ages 18–24 in the United States: Results from the 2001–2002 NESARC survey. *Alcohol Research & Health* 28, 269–280.

Cooper, M. L., Russell, M., Skinner, J. B., & Windle, M. (1992). Developmentand validation of a three-dimensional measure of drinking motives. *Psychological Assessment,4,*123-132.

Dwyer, A. L., & Cummings, A. L. (2001). Stress, self-efficacy, social support, and coping strategies in university students. *Canadian Journal of Counselling, 35,*208-220.

Ellickson, P. L., McGuigan, K. A., Adams, V., Bell, R. M., & Hays, R. D. (1996). Teenagers and alcohol misuse in the Unites States: By definition, it's a big problem. *Addiction,91,* 1489-1504.

Hildebrand, K. M., Johnson, D. J., & Bogle, K. (2001). Comparison of patterns of alcohol use between high school and college athletes and non-athletes. *College Student Journal,35,* 358-365.

Huselid, R. F.,&Cooper, L. M. (1992). Gender roles as mediators of sex differences in adolescent alcohol use and abuse.*Journal of Health and Social Behavior,33,*348-362.

Jerry-Szpak, J., & Brown, H. P. (1994). Alcohol use and misuse: The hidden curriculum of the adolescent athlete. *Journal of Child and Adolescent Substance Abuse,31,* 57-67.

Johnston, L. D., O'Malley, M.,&Bachman, J. G. (1993). Period, age, and cohort effects on substance use among American youth, 1976-82.*American Journal of Public Health,74,*682-688.

Johnston, L. D., O'Malley, P. M., Bachman, J. G., & Schulenberg, J. E. (2007). Data tables from the 2007 Monitoring the Future Survey. Ann Arbor, MI: University of Michigan News and Information Services. [On-line]. Available: www.monitoringthefuture.org

Lazarus, R. S., & Folkman, S. (1984). *Stress, appraisal and coping.* New York: Springer.

Martens, M. P., Dams-O'Connor, K., & Beck, N. C. (2006). A systematic review of college student-athletedrinking: Prevalence rates, sport-related factors, and interventions.*Journal of Substance Abuse Treatment, 31,* 305-316.

Martens, M. P., Dams-O'Connor, K., & Duffy-Paiement, C. (2006). Perceived alcohol use among friends and alcohol consumption among college athletes. *Psychology of Addictive Behaviors, 20,* 178-184.

O'Brien, K. S., Ali, A., Cotter, J., O'Shea, R. P., & Stannard, S. (2007). Hazardous drinking in New Zealand sportspeople: Level of sporting participation and drinking motives. *Alcohol and Alcoholism, 42,*376-382.

O'Brien, C. P. & Lyons, F. (2000). Alcohol and the athlete. *Sports Medicine,29,* 295-300.

Perczek, R., Carver, C. S., Price, A. A., & Pozo-Kaderman, C. (2000). Coping, mood, and aspects of personality in Spanish translation and evidence of convergence with English versions. *Journal of Personality Assessment, 74,* 63-87.

Phelps, S. B., & Jarvis, P. A. (1994). Coping in adolescence: Empirical evidence for a theoretically based approach to assessing coping. *Journal of Youth and Adolescence, 23,* 359-371.

Piko, B. (2001). Gender differences and similarities on adolescents' ways of coping. *Psychological Record, 51,* 223-235.

Pritchard, M. E., & McIntosh, D. N. (2003). What predicts psychological outcomes among law students: A longitudinal panel study. *Journal of Social Psychology, 143, 727-745.*

Rao, K., Moudad, S., & Subbakrishna, D. K. (2000). Appraisal of stress and coping behaviour in college students. *Journal of the IndianAcademy of Applied Psychology, 26,* 5-13.

Schaffer, J., & Pritchard, M. E. (2003). Impact of stress on health and coping tactics in relation to sex. *The Psi Chi Journal of Undergraduate Research, 8,* 12-20.

Sheu, H., &Sedlacek, W. E.(2004). An exploratory study of help-seeking attitudes and coping strategies among college students by race and gender. *Measurement & Evaluation in Counseling & Development,37,* 130-143.

The National Center on Addiction and Substance Abuse at Columbia University (2007). *National Survey of American Attitudes on Substance Abuse XII: Teens and Parents.*www.casacolumbia.org/

Turrisi, R., Mastroleo, N. R., Mallett, K. A., Larimer, M. E., & Kilmer, J. R. (2007). Examination of the mediational influences of peer norms, environmental influences, and parent communications on heavy drinking tendencies in athletes and nonathletes. *Psychology of Addictive Behaviors, 21,* 453-461.

Wagenaar A. C., Harwood, E., &Bernat, D. (2002)*The Robert Wood Johnson Foundation 2001 Youth Access to Alcohol Survey: Summary Report.* Minneapolis: University of Minnesota, Alcohol Epidemiology Program.

Watson, J. C. (2002). Assessing the potential for alcohol-related issues among college student-athletes. *Athletic Insight: The Online Journal of Sport Psychology, 4,* http://www.athleticinsight.com

Wills, T. A., Sandy, J. M., Yaeger, A. M., Cleary, S. D., & Shinar, O. (2001). Coping dimensions, life stress, and adolescent substance use: A latent growth analysis. *Journal of Abnormal Psychology, 110,* 309-232.

Wills, T. A., Vaccaro, D., & Benson, G. (1995). Coping and competence in adolescent alcohol and drug use. In J. L. Wallander & L. J. Siegel (Eds.), *Adolescent health problems: Behavioral perspectives. Advances in pediatric psychology* (pp. 160-178). New York: Guilford Press.

Wilson, G. S., Pritchard, M. E., & Schaffer, J. (2004). Athletic status and drinking behavior in college students: The influence of gender and coping styles. *Journal of AmericanCollege Health,52,* 269-273.

In: Introduction to Sport Psychology
Editor: Robert Schinke

THE EFFECTS OF SCHOLARSHIP STATUS ON INTRINSIC MOTIVATION

Mark W. Aoyagi[*a] *and Richard H. Cox*[b]

[a]University of Denver
[b]University of Missouri-Columbia, USA

ABSTRACT

The purpose of this study was to test the predictions of cognitive evaluation theory (CET) by exploring the relationship between Division 1 student-athletes' ($N = 122$) perceptions of scholarships and intrinsic motivation (IM). Student-athletes were asked to rate the extent to which they perceived their own scholarship and athletic scholarships in general as informational (i.e., competence feedback) and controlling. IM was measured with the Intrinsic Motivation Inventory. Results showed: a) athletes' perceptions of scholarships as competence feedback predicted the perceived competence aspect of IM, b) athletes' perceptions of scholarships as controlling did not predict IM, and c) there were no differences on IM based on percentage of teammates on scholarship. Implications of the study included a better understanding of student-athletes' perceptions of scholarships, support for aspects of CET, and considerations in the measurement of IM.

THE EFFECTS OF SCHOLARSHIP STATUS ON INTRINSIC MOTIVATION

Athletic achievement motivation has garnered a great deal of interest in the sport psychology literature. Much of the research produced on motivation has focused around the positive effects of increased intrinsic motivation. Intrinsic motivation is most commonly defined as participating in an activity for its own sake and the inherent pleasure therein (e.g., Amorose & Horn, 2001; Vallerand, Gauvin, & Halliwell, 1986; Vallerand & Losier, 1999). The most studied theory pertaining to intrinsic motivation is Deci and Ryan's (1985) cognitive evaluation theory.

Cognitive evaluation theory is contained within self-determination theory (Deci & Ryan, 1985) and advances two key factors that may positively effect intrinsic motivation. These factors are: (a) the extent to which individuals perceive their actions and choices to be self-determined (i.e., within their control) and (b) individuals' perceptions of competence within

*Correspondence concerning this article should be addressed to Mark Aoyagi, Graduate School of Professional Psychology, University of Denver, 2460 South Vine Street, Denver, Colorado80208. E-mail: maoyagi@du.edu

the specific context of interest. Further, cognitive evaluation theory predicts that rewards can affect intrinsic motivation differently depending upon how they are perceived by the recipient of the rewards. If rewards are perceived by the recipient as positive feedback (i.e., as indicative of competence), then they will positively affect intrinsic motivation. Conversely, if rewards are perceived by the recipient as controlling then intrinsic motivation would be reduced.

Within collegiate sport, arguably the most significant reward is that of an athletic scholarship. There have been several notable studies that have investigated the effects of athletic scholarships on intrinsic motivation. The first known study of this nature compared the intrinsic motivation of scholarship and non-scholarship male athletes (Ryan, 1977). In this study, it was hypothesized that because scholarship athletes were being paid (i.e., the scholarship) to play sport they would score lower in intrinsic motivation then non-scholarship athletes. Results supported this hypothesis. However, in an extension of his previous work Ryan (1980) found some interesting qualifiers to his earlier research. In the second study, which included male athletes from football and wrestling and female athletes from several sports, only scholarship football players reported lower levels of intrinsic motivation as compared to non-scholarship athletes. Female athletes and male wrestlers were found to have higher intrinsic motivation than non-scholarship athletes. Ryan (1980) explained these findings by suggesting that because there were only a small number of athletes on scholarship on the male wrestling team and the female teams, the scholarships were perceived by these athletes as competence feedback and thus facilitated intrinsic motivation. On the other hand, Ryan (1980) felt that because most football players were on scholarship their scholarships may have been perceived as controlling rather than as a reward for competence. So, from these studies it was hypothesized that the proportion of athletes on a team with scholarships can influence the effect of scholarships on an athlete's intrinsic motivation.

A more recent study investigating the effects of scholarships on intrinsic motivation was conducted by Amorose and Horn (2000). They studied male and female athletes from a variety of sports and divided them into three groups: full scholarship, partial scholarship, and no scholarship. Also, athletes were asked their perceptions of the percentage of their teammates who were on scholarship. It was found that scholarship athletes scored higher than non-scholarship athletes on intrinsic motivation, and no significant effects were found concerning the percentage of teammates on scholarship and intrinsic motivation among scholarship athletes. In this study, intrinsic motivation was measured with the Intrinsic Motivation Inventory (IMI; McAuley, Duncan, & Tammen, 1989). Although this study appears to contradict Ryan's studies, there are a number of explanations for the discrepancies. First, the Amorose and Horn study contained male athletes from a wider range of sports than either of the Ryan studies. Second, the methods for assessing intrinsic motivation were different in the Amorose and Horn study (IMI) and the Ryan studies (surveys asking about interest and enjoyment in sport). Finally, Amorose and Horn concede that their findings concerning the scholarship percentage should be interpreted cautiously. Due to the pattern of responding, a median split resulted in grouping the athletes into those perceiving 75% or more of their teammates being on scholarship and those perceiving 70% or less of their teammates being on scholarship. These grouping are less than ideal for investigating Ryan's beliefs concerning the effects of the proportion of scholarship athletes on a team on intrinsic motivation.

A second study by Amorose and Horn (2001) examined male and female athletes from a variety of sports who were all in their first year of collegiate competition. The authors hypothesized that the effects of a scholarship (i.e., perceptions of competence feedback or as controlling) would be more pronounced among first year players. A pre-post design was utilized with all athletes measured prior to and at the conclusion of their competitive season. Results revealed non-significant effects for scholarship status, time of measurement, and their interaction. Thus, in this study there were no differences on intrinsic motivation as a result of scholarship status. The authors suggested the lack of differences may be due to the fact that a majority of athletes sampled reported only receiving a partial scholarship. It was hypothesized that a partial scholarship may not exert enough of an effect to produce changes in intrinsic motivation.

Other recent studies have expanded our understanding of the relationship between scholarships and motivation by examining both intrinsic and extrinsic motivation. Kingston, Horrocks, and Hanton (2006) found that scholarship athletes could be discriminated from non-scholarship athletes by both intrinsic motivation and by the least self-determined (i.e., introjected regulation and external regulation) forms of extrinsic motivation. The authors concluded that athletes may have perceived their scholarships as controlling, and thus undermining of intrinsic motivation. Similarly, Medic, Mack, Wilson, and Starkes (2007) found that male athletes with scholarships scored significantly higher on the extrinsic factors of introjected regulation and external regulation. It is interesting to note that although the sample included male and female athletes with and without scholarships, it was only scholarship male athletes that exhibited the higher extrinsic motivation. Further, when non-scholarship athletes were asked about their motivation in a scenario where scholarships were made available to them, they reported a decrease in intrinsic motivation. Again, the authors determined the results suggested that athletic scholarships could be controlling and hence reduce intrinsic motivation.

A shortcoming of the research reported thus far has been that athletes were not specifically asked how they perceived their scholarships. Amorose and Horn (2000) used results from the perceived competence, perceived choice, and interest-enjoyment subscales of the IMI to indicate that scholarship athletes displayed greater perceived competence and did not differ in terms of self-determination from non-scholarship athletes. However, there was no way of knowing if these findings were a result of the athletes having a scholarship or simply some other confounding variable (e.g., skill level). Likewise, Kingston et al. (2006) and Medic et al. (2007) explain their findings based on the belief that scholarships were perceived as controlling, but this belief is based on speculation as they did not actually determine the athletes' perceptions. Thus, the present study will add to the research concerning the effects of scholarships on intrinsic motivation by asking athletes for their perceptions of scholarships. It was hypothesized that: 1) There will be a positive relationship between athletes' perceptions of scholarships as informational (i.e., as competence feedback) andthe subscales of the IMI, 2) There will be a negative relationship between athletes' perceptions of scholarships as controlling and the subscales of the IMI, and 3) Scholarship athletes perceiving a lower proportion of their teammates having scholarships will score higher on the IMI than athletes perceiving a large proportion of their teammates being on scholarship (Ryan, 1980).

METHOD

Participants

The sample (N = 122) consisted of 52 male and 70 female varsity athletes from a large Division I university in the Midwestern United States who voluntarily participated. The athletes ranged in age from 18 to 23 ($M = 20.10$, $SD = 1.31$) and most identified themselves as Caucasian (91.0%) with the remainder identifying as African American (4.9%), Hispanic American (1.6%), and Asian American (1.6%). One person did not specify a racial/ethnic background. The athletes represented a wide variety of sports (i.e., golf, soccer, gymnastics, baseball, softball, swimming, volleyball, tennis, wrestling, basketball, and track and field). Additionally, 99 of the athletes reported having an athletic scholarship and 23 did not have an athletic scholarship. All participants were treated ethically and fairly according to APA guidelines and the campus Institutional Review Board.

INSTRUMENTS

Demographic questionnaire. A demographic questionnaire asked participants to identify their gender, age, ethnicity, year in school, primary sport, whether or not they had an athletic scholarship, and if so, the percentage of the scholarship. Athletes were asked to rate their perceptions of scholarships in general (e.g., I feel that athletic scholarships are given based on how well an athlete performs at his/her sport) as well as their perceptions of their own scholarship (e.g., I feel that <u>my</u> athletic scholarship was given to me based on how well I perform at my sport) in terms of both competence (see examples above) and control (e.g., Most athletes who are on an athletic scholarship are asked to do things they would prefer not to do, but feel that they must because they are on scholarship). Responses were scored on a four-point Likert scale anchored by 1 = *Strongly disagree* and 4 = *Strongly agree*. Participants also indicated the percentage of their teammates they perceived as having an athletic scholarship.

Intrinsic Motivation Inventory. Intrinsic motivation was assessed with the sport version of the Intrinsic Motivation Inventory (IMI; McAuley et al., 1989). The IMI was chosen primarily to provide consistency between the current study and previous studies (i.e., Amorose & Horn, 2000, 2001). The IMI contains four subscales: (a) interest-enjoyment, (b) perceived competence, (c) effort-importance, and (d) pressure-tension with four items in each subscale. According to McAuley et al. (1989) each subscale was reported to have adequate internal consistency (alpha coefficients = .80, .80, .84, and .68, respectively) as did the entire scale (alpha = .85). Based on the recommendations of McAuley et al. (1989) and the work of Amorose and Horn (2000, 2001) a fifth subscale (four items) of perceived choice was also included. Items are scored on a 7-point Likert scale ranging from 1 = *Strongly disagree* to 7 = *Strongly agree*.

PROCEDURE

Coaches from various athletic teams were approached and asked to allow their athletes to participate in a research project. Upon assent from the coaches, athletes were asked to voluntarily take part in a study approved by the Campus Institutional Review Board. A time was arranged when members of the team could gather and complete the background questionnaire and the IMI. Prior to completing the questionnaires, athletes were asked to sign an informed consent form agreeing to participate in the project. After completing the consent form and surveys the athletes were thanked for their time and given a debriefing statement containing the purpose of the study and how to contact the researchers.

DATA ANALYSIS

Preliminary analyses consisted of data screening, testing the assumptions of multiple regression, and calculation of Cronbach's alpha for each of the IMI subscales. Then, t tests were conducted for the purpose of describing the sample. First, independent-samples t tests examined if male and female athletes differed in their motivation, followed by independent-samples t tests to determine whether scholarship and non-scholarship athletes differed in intrinsic motivation. Finally, independent-samples t tests were conducted to examine differences between scholarship and non-scholarship athletes on perceptions of scholarships, and a dependent-sample t test examined scholarship athletes' perceptions of their own scholarship as compared to athletic scholarships in general.

In order to test Hypotheses 1 and 2, multiple regression analyses were conducted to determine the proportion of variance accounted for in the dependent variables (i.e., subscales of the IMI) by the independent variables (i.e., perceptions of scholarships as controlling and as competence feedback) as well as the contributions of each independent variable to the prediction. This resulted in two sets of multiple regressions: one with athletes' perceptions of athletic scholarships in general as the independent variables and the second with athletes' perceptions of their own scholarship as the independent variables. Due to the number of regression analyses (10), Bonferroni correction was utilized to set the alpha level at .005. Hypothesis 3 was tested with an independent-samples t test comparing scholarship athletes' perception of the proportion of their teammates having a scholarship on intrinsic motivation. In order to attain relatively equal sample sizes, High was defined as > 75% ($n = 41$) and Low as ≤ 75% ($n = 58$).

RESULTS

Preliminary Analyses

The data were initially screened for missing values, outliers, data entry errors, and the assumptions of multiple regression. A total of 33 participants were removed from the data set due to missing or incomplete data and an additional participant was identified as a multivariate outlier and subsequently removed. This resulted in the final data set of 122 participants as reported in the Method section. The variables interest-enjoyment (-.96), perceived competence   (-.76), effort-importance (-1.09), and perceived choice (-.63) all displayed significant negative skewness. As a result, each variable was reflected and then inversely transformed, which resolved the skewness (-.06, .54, -.22, and .46, respectively). Univariate correlations among the study variables ranged from .01 to .68 and thus multicollinearity was not considered to be an issue as all correlations were less than .70.

Table 1.*Descriptive Statistics and Alpha Coefficients for Study Variables*

Variable	M	SD	α
Dependent variables			
Interest-enjoyment	6.21	0.89	.71
Perceived competence	5.94	0.86	.65
Effort-importance	6.24	0.92	.58
Pressure-tension	4.09	1.15	.57
Perceived choice	5.75	1.12	.61
Predictor variables			
Perception of athletic scholarships in general as controlling	2.20	0.86	-
Perception of athletic scholarships in general as competence feedback	3.24	0.73	-
Perception of own scholarship as controlling	1.89	0.81	-
Perception of own scholarship as competence feedback	3.35	0.74	-

Note. Alpha coefficients were not calculated for the predictor variables because they are single-item measures.

Internal consistency of the IMI subscales was assessed using Cronbach's alpha, and only the interest-enjoyment subscale of the IMI demonstrated reliability greater than the suggested acceptable level of .70 (Nunnally, 1978). However, two other subscales (i.e., perceived competence and perceived choice) exceeded .60, which has been identified as a marginally acceptable level of reliability for subscales with few items (Amorose & Horn, 2000). The remaining subscales of effort-importance and pressure-tension fell below the .60 threshold and thus results pertaining to these subscales should be interpreted with caution. Table 1 presents alpha coefficients for each of the IMI subscales as well as descriptive statistics for all of the study variables.

DESCRIPTIVE ANALYSES

In order to describe motivational differences in the sample based on sex and scholarship status, independent-samples t tests were conducted. For each subscale of the IMI, there was no significant difference based on sex. Similarly, there were no significant differences between scholarship and non-scholarship athletes on any of the IMI subscales with the exception of perceived competence. For perceived competence, scholarship athletes ($M = 6.03$, $SD = .81$) scored higher than non-scholarship athletes ($M = 5.59$, $SD = .96$), $t(120) = 2.25$, $p < .05$, ES = .50.

Next, independent-samples t tests were conducted to determine differences between scholarship and non-scholarship athletes on perceptions of scholarships. These tests revealed that scholarship athletes ($M = 2.28$, $SD = .83$) were significantly more likely to view athletic scholarships in general as controlling than non-scholarship athletes ($M = 1.86$, $SD = .89$), $t(118) = 2.07$, $p < .05$, ES = .49, but there were no significant differences between scholarship ($M = 3.24$, $SD = .74$) and non-scholarship athletes ($M = 2.23$, $SD = .69$) on perceptions of athletic scholarships as competence feedback, $t(119) = .09$. Lastly, a dependent-sample t test found that scholarship athletes were significantly less likely to view their own athletic scholarship ($M = 1.89$, $SD = .81$) as controlling than they were to view athletic scholarships in general as controlling ($M = 2.28$, $SD = .83$), $t(92) = -4.59$, $p < .01$, ES = .48.

HYPOTHESIS TESTING

The first set of five standard multiple regression analyses included athletes' perceptions of athletic scholarships in general as controlling and as competence feedback as the predictor variables and the IMI subscales as the dependent variables. As can be seen in Table 2, none of the beta coefficients were significant for perceptions of athletic scholarships as controlling, and only perceived competence was significant for perceptions of athletic scholarships as competence feedback. None of the multiple correlations were significant.

The second set of standard multiple regression analyses examined athletes' perceptions of their own scholarships as controlling and as competence feedback as the predictor variables and the IMI subscales as the dependent variables. Table 3 presents the results of these analyses where it can be seen that no beta coefficients or multiple correlations were significant.

The results from the independent-samples t test comparing high ($> 75\%$) and low ($\leq 75\%$) perceived proportion of teammates on scholarship found perceived competence, $t(97) = 1.98$, $p = .05$, ES = .39 to be the only significant difference (See Table 4). None of the other subscales were significant, although total intrinsic motivation, $t(97) = 1.90$, $p = .06$, ES = .37, was very close to achieving significance. Additionally, as can be seen in Table 4, the pattern of the means is uniformly higher for each aspect of intrinsic motivation in the low group as compared to the high group.

Table 2.Multiple Regressions for Perceptions of Athletic Scholarships on Intrinsic Motivation

Dependent variable	Controlling			Competence Feedback			Model	
	B	SE B	β	B	SE B	β	R	R²
Interest-enjoyment	-.040	.030	-.123	.067	.035	.175	.207	.043
Perceived competence	.006	.024	.023	.086	.028	.270*	.273	.074
Effort-importance	.000	.030	.000	.078	.035	.204	.204	.041
Pressure-tension	-.174	.124	-.129	.002	.145	.001	.129	.017
Perceived choice	.011	.030	.034	.068	.035	.180	.185	.034

Note. *p< .005.

Table 3. Multiple Regressions for Perception of Own Scholarship on Intrinsic Motivation

Dependent variable	Controlling			Competence Feedback			Model	
	B	SE B	β	B	SE B	β	R	R²
Interest-enjoyment	-.061	.036	-.175	.023	.040	.061	.184	.034
Perceived competence	-.047	.029	-.166	.053	.032	.168	.233	.055
Effort-importance	-.020	.035	-.058	.066	.038	.179	.187	.035
Pressure-tension	.117	.156	.078	.022	.172	.013	.080	.006
Perceived choice	-.018	.037	-.052	.056	.040	.145	.153	.023

Table 4. Statistical Summary for Scholarship Athletes' Perceived Proportion of Teammates on Scholarship and Intrinsic Motivation

Dependent variable	High (> 75%) ($n = 41$)		Low ($\leq$ 75%) ($n = 58$)		Independent-samples t test ($df = 97$)	
	M	SD	M	SD	t	p
Interest-enjoyment	6.07	1.04	6.27	0.79	1.11	0.27
Perceived competence	5.84	0.92	6.16	0.71	1.98	0.05
Effort-importance	6.12	0.94	6.36	0.80	1.41	0.16
Pressure-tension	4.32	1.04	4.00	1.28	-1.33	0.19
Perceived choice	5.59	1.12	5.86	1.11	1.17	0.25
Total intrinsic motivation	5.46	0.73	5.73	0.69	1.90	0.06

DISCUSSION

This study found mild support for the hypothesis that college athletes' perceptions of athletic scholarships as competence feedback are associated with greater levels of intrinsic motivation. The significant positive relationship between athletes' perceptions of athletic scholarships as competence feedback and perceived competence is consistent with cognitive evaluation theory's (Deci & Ryan, 1985) prediction that intrinsic motivation will result from the perception of rewards as competence feedback. However, the non-significant relationships found in this study between athletes' perceptions of athletic scholarships as controlling and intrinsic motivation are contrary to the predictions of cognitive evaluation theory.

Perhaps the best explanation for the lack of a relationship between athletes' perceptions of athletic scholarships as controlling and intrinsic motivation is to take a closer look at the variables themselves. The mean response (see Table 1) for athletes' perceptions of athletic scholarships as controlling is slightly above "*mostly disagree*" indicating that athletes do not tend to view athletic scholarships as controlling. Furthermore, the mean responses for the IMI subscales are all close to 6 on a 7-point scale. Thus, the student-athletes in this study appear to be highly intrinsically motivated and tend not to perceive athletic scholarships as controlling. These two factors combine to make it highly unlikely that a negative relationship between perceptions of athletic scholarships as controlling and intrinsic motivation would be found.

The results also revealed that scholarship athletes were more likely to view athletic scholarships as controlling than were non-scholarship athletes; however, there were no differences in terms of perceptions of athletic scholarships as competence feedback. Further, the findings indicate that scholarship athletes are less likely to perceive their own scholarship as controlling than they are to perceive athletic scholarships in general as controlling. Thus, the athletes sampled in the current investigation do not appear to view their own athletic scholarship as controlling, but do seem to acknowledge that athletic scholarships can be perceived as controlling. While perceptions of athletic scholarships as competence feedback and as controlling cannot necessarily be assumed to be mutually exclusive, the athletes' surveyed in the current investigation were much more likely to view athletic scholarships as competence feedback than as controlling.

Contrary to previous research (Amorose & Horn, 2000), there was some evidence to support the hypothesis that a lower percentage of teammates on scholarship would result in greater levels of intrinsic motivation. The genesis for this hypothesis was Ryan's (1980) finding that athletes on a team with a high percentage of scholarship athletes (i.e., football) scored lower on intrinsic motivation than other athletes. Thus, Ryan's belief was that if a scholarship athlete were on a team with few other scholarship athletes, he/she would be more likely to view the scholarship as competence feedback. Interestingly, in the current study it was in perceived competence that athletes perceiving a lower proportion of their teammates having an athletic scholarship scored higher than athletes perceiving a large proportion of their teammates being on athletic scholarship. In other words, scholarship athletes who perceive a low percentage of their teammates have athletic scholarships feel more competent than scholarship athletes who perceive a high percentage of their teammates also have athletic scholarships. Further, the total intrinsic motivation score narrowly missed significance, and also supported athletes from perceived low-proportion of athletic scholarship teams having more intrinsic motivation than those from high proportion teams.

These differences are perhaps even more significant given the use of the IMI to measure intrinsic motivation in this investigation. The IMI was originally developed to measure intrinsic motivation with regard to experimental tasks (Plant & Ryan, 1985; Ryan, 1982; Ryan, Mims, & Koestner, 1983) and was adapted to the sport environment using physical education students (McAuley et al., 1989). Thus, it can be surmised that the IMI has primarily been validated on populations with questionable personal investment in the tasks they were completing. In the current study, participants were student-athletes competing at a very high level (i.e., Division 1 college athletics) and investing large amounts of time and energy into their sport. Likely as a result, the mean scores on the IMI subscales were very high resulting in a restricted range of responses and limited variability in the data. Because the IMI scores were uniformly high, it would be surprising to find statistical differences between any of the groups. Given these conditions, the fact that there were significant differences found in the current study is amplified.

Moreover, the limited variability in the IMI responses could also serve to suppress some of the relationships observed between athletes' perceptions of scholarships and intrinsic motivation. So, the observed relationships may actually be stronger in magnitude than what was reported in the current study. Thus, although the amount of variance explained in the multiple correlations may be small, when it is considered within the overall context of the limited variability in the dependent variables, the meaningfulness of the multiple correlations may be stronger than the raw R^2 values would indicate.

While the current study has offered some new perspectives and interpretations on the effects of scholarships and intrinsic motivation, it is not without limitations. Perhaps the largest limitation to the study was the low reliability coefficients for the IMI subscales. Again, this finding is likely a result of the IMI being used on a population with different characteristics than what the instrument was originally developed for. The participants in the current study were highly invested in sport, while the participants used to develop the IMI were likely not invested in their task as discussed earlier. The resulting low alpha coefficients also served to suppress the correlations found in the study, and thus it is difficult to say how much more meaningful the relationships observed in the study may have been.

Future researchers should focus on finding or developing an instrument to measure intrinsic motivation that is more appropriate for a highly invested population such as student-athletes. Also deserving of further research is the finding that scholarship athletes view scholarships in general as more controlling than their own scholarship. While there is no compelling evidence in the current investigation to explain why scholarship athletes would perceive athletic scholarships as more controlling than non-scholarship athletes, yet not perceive their own scholarship as controlling, it is certainly a topic deserving of future investigation. Researchers may want to consider the possible effects of media and other outside influences insinuating the idea that scholarship athletes are controlled by their scholarships. Perhaps qualitative research would provide the best insight into this research question.

Finally, future researchers should account for the effects of the coach in athletes' perceptions of scholarships. Aside from being the strongest influence in the athletic environment (Vernacchia, McGuire, & Cook, 1996), the coach is also the person responsible for determining who receives athletic scholarships and how much they receive. Thus, it is impossible to overstate the potential effects that coach factors may have on the relationships and effects associated with scholarships.

REFERENCES

Amorose, A. J., & Horn, T. S. (2000). Intrinsic motivation: Relationships with collegiate athletes' gender, scholarship status, and perceptions of their coaches' behavior. *Journal of Sport and Exercise Psychology, 22,* 63-84.

Amorose, A. J., & Horn, T. S. (2001). Pre- to post-season changes in the intrinsic motivation of first year college athletes: Relationships with coaching behavior and scholarship status. *Journal of Applied Sport Psychology, 13,* 355-373.

Deci, E. L., & Ryan, R. M. (1985). *Intrinsic motivation and self-determination in human behavior.* New York: Plenum.Kingston, K. M., Horrocks, C. S., & Hanton, S. (2006). Do multidimensional intrinsic and extrinsic motivation profiles discriminate between athlete scholarship status and gender? *European Journal of Sport Science, 6,* 53-63.

McAuley, E., Duncan, T., & Tammen, V. (1989). Psychometric properties of the Intrinsic Motivation Inventory in a competitive sport setting: A confirmatory factor analysis. *Research Quarterly for Exercise and Sport, 60,* 48-58.

Medic, N., Mack, D. E., Wilson, P. M., & Starkes, J. L. (2007). The effects of athletic scholarships on motivation in sport. *Journal of Sport Behavior, 30,* 292-306.

Nunnally, J. C. (1978). *Psychometric theory* (2nd ed.). New York: McGraw-Hill.

Plant, R., & Ryan, R. M. (1985). Self-consciousness, self-awareness, ego-involvement, andintrinsic motivation: An investigation of internally controlling styles. *Journal of Personality, 53,* 435-449.

Ryan, E. D. (1977). Attribution, intrinsic motivation, and athletics. In L. I. Gedvilas & M. E. Kneer (Eds.), *Proceedings of the National Association for Physical Education of College*

*Men National Association for Physical Education of College Women National Conference.*Chicago: University of Illinois at Chicago Circle.

Ryan, E. D. (1980). Attribution, intrinsic motivation, and athletics: A replication and extension. In C. H. Nadeau, W. R. Halliwell, K. M. Newell, & G. C. Roberts (Eds.), *Psychology of Motor Behavior and Sport,* (pp. 19-26). Champaign, IL: Human Kinetics.

Ryan, R. M. (1982). Control and information in the intrapersonal sphere: An extension of cognitive evaluation theory. *Journal of Personality and Social Psychology, 43,* 450-461.

Ryan, R. M., Mims, V., & Koestner, R. (1983). Relation of reward contingency and interpersonal context to intrinsic motivation: A review and test using cognitive evaluation theory. *Journal of Personality and Social Psychology, 45,* 736-750.

Vallerand, R. J., Gauvin, L. I., & Halliwell, W. R. (1986). Negative effects of competition on children's intrinsic motivation. *The Journal of Social Psychology, 126,* 649-657.

Vallerand, R. J. & Losier, G. F. (1999). An integrative analysis of intrinsic and extrinsic motivation in sport. *Journal of Applied Sport Psychology, 11,* 142-169.

Vernacchia, R., McGuire, R., & Cook, D. (1996). *Coaching mental excellence: It does matter whether you win or lose.* Portola Valley, CA: Warde.

AUTHOR NOTE

Mark W. Aoyagi, Graduate School of Professional Psychology, University of Denver and Richard H. Cox, Department of Educational, School, and Counseling Psychology, University of Missouri-Columbia.

In: Introduction to Sport Psychology
Editor: Robert Schinke

ISBN: 978-1-61761-973-1
© 2011 Nova Science Publishers, Inc.

THE INFLUENCE OF MOTIVATIONAL CLIMATE AND GOAL ORIENTATION ON BURNOUT: AN EXPLORATORY ANALYSIS AMONG DIVISION I COLLEGIATE STUDENT-ATHLETES

Brandonn S. Harris[*1] *and Meredith L. Smith*[2]

[1]Kansas State University, USA
[2]West Virginia University, USA

ABSTRACT

A review of the burnout literature reveals a paucity of research examining the relationship between goal orientation, motivational climate, and burnout among collegiate student-athletes. The present research investigated the relationship of these constructs among Division I student-athletes from a mid-Atlantic university. Gender differences in burnout were also examined. Student-athletes (N=74) completed inventories assessing burnout, motivational climate, and goal orientation. Significant relationships between burnout and motivational climate were observed. Athletes perceiving high ego-lowtask climates reported the greatest burnout levels. Female athletes also reported significantly greater burnout levels. Motivational climate and gender also predicted burnout among participants. Results provide support for examining burnout within an Achievement Goal Theory framework. The importance of the potential social impact of coaches and gender on collegiate athlete burnout is discussed.

INTRODUCTION

Within the field of sport and exercise psychology, a great deal of research attention has been given to the areas of sport motivation and sport burnout. Previous research has identified correlates of athlete burnout as including a loss of motivation and enjoyment, internal and external sources of pressure, physical and mental exhaustion, mood changes, increased anxiety, low feelings of sport accomplishment, and apathy towards their sport involvement (Goodger, Gorely, Lavallee, & Hardwood, 2007; Raedeke & Smith, 2001). Because athletes experiencing burnout can end up mentally and physically withdrawing from a sport they once

---

[*]Send all correspondence to: Brandonn S. Harris, Ph.D. Kansas State University; College of Education; Department of Special Education, Counseling, and Student Affairs; 329 Bluemont Hall; 1100 Mid-Campus Drive; Manhattan, KS 66506-5301; Phone: 785.532.5784; Fax: 785.532.7304; bsharris@ksu.edu

enjoyed, it appears important to better understand burnout and all of the potential contributing factors leading to its occurrence. Considering researchers have identified burnout as a subtype of the general construct of motivation (Gould, 1996), it appears that the incorporation of constructs stemming from the sport motivation literature may provide great utility for exploring the athlete burnout experience.

LITERATURE REVIEW

Only recently has a trend in athlete burnout research involved the utilization of achievement motivation theories as a means for examining burnout. This emerging line of research has included the incorporation of Deci and Ryan's (1985) Self Determination Theory (e.g., Cresswell & Eklund, 2005a, 2005b, 2005c; Lemyre, Treasure, & Roberts, 2005) and Nicholls' (1984) Achievement Goal Theory (e.g. Chi & Chen, 2003; Wyner, 2005). A review of the burnout and motivation lines of research reveals relatively limited attention given to the relationship between goal orientation, motivational climate, and burnout among Division I athletes. To date, only two published studies have examined these constructs concurrently using samples of Division III athletes (Wyner) and professional Taiwanese basketball players (Chi & Chen). However, when examining this line of research, it seems probable that motivational climate and orientation could be related to burnout development in Division I athletes as well. This is particularly true given the high demands and pressures associated with Division I athletics, in addition to the unique challenges that student-athletes experience as a result of their intercollegiate athletic participation (Ferrante, Etzel, & Lantz, 2002). Therefore, it appears that research attention should be given to this area considering the strong implications of these constructs' influences on athletes' sport participation and experiences.

Athlete Burnout

Due to the detrimental effects that burnout has on athletes' well-being both in and out of sport, it is important to understand how and why this phenomenon occurs. Athlete burnout has been previously linked to heavy training loads (Silva, 1990) and poor social interactions and support with people close to the athlete (Coakley, 1992; Udry, Gould, Bridges, & Tuffey, 1997). Burnout has also been suggested to be more multidimensional in nature (Smith, 1986; Tenenbaum, Jones, Kitsantas, Sacks, & Berwick, 2003a, 2003b), resulting from poor adaptations to external or environmental demands, physical demands (i.e., training), social interactions, general life stressors that occur outside of sport, and secondary stressors. All of these stressors can be emotional, cognitive, or due to unrealistic goals that the athlete may experience (Tenenbaum et al., 2003a).

In addition to these aforementioned causes, another socially-based source of burnout development may stem from coach-athlete interactions. Vealey, Armstrong, Comar, and Greenleaf (1998) examined the influences perceived coaching behaviors had on female collegiate athletes' burnout and competitive anxiety. Authors found several coaching behaviors that related to athletes' burnout. Specifically, athletes scoring higher on the burnout dimensions of negative self-concept, emotional and physical exhaustion, devaluation, and psychological withdrawal perceived coaching behaviors to be less empathetic, using more dispraise and an autocratic coaching style, and emphasizing winning more than development. Harris and Ostrow (2007) demonstrated similar findings as collegiate swimmers' burnout scores were found to be higher among those perceiving autocratic decision-making styles. Moreover, Price and Weiss (2000) also found that female varsity soccer players experiencing low perceived sport competence and pleasure, in addition to higher anxiety and burnout levels, also reported coaching behaviors characterized by less instruction or training, social support, and positive feedback. With the coach oftentimes regarded as a critical individual in the development of a particular type of motivational climate (White, Kavassanu, & Guest, 1998), these results provide further support for the significant role that the coach plays in the development of athlete burnout (Harris & Ostrow; Vealey et al., 1998). Therefore, it appears that when examining potential influences of athlete of burnout, the sport climate that is created by the coach may be an additional factor worthy of consideration. Nicholls' (1984) Achievement Goal Theory provides sport psychology researchers with a very good theoretical framework to utilize in examining the influence of sport climate on burnout among collegiate student-athletes.

Achievement Goal Theory

Achievement Goal Theory (Nicholls, 1984) suggests two factors interact to impact an athlete's motivation or achievement behavior. These factors include perceived ability (high or low) and achievement goals (task- versus ego-oriented goals). A task orientation involves athletes using themselves and their previous performances as their reference for achievement. Contrastingly, athletes who endorse an ego-orientation seek to demonstrate competence and achievement by referencing their performance to that of other individuals; these athletes believe ability has been exemplified when they outperform others (Ames, 1992; Duda & Treasure, 2000; Nicholls, 1984). Duda and Treasure noted that an ideal motivational profile might include both a high task and ego orientation due to the several sources and opportunities to demonstrate competence provided by both orientations (e.g., improvement/effort or winning a competitive event). An athlete high in ego orientation and low in task orientation has been suggested to be at risk for motivational difficulties, including sport dropout (Seifriz, Duda, & Chi, 1992).

Task and ego constructs can also characterize the types of motivational climates an athlete is exposed to while participating in sport. Newton and Duda (1999) noted that ego-oriented climates have been associated with manifesting beliefs among athletes that poor performances will be punished by coaches while high ability athletes would receive more positive attention or recognition. These authors further noted that an emphasis placed on improvement and working together, like that often seen in a task-oriented climate, enhances an athlete's sense of self-determination and competence. Both factors are significant in motivating an athlete to continue their sport involvement (Deci & Ryan, 1985). A task climate and goal orientation also allows athletes to challenge themselves to improve their skill, which has been identified as a motivational factor leading to continued sport participation (Barber, Sukhi, & White, 1999; Chambers, 1991; Gill, Gross, Huddleston, 1983; Pugh, Wolff, & DeFrancesco, 2000; Wann, 1997). Task-involving activities are also likely to be interpreted as informational, which can increase self-esteem and competence while enhancing intrinsic motivation and sport adherence (Deci & Ryan).

Achievement Goal Theory and Athlete Burnout

A review of the burnout literature reveals a paucity of research that examines the relationship between goal orientation, motivational climate, and burnout among athletes. However, when examining the literature pertaining to the implications and development of motivational climate and goal orientation on athletes' continued sport participation and satisfaction, it seems probable that climate and orientation could be related to burnout development. This becomes apparent when exploring the behaviors and affect of athletes who endorse a particular goal orientation and/or are exposed to a certain motivational climate, which the present researchers are proposing as being similar to the symptoms and characteristics associated with athlete burnout.

For example, a mastery or task climate may be beneficial because it can enhance the enjoyment athletes experience playing their sport (Boixadós, Cruz, Torregrosa, & Valiente, 2004). In a survey of youth male soccer players, these authors found that athletes who perceived a mastery or task involved climate showed more intrinsic motivation, satisfaction, and fair play attitudes compared to athletes who perceived a more ego-oriented climate (Boixadós et al.). These views may result in athletes' enhanced self-efficacy and sport performances. Similarly, athletes who believe they are receiving the expected outcome based on the effort they are putting into their sport are more likely to be satisfied and may be less likely to develop burnout (Schmidt & Stein, 1991). Thus, it appears that athletes who are participating in task climates may be less likely to develop burnout due to overall satisfaction in their sport.

Athletes who endorse a task goal orientation and/or perceive their climate to be task in nature have also reported lower levels of state anxiety compared to those with an ego orientation and/or climate (McArdie & Duda, 2002; Vazou, Ntoumanis, & Duda, 2006). Trait anxiety has also been suggested to relate to burnout as athletes reporting higher levels of trait anxiety have concurrently reported greater levels of burnout (Raedeke & Smith, 2001; Vealey et al., 1998; Wiggins, Lai, & Detters, 2005). Because trait anxious athletes are also likely to report higher levels of cognitive and somatic state anxiety (Martens, Burton, Vealey, Bump, & Smith, 1990), and state anxiety is associated with an ego orientation and/or climate, it is possible that a relationship exists between goal orientation, motivational climate, and burnout in athletes.

Athletes participating in ego climates have also been found to evidence more neurotic perfectionism (Carr, Phil, & Wyon, 2003). Perfectionism has also been identified as a contributing factor in the development of burnout among athletes as they may be more likely to set unrealistic goals and overexert themselves in the pursuit of them (Feigley, 1984; Fender, 1989; Henschen, 1998). Due to the commonality between the presence of perfectionism in both an ego orientation/climate and athlete burnout, it would seem important to investigate the potential direct relationship between ego goal orientations/climates and burnout among athletes.

To date there have only been two studies that have examined the constructs of burnout, motivational climate, and goal orientation concurrently. Wyner (2005) examined goal orientation and climate in Division III athletes. Results suggested that athletes with high task and low ego orientations had the lowest levels of burnout, followed by high task and high ego athletes. Athletes whose orientation was low task and low ego had the most severe burnout levels. Additionally, it was found that congruence between team climates and athlete orientations acted as a buffer to burnout development. This was found to be particularly true for female athletes (Wyner). Chi and Chen (2003) found similar evidence between goal orientation and climate and burnout in Taiwanese professional basketball players. Specifically, task oriented climates were found to be negatively related to burnout and athletes exhibiting a high task/low ego goal orientation exhibited less psychological withdrawal and devaluation by coaches and teammates compared to high ego/low task orientations. Gender differences were also revealed, with high task/low ego male athletes showing less emotional and physical exhaustion in addition to less psychological withdrawal and devaluation by coaches and teammates (Chi & Chen).

Although this area of study is still in its infancy, the aforementioned research examining the relationship between goal orientation and/or motivational climate and burnout among athletes suggests there may be a strong connection between these constructs. There appears to be overlapping characteristics associated with particular climates or orientations and burnout, which is worthy of further investigation. Due to the limited research that has examined climate/orientation and burnout concurrently in Division I American athletes, the purpose of the present research was to investigate the relationship of these three constructs among this population. Secondary purposes were to examine gender differences on burnout development. It was hypothesized that a positive correlation would be found between an ego climate/goal orientation and burnout. Conversely, a negative association was expected between task climates/goal orientation and burnout. It was also hypothesized that athletes higher in task orientation would report less burnout compared to those higher in ego orientation. Similarly, athletes higher in task climate were also expected to report less burnout compared to those higher in ego climate. It was also hypothesized that motivational climate would be a significant predictor of burnout levels among athletes. Goal orientation was also anticipated be a significant predictor of burnout levels among athletes. Because gender differences in burnout have received limited research attention among athletes, research examining gender differences in coach burnout was utilized to formulate hypotheses for the current sample of athletes (e.g. Kelley, 1994; Kelley, Eklund, & Ritter-Taylor, 1999; Pastore & Judd, 1993; Vealey, Udry, Zimmerman, & Soliday, 1992). Based on this literature, it was hypothesized that females in the present study would demonstrate significantly more burnout compared to their male athlete counterparts. Gender was also expected to predict burnout levels among athletes.

METHOD

Participants

The participants for this study consisted of 74 athletes (32 male and 42 female) from a large, mid-Atlantic Division I land-grant university with approximately 30,000 students and a reputation for rigorous undergraduate and graduate academic programs. Athletes were recruited from women's gymnastics ($n=12$), men's ($n=10$) and women's ($n=13$) basketball, men's soccer ($n=22$), women's volleyball ($n=9$), and women's tennis ($n=8$). These teams were selected as they had either completed their competitive season or were approaching the end of their season, allowing enough time for the motivational climate of the team to develop. Forty-three percent of the sample was between the ages of 18-19 years. The age of the majority of the sample was between 20-22 years old (55%). Only 1% of the sample fell between the ages of 23-25 years old. On average, athletes reported participating in their sport for 12.19 years (*SD*=4.15).

Instrumentation

A demographic questionnaire was created by the researchers that assessed participants' age, total years of participation in their sport, and number of years participation at their current institution.

Athlete Burnout Questionnaire

The Athlete Burnout Questionnaire (ABQ; Raedeke & Smith, 2001) was used to measure burnout levels. The ABQ consists of 15 questions, with 5 questions that focus on each of the three areas believed to be associated with the experience of burnout: reduced sense of accomplishment, emotional/physical exhaustion, and devaluation of sport. The responses are recorded on a 5-point Likert-type scale, ranging from 1 (*almost never*) to 5 (*almost always*), with higher numbers indicating higher burnout levels, except for items 1 and 14, which are reverse scored. The psychometric properties of this instrument have been deemed adequate as construct validity and test-retest reliability were established during the inventory's construction (Raedeke & Smith, 2001).To examine the internal consistency of the ABQ's subscales for the present study, Cronbach's alpha coefficients were calculated. Coefficients were .91, .78, and .86 for the exhaustion, reduced accomplishment, and devaluation subscales, respectively. Kaplan and Saccuzzo (1997) suggested that reliability estimates between .70 and .80 indicate adequate for internal consistency of a measure.

Task and Ego Orientation in Sport Questionnaire (TEOSQ)

To determine each athlete's motivational orientation, the Task and Ego Orientation in Sport Questionnaire was used (TEOSQ; Duda, 1989). The TEOSQ is a 13-item inventory that was used to assess the sport orientation of athletes and contains two subscales which include task and ego orientations. Athletes respond to each item using a Likert scale with anchors at 1 (*strongly disagree*) and 5 (*strongly agree*). The TEOSQ is a sport-specific version of an inventory originally created by Nicholls (1989) to assess task and ego orientation in an academic context. Although modified from its original version, this sport-specific measure has yielded adequate psychometric properties including construct and concurrent validity (Duda, 1989). Internal consistency analyses for the TEOSQ yielded Cronbach's alpha coefficients of .84 and .88 for the task and ego orientation subscales in the present study, respectively.

Perceived Motivational Climate in Sport Questionnaire-2 (PMCSQ-2)

To assess athletes' perception of the motivational climate present in their sport, the Perceived Motivational Climate in Sport Questionnaire was utilized (PMCSQ-2; Newton, Duda, & Yin, 2000). Originally developed from Ames and Archer's (1988) Classroom

Achievement Goals Questionnaire and the original version of the PMCSQ (Seifriz et al., 1992), the PMCSQ-2 contains a total of 33 items and two subscales (i.e. ego and task climates). Athletes responded to each item using a Likert scale ranging from 1 (*strongly disagree*) to 5 (*strongly agree*). Recent research has demonstrated adequate validity and reliability of the PMCSQ-2 (Carr & Wyon, 2003; Smith, Fry, Ethington, & Li, 2005). Cronbach's alpha coefficients for the PMCSQ-2 in the present study were .91 and .88 for the task and ego climate subscales, respectively.

Procedure

Following IRB and coach approval to solicit athletes' participation, one of the researchers met with the athletes or a team representative (e.g., academic advisor) to explain the nature of the study. The meeting with the athletes took place before or after a team meeting called by the coach. Measures were administered by the researchers or academic advisors that had been trained in the test administration procedures. For men's and women's basketball academic advisors administered the surveys when athletes came in to meet with them. This was done because these teams had completed their season and were no longer meeting as a team on a consistent basis. No coaches or coaching personnel were present during the explanation and completion of the surveys by the athletes. Those athletes who agreed to participate were given a packet with the consent letter, demographic questionnaire, ABQ, TEOSQ, and PMCSQ-2. All measures were counterbalanced. The total time required to complete the surveys was typically 10-15 minutes.

RESULTS

The analyses that were selected for the present research were used to accommodate the smaller sample size obtained. Regarding the analyses involving gender and burnout, three independent samples *t*-tests were used with the incorporation of a Bonferroni correction that adjusted the significance level to avoid committing a type I error if rejecting the null hypothesis. This approach was selected as opposed to using one MANOVA due to the smaller sample size. Additionally, non-parametric statistics (e.g., Kruskal-Wallis H and Mann-Whitney U tests) were also utilized to account for the smaller sample size and uneven cell sizes when a normal distribution of scores cannot be assumed. This was the case once athletes were placed into one of four different types of motivational climates and goal orientations using the median subscale scores for the PMCSQ-2 and TEOSQ. While the ideal standard would be to utilize a percentage of each subscales' standard deviation to separate high and low scores on the PMCSQ-2 and TEOSQ, this procedure was not feasible as it would have eliminated too large of the sample for subsequent analyses.

The Relationship between Motivational Climate/Goal Orientation and Burnout

It was hypothesized that a positive correlation would be found between an ego climate/goal orientation and burnout. Conversely, a negative association was expected between task climates/goal orientation and burnout. Pearson Product-Moment Correlations were calculated to examine the relationship that motivational climate and goal orientation had with burnout among participants (see table 1). Results of the analyses revealed significant, moderate relationships between perceived motivational climate and the devaluation and reduced sense of sport accomplishment burnout subscales. More specifically, the perception of an ego climate was found to be positively correlated with devaluation ($r=.41$, $p<.001$) and the reduced accomplishment ($r=.37$, $p<.01$) subscales. The perception of a task climate was negatively related with sport burnout as denoted by the devaluation ($r=-.48$, $p<.001$) and reduced accomplishment ($r=-.40$, $p<.01$) subscales. No significant relationships were found between goal orientation and burnout.

Table 1. Correlation matrix for burnout subscales, motivational climate, and goal orientation

	1	2	3	4	5	6	7
1. Exhaustion	---	.33*	.47**	-.16	.20	-.15	.08
2. Reduced Accomplishment	---	---	.75**	-.40*	.37*	.01	.14
3. Sport Devaluation	---	---	---	-.48**	.41**	-.1	.06
4. Task Climate	---	---	---	---	-.36*	.13	.09
5. Ego Climate	---	---	---	---	---	.00	.06
6. Task Orientation	---	---	---	---	---	---	.23*
7. Ego Orientation	---	---	---	---	---	---	---

Note. * denotes significance at the $p<.01$ level.**denotes significance at the $p<.001$ level.

Gender Differences in Burnout Among Collegiate Student-Athletes

It was hypothesized that female athletes in the present study would report significantly more burnout compared to their male athlete counterparts. To test this hypothesis, three independent sample t-tests were conducted to examine the differences in burnout subscales between male and female athletes. Gender served as the independent variable in all three analyses with each burnout subscale serving as the dependent variable in an analysis. To account for the potential of type I error to occur when running multiple analyses, a Bonferroni correction was used resulting with the alpha level being set at $p=.017$ when interpreting results.

The results of the analyses revealed that women demonstrated significantly more burnout on all three subscales of the ABQ compared to their male counterparts (see table 2). Women reported experiencing significantly greater levels of exhaustion ($t(72)=-2.66$, $p<.01$, Cohen's $d=.63$), reduced sport accomplishment ($t(72)=-2.87$, $p<.01$, Cohen's $d=.66$), and sport devaluation ($t(72)=-3.79$, $p<.001$, Cohen's $d=.89$).

Table 2. Descriptive statistics for gender differences on burnout subscales

	Males (n=32)		Females (n=42)		
	M	SD	M	SD	Cohen's d
Exhaustion	2.92	.83	3.44	.83	.63*
Reduced Accomplishment	2.21	.70	2.70	.78	.66*
Sport Devaluation	1.87	.82	2.64	.91	.89**

Note. * denotes significance at the p<.01 level. **denotes significance at the p<.001 level.

Differences in Burnout with Regards to Goal Orientation

It was expected that athletes higher in a task goal orientation would report less burnout compared to those reporting more of an ego goal orientation. To examine these differences in burnout among athletes with varying motivational goal orientations, three Kruskal-Wallis H tests were utilized with goal orientation serving as the independent variable and one of three burnout subscales serving as the dependent variable for each analysis (see table 3). Participants' scores on the TEOSQ were categorized as being either: 1) high task-high ego, 2) high task-low ego, 3) low task-high ego, or 4) low task-low ego based upon their value compared to the median score of 4.00 on the task orientation subscale and 2.83 on the ego orientation subscale on the TEOSQ. Once scores were categorized into their orthogonal category, it was revealed that participants' goal orientation types fell into each of the four groups but the cell sizes were unequal between all four groupings and were too small to assume a normal distribution of the data. Therefore, this non-parametric test was utilized for these comparisons as it is the appropriate statistical accommodation given these circumstances. Although preliminary analyses revealed differences in burnout found among the variables gender and time-of-season, this non-parametric test does not allow for the inclusion of covariates.

Table 3. Descriptive statistics for goal orientation and climate differences on burnout subscales

	High Task-High Ego (n=20/13)[a]		High Task-Low Ego (n=12/20)[a]		Low Task-High Ego (n=12/19)[a]		Low Task-Low Ego (n=21/14)[a]	
	M	SD	M	SD	M	SD	M	SD
Goal Orientation								
Exhaustion	3.17	.86	2.83	.92	3.32	.75	3.33	.90
Reduced Accomplishment	2.51	.65	2.23	.76	2.90	.94	2.51	.71
Sport Devaluation	2.09	.77	2.03	1.03	2.83	.97	2.40	.91
Motivational Climate								
Exhaustion	3.00	1.02	3.04	.87	3.62	.82	3.21	.62
Reduced Accomplishment*	2.38	.63	2.13	.63	2.97	.76	2.57	.89
Sport Devaluation*	2.04	.67	1.71	.59	3.13	.99	2.47	.79

Note. [a]These are the cell sizes for each grouping as it pertains to goal orientation/motivational climate following the median split procedure that utilized the median score for each respective subscale of the TEOSQ and PMCSQ-2. *indicates that at least two groups significantly differed on the burnout subscale.

Results of the three Kruskal-Wallis analyses revealed no significant differences between individuals with any of the four types of goal orientations on the exhaustion subscale $X^2(3)=2.66$, reduced accomplishment subscale$X^2(3)=3.75$, or devaluation subscale $X^2(3)=5.80$.

Differences in Burnout with Regards to Motivational Climate

It was anticipated that athletes reporting more of a task climate would also report less burnout compared to those athletes reporting more of an ego climate. Three Kruskal-Wallis H tests were utilized to examine differences between varying motivational climates of student-athletes and their reported levels of burnout (see Table 3). Participant's scores on the PMCSQ-2 were categorized as being either: 1) high task-high ego, 2) high task-low ego, 3) low task-high ego, or 4) low task-low ego based upon their value compared to the median score of 3.94 and 3.32 for the task and ego climate subscales on the PMCSQ-2, respectively. Once scores were placed into their orthogonal category, it was revealed that participants' perceived motivational climate type into each of the four groups but the cell sizes were unequal between all four groupings and were too small to assume a normal distribution of the data. Therefore, this non-parametric test was utilized for these comparisons as it is the appropriate statistical accommodation given these circumstances. Gender and time-of-season were not included in these analyses as covariates due to the inability of this nonparametric statistic to account for covariates in this type of analysis.

Results of the analyses indicated that athletes with differing types of perceived motivational climates reported significantly different levels of burnout on the reduced accomplishment $X^2(3)=11.30$, $p<.05$ and sport devaluation subscales $X^2(3)=21.46$, $p<.001$. No significant differences were found to exist on the exhaustion subscale $X^2(3)=6.08$. Because the Kruskal-Wallis H test does not allow for post-hoc analyses to be conducted to determine which groups differed from one another, individual Mann-Whitney U tests were utilized to determine which climate groupings reported significantly different levels of burnout on the reduced accomplishment and devaluation subscales. A Bonferroni correction was used to account for using multiple analyses resulting with the alpha level being set at $p=.01$ when interpreting results.

Results of the Mann-Whitney U tests indicated that athletes perceiving a high ego-low task climate reported significantly more reduced accomplishment ($U=68.00$, $p<.01$) and sport devaluation ($U=78.00$, $p<.001$) compared to those perceiving a high task-low ego climate. Athletes in the high ego-low task climate group also reported significantly more sport devaluation compared to those perceiving a high task-high ego climate ($U=49.00$, $p<.01$). The difference between these two groups of athletes on the reduced accomplishment scale approached statistical significance ($p=.03$) but fell short of achieving the .01 criteria. This was also evidenced when comparing athletes in the high ego-high task group with those in the low ego-low task group ($p=.04$).

Motivational Climate and Gender as Predictors of Athlete Burnout

It was hypothesized that motivational climate, goal orientation, and gender would significantly predict athlete burnout. To determine the utility of motivational climate and gender as predictors of burnout among student-athletes, three stepwise multiple regression analyses were conducted. Because goal orientation was not found to be significantly related to athlete burnout, the subscales of the TEOSQ were not included as predictor variables. For all three analyses, gender and motivational climate (task and ego climate) served as predictor variables with one burnout subscale (exhaustion, reduced accomplishment, and sport devaluation) serving as the criterion variable in each of the analyses.

For the emotional and physical exhaustion burnout subscale, one model emerged as significantly predicting burnout among collegiate student athletes. This model only included gender as significantly predicting exhaustion ($F(1,73)=7.08$, $p<.01$). Further, this model was found to only account for just under 9% of the variance of the criterion variable ($R^2=.09$), suggesting that for Division I collegiate student-athletes, task and ego climates do not predict the exhaustion component of burnout while gender only minimally accounts for the exhaustive experience with regards to sport burnout.

The results of the regression analysis for the reduced sense of sport accomplishment revealed two models that were able to significantly predict this component of burnout in student-athletes. The most parsimonious of the two models included both task and ego climates as significant predictors of reduced accomplishment ($F(2, 73)=9.71$, $p<.001$) and accounted for just under 22% of the variance in the criterion variable ($R^2=.22$). Task climate accounted for the majority of the variance in this model with 15.6%. Ego climate accounted for 5.9% in this model.

Three models emerged as significant predictors of the sport devaluation component of athlete burnout. The most parsimonious of the three models included task climate, ego climate, and gender as significant predictors of the criterion variable ($F(3, 73)=12.04$, $p<.001$). Further, this model was found to account for about 60% of the variance in sport devaluation ($R^2=.58$). Task climate, ego climate, and gender each accounted for 48.4%, 6.1%, and 3.8% of the variance, respectively.

DISCUSSION

The present exploratory study sought to examine the impact of motivational climate and goal orientation on the occurrence of burnout in Division I collegiate student-athletes. A secondary purpose included examining gender differences in burnout among participants. Regarding the impact of motivational climate and goal orientation on burnout, it was hypothesized that athletes higher in task orientation and/or perceived climate will report less burnout compared to those higher in ego orientation and/or climate. It was also hypothesized that motivational climate and goal orientation will be significant predictors of burnout levels among athletes. Results partially supported these hypotheses. The results of the Kruskal-Wallis H and Mann-Whitney U tests revealed that athletes who reported perceiving a motivational climate that was higher in ego and lower in task characteristics also reported more burnout than those perceiving a climate that was higher in task and lower in ego characteristics, or higher in both task and ego characteristics. Additionally, motivational climate was found to significantly predict burnout among the participants and accounted for between 9%-60% of the variance among the three burnout subscales. Taken together, these results appear to provide additional preliminary support for the impact that motivational climate has on the development or deterrence of burnout among collegiate athletes.

These results also provide some additional support for the limited research previously conducted in this area. For example, Chi and Chen (2003) found evidence of a relationship between goal orientation and climate and burnout in Taiwanese professional basketball players. Their study revealed that task oriented climates were negatively related to burnout. While it is of interest that goal orientation did not significantly relate to or explain differences in mean burnout scores among the present study's participants, the findings regarding motivational climate and burnout seem to support those results found by Chi and Chen in addition to providing further support for burnout being examined within an Achievement Goal Theory context.

The nature of task versus ego motivational climates may provide answers as to why the link between these climates and burnout among Division I student-athletes was demonstrated in the present study. Newton and Duda (1999) noted in their research that an emphasis placed on improvement and working together, like that often seen in a task-oriented climate, enhances an athlete's sense of self-determination and competence which have been deemed as significant in motivating an athlete to continue their sport involvement (Deci & Ryan, 1985). A task climate and goal orientation also allows athletes to challenge themselves to improve their skill, which has also been identified as a factor leading to sustained sport involvement (Barber et al, 1999; Chambers, 1991; Gill et al., 1983; Pugh et al., 2000; Wann, 1997). It is conceivable that in addition to enhancing athletes' self-determination and sport competence, task climates may also reduce the degree of burnout present among student-athletes, as was suggested by the results of the present study.

While the research of Chi and Chen (2003) and that of Wyner (2005) found relationships between goal orientation and burnout, the present study did not. Results did not support the hypothesized relationship between these constructs. For the current sample, it appeared that motivational climate was a more relevant factor influencing the occurrence of burnout in Division I athletes. In explaining the significant relationship found between motivational climate and burnout, it seems feasible to look at the impact that the coach has on the sport environment as a possible source of this relationship. This is particularly true as previous research has identified coaches as primary figures in determining the type of motivational climate present on a sport team (White et al., 1998).

In fact, the impact of coaches on the development of athlete burnout has been investigated in previous sport burnout literature. For example, Vealey et al. (1998) examined the influence of perceived coaching behaviors on athlete burnout. Their results indicated that athletes who scored higher on a burnout inventory also perceived their coach's leadership style to be more autocratic in nature. Price and Weiss (2000) also found that athletes reported higher levels of burnout in response to perceived autocratic coaching behaviors and less burnout in response to a democratic style of decision-making. Thus, it is possible that a coach's impact on the burnout levels of their athletes extends beyond their style of decision-making to include the motivational environment they promote within their team. Otherwise stated, this line of burnout research may suggest that coach influences (e.g., leadership style, motivational climate) might partially contribute to an extreme training environment that

Vealey et al. (1998) noted athletes have previously cited as the most significant cause of burnout.

In the current study, the experience of burnout was found to significantly differ between men and women; females had higher burnout scores on all three subscales of the Athlete Burnout Questionnaire compared to male athletes. These results support the present study's hypothesis regarding gender and burnout. Gender was also found to be a significant predictor of sport devaluation. However, gender was not found to be a significant predictor of reduced accomplishment and only minimally predicted physical/emotional exhaustion. While there is a paucity of literature examining athlete burnout and gender, the coaching literature has revealed gender differences in burnout. For example, it has been suggested that female coaches experienced significantly higher levels of burnout than their counterparts, specifically in the emotional exhaustion and personal accomplishment subscales (Caccese & Mayerberg, 1984; Kelley, 1994; Vealey et al., 1992). Since the findings of this exploratory study demonstrated similar gender differences, it seems possible females might have a tendency to experience a greater degree of burnout compared to males.

One sociological explanation for this potential gender difference in burnout involves the environment and perception of female athletes in present American culture. Coakley (2007) noted that although women's participation in athletics has increased drastically since the 1960s, there is currently a belief that women's sports are seen as secondary to the male sports that appear to be more legitimized through its physicality and intimidation. Coakley further postulated that these issues of power and performance that are typically associated with male sports serve as a comparison for evaluation and ultimately disadvantage women when gauging the success of female athletes. Therefore, this perception that female athletes are not as deemed to be equivalently supported and recognized as are their male counterparts may lead some female athletes to conclude they have to exert more effort to receive comparable attention or support. This increase in emotional and physical effort could, in part, contribute to the experience of more emotional and physical exhaustion. The perceived inequality between male and female athletics may also result in female athletes viewing their sport accomplishments as being not as important compared to similar accomplishments demonstrated by their male counterparts. This could conceivably result in feelings of reduced accomplishment and sport devaluation and contribute to increased burnout levels among female athletes.

Limitations

One limitation of the present study involves the sample size that was obtained from only one collegiate institution. Due to the smaller sample, there may be findings that are too small to detect and would require a large effect size to reveal. Further, although the number of males and females sampled were similar, there were fewer male teams represented, limiting the generalizability of the present research

Additionally, the smaller sample required that a median split be used to create goal orientation and climate categories. This procedure does not produce groupings that were as differentiated from one another had the standard deviation been used to create such categories. Considering the exploratory nature of the present study and the results that were demonstrated, future research in this area should focus on recruiting larger samples of

Division I athletes from several institutions. Further, larger sample sizes would permit the standard deviation value to be utilized in creating goal orientation and climate classifications which might increase the differentiation between high and low categories of motivational climate and goal orientation.

For the present analyses, gender and time-of-season would have ideally been utilized as covariates. However, it was not possible to do so as Kruskal-Wallis H and Mann-Whitney U analyses do not allow for the incorporation of covariates. Therefore, it is important that readers exert some degree of caution when interpreting the study's results. Future research in this area should attempt to continue to account for any known covariates when statistically feasible, that could have a confounding influence on the data analyses.

Implications and Future Directions

This exploratory study is the first to examine goal orientation and motivational climate in Division I athletes, and is also one of the few to examine gender differences in athlete burnout. While burnout is a phenomenon that can affect almost any type of athlete, it appears that female athletes may be more at risk. It is important for future athlete burnout research to examine why females may be more prone to burnout compared to their male counterparts so that professionals are able to provide gender-appropriate guidance or interventions. Such possible explanations may include coping skills, climates created by coaches, the perception of women's sports and athletes in society, or factors outside of sport (e.g. social and/or academic pressures). While the present study revealed differences in burnout between types of motivational climates, it did not assess the impact that a matching climate and goal orientation has on burnout. Future research should also continue to investigate the impact that having a compatible or matching goal orientation and climate has on the occurrence of burnout.

This research also adds to the existing research in this area (Chi& Chen, 2003; Wyner, 2005), which suggests that the climate created by the coach may be an important contributing factor to athlete burnout development. It may be beneficial to educate coaches on creating more of a task-oriented climate to help their athletesremain satisfied and interested in sport. Additionally, it may be important to teach athletes cognitive-behavioral coping skills to help them more effectively deal with climates dominant in ego characteristics to help limit the potential for burnout to occur.

REFERENCES

Ames, C. (1992). Achievement goals, motivational climate, and motivational processes. In G. C. Roberts (Ed.), *Motivation in sport and exercise*(pp. 161- 176). Champaign, IL: Human Kinetics.

Ames, C., & Archer, J. (1988). Achievement goals in the classroom: Students' learning strategies and motivational processes. *Journal of Educational Psychology, 80,* 260-267.

Barber, H., Sukhi, H., & White, S. (1999). The influence of parent-coaches on participant motivation and competitive anxiety in youth sport participants. *Journal of Sport Behavior, 22,* 162-180.

Boixadós, M., Cruz, J, Torregrosa, M., & Valiente, L. (2004). Relationship among motivational climate, satisfaction, perceived ability, and fair play attitudes in young soccer players. *Journal of Applied Sport Psychology, 16,* 301-317.

Carr, S., Phil, M., & Wyon, M. (2003). The impact of motivational climate*Journal of Dance Medicine & Science, 7* (4), 105-114.

Carr, S. & Wyon, M. (2003). Motivational climate and goal orientation, trait anxiety and perfectionism in dance students: The link between contextual climate and motivational traits. *Journal of Sport Sciences, 21,* 343-344.

Caccese, T., & Mayerberg, C. (1984). Gender differences in perceived burnout of college coaches. *Journal of Sport Psychology, 6,* 279-288.

Chambers, S. (1991). Factors affecting elementary school students' participation in sports. *The Elementary School Journal, 91,* 413-419.

Chi, L., & Chen, Y-L. (2003). The relationship of goal orientation and perceived motivational climate to burnout tendency among elite basketball players [Abstract]. *Journal of Sport & Exercise Psychology, 25* (suppl. 1), S40-S41.

Coakley, J. (1992). Burnout among adolescent athletes: a personal failure or social problem? *Sociology of Sport Journal, 9,* 271-285.

Coakley, J. (2007). *Sports in society: Issues and controversies.* Boston: McGraw Hill.

Cresswell, S. L., & Eklund, R. C. (2005a). Motivation and burnout among top amateur rugby players. *Medicine & Science in Sports & Exercise, 37,* 469-477.

Cresswell, S.L., & Eklund, R.C. (2005b). Changes in athlete burnout and motivation over a 12-week league tournament. *Medicine & Science in Sports & Exercise, 37,* 1957-1966.

Cresswell, S.L., & Eklund, R.C. (2005c). Motivation and burnout in professional rugby players. *Research Quarterly for Exercise and Sport, 76,* 370-376.

Deci, E., & Ryan, R. (1985). *Intrinsic motivation and self-determination in human behavior.* New York: Plenum.

Duda, J. (1989). The relationship between task and ego orientation and the perceived purpose of sport among male and female high school athletes. *Journal of Sport & Exercise Psychology, 11,* 318-335.

Duda, J., & Treasure, D. (2000). Toward optimal motivation in sport: Fostering athletes' competence and sense of control. In J. Williams (Ed.), *Applied sport psychology: Personal growth to peak performance*(pp.43-62). Mountain View, CA: Mayfield Publishing Company.

Feigley, D. (1984). Psychological burnout in high-level athletes. *The Physician and Sportsmedicine, 12,* 109-119.

Fender, L. (1989). Athlete burnout: Potential for research and intervention strategies. *The Sport Psychologist, 3,* 63-71.

Ferrante, A.P., Etzel, E., & Lantz, C. (2002). Counseling college student-athletes: The problem, the need. In E.F. Etzel, A.P. Ferrante, & J.W. Pinkney (Eds.), *Counseling college student-athletes: Issues and interventions* (pp. 3-26). Morgantown, WV: Fitness Information Technology.

Gill, D., Gross, J., & Huddleston, S. (1983). Participation motivation in youth sports. *International Journal of Sport Psychology, 14,* 1-14.

Goodger, K., Gorely, T., Lavallee, D., & Harwood, C. (2007). Burnout in sport: A systematic review. *The Sport Psychologist, 21,* 127-151.

Gould, D. (1996). Personal motivation gone awry: Burnout in competitive athletes. *Quest, 48,* 275-289.

Harris, B.S., & Ostrow, A.C. (2007). Coach and athlete burnout: The role of coaches' decision-making style. *Journal of Contemporary Athletics, 2,* 393-412.

Henschen, K. (1998). Athletic staleness and burnout: Diagnosis, prevention, and treatment. In J. Williams (Ed.), *Applied sport psychology: Personal growth to peak performance* (pp. 398-408). Mountain View, CA: Mayfield Publishing Company.

Kaplan, R.M., & Saccuzzo, D.P. (1997). *Psychological testing: Principles, applications, and issues.* Pacific Grove, CA: Brooks/Cole Publishing Company.

Kelley, B. (1994). A model of stress and burnout in collegiate coaches: Effects of gender and time of season. *Research Quarterly for Exercise and Sport, 65,* 48-58.

Kelley, B., Eklund, R., & Ritter-Taylor, M. (1999). Stress and burnout among collegiate tennis coaches. *Journal of Sport & Exercise Psychology, 21,* 113-130.

Lemyre, P., Treasure, D., & Roberts, G. (2006). Influence of variability in motivation and affect on elite athlete burnout susceptibility. *Journal of Sport & Exercise Psychology, 28,* 32-48.

Martens, R., Burton, D., Vealey, R., Bump, L., & Smith, D. (1990). The competitive state anxiety inventory-2 (CSAI-2). In R. Martens, R. Vealey, & D. Burton (Eds.), *Competitive anxiety in sport* (pp. 117-178). Champaign, IL: Human Kinetics.

McArdie, S., & Duda, J.K. (2002). Implications of the motivational climate in youth sports. In F.L. Smoll & R.E. Smith (Eds.), Children and youth in sport: A biopsychosocial perspective (2nd ed., pp. 409-434). Dubuque, IA: Kendall/Hunt.

Newton, M., & Duda, J. (1999). The interaction of motivational climate, dispositional goal orientations, and perceived ability in predicting indices of motivation. *International Journal of Sport Psychology, 30,* 63-82.

Newton, M., Duda, J.L., & Yin, Z. (2000). Examination of the psychometric properties of the perceived motivational climate in sport questionnaire-2 in a sample of female athletes. *Journal of Sport Sciences, 18,* 275-290.

Nicholls, J. (1984). Conceptions of ability and achievement motivation. In R. Ames & C. Ames (Eds.), *Research on motivation in education: Student motivation* (pp. 39-73). New York: Academic Press.

Nicholls, J. (1989). *The competitive ethos and democratic education.* Cambridge, MA: Harvard University Press.

Pastore, D., & Judd, M. (1993). Gender differences in burnout among coaches of women's athletic teams at 2-year colleges. *Sociology of Sport Journal, 10,* 205-212.

Price, M., & Weiss, M. (2000). Relationships among coach burnout, coach behaviors, and athletes' psychological responses. *The Sport Psychologist, 14,* 391-409.

Pugh, S., Wolff, R., & DeFrancesco, C. (2000). Measuring sports participation motivation. *International Journal of Sport Psychology, 18,* 112-119.

Raedeke, T., & Smith, A. (2001). Development and preliminary validation of an athlete burnout measure. *Journal of Sport & Exercise Psychology, 23,* 281-306.

Schmidt, G., & Stein, G. (1991). Sport commitment: A model integrating enjoyment, dropout, and burnout. *Journal of Sport & Exercise Psychology, 8,* 254-265.

Seifriz, J., Duda, J., & Chi, L. (1992). The relationship of perceived motivational climate to intrinsic motivation and beliefs about success in basketball. *Journal of Sport & Exercise Psychology, 14,* 375-391.

Silva, J. M. (1990). An analysis of the training stress syndrome in competitive athletics. *Applied Sport Psychology, 2,* 5-20.

Smith, R. E. (1986). Toward a cognitive-affective model of athletic burnout. *Journal of Sport Psychology, 8,* 36-50.

Smith, S.L., Fry, M.D., Ethington, C.A., & Li, Y. (2005). The effect of female athletes' perceptions of their coaches' behavior on their perceptions of the motivational climate. *Journal of Applied Sport Psychology, 17,* 170-177.

Tenenbaum, G., Jones, C., Kitsantas, A., Sacks, D., & Berwick. (2003a). Failure adaptation: Psychological conceptualization of the stress response process in sport. *International Journal of Sport Psychology, 34,* 1-26.

Tenenbaum, G., Jones, C., Kitsantas, A., Sacks, D., & Berwick. (2003b). Failure adaptation: An investigation of the stress response process in sport. *International Journal of Sport Psychology, 34,* 27-62.

Udry, E., Gould, D., Bridges, D., & Tuffey, S. (1997). People helping people? Examining the social ties of athletes coping with burnout and injury stress. *Journal of Sport & Exercise Psychology, 19,* 368-395.

Vazou, S., Ntoumanis, N., & Duda, J.L. (2006). Predicting young athletes' motivational indices as a function of their perceptions of the coach- and peer-created climate. *Psychology of Sport and Exercise, 7,* 215-233.

Vealey, R.S., Armstrong, L., Comar, W., & Greenleaf, C.A. (1998). Influences of perceived coaching behaviors on burnout and competitive anxiety in female college athletes. *Journal of Applied Sport Psychology, 10,* 297-318.

Vealey, R., Udry, E., Zimmerman, V., & Soliday, J. (1992). Intrapersonal and situational predictors of coaching burnout. *Journal of Sport & Exercise Psychology, 14,* 40-58.

Wann, D. (1997). Sport socialization and the motivation to participate in sport. In D. Wann (Ed.), *Sport psychology* (pp. 42-55). Upper Saddle River, NJ: Prentice-Halline.

White, S., Kavassanu, M., & Guest, S. (1998). Goal orientations and perceptions of the motivational climate created by significant others. *European Journal of Physical Education, 3,* 212-228.

Wiggins, M., Lai, C., & Detters, J. (2005). Anxiety and burnout in female collegiate ice hockey and soccer players. *Perceptual and Motor Skills, 101,* 519-524.

Wyner, D. R. (2005). Personal and situational factors associated with collegiate athlete burnout: An achievement goal theory perspective. (Doctoral dissertation, Emory University, 2003). *Dissertation Abstracts International, 65,* 4310.

ISBN: 978-1-61761-973-1
© 2011 Nova Science Publishers, Inc.

THE ASSOCIATIONS OF COMPETITIVE TRAIT ANXIETY AND PERSONAL CONTROL WITH BURNOUT IN SPORT

Mark W. Aoyagi[a], Kevin L. Burke[b], A. Barry Joyner[c], Charles J. Hardy[c], and Michelle S. Hamstra[c]

[a]University of Denver, [b]East Tennessee State University, USA
[c]Georgia Southern University, USA

ABSTRACT

The incidence of athlete burnout among competitive athletes from youth, high school, and collegiate age groups as well as the associations between competitive trait anxiety and personal control with athlete burnout were explored. The sample consisted of 153 competitive athletes (58 men, 95 women) from three age groups. The Eades Athlete Burnout Inventory (Eades, 1990), Sport Anxiety Scale (Smith, Smoll, & Schutz, 1990), and a modified version of the Control Over One's Sport Environment scale (Tetrick & Larocco, 1987) were completed by 30 youth (ages

10-13 years), 67 high school (ages 14-18 years), and 56 college (ages 18-22 years) athletes. Also, a directional scale was added to the Sport Anxiety Scale on which athletes rated the extent to which items were perceived as helpful or hurtful to performance. Results revealed that overall the sample reported a low incidence of burnout ($M = 62.88$, $SD = 33.67$). A moderate to strong positive relationship ($r = .645$) between athlete burnout and competitive trait anxiety was found as well as a moderate negative correlation ($r = -.433$) between athlete burnout and perceived control. Youth athletes ($M = 28.21$, $SD = 18.41$) scored significantly ($p < .05$) lower on the EABI than high school ($M = 69.66$, $SD = 21.93$) and college ($M = 72.95$, $SD = 39.24$) athletes, and women ($M = 68.89$, $SD = 37.49$) reported significantly ($p < .05$) higher burnout scores than men ($M = 52.19$, $SD = 22.19$). Somatic anxiety was perceived to be helpful to performance ($M = 2.50$, $SD = 12.95$) while worry ($M = -1.75$, $SD = 11.34$) and concentration disruption ($M = -1.01$, $SD = 8.54$) were perceived as detrimental to performance. Implications of results and directions for future research are discussed.

THE ASSOCIATIONS OF COMPETITIVE TRAIT ANXIETY AND PERSONAL CONTROL WITH BURNOUT IN SPORT

Burnout is a popular catchphrase in today's vernacular, and the frequency of its use may have trivialized the severity of this phenomenon. From a scientific standpoint, burnout is a syndrome of emotional exhaustion, depersonalization, and reduced personal accomplishmenttypically occurring among individuals who work in helping professions (Maslach, 1982). The term burnout was originally coined by Herbert J. Freudenberger (1974) who noticed that workers on a clinic staff seemed particularly prone to exhaustion so severe they would become inoperative. This idea of susceptibility to burnout was later expanded to include all individuals working in the human service and helping professions (Maslach, 1976). The Maslach Burnout Inventory (MBI) (Maslach & Jackson, 1981) quickly became the most popular instrument used for these purposes. The MBI proved to be a reliable and valid measure of burnout for workers in the helping professions, and continues to be the instrument of choice with this population.

From its roots in the helping professions, interest in burnout research extended into the sporting world. Logically, the first groups to be studied were coaches and athletic trainers because their responsibilities were similar to those of helping professionals. Many researchers found that the burnout syndrome as measured by the MBI was prevalent among both coaches (Caccese & Mayerberg, 1984; Capel, Sisley, & Desertrain, 1987; Vealey, Udry, Zimmerman, & Soliday, 1992) and athletic trainers (Capel, 1986). As interest in burnout in sport continued to increase, studies began to explore burnout in athletes.

Athlete burnout is defined as a psychological, emotional, and physical withdrawal from a formerly enjoyable sport as a result of chronic, excessive stress (Gould, Udry, Tuffey, & Loehr, 1996; Smith, 1986). As emphasized by this definition, burnout describes only those athletes quitting sport participation for a specific reason, namely stress. Therefore, burnout is differentiated from dropout which occurs when athletes leave sport for a variety of reasons, typically because of the comparative attractiveness of alternative activities (Smith, 1986).

There are four models that attempt to explain psychological burnout. Smith's (1986) Cognitive-Affective Stress Model states that chronic stress will result in the behavioral manifestation of burnout (Smith, 1986). That is, athletes exposed to high levels of stress over a long period of time will eventually leave sport or be unable to continue. Silva's (1990) Negative Training Stress Response Model approaches burnout from a more physiological perspective. Silva contends that negative adaptation can occur with excessive training demands, which may lead to burnout. Coakley's (1992) Unidimensional Identity Development and External Control Model approaches burnout from a sociological standpoint. The model states that burnout is due to two factors in sport: a) the structure of sport leads to a unidimensional self-concept, and b) athletes feel powerless to control their own lives. In this model, sport restricts athletes' development (e.g., unidimensional self-concept) which leads to feelings of powerlessness and eventually to burnout. Raedeke's (1997) Sport Commitment Model is based on the belief that athletes will be more likely to experience burnout if they participate because they have to rather than because of a personal choice. Raedeke views three factors as primary influences on athlete commitment: a) satisfaction based on the rewards and costs of sport, b) attractiveness of alternative options, and c) resources invested by the athlete in sport.

Initial research on athlete burnout utilized qualitative methodology and found that athletes were reporting an extremely high incidence of burnout. A pair of studies in which athletes were asked if they had ever experienced burnout indicated that 100% (Cohn, 1990) and 46.9% (Silva, 1990) of athletes experienced burnout. The participants in these studies were 10 high school competitive golfers and 68 intercollegiate athletes from a variety of sports, respectively. However, research on burnout in athletes was limited by the lack of a valid instrument to measure the phenomenon. The MBI was not used with athletes because it was perceived as valid only for human service providers (Dale & Weinberg, 1990; Raedeke, 1997). Another measure, the Eades Athlete Burnout Inventory (EABI) (Eades, 1990) has been utilized in recent research on athlete burnout, and has been shown to be a valid and reliable measure (Gould et al., 1996; Vealey, Armstrong, Comar, & Greenleaf, 1998). Results from studies of 236 competitive age group swimmers (ages 13 to 18) (Raedeke) and 149 female college athletes (Vealey et al., 1998) found burnout as measured by the EABI to be on the lower end of the possible range of scores.

Despite requests in the literature for research on the incidence of athlete burnout (Fender, 1989; Gould et al., 1996), only one study was found to report prevalence data. Gustafsson, Kentta, Hassmen, and Lundqvist (2007) found elevated burnout scores as measured by the EABI in between 1% and 9 % of their sample of 980 elite adolescent athletes. Further, there are certain variables that appear to play a major role in burnout which merit investigation. In Smith's (1986) Cognitive-Affective Stress Model of burnout, burnout processes are influenced by personality and motivational factors. Due to the model's stress-based framework, trait anxiety is considered an influential component of the personality factors (Gould et al.). Research has supported the influence of trait anxiety on burnout. Trait anxiety has been found to be the most significant predictor of burnout in coaches (Vealey et al., 1992), and also predictive of athlete burnout (Vealey et al., 1998). Moreover, athletes who perceived anxiety to be debilitative reported higher levels of burnout than those perceiving anxiety as facilitative (Wiggins, Lai, & Deiters, 2005).

Another variable that may play an important role in athletics is personal control. While mostly ignored in sport science research, personal control has been recently investigated in sport for potential influences in perceptions of momentum, optimism, pessimism, and superstitions (Burke, et al., 2006; Smisson, Burke, Joyner, Munkasy, & Blom, 2007). Control was speculated to increase the likelihood of burnout in the Cognitive-Affective Stress Model of burnout (Smith, 1986), and was one of the primary sources of burnout in Coakley's (1992) sociological framework of athlete burnout. Research examining perceived control in sport has supported a link between control and burnout. Raedeke (1997) used a cluster analysis to group swimmers based on certain characteristics (e.g., perceived control, enjoyment, benefits, costs). Athletes in the clusters characterized by low perceived control scored significantly higher on burnout dimensions as measured by the EABI.

Research on athlete burnout has added to the understanding of the problem, but there is still much to be learned. Further, the results of the Vealey et al. (1998) and Raedeke (1997) studies demonstrated the impact trait anxiety and personal control may have on athlete burnout. However, additional research is needed to investigate possible links between trait anxiety, personal control, and burnout. In line with Coakley (1992) and Smith's (1986) models of burnout, the purpose of this study is to investigate the incidence of burnout among competitive athletes from different age groups, and to examine the relationships between trait anxiety, personal control, and burnout. It is hypothesized that 1) there will be a significant positive correlation between competitive trait anxiety and burnout, 2) there will be a significant negative correlation between personal control and burnout, 3) there will not be a significant difference between males and females on athlete burnout, 4) college athletes and high school athletes will be significantly higher in burnout than youth athletes, 5) college athletes and high school athletes will score significantly higher on the emotional/physical exhaustion subscale of the EABI than youth athletes, 6) college athletes will score significantly higher on the psychological withdrawal from and devaluation of sport subscale of the EABI than either high school or youth athletes, and 7) college athletes will score significantly higher on the depersonalization by coach and teammates subscale of the EABI than either high school or youth athletes.

METHOD

Participants

A total of 153 competitive athletes volunteered to participate in the study from a youth swim team ($n = 11$), youth soccer teams ($n = 19$), varsity high school swim teams ($n = 47$), varsity high school soccer teams ($n = 20$), a college swim team ($n = 19$), and a college soccer team ($n = 37$). The sample contained 58 males and 95 females with ages ranging from 10-13 ($M = 11.27$, $SD = .87$) years in youth sport athletes, 14-18 ($M = 15.75$, $SD = 1.17$) years in high school athletes, and 18-22 ($M = 19.23$, $SD = .89$) years in college athletes (See Table 1 for further descriptive statistics of age group, gender, and sport). In terms of season, 46 athletes were in the off-season, 11 at the start of the season, 89 at mid-season, and 7 at the end of the season. The majority of athletes ($n = 87$, 56.9%) reported practicing more than five days per week, 15 (9.8%) practiced once or twice a week, with the rest ($n = 51$, 33.3%) practicing between three and five days per week. The most common practice sessions were 90 - 120 minutes in length ($n = 90$, 58.8%) with 36 (23.5%) athletes reporting practices shorter than 90 minutes and 27 (17.6%) athletes indicating practice sessions of more than 120 minutes. Most athletes played one competitive sport ($n = 96$, 62.7%), and had participated in sport for approximately eight years ($M = 8.42$, $SD = 4.68$). All participants were located in the United States with high school swimmers from competitive teams in Utah and all other sample teams from Georgia. All participants, including parents where necessary, signed informed consent.

Table 1. Number of participants by age group, sport, and gender

	Youth		High School		College		Total
	Swimming	Soccer	Swimming	Soccer	Swimming	Soccer	
Males	3	7	19	11	0	18	58
Females	8	12	28	9	19	19	95
Total	11	19	47	20	19	37	153

INSTRUMENTS

A demographic questionnaire was utilized to obtain information regarding participants' age, gender, sport, stage of season (e.g., off-season, mid-season), number of practice sessions per week, length of typical practice session, number of sports played competitively, number of years playing competitive sport, and whether or not sports were played during free time.

Burnout was assessed with the Eades Athlete Burnout Inventory (EABI) (Eades, 1990). The EABI consists of 36 statements to which athletes respond on a 7-point Likert scale (0 = never; 6 = every day). Scores are tallied on six subscales: negative self-concept of athletic ability, emotional and physical exhaustion, psychological withdrawal from and devaluation of sport participation, depersonalization by coach and teammates, congruent athlete-coach expectations for and evaluations of the athlete's performance, and personal and athletic accomplishment. Internal consistency (α) ranged from .57 to .89 for the subscales, but in a later study were found to range from .70 to .91 (Vealey et al., 1998). Validity was established as relationships between EABI scores and sport experiences (e.g., high levels of stress, number of injuries) hypothesized to be associated with burnout followed predicted patterns (Eades, 1990).

Competitive trait anxiety was measured with the Sport Anxiety Scale (SAS) (Smith et al., 1990). The SAS has 21 items asking athletes how they typically feel before or during competition. Scores are recorded on a 4-point Likert scale (1 = not at all; 4 = very much so) and categorized on three subscales: worry, somatic anxiety, or concentration disruption. A directional scale was added to the SAS on which respondents rated the extent to which they felt each statement was facilitative or debilitative to performance. The direction scale was a 6-point Likert scale (-3 = very hurtful; +3 = very helpful). Test-retest reliability (.68 to .71) and internal consistency has been established for the worry (α = .86), somatic anxiety (α = .90), and concentration disruption (α = .80) subscales. The SAS has demonstrated appropriate levels of convergent and discriminant validity (Smith et al., 1990).

Personal control was assessed with a modified version of the Control Over One's Work Environment scale (COOWE; Tetrick & LaRocco, 1987). The altered scale was titled Control Over One's Sport Environment (COOSE) and contained six items that athletes respond to on a 7-point Likert scale (1 = very little; 7 = a great extent). The only modifications made to the COOWE were changes in wording to make the scale applicable to sport (e.g., "to what extent do you have influence over the things that affect you on the job" was changed to "to what extent do you have influence over the things that affect you in sport"). Internal consistency for the COOWE was established as α = .83 (Tetrick & LaRocco).

PILOT STUDY

The instruments in the study were primarily designed for use with adults, and thus a pilot study utilizing 10 children between the ages of 10 and 12 years was conducted to explore the children's ability to comprehend the items on the instruments. Parental consent was obtained from the parents of the children. The children were asked to complete the background questionnaire, EABI, SAS, and COOSE. The children were instructed to ask questions about any items they did not understand. The pilot study indicated the children could read and complete the questionnaires in a satisfactory manner.

PROCEDURE

Coaches of the competitive teams were asked to allow athletes to take part in a study examining burnout. Once the coaches agreed, the team members were then asked to volunteer to participate in a study examining athletic participation, which would require approximately 30 to 45 minutes. Volunteers were then gathered together at a preselected time (typically after a practice session) and asked to complete an informed consent document. Youth sport participants were given the parental consent form ahead of time and returned the signed document at the meeting time. Once all participants had completed informed consent, brief instruction was given on how to complete the questionnaires (e.g., completing the blanks where appropriate and circling the numbers where appropriate). Participants were asked to complete all questions on all instruments. Participants were allowed to ask questions at any time if they had trouble with comprehension. Upon completion of the questionnaires, the athletes were thanked for participating.

RESULTS

Pearson correlations were utilized to examine the relationships between competitive trait anxiety and burnout, and personal control and burnout. A two-way ANOVA with gender and age group (youth, high school, or college) as the independent variables and the scales of the EABI, SAS, and COOSE as the dependent variables was utilized to explore differences between these groups. Scheffe's post-hoc analysis was run to explore age group differences. Alpha level was set at .05 for all statistical analyses.

Table 2. Descriptive Statistics for the Eades Athlete Burnout Inventory, Sport Anxiety Scale, and Control Over One's Sport Environment Scale

Measure	M	Mdn	SD
EABI Subscale			
Neg. self-concept	13.72	11.50	10.77
Exhaustion	21.03	21.00	12.49
Psych. withdrawal	10.57	10.00	7.30
Depersonalization	7.16	6.00	5.32
Congruence	12.92	13.00	3.79
Accomplishments	12.67	13.00	3.74
Total	62.88	60.50	33.67
SAS Subscale			
Somatic Anxiety	19.44	18.00	6.37

Worry	16.07	15.00	5.56
Concentration Disruption	8.65	8.00	2.80
Total	44.17	43.00	12.72
Directional Scale			
Somatic Anxiety	2.50	3.00	12.95
Worry	-1.75	-2.00	11.34
Concentration Disruption	-1.01	-2.00	8.54
Total	-0.26	-1.00	28.41
COOSE	27.66	29.00	6.57

Descriptive statistics revealed that overall this sample displayed a low incidence of burnout. The majority of athletes scored in the lower third of the possible range of scores ($n = 101$, 66.4%). Only four athletes (2.6%) scored in the upper third of scores, while the remainder of athletes scored in the middle third ($n = 47$, 30.9%). (One participant did not complete all items on the EABI and was eliminated from the analysis.) Anxiety means were very similar to those reported by Smith, Smoll, and Schutz (1990). High school girls' ($M = 49.19$, $SD = 9.47$) and boys' ($M = 43.00$, $SD = 18.76$) scores in this study were consistent with Smith et al. scores for high school girls ($M = 44.54$, $SD = 12.12$) and boys ($M = 43.44$, $SD = 10.81$). Results from the direction scale revealed that anxiety was generally perceived as slightly detrimental to performance ($M = -.26$, $SD = 28.41$). However, somatic anxiety was perceived to be facilitative ($M = 2.50$, $SD = 12.95$) while worry ($M = -1.75$, $SD = 11.34$) and concentration disruption ($M = -1.01$, $SD = 8.54$) were perceived as debilitative. See Table 2 for a summary of descriptive statistics.

Table 3. Pearson Correlations for the Eades Athlete Burnout Inventory, Sport Anxiety Scale, and Control Over One's Sport Environment Scale

	T.B.	I	II	III	IV	V	VI	T.A.	S.A.	Worry	C.D.	C.O.
T.B.	1.00											
I	0.89**	1.00										
II	0.84**	0.73**	1.00									

Table 3 – (Continued)

III	0.77**	0.55**	0.50**	1.00								
IV	0.79**	0.67**	0.55**	0.56**	1.00							
V	-0.38**	0.19**	-0.03	0.40**	0.36**	1.00						
VI	0.63**	0.51**	0.34**	0.50**	0.42**	0.44**	1.00					
T.A.	0.65**	0.70**	0.64**	0.32**	0.47**	0.02	0.35**	1.00				
S.A.	0.47**	0.52**	0.51**	0.18*	0.31**	-0.04	-0.22**	0.91**	1.00			
W.	0.69**	0.74**	0.66**	0.34**	0.51**	0.05	0.41**	0.90**	0.68**	1.00		
C.D.	0.50**	0.49**	0.43**	0.37**	0.41**	0.08	0.28**	0.71**	0.50**	0.55**	1.00	
C.O.	-0.43**	-0.32**	-0.36**	-0.38**	-0.29**	-0.27**	-0.36**	-0.26**	-0.24**	-0.24**	-0.16	1.00

Note. T.B. = Total Burnout, T.A. = Total Anxiety, S.A. = Somatic Anxiety, W. = Worry
C.D. = Concentration Disruption, C.O. = Control Over One's Sport Environment, I = Neg. self-concept,
II = Exhaustion, III = Psych. withdrawal, IV = Depersonalization, V = Congruence, VI = Accomplishments.
* = $p< .05$. ** = $p< .01$.

Pearson correlations revealed a moderate to strong positive relationship between total athlete burnout and total competitive trait anxiety ($r = .645$, $p< .01$). The worry subscale of the SAS also demonstrated a strong positive relationship with athlete burnout ($r = .689$, $p< .01$). Personal control had a moderate negative correlation with athlete burnout ($r = -.433$, $p< .01$). Negative self-perception of athletic ability demonstrated a strong positive correlation with competitive trait anxiety ($r = .695$, $p< .01$), and in particular the worry subscale ($r = .742$, $p< .01$). Emotional and physical exhaustion had a moderate to strong correlation with competitive trait anxiety ($r = .638$, $p< .01$); again the worry subscale was most strongly related ($r = .662$, $p< .01$). See Table 3 for a summary of EABI, SAS, and COOSE correlations.

Results from the two-way ANOVA found that the psychological withdrawal subscale of the EABI was the only measure to show a significant ($p = .01$) interaction. There was no difference between high school boys ($M = 11.31$, $SD = 5.06$) and girls ($M = 11.61$, $SD = 4.63$), but male youth athletes ($M = 11.11$, $SD = 5.04$) scored much higher than female youth athletes ($M = 6.68$, $SD = 6.11$). Interestingly, collegiate women and men were the opposite as women ($M = 12.63$, $SD = 10.67$) were more psychologically withdrawn than men ($M = 6.59$, $SD = 5.36$). These results may be partially explained by the relatively high standard deviations within the groups.

Table 4. Youth, high school, and college athletes means and standard deviations on the Eades Athlete Burnout Inventory, Sport Anxiety Scale, and Control Over One's Sport Environment (COOSE)

	Youth		High School		College	
	M	*SD*	*M*	*SD*	*M*	*SD*
Total Burnout	28.21	18.41	69.66**	21.93	72.95**	39.24
Neg. self-concept	3.29	4.40	15.31**	8.84	17.40**	11.95
Exhaustion	6.71	6.27	25.08**	10.37	24.44**	12.02
Psych. withdrawal	8.11	6.07	11.48	4.78	10.76	9.72
Depersonalization	3.46	3.64	7.19**	3.84	8.75**	6.41
Congruence	13.82	3.49	13.56	3.48	12.00	3.80
Accomplishments	15.54	3.67	11.84**	3.25	12.40**	3.49
Total Anxiety	33.21	9.09	46.56**	10.53	47.33**	13.81
Somatic Anxiety	14.96	4.82	20.13**	5.92	21.09**	6.64
Worry	10.86	3.06	17.42**	4.67	17.20**	5.91
C.D.	7.39	2.54	9.02*	2.23	9.03*	3.31
COOSE	30.07	6.57	27.06	6.49	26.98	6.52

Note. C.D. = Concentration Disruption. $*p < .05.$ $**p < .01.$

Main effects for age group were similar. All EABI scales yielded a significant age group effect with the exception of the psychological withdrawal and congruence between athlete's and coach's expectations for and evaluations of athletic accomplishment. Further, a significant age group effect was found for all of the SAS scales as well. Scheffe's post-hoc analysis revealed that for the personal and athletic accomplishments scale, youth athletes scored significantly higher than high school or college athletes, and high school and college athletes were not significantly different. On all other significant age group effects youth athletes were significantly lower than both college and high school athletes, and college and high school athletes were not significantly different. There was not a significant age group effect for COOSE ($p = .09$). Table 4 contains means and standard deviations for each age group.

Gender main effects followed a similar pattern to the age group effects. Women scored significantly higher than men on total burnout, negative self-perception of athletic ability, emotional and physical exhaustion, and all SAS scales. Men scored significantly higher than women on the personal and athletic accomplishments subscale of the EABI. See Table 5 for means, standard deviations, and p values of the gender effects.

Table 5. Gender effects on Eades Athlete Burnout Inventory, Sport Anxiety Scale, and Control Over One's Sport Environment (COOSE)

	Men		Women		
	M	*SD*	*M*	*SD*	*p*
Total Burnout	52.19	22.19	68.89	37.49	0.003
Neg. self-concept	8.75	6.38	16.59	11.81	0.0001
Exhaustion	17.67	11.11	23.31	12.96	0.002
Psych. withdrawal	9.73	5.52	11.02	8.15	0.629
Depersonalization	6.23	4.06	7.53	5.80	0.252
Congruence	12.37	3.51	13.38	3.72	0.088
Accomplishments	13.83	3.52	12.17	3.63	0.005
Total Anxiety	38.92	10.59	47.27	12.99	0.0001
Somatic Anxiety	17.23	5.65	20.76	6.47	0.001
Worry	13.79	4.30	17.34	5.76	0.0001
C.D.	7.90	2.44	9.16	2.89	0.002
COOSE	28.69	6.58	27.01	6.54	0.111

Note. C.D. = Concentration Disruption.

It was found that there were no significant gender differences for the directional scale of the SAS; however, there were significant age group effects. Youth athletes scored total anxiety, worry, and concentration disruption as significantly more facilitative than either high school or collegiate athletes. Youth athletes also scored somatic anxiety as significantly more facilitative than collegiate athletes, but were not significantly different from high school athletes. There were no significant differences between high school and collegiate athletes on any of the directional scales. See Table 6 for a summary of directional scores.

Table 6. Youth, high school, and college athletes means and standard deviations for the directional scales of the Sport Anxiety Scale

	Youth		High School		College	
	M	*SD*	*M*	*SD*	*M*	*SD*
Total Anxiety	18.37	30.06	-2.52	23.19	-8.73	29.28
Somatic Anxiety	8.27	12.76	1.66	12.02	.01	14.83
Worry	6.17	10.20	-2.52	9.56	-5.63	12.05
Concentration Disruption	3.93	8.73	-1.66	7.79	-3.19	8.39

DISCUSSION

One of the main purposes of this study was to investigate the incidence of burnout among competitive athletes. Results revealed that mean burnout in this study was lower than means reported by Eades ($M = 81.70$, $SD = 32.43$) (1990), and thus the subsequent analyses should be interpreted with appropriate caution given the low burnout scores. Two particularly interesting findings were the extremely low incidence of burnout among youth athletes, and the significant gender effect. It should be noted that the young athletes in this study, while competitive, were not elite national level athletes which are often the victims mentioned anecdotally. Further, the majority of young athletes may not be exposed to the high levels of stress associated with elite competition. Thus, this sample may have been more representative of a typical competitive youth sport experience.

The gender effect was surprising because past research has produced equivocal results in terms of gender (Dale & Weinberg, 1990). The pattern with which women scored higher in burnout and competitive trait anxiety is noteworthy and warrants future research. One possible explanation is that as female sports have become more nationally recognized, the number of potential stressors has increased.Still, this is purely speculation and researchers are encouraged to further explore burnout among female athletes.

As expected, competitive trait anxiety had a significant, positive relationship with athlete burnout and personal control had a significant, negative relationship with athlete burnout. In general, worry appeared to be the most closely associated aspect of competitive trait anxiety to athlete burnout. The relationships between worry, negative self-perception of athletic ability, and emotional and physical exhaustion with athlete burnout were consistent with the Cognitive-Affective Stress Model (Smith, 1986). While the relationship of athlete burnout to personal control was not as strong, it was still significant. It was somewhat surprising that youth athletes scored slightly higher than high school or college athletes on perceived control given Coakley's (1992) model. Lack of personal control among young athletes was a central tenet of the Coakley model, and future research on this topic is certainly warranted.

Age group produced some interesting results as all significant differences showed youth scoring lower in burnout than high school or college athletes. This is particularly encouraging considering the low incidence of burnout in the sample. Therefore, burnout may not be a common problem among competitive youth athletes. High school and college athletes were not significantly different on any of the measures.

As expected, college and high school athletes were significantly higher in emotional and physical exhaustion than youth athletes. This likely reflects the increased time commitments and physical demands placed on high school and college athletes. However, college athletes did not score significantly higher in psychological withdrawal from and devaluation of sport. While college athletes may experience a higher degree of burnout than youth athletes, they still appreciate the opportunity to play collegiate sport. College athletes scored significantly higher in depersonalization by coach and teammates than youth athletes; however, they did not score significantly higher than high school athletes. This seems to indicate that competition for playing time and roster positions may be as stressful at the high school level as it is on the college level.

Adding the directional scale to the SAS provided valuable information regarding athletes' perceptions of anxiety. The perception of somatic anxiety being helpful to performance is an important distinction as anxiety is often considered harmful. However, somatic anxiety was still positively correlated with athlete burnout. This could in part be explained by the low scores on athlete burnout reported by the sample. Youth athletes scoring of anxiety as more facilitative than high school or college athletes may reflect a developmentally limited ability in youths to discriminate aspects of performance. Future research on athletes' perceptions of competitive anxiety should help to clarify these findings.

Other areas for future research include exploring the prevalence of burnout among different sports, populations, and competitive experiences. Smith (1986), Silva (1990), Coakley (1992), and Raedeke (1997) provide several frameworks from which athlete burnout may be researched, and these models need to be better utilized as a basis for empirical exploration. Variables such as type of sport (i.e., individual or team), optimism and pessimism (Burke, Joyner, Czech, & Wilson, 2000; Czech, Burke, Joyner, & Hardy, 2002),perfectionism, level of commitment, social support, and coach-athlete communication offer rich opportunities for meaningful research. Perceived control appears to play an important role in athlete burnout; however, research may be limited by the lack of an appropriate instrument to measure perceived control within sport. Perhaps qualitative research on this topic would help to produce a more valid measure of perceived control.

REFERENCES

Burke, K. L., Czech, D. R., Knight, J. L., Scott, L. A., Joyner, A. B., Benton, S. G., & Roughton,H. K. (2006). An exploratory investigation of superstition, personal control, optimismandpessimism in NCAA Division I intercollegiate student-athletes. *Athletic Insight: TheOnline Journal of Sport Psychology, 8 (2)*. Retrieved fromhttp://www. athleticinsight.com/Vol8Iss2/Superstition.htm

Burke, K. L., Joyner, A. B., Czech, D. R., & Wilson, M. J. (2000). An investigation of concurrent validity between two optimism/pessimism questionnaires: The life orientation test-revised and the optimism/pessimism scale. *Current Psychology, 19,* 129-136.

Caccese, T. M., & Mayerberg, C. K. (1984). Gender differences in perceived burnout of college coaches. *Journal of Sport Psychology, 6,* 279-288.

Capel, S. A. (1986). Psychological and organizational factors related to burnout in athletic trainers. *Research Quarterly for Exercise & Sport, 57,* 321-328.

Capel, S. A., Sisley, B. L., & Desertrain, G. S. (1987). The relationship of role conflict and role ambiguity to burnout in high school basketball coaches. *Journal of Sport Psychology, 9,* 106-117.

Coakley, J. (1992). Burnout among adolescent athletes: A personal failure or social problem? *Sociology of Sport Journal, 9,* 271-285.

Cohn, P. J. (1990). An exploratory study on sources of stress and athlete burnout in youth golf. *The Sport Psychologist, 4,* 96-106.

Czech, D. R., Burke, K. L., Joyner, A. B., & Hardy, C. J. (2002). An exploratory investigation of optimism, pessimism and sport orientation among NCAA Division I college athletes. *International Sports Journal, 6,*136-145.

Dale, J., & Weinberg, D. (1990). Burnout in sport: A review and critique. *Journal of Applied Sport Psychology, 2,* 67-83.

Eades, A. M. (1990). *An investigation of burnout in intercollegiate athletes: The development of the Eades Athlete Burnout Inventory.* Unpublished master's thesis, University of California, Berkeley.

Fender, L. K. (1989). Athlete burnout: Potential for research and intervention strategies. *The Sport Psychologist, 3,* 63-71.

Freudenberger, H. J. (1974). Staff burnout. *Journal of Social Issues, 30,* 159-165.

Gould, D., Udry, E., Tuffey, S., & Loehr, J. (1996). Burnout in competitive junior tennis players: I. A quantitative psychological assessment. *The Sport Psychologist, 10,* 322-340.

Gustafsson, H., Kentta, G., Hassmen, P., & Lundqvist, C. (2007). Prevalence of burnout in competitive adolescent athletes. *The Sport Psychologist, 21,* 21-37.

Maslach, C. (1976). Burned-out. *Human Behavior, 5,* 16-22.

Maslach, C. (1982). *Burning out: The emotional cost of caring.* Englewood, NJ: Prentice Hall.

Maslach, C., & Jackson, S. (1981). *Maslach Burnout Inventory.* Palo Alto, CA: Consulting Psychologists Press.

Raedeke, T. D. (1997). Is athlete burnout more than just stress? A sport commitment perspective. *Journal of Sport & Exercise Psychology, 19,* 396-417.

Silva, J. M. (1990). An analysis of the training stress syndrome in competitive athletics. *Journal of Applied Sport Psychology, 2,* 5-20.

Smisson, C. P., Burke, K. L., Joyner, A. B., Munkasy, B. A., & Blom, L.C. (2007). Spectators' perceptions of momentum and personal control: Testing the antecedents-consequences model. *Athletic Insight: The Online Journal of Sport Psychology, 9* (1). Retrieved   from http://www.athleticinsight.com/Vol9Iss1/MomentumSpectatorsPerception.htm

Smith, R. E. (1986). Toward a cognitive-affective model of athletic burnout. *Journal of Sport Psychology, 8,* 36-50.

Smith, R. E., Smoll, F. L., & Schutz, R. W. (1990). Measurement and correlates of sport-specific cognitive and somatic trait anxiety: The sport anxiety scale. *Anxiety Research, 2,* 263-280.

Tetrick, L. E., & LaRocco, J. M. (1987). Understanding, prediction, and control as moderators of the relationships between perceived stress, satisfaction, and psychological well-being. *Journal of Applied Psychology, 72,* 538-543.

Vealey, R. S., Armstrong, L., Comar, W., & Greenleaf, C. A. (1998). Influence of perceived coaching behaviors on burnout and competitive anxiety in female college athletes. *Journal of Applied Sport Psychology, 10,* 297-318.

Vealey, R. S., Udry, E. M., Zimmerman, V., & Soliday, J. (1992). Intrapersonal and situational predictors of coaching burnout. *Journal of Sport and Exercise Psychology, 14,* 40-58.

Wiggins, M. S., Lai, C., & Deiters, J. A. (2005). Anxiety and burnout in female collegiate ice hockey and soccer athletes. *Perceptual and Motor Skills, 101,* 519-524.

In: Introduction to Sport Psychology
Editor: Robert Schinke

ISBN: 978-1-61761-973-1
© 2011 Nova Science Publishers, Inc.

Initial Examination of a Brief Assessment of Recovery and Stress (BARS)

Linda A. Keeler[a], Edward F. Etzel[b] and Lindsey C. Blom[c]

[a]CaliforniaStateUniversity, United states of America
[b]West Virginia University, United states of America
[c]Ball State University, United states of America

ABSTRACT

Approximately20% to 70% of athletes may experience some type of performance staleness during their trainingseasons or careers (Morgan, O'Connor, Sparling, & Pate, 1987; Nederhof, Lemmink, Visscher, Meeusen, & Mulder, 2006). While monitoring an athlete's training load, or "stress" can help prevent staleness (Kellmann & Kallus, 2001), it can also be costly, invasive, one-dimensional and time consuming. The purpose of this investigation was to construct and examine an abbreviated self-report measure of underrecovery,the "Brief Assessment of Recovery Stress" (BARS) that would be convenient and useful for applied sport psychologists. BARS is a 19-item, Likert type self-report instrument designed to efficiently assess stress recovery status perceptions more quickly than the Recovery-Stress Questionaire-76 Sport (RESTQ-76; Kellmann & Kallus). Participants were 387 undergraduate college student-athletes and non-athletes from a large southern and mid-Atlantic university. Results suggest that BARS, in its early form, is a reliable,practical instrument.

INITIAL EXAMINATION OF A BRIEF ASSESSMENT OF RECOVERY AND STRESS (BARS)

Various language has been used synonymously in research on training and its consequences (Kenttä & Hassmén, 1998; McKenzie, 1995; O'Connor, 1998). Terms such as underrecovery, overtraining, staleness, burnout and failure adaptation have been used interchangeably in the literature. Thus, models and instruments developed to characterize and measure these training states are often confusing. Furthermore, instruments developed to assess training impact vary in nature from physical ·to multi-dimensional psychological measurements. They can be costly, invasive and time consuming. Sport professionals working in applied settings may not have the resources or access to physiologically monitor the impact of training loads. Thus, a convenient, brief measurement of factors relating to maladaptive training responses would seem to be quite beneficial. In this study, researchers attempted to validate an initial version of the "Brief Assessment of Recovery and Stress" (BARS), which is a short self-report questionnaire based on the scales of the RESTQ-76 Sport (Kellmann & Kallus, 2001).

The concepts of underrecovery, overtraining, staleness and burnout are related but are not identical. One difficulty in deciphering the overlap between these concepts is the different operational definitions used in the literature; thus it is perhaps more constructive to focus on the processes they refer to rather than the terms themselves. Overtraining is considered a training method, where the athlete is overloaded with high training demands in order to cause the natural adaptation process to occur in the body (Hooper, MacKinnon, Howard, Gordon, & Bachmann, 1995; Morgan, Brown, Raglin, O'Connor, & Ellickson, 1987). By taxing the system with higher demands, the body naturally compensates and adapts to perform at higher levels. This phenomenon is known as the "supercompensation principle" (Kenttä & Hassmén, 1998, p. 1) and the "Specific Adaptation to Imposed Demands" (SAID) principle (Silva, 1990). For the sake of remaining consistent with the operational definitions associated with the RESTQ, the term overtraining will be used in this manuscript to represent this purposeful training method.

Systematic recovery is a biopsychosocial process that enables a person to return to baseline performance levels (Kellmann & Kallus, 2001) after periods of stress or absence of stress (e.g., under activation or monotony). A more recent term, "underrecovery" refers to inefficient recovery necessary in response to applied training loads (Kellmann, 2002). In other words, to be "underrecovered" means that a person has not returned to a sufficient recovery state so as to be ready to meet new training loads. Thus, underrecovery is not one and the same with overtraining.

Staleness can be viewed as a relatively early state of underrecovery (Morgan, Brown et al., 1987) in which a person's ability to adapt or failure to compensate for excessive training demands results in fatigue (mentally and/or physically) and performance plateaus (Kellmann, 2002). Symptoms of staleness can also include depressed mood, apathy, decreased self-esteem, mood fluctuations, weight loss, sleep disturbance, and loss of appetite (e.g., Kuipers & Kiezer, 1988). These symptoms negatively impact performance. Morgan, Brown, and colleagues (1987) pointed out an effective way of differentiating the two: overtraining can be planned and positive, whereas staleness is unwanted and negative. In a cross-cultural examination of swimmers, 34.6% of athletes had reported being stale at one time (Raglin, Sawamura, Alexiou, Hassmén, & Kenttä, 2000), whereas approximately two-thirds of elite runners had experienced staleness during their careers (Morgan, O'Connor et al., 1987). Burnout is another related term that has inaccurately been erroneously used. In contrast, burnout is an end state that is typically caused by prolonged underrecovery leading to physiological, emotional, and psychological exhaustion (Silva, 1990). Suggested differences between burned out athletes and those who are stale include lost motivation (Smith, 1986), emotional/physical exhaustion, a significantly reduced sense of accomplishment and sport devaluation (Raedeke & Smith, 2001).

The task of the sport practitioner involved in monitoring athlete recovery is to be able to recognize signs of underrecovery and staleness, promote recovery behaviors and hopefully avoid athlete burnout. Having a convenient tool on hand to monitor underrecovery symptoms for preventive purposes would seem to be advantageous to sport professionals, especially given the apparent prevalence of underrecovery and its negative consequences (Morgan, O'Connor et al., 1987).

THEORETICAL FRAMEWORKS

A basic principle of recovery is that training stress demands require sufficient recovery behaviors over time to avoid underrecovery. Along these lines Kellmann (1991, as cited in Kellmann, 2002) proposed a "scissors" model of underrecovery. In this model, stress and recovery go hand in hand along different continuums. According to the aforementioned researcher, as training stress demands increase, recovery demands also increase and require a systematic investment of greater personal effort and resources to handle them. The resources identified by Kellmann and Kallus (2001) that contribute to recovery include general life elements (i.e., general success, social relaxation, physical relaxation, general well-being and sleep quality) and sport-specific elements (i.e., a sense of being in shape, personal accomplishment, self-efficacy, and self-regulation). These resources comprise the *sleep and rest* and *relaxation and emotional support* categories of approaches to recovery that Kenttä and Hassmén (1998) discuss.

Recently, the failure adaptation model was developed by Tennenbaum, Jones, Kitsantas, Sacks, and Berwick (2003a). They attempted to provide a comprehensive model of failure adaptation (i.e., overtraining syndrome or underrecovery) that attempts to account for stress sources, modifying personal factors, and the addition of perceptions and coping strategies that affect adaptation. Tennenbaum and colleagues found stress can come from a variety of sources, not just physical causes, and the response to the stress depends on a person's appraisal of the stress and how the stress is handled. This model has been tested using a case study method and a battery of objective tests such as The Sports Pressure Checklist, The Profile of Mood States, and The Sport Competition Anxiety Test (Tennenbaum, Jones, Kitsantas, Sacks, & Berwick, 2003b). Consequently, the authors reaffirmed the need to account for non-training stressors in the comprehensive assessment and monitoring of overtraining, staleness, or burnout. Because the use of multiple assessment methods is often not practical in an applied setting, there appears to be a need for additional research in the area to reduce the instruments essential to efficiently monitoring recovery status. If one psychological measure could effectively detect such occurrence, the ease of use and the non-invasive method of testing would be beneficial to those looking for a repeated measures monitoring tool.

MEASURES

Physiological measures. As noted above, underrecovery typically results in emotional and physical negative adaptations, which manifest physiologically in the malfunction of the central nervous system (CNS), autonomic nervous system (ANS), and the neuroendocrine system (Froehlich, 1993). Commonly cited methods to assess physiological adaptations include measuring stress hormones, antibodies, catecholamines, and resting or sleeping heart rates (Froehlich, 1993; Gleeson, 2002; Hooper et al., 1995). Some of the most popular forms of measuring the training response are plasma creatine kinase levels (CK), muscle lactate, and resting heart rate. High levels of CK in blood samples, low levels of blood lactate in the muscles (Gleeson, 2002) and a significant increase or decrease in resting heart rate (Dressendorfer, Wade, & Scaff, 1985; Gleeson, 2002; Kuipers & Keizer, 1988; Smith & Norris, 2002) can all be symptoms of underrecovery. Even though there is a relative abundance of research in this area, there does not appear to be one standard set of tests that reliably measures underrecovery. (Gleeson, 2002; Raglin & Morgan, 1994; Urhausen & Kindermann, 2002). Furthermore, physiological methods are typically invasive and retrospective limiting the practicality of this assessment method (Armstrong & VanHeest, 2002; Meeusen et al., 2006).

Psychological measures. Several questionnaires have been developed and validated that are used to monitor an athlete's perceptions of training loads and recovery. Borg (1998) proposed that measuring physical exertion should measure physical output as well as perceptions of effort. The Rating of Perceived Exertion Scales (RPE; Borg) were constructed using categorical scales to measure state training intensity ranging from *no exertion at all* to *maximal exertion*. Some researchers have found the measure to be reliable and valid measures of training loads (Borg; Noble & Robertson, 1996), yet others surmise that it is not practical for other purposes such as detecting a staleness (Urhausen & Kindermann, 2002). One limitation of the RPE is that it is uni-dimensional, in that it only measures one construct, perceived exertion. RPE does not measure recovery or other non-physical sources of stress during the training process that appear to be related to underrecovery.

To address one of the issues with the RPE, Kenttä (1996) created the Total Quality Recovery (TQR) scale to measure perceived recovery ratings. The scale's construction mirrored Borg's RPE but incorporated the important concept of recovery. Unfortunately, no identified studies in English have used the TQR. Therefore, the psychometric properties remain uncertain.

The Profile of Mood States (POMS) is a global assessment of mood comprised of a 65-item adjectives checklist (McNair, Lorr, & Droppleman, 1971). The POMS has been used as a reliable self-report measure to monitor changes in athletes' training stress (Morgan, Brown et al., 1987). Unfortunately, the POMS only provides a list of consequential mood disturbances and does not provide insight as to the origin of mood change. Raglin and Morgan (1994) developed a shortened version of the POMS to measure training-induced distress titled the Training Distress Scale (TDS). The TDS is used to identify distressed athletes, but additional studies are needed to further support its application use in interventions (Raglin & Morgan).

In order to provide more insight into the main stressors, Kallus (1995) originally created a German version of the Recovery-Stress Questionnaire (RESTQ), based on the "scissors model" proposed by Kellmann (1991; as cited in Kellmann & Kallus, 2001). It has since been modified to be sport specific (RESTQ-Sport; Kellmann & Kallus). Respondents are asked to answer each phrase (e.g., "I had the impression there were too few breaks") by circling a number from zero to six with anchors of *never* to *always* indicating the level experienced within the past three days. The RESTQ-Sport has two versions - one with 77 items and another with 53 items (note: the two versions are called RESTQ-76 and RESTQ-52 respectively since one additional, non-scored filler item is also included on each version). Each version includes 19 scales measuring stressful and restful categories including up to four items per scale depending on the version (Kellmann & Kallus).

Internal consistency was found to be adequate in most of the 19 scales. Information about RESTQ-Sport's construct validity was reported using intercorrelations between the scales (Kellmann & Kallus, 2001). One stress and one recovery factor for the general and sport-specific subscales emerged in a Principle Component Analysis with a Varimax rotation. Additional convergent validity has been found with the Multidimensional Physical Symptom

List, the POMS, and the State-Trait Anxiety Inventory (Erdmann & Janke, 1982; McNair et al., 1971; Spielberger, Gorsuch, & Lushene, 1970; as cited in Kellmann & Kallus, 2001). The RESTQ-Sport has been used in a variety of studies that aimed at monitoring and regulating stress and recovery states of athletes (Kellmann, Altenburg, Lormes, & Steinacker, 2001; Kellmann & Günther, 2000).

Since items on the RESTQ-Sport are more action-oriented and revealing of how an athlete may be struggling (i.e., either too much stress or too little recovery), an intervention can easily be matched to treat the specific symptoms or stop the source(s) of the stressor. The administration is relatively easy in comparison to physiological measures. However, the 10-15 minutes it takes to complete could be tedious for the athlete, coach, trainer or sport consultant if done every three days as suggested given time constraints common in training. Utilization of the short-form, RESTQ-52, by two of the current authors showed the instrument to be helpful yet impractical for frequent repeated measures to a collegiate sport team over the span of a season. Comments from athletes and coaches suggested that a shorter survey was preferred. A brief, one-page questionnaire of recovery and stress would seem to be more time and cost effective for repetitive use by those interested in monitoring training loads, recovery and possible prevention of staleness and burnout.

Kellmann, Botterill, and Wilson (1999, as cited in Kellmann, Patrick, Botterill, & Wilson, 2002) constructed the shorter, 7-item Recovery-Cue from TQR and RESTQ-Sport items in order to assess perceived exertion, perceived recovery and recovery effort that would meet the shorter criteria. Botterill and Wilson (2002) reported that the Recovery-Cue has been used with a variety of Canadian National Teams and has been widely accepted as part of a monitoring system. The benefits to a monitoring form like this seem clear, however, no psychometric properties were provided in the review of this form, so the need for a critically-examined, holistic self-report measure is warranted. Accordingly, the purpose of this study was to conduct initial reliability and validity analyses on an early version of the Brief Assessment of Recovery and Stress (BARS). The BARS is a short scale based on the RESTQ-Sport that was designed for repetitive use to monitor stress and recovery in athletes.

METHOD

The purpose of this investigation was to construct and examine the psychometric properties of an abbreviated self-report measure of training stress and recovery perceptions, "Brief Assessment of Recovery and Stress" (BARS). It was hope that BARS could ultimately be used to reliably and efficiently assess training stress and recovery status in athletes and other active people.

PARTICIPANTS

Participants were 387undergraduate college student-athletes and non-athletes enrolled at two United States Universities: a large southern university and a large mid-Atlantic land-grant university. Three hundred and forty-three of the 387 participants (114 females, 228 males) chose to indicate their sex in the demographic section of the questionnaire. Two hundred and seventy-four non-athletes and 113 athletes reported their athletic status. Of the 91% of participants who reported their age, 64% were aged 19-21 with ages ranging from 17 to over 21 years. The inclusion of non-athletes in the study was felt appropriate, as the purpose of the statistical analyses was to establish factors within BARS and examine the correlations between two scales. Further, sport terminology was essentially omitted and the purpose was not to establish normative data, thus distinction between athletic status was not justified.

INSTRUMENTS

Recovery-Stress Questionaire-76 Sport (RESTQ-76 Sport). RESTQ-76 Sport is a 77-item self-report, 7-point Likert type scale (0 = never, 6 = always) that provides a systematic "snapshot" of a respondent's perceptions of her or his stress-recovery state. Consistent with their theoretical premise, Kellmann and Kallus (2001) have included items in the RESTQ-76 Sport that measure various stressors as well as various recovery efforts (e.g., social relaxation) or situations (e.g., being in shape) that athletes may encounter during their training and competition process. The items are categorized into four different broad areas (General Stress, General Recovery Efforts, Sport Specific Stress, and Sport Specific Recovery Efforts). The four broad areas are further divided into nineteen different scales as follows:

1. General Stress (7-scales): general stress, emotional stress, social stress, conflicts/pressure, fatigue, lack of energy, and physical complaints;
2. General Recovery Efforts (5-scales): success, social recovery, physical recovery, general well-being, and sleep quality;
3. Sport Specific Stress (3-scales): disturbed breaks, emotional exhaustion, and injury;
4. Sport Specific Recovery Efforts (4-scales): being in shape, personal accomplishment, self-efficacy, and self-regulation.

Each of these scales has four items associated with it. Sixteen of the nineteen RESTQ-Sport scales for an American athlete sample possessed internal consistencies values above .71. The three factors that possessed relatively low alpha coefficients were: 1) conflicts/pressure, 2) personal accomplishment, and 3) disturbed breaks (i.e., alpha coefficients .58, .62, and <.50 respectively; Kellmann & Kallus, 2001).

Brief Assessment of Recovery and Stress (BARS). BARS is a preliminary nineteen item self-report, seven point, Likert type instrument (0=never, 6=always). The primary investigators crafted BARS in an effort to assess stress recovery status more efficiently than the 77 question RESTQ-76 Sport or its "cousin", the abbreviated, 53-question RESTQ-52 Sport. The nineteen BARS items were constructed using the exact wording of the 19 RESTQ Sport subscales. In other words, each RESTQ Sport subscale is addressed in BARS through one item. This is a similar approach that was used in creating the Brief Assessment of Mood from the POMS (Dean, Whelan, & Myers, 1990). Three additional items at the end of the BARS form asked about selected participant background information including sex, current athlete status (i.e., active athlete or non-athlete) and age. No information was collected that could have led to participant identification.

PROCEDURES

Internal Review Board approval and class instructors granted permission prior to the commencement of this study. Either one of the investigators or a trained research assistant solicited the involvement of students who were in introductory sport studies classes. During a regularly-scheduled class meeting, all students were given a cover letter explaining the survey and were told that items on the survey covered perceptions of training and recovery behavior in sport and life. Students were also told that participation was voluntary and answers would be kept secure and confidential. After completion of the surveys, students were thanked for their participation. Data were collected over the course of the spring and fall semesters.

RESULTS

Descriptive Statistics

Descriptive statistics were calculated for BARS by gender, athlete status and the overall sample (see Table 1). Pair-wise comparisons were calculated using Cohen's d to estimate effect sizes for all significant ($p<.01$) mean differences between men and women and athlete and non-athletes. All other pair-wise comparisons were non-significant.

Table 1. BARS Descriptive Data by Gender, Athlete Status and Overall Sample

Item	Female (n = 114)		Male (n = 228)			Athlete (n = 113)		Non-Athlete (n = 229)			Overall (N = 382)	
	M	SD	M	SD	ES	M	SD	M	SD	ES	M	SD
General stress	3.11	1.51	2.83	1.41		2.78	1.48	3.01	1.44		2.96	1.46
Emotional stress	3.01	1.51	2.53	1.46	.021	2.74	1.59	2.69	1.47		2.72	1.53
Social stress	2.29	1.42	2.09	1.46		2.14	1.54	2.18	1.41		2.20	1.46
Conflicts/pressure	2.63	1.43	2.64	1.53		2.72	1.62	2.60	1.46		2.63	1.52
Fatigue	2.82	1.44	2.82	1.50		3.07	1.56	2.72	1.45		2.83	1.54
Lack of energy	2.65	1.39	2.63	1.47		2.86	1.43	2.55	1.45		2.70	1.48
Physical complaints	2.23	1.46	2.11	1.42		2.50	1.58	2.02	1.38	.024	2.24	1.50
Burnout/emotional exhaustion	2.47	1.74	2.16	1.56		2.55	1.73	2.16	1.59	'	2.31	1.62
Disturbed breaks	2.29	1.44	2.20	1.37		2.19	1.37	2.28	1.44		2.28	1.41
Injury	1.32	1.53	1.32	1.58		1.79	1.76	1.07	1.38	.047	1.40	1.59
Success	3.46	1.19	3.52	1.34		3.70	1.39	3.42	1.22		3.53	1.29
Being in shape	2.54	1.49	3.36	2.44	.037	3.61	1.67	2.84	2.39	.027	3.10	2.11
Personal accomplishments	3.05	1.31	3.51	1.30	.030	3.58	1.42	3.24	1.25		3.37	1.32
Self-efficacy	3.02	1.23	3.48	1.24	.040	3.48	1.34	3.26	1.21		3.34	1.25
Self-regulation	3.01	1.30	3.45	1.16	.049	3.46	1.30	3.22	1.20		3.33	1.24
Social relaxation	2.97	1.31	3.29	1.38		3.12	1.46	3.25	1.32		3.21	1.36
Physical relaxation	2.74	1.18	3.09	1.32		2.92	1.43	3.01	1.21		2.97	1.30
General well-being	3.38	1.28	3.59	1.33		3.52	1.50	3.50	1.22		3.46	1.32
Sleep quality	2.69	1.21	2.96	1.57		2.80	1.57	2.90	1.44		2.87	1.47

Note. Effect size estimates (Cohen's d) reported for all significant ($p<.01$) mean differences between men and women and athlete and non-athlete. All other pairwise comparisons were non-significant.

Principal Component Analysis

Table 2. Principle Components Analysis with Varimax Rotation of the BARS with Injury Deleted.

Item	Stress (Factor 1)	Self-Efficacy (Factor 2)	Relaxation (Factor 3)
General stress	**.80**	-.07	-.13
Emotional stress	**.78**	-.15	-.10
Social stress	**.70**	-.14	-.14
Conflicts/pressure	**.73**	-.01	-.13
Fatigue	**.73**	.03	-.21
Lack of energy	**.77**	-.06	-.31
Physical complaints	**.65**	-.00	-.26
Burnout/emotional exhaustion	**.74**	-.13	-.10
Disturbed breaks	**.57**	-.14	.30
Success	-.01	**.73**	.18
Being in shape	-.15	**.58**	-.03
Personal accomplishments	-.09	**.77**	.24
Self-efficacy	-.08	**.80**	.18
Self-regulation	.03	**.78**	.17
Social relaxation	-.13	.45	**.43**
Physical relaxation	-.24	.23	**.73**
General well-being	-.28	.38	**.63**
Sleep quality	-.20	.21	**.73**
Eigenvalues	6.21	3.02	1.11
% of variance explained	34.48	16.75	6.16

RELIABILITY

Table 3. Cronbach Alpha Coefficients for BARS Emerging Factors

Items	Correlated item total r	Alpha if item deleted	Total scale alpha
General stress	.74	.88	.89
Emotional stress	.72	.88	
Social stress	.64	.88	
Conflicts/pressure	.66	.88	
Fatigue	.67	.88	
Lack of energy	.76	.87	
Physical complaints	.61	.89	
Burnout/emotional exhaustion	.68	.88	
Disturbed breaks	.42	.90	
Success	.58	.73	.78
Being in shape	.40	.84	
Personal accomplishments	.66	.71	
Self-efficacy	.67	.71	
Self-regulation	.62 ·	.72	
Social relaxation	.49	.70	.77
Physical relaxation	.62	.76	
General well-being	.64	.68	
Sleep quality	.56	.73	

Note. N = 387

Following data collection, Bartlett's test of sphericity (.893/1.00) and Kaiser-Meyer-Olkin (KMO) test of sampling adequacy (<.0001) were employed. Both indicated that the data set was suitable for analysis. To examine the factor integrity of BARS, a principal component analysis with Kaiser's Varimax rotation method was conducted. The initial analysis of all nineteen items revealed four factors, with the Injury item as an outlier in the fourth factor. Thus, this factor was deleted and the data was reanalyzed with a PCA with eighteen items. Three factors emerged with Eigenvalues >1, yielding sound empirical support and an interpretable solution (see Table 2). Overall, the three-factor solution accounted for 57% of the variance. The first factor was designated "Stress" because the nine items relate to sources of stress. This factor accounted for 34.5% of the overall variance. It appeared that the remaining two factors were both associated with recovery. The second factor, "Self-Efficacy Recovery," had five items that appear to relate to one's psychological recovery and confidence in his or her recovery. This factor accounted for 16.8% of the overall variance. Finally, the third factor was labeled "Relaxation Recovery," because the four associated items link to direct methods of recovery involving rest. This factor accounted for 6.2% of the variance. Social relaxation was kept in the Relaxation Recovery component despite double loading on the Self-Efficacy component since this is logical conceptually. A second PCA without this item was performed, which resulted in negligible (i.e. one tenth) differences in variances and eigenvalues. Clearly, future research critically examining this item is necessary. Separate Cronbach alpha reliability coefficients were calculated to determine the internal consistency of participant's responses to the nine Stress, five Self-Efficacy Recovery, and four Relaxation Recovery items (see Table 3). Reliability coefficients were deemed acceptable for the majority of the items. Three items, one from each factor, (i.e., Disturbed Breaks, [Stress factor], Being in Shape [Self-Efficacy Recovery factor], and Social Relaxation [Relaxation Recovery factor]) did not emerge as psychometrically sound as others. These items may need to be re-worded in future study.

CONVERGENT VALIDITY

Pearson Product correlations were calculated between the 19 BARS items and RESTQ-76 individual subscales (see Table 4). All correlations were positive and significant (p < .01), and ranged from in strength from low (Social Relaxation r = .353) to moderate (Physical Complaints r = .592).

DISCUSSION

The central purpose of this study was to examine the preliminary psychometric properties of BARS. Results from the PCA indicated that a three-factor solution (i.e., Stress, Self-Efficacy Recovery, and Relaxation Recovery) best represented the data. Additional analyses provided reasonable support for internal consistency for BARS.

The three-factor solution that we observed for BARS differs slightly from the two identified factors (i.e., general stress and recovery) for both the general and sport-specific subscales of the RESTQ-Sport reported by Kellmann and Kallus (2001). Overall, the current data did not provide sufficient support to justify only these two subscales (see Table 2). Furthermore, there were small differences between BARS and RESTQ-Sport factor solutions for the recovery factor. Kellmann and Kallus (2001) discuss two recovery scales - general recovery and sport-specific recovery. In comparison, the analyses from this study produced what the authors term a "Self-Efficacy Recovery" (i.e., success, being in shape, personal accomplishment, self-efficacy, and self-regulation) and a "Relaxation Recovery" (i.e., social relaxation, physical relaxation, general well-being, and sleep quality) factor. The item that loads differently in the two studies is the Success item. In this study the item loaded on the Self-Efficacy Recovery factor with items such as Personal Accomplishment and Self-Regulation. In contrast, this item loaded on to Kellmann and Kallus' general recovery factor with Social Recovery and Sleep Quality. It could be that the Self-Efficacy Recovery element includes those items that act as a buffer between recovery efforts and stress. In other words, recovery efforts may be more effective when one is in shape, self-regulates, experiences success, etc. This factor may also reflect a person's "hardiness," which has been recently shown to relate to adaptation in training (Wilson & Raglin, 2004). Further exploration and interpretation of this factor is necessary.

Table 4. Pearson Product Correlations of BARS Items and RESTQ-76 Sport Subscales

Subscales	r
General stress	.56*
Emotional stress	.57*
Social stress	.45*
Conflicts/pressure	.53*
Fatigue	.56*
Lack of energy	.47*
Physical complaints	.59*
Burnout/emotional exhaustion	.46*
Disturbed breaks	.42*
Success	.49*
Being in shape	.39*
Personal accomplishments	.46*
Self-efficacy	.51*
Self-regulation	.37*
Social relaxation	.35*
Physical relaxation	.40*
General well-being	.53*
Injury	.48*

*$p < .01$

Alternatively, the Stress factor loadings for the BARS instrument were very comparable to the combinedRESTQ-Sport general and sport-specific stress factor loadings. The RESTQ-Sport general stress scale had seven items and the sport-specific stress scale had three items. Factor analysis for BARS combined nine of these items, with the Injury item as an outlier on a weak fourth factor. This could be due to a very small number of participants that actually did perceive themselves as experiencing an injury, thus this item's variance was positively skewed. Interestingly, the alpha coefficients for the Disturbed Breaks item were low for both instruments. Further work on this item needs to be completed.

There appear to be three central research implications that emerged from this study. First, the results suggest that BARS has the potential to be a useful psychological measure that can aid in the brief holistic screening and monitoring of self-reported stress and recovery. Past measurements of underrecovery, overtraining, or staleness have been predominantly physiologically based, psychologically uni-dimensional, time consuming or not practical (Urhausen & Kindermann, 2002). Over time, there appears to have been a shift to more holistic assessment and monitoring of an athlete's stress and recovery efforts in the training response paradigm. An increase in psychological testing in this area has shown to be beneficial and perhaps more reliable than physiological monitoring (Raglin & Wilson, 2000).

Consequently, it seems that only measuring training loads or physical markers of recovery may not be a consistently accurate indicator of athlete training status. BARS could be used independently or in conjunction with a physiological assessment.

Secondly, the development of BARS also expands the area of stress and recovery assessment by providing sport professionals such as sport psychology consultants and coaches with the readily accessible insight into where stressors and/or lack of recovery concerns are originating. The economy of BARS administration and scoring can be helpful in two ways. As Kenttä and Hassmén (1998) stated, one of the main benefits is that this type of psychological screening tool can be regularly used in a preventative way rather than just a means for diagnosis. Thus, sport professionals may be able to use BARS, like the RESTQ-Sport, to help avert staleness and facilitate recovery in targeted areas.

Furthermore, because of the relative specificity of BARS, an individual athlete's and the collective team's stressors and recovery behavior perceptions can be monitored. Indeed, an important concept in the stress response relationship is that it varies with each individual. A certain type and amount of training load in one athlete may result ·in positive adaptations, whereas the same training in another athlete may result in undesirable adaptations (e.g., staleness). Coaches may find BARS to be a practical way of fine tuning training and recovery to account for the individual needs of team members.

Finally, one of the most important implications for the development of BARS is the ease in which it can be administered. As a concise 19-item instrument, athletes can complete it in only two or three minutes without burdening them or their coaches for time, which is typically seen as a precious commodity in the world of sport and athletics. Measuring both stress and recovery in training and non-training domains in an unobtrusive and costly manner appears worthwhile (Kenttä & Hassmén, 1998).

LIMITATIONS

There are several limitations to the study primarily linked to sampling. First, the participants surveyed were from samples of convenience that included a combination of active collegiate athletes and other students who perceived themselves as non-active athletes. A differentiation was not made between types of athletes (e.g. varsity, club, intramural) and not objectively verified. However, differences in means on the individual subscales between these two groups were at a minimum. Future researchers may want to limit their participant pool to only active athletes. There were also considerably more males than female participants, thus greater balance by sex of future participants seems warranted. Finally, the relatively restricted age range of participants limits the results of this study.

FUTURE DIRECTIONS

Results from this study of the psychometric properties of the initial version of BARS suggest it has potential for use by sport psychology consultants, coaches and researchers. Logical next steps in refining BARS include administrations to larger numbers of diverse, active athletes and samples of both sexes. The conduct of more sophisticated statistical analyses of BARS's psychometric properties. (e.g., predictive, concurrent, and divergent validities) would also seem useful to this process. The content of some BARS items require re-examination. For example, the two items (i.e., Disturbed Breaks and Being in Shape) that were shown to be weak need to be scrutinized more closely and possibly modified. Further, a continuation of the exploration of other areas of stress (e.g., family stress and illness) and recovery (e.g., nutrition/hydration quality and active rest) are necessary to determine if additional items should be added (Kenttä & Hassmén, 1998). Future research should also involve contrasting the efficacy of BARS with other training stress and recovery scales.

REFERENCES

Armstrong, L. E., & VanHeest, J. L. (2002). The unknown mechanism of the overtraining syndrome: Clues from depression and psychoneuroimmunology. *Sports Medicine, 32*, 185-209.

Botterill, C., & Wilson, C. (2002). Overtraining: Emotional and interdisciplinary dimensions. In M. Kellmann (Ed.), *Enhancing recovery: Preventing underperformance in athletes* (pp. 143-159). Champaign, IL: Human Kinetics.

Borg, G. (1998). *Borg's Perceived Exertion and Pain Scales.* Champaign, IL: Human Kinetics.

Dean, J., Whelan, J. P., & Meyers, A. W. (1990, September). *An incredibly quick way to assess mood states: The incredibly short POMS.* Paper presented at the Association for the Advancement of Applied Sport Psychology, San Antonio.

Dressendorfer, R.H., Wade, C.E., & Scaff, J.H. (1985). Increased morning heart rate in runners. A valid sign of overtraining? *The Physician and Sports Medicine, 13*, 77-86.

Froehlich, J. (1993). Overtraining syndrome. In J. Heil (Ed.), *Psychology of sport injury* (pp. 59-70). Champaign, IL: Human Kinetics.

Gleeson, M. (2002). Biomechanical and immunological markers of overtraining. *Journal of Sports Science and Medicine, 1*, 31-41.

Hooper, S. L., MacKinnon, T., Howard, A., Gordon, R. D., & Bachmann, A. W. (1995). Markers for monitoring overtraining and recovery. *Medicine and Science in Sports & Exercise, 27*, 106-112.

Kallus, K.W. (1995). *Der Erholungs-Belastungs-Fragebogen [The Recovery-Stress Questionnaire].* Frankfurt: Swets & Zeitlinger.

Kellmann, M. (2002). Underrecovery and overtraining: Different concepts-similar impact? In M. Kellmann (Ed.), *Enhancing recovery: Preventing underperformance in athletes* (pp. 3-24). Champaign, IL: Human Kinetics.

Kellmann, M., Altenburg, D., Lormes, W., & Steinacker, J. M. (2001). Assessing stress and recovery during preparation for the world championships in rowing. *The Sport Psychologist, 15*, 151-167.

Kellmann, M., & Gunther, K. (2000). Changes in stress and recovery in elite rowers during preparation for the Olympic games. *Medicine and Science in Sports & Exercise, 32*, 676-683.

Kellmann, M., & Kallus, K. W. (2001). *Recovery-stress questionnaire for athletes: User manual.* Champaign, IL: Human Kinetics.

Kellmann, M., Patrick, T., Botterill, C., & Wilson, C. (2002). The Recovery-Cue and its use in applied settings: Practical suggestions regarding assessment and monitoring of recovery. In M. Kellmann (Ed.), *Enhancing recovery: Preventing underperformance in athletes* (pp. 219-229). Champaign, IL: Human Kinetics.

Kenttä, G. (1996). *Överträingingssyndrom: en psykofysiologisk process (Overtraining: a psychophysicological process)* Swedish: Luleä. Sweden: Högskolan I Luleä.

Kenttä, G. & Hassmén, P. (1998). Overtraining and recovery: A conceptual model. *Sports Medicine, 26*, 1-16.

Kuipers, H., & Keizer, H. A. (1988). Overtraining in elite athlete: Review and directions for the future. *Sports Medicine, 6*, 79-92.

Lehmann, M., Netzer, N., Steinacker, J. M., & Opitz-Gress, A. (1998). Physiological responses to short- and long-term overtraining in endurance athletes. In R. B. Kreider, A. C. Fry, & M. L. O'Toole (Eds.), *Overtraining in sport* (pp. 19-46). Champaign, IL: Human Kinetics.

McKenzie, D. (1995). Overtraining. In J. S. Torg & R. J. Shephard (Eds.) *Current Therapy in Sports Medicine* (3rd ed., pp. 526-530). New York: Mosby.

McNair, D. M., Lorr, M., & Droppleman, L.F. (1971). *EdITS manual for the Profile of Mood States*. San Diego: Educational and Industrial Testing Service.

Meeusen, R., Duclos, M., Gleeson, M., Rietjens, G., Steinacker, J., & Urhausen, A. (2006). The overtraining syndrome- facts & fiction. *European Journal of Sport Sciences, 6, 263*.

Morgan, W. P., Brown, D. R., Raglin, J. S., O'Connor, P. J., & Ellickson, K. A. (1987). Psychological monitoring of overtraining and staleness. *British Journal of Sports Medicine, 21*, 107-114.

Morgan, W. P., O'Connor, P. J., Sparling, P. B., & Pate, R. R. (1987). Psychological characterization of the elite female distance runner. *International Journal of Sports Medicine, 8*, 124-131.

Nederhof, E., Lemmink, K., Visscher, C., Meeusen, R., & Mulder, T. (2006). Psychomotor speed: Possibly a new marker for overtraining syndrome. *Sports Medicine, 36*, 817-828.

Noble, B. J., & Robertson, R. J. (1996). *Perceived exertion*. Champaign, IL: Human Kinetics.

O'Connor, P. J. (1998). Overtraining and staleness. In W. P. Morgan (Ed.), *Physical activity and mental health* (pp. 145-160). New York: Hemisphere.

Raedeke, T. D., & Smith, A. L. (2001). Development and preliminary validation of an athlete burnout measure. *Journal of Sport & Exercise Psychology, 23*, 281-306.

Raglin, J., & Morgan, W. P. (1994). Development of a scale for use in monitoring training-induced distress in athletes. *International Journal of Sports Medicine, 15*, 84-88.

Raglin, J., Sawamura, S., Alexiou, S., Hassmén, P., & Kenttä, G. (2000). Training practices and staleness in 13-18-year-old swimmers: A cross-cultural study. *Pediatric Exercise Science, 12*, 61-70.

Raglin, J. & Wilson, G. (2000). Overtraining in athletes. In Y. Hanin (Ed.). *Emotions in sport.* (pp. 191-207). Champaign, IL: Human Kinetics.

Silva, J. M. (1990). An analysis of the training stress syndrome in competitive athletics. *Journal of Applied Sport Psychology, 2*, 5-20.

Smith, R. E. (1986). Toward a cognitive-affective model of athletic burnout. *Journal of Sport Psychology, 8*, 36-50.

Smith, D. J., & Norris, S. R. (2002). Training load and monitoring an athlete's tolerance for endurance training. In M. Kellmann (Ed.), *Enhancing recovery: Preventing underperformance in athletes* (pp. 81-101). Champaign, IL: Human Kinetics.

Tennenbaum, G., Jones, C. M., Kitsantas, A., Sacks, D. N., & Berwick, J. P. (2003a). Failure adaptation: Psychological conceptualization of the stress response process in sport. *International Journal of Sport Psychology, 34,* 1-26.

Tennenbaum, G., Jones, C. M., Kitsantas, A., Sacks, D. N., & Berwick, J.P. (2003b). Failure adaptation: An investigation of the stress response process in sport. *International Journal of Sport Psychology, 34,* 27-62.

Urhausen, A., & Kindermann, W. (2002). Diagnosis of overtraining: What tools do we have? *Sports Medicine, 32*(2), 95-102

Wilson, G. S. & Raglin, J. S. (2004). The predictive value of hardiness and optimism for the identification of past staleness responses in high school age male and female distance runners. *New Studies in Athletics,* 19, 41-46.

AUTHOR NOTE

Correspondence concerning this manuscript should be sent to Dr. Linda A. Keeler, CaliforniaStateUniversity, Chico, Department of Kinesiology, Yolo Hall 256, Chico, CA, 95929-0330, or emailed to lkeeler@csuchico.edu. Lead author phone: (530) 898-4072 and fax: (530) 898-4932.

The authors would like to express their appreciation to Dr. Kristen Dieffenbach of West VirginiaUniversity's College of Physical Activity and Sport Science for her feedback on this article.

In: Introduction to Sport Psychology
Editor: Robert Schinke

ISBN: 978-1-61761-973-1
© 2011 Nova Science Publishers, Inc.

MISSION STATEMENTS IN SPORT AND THEIR ETHICAL MESSAGES: ARE THEY BEING COMMUNICATED TO PRACTITIONERS?

Martin Camiré, Penny Werthner, and Pierre Trudel
School of Human Kinetics, University of Ottawa, Ottawa, Canada

ABSTRACT

Mission statements are widely employed as a tool for strategic organizational planning. In sport, various types of organizations utilize their mission statements to communicate objectives that range from the development of responsible citizens to the importance of establishing professional standards of ethical practice for members. Research has shown that a mission statement's usefulness is related to organizational members' knowledge of it. In sport, it is not known if mission statements and the ethical messages they convey are effectively disseminated from those who develop them to the practitioners who implement them (e.g., coaches, athletes, sport psychologists, mental trainers). Therefore, using a case study approach, the purpose of this study was to trace the process of how one academic institution's mission statement was communicated to and understood by sport stakeholders. Results indicated that administrators were knowledgeable of the school's mission statement and that many coaches were at least familiar with the mission statement whereas parents and athletes reported very little or no knowledge. The findings of this study suggest possible issues in the communication of mission statements and implications for sport psychology organizations are discussed.

MISSION STATEMENTS IN SPORT AND THEIR ETHICAL MESSAGES: ARE THEY BEING COMMUNICATED TO PRACTITIONERS?

Living in a highly competitive and ever-changing world that is driven by knowledge (Bart, 2004), organizations must continuously find ways to direct and enhance the performance of their members. Organizations employ a number of tools and techniques for strategic organizational planning and among these, the mission statement has been and continues to be one of the most widely used (Bart & Hupfer, 2004). A mission statement is "in its most basic form…a formalized document defining an organization's unique and enduring purpose" (Bart & Tabone, 1999, p.19). According to Bart and Baetz (1998), there is no consensus as to what mission statements should or should not include but most are composed of a 'raison d'être' as well as an organization's values, beliefs, and philosophy.

The two main purposes of mission statements should be "to provide a focused guide for decision making and to motivate and inspire employees toward common objectives" (Bart & Tabone, 1999, p.19). Mission statements are also used to balance the competing interests of different stakeholders and to create behavioral standards of ethical conduct (Vandijck, Desmidt, & Buelens, 2007).

In the world of sport, mission statements are used by a variety of organizations (e.g., national sport organizations, multi-sport associations, sport psychology organizations). Given that organizations operate at varying levels and offer their services to different populations,their mission statements communicate different purposes. Large international organizations, such as the United Nations (UN) and the International Olympic Committee (IOC), have broad objectivesand attribute to sporta distinctive role in the realization and achievement of greater social inclusion and peace (Bailey, 2008). Sport is viewed as an essential component in addressing global issues such as violence, disease, poverty, social injustices, and inequality (Mandigo, Corlett, & Anderson, 2008)..For example, the UN (2004) states that sportis a tool to "contribute to economic and social development,'improving health and personal growth...help build a culture of peace and tolerance by bringing people together" (¶ 4).In its mission statement, the IOC (2004) states that through the philosophy of Olympism, sport can be "at the service of the harmonious development of man, with a view to promoting a peaceful society concerned with the preservation of human dignity" (p.9).

National level sport organizations, some of which oversee the practice of sport in academic institutions, suggest through their mission statements thatthe educational benefits of sport participation are at the forefront. For example, the mission of the National Collegiate Athletic Association (NCAA, 2007) is to "govern competition in a fair, safe, equitable and sportsmanlike manner, and to integrate intercollegiate athletics into higher education so that the educational experience of the student-athlete is paramount" (Core Purpose, ¶ 1). Although the educational benefits of sport participation are of great importance, national level school sport organizations also seek to develop well-rounded citizens who behave in an ethically responsible manner. For example, the Canadian School Sport Federation's (CSSF, 2004) purpose is to "encourage, promote and be an advocate for good sportsmanship, citizenship and the total development of student athletes through interscholastic sport" (p.4). Similar patterns can be observed in the mission statements of national sport organizations overseeing sports practiced at the community level. For example, Hockey Canada (2008) believes "in the values of fair play and sportsmanship, including the development of respect for all people by all participants" (Mandate and Mission).

Smaller regional school sport organizations also appear to have a mandate of promoting ethical values such as respect, sportsmanship, and fair play. However, given that they are generally responsible for lower levels of competition and that they deal with younger populations, objectives are also aimed towards the promotion of values such as pleasure and safety. For example, the National Capital Secondary School Athletic Association (NCSSAA, 2005) in the Ottawa region states it aims "to contribute to the health, happiness and general welfare of the student-athlete by sponsoring well-organized and properly supervised athletic activities" (p.1).

Sport psychology organizationshave also developed mission statements to communicate their goals, values, and philosophy. The International Society of Sport Psychology (ISSP) states it is an organization "devoted to promoting research, practice, and development in the discipline of sport psychology throughout the world" (ISSP, 2005, About ISSP). The newly created Canadian Sport Psychology Association (CSPA, 2007) developed its mission statement based on that of the ISSP and adds that the practice of sport psychology should "lead to performance enhancement...as well as the holistic development of individuals who are not just 'athletes' performing in sport but 'persons' performing in life" (About CSPA). Given that a number of sport psychology organizations have a mandate to certify individuals who provide professional services, they have developed ethical codes, consistent with their organizational values, to establish, promote, and enhance professional standards. The ISSP, CSPA, and Association for Applied Sport Psychology (AASP) have all established codes of ethics to guide the decision-making processes and professional behaviors of their members. These codes share many similarities and are based on fundamental principles such as competence, integrity, professional and scientific responsibility, and social responsibility.

Research in the world of business and healthcare has shown that mission statements that emphasize and communicate the organization's value system have a significant positive relationship with performance (Bartkus, Glassman, & McAfee, 2005). However, a number of other factors influenceorganizational members' usage of and satisfaction with the mission. Bart and Baetz (1998) found that in order for a mission to have an impact on members, it must be relevant to daily practice and transferable to action and not "just a bunch of nice sounding words thrown on a piece of paper" (p.842). In addition, these researchers found that internal stakeholder involvement in the process of developing the mission was significantly correlated with higher levels of influence on employee behavior. Although all these factors are critical, a mission statement's usefulness remains fundamentally contingent on organizational members' awareness of it (Williams, Smythe, Hadjistavropoulos, Malloy, & Martin, 2005). In spite of this crucial fact, there is evidence demonstrating that missions are not always effectively communicated. A study conducted in Flemish hospitals showed that more than 40% of nurses were unaware that their organization even had a mission statement (Desmidt, Prinzie, & Heene, 2008).

In sport, there is an absence of information available regarding what happens to mission statements once they are developed and officially adopted by organizations. Given that sport organizations' mission statements often emphasizethe development of well-rounded citizens and the promotion of ethical values, standards, and practices, it becomes crucial to understand how mission statements are known and communicated in sporting environmentswhere many of the stakeholders are, especially in Canada, volunteer or part-time. For this study, a case study approach (Yin, 1994) was employed given its usefulness when attempting to investigate the contextual conditions of a phenomenon that is not well understood. The purpose of this study was to trace the process of howone academic institution's mission statement was communicated to andunderstood by sport stakeholders.

METHOD

Context

This study explored the mission statement knowledge of stakeholders from one academic institution. Participants (i.e., administrators, coaches, parents, athletes) were all affiliated with a private French-speaking high school from a mid-sized city in the province of Quebec in Canada. The institution is one of two private schools in the region and is, according to an annual ranking, considered to be among the top academic high schools in the province (Kozhaya & Cowley, 2006). Parents can be actively involved in the school's activities as a 20 member parents' association organizes monthly meetings to represent and promote the interests of all. The school has an enrolment of approximately 1,000 students and one third of the students participate in after-school sports. The sport program has a long tradition of excellence and is managed by an athletic director overseeing the program's operations as well as four coordinators who are responsible for adnministering each of the four sports offered at the school,which are basketball, volleyball, soccer, and badminton. The desire of the institutional leaders to positively develop students and to nourish a culture of excellence, in both academics and sports, is reflected in the school's mission statement, which was developed in 1993 and is posted and available on the school's website. The mission statement asserts that:

> The mission of the school rests on principles which aim to develop boys and girls so they can flourish in an environment favorable to the total development of their personalities. Whether it is on an intellectual, physical, social, moral, religious, or emotional level, the school will ensure that they become accomplished human beings who are engaged in their surroundings as well as responsible citizens. (*free translation from French*)

PARTICIPANTS

A total of 57 participants were purposefully selected (Patton, 2002) to take part in this study. The main criteria consisted of recruiting athletes and coaches who were currently involvedin high school sports or had been involved during the academic year and parents who hadat least one child practicing high school sports. The participants included two school administrators (principal and athletic director), 15 coaches, 20 student-athletes, and 20 parents. Interviews with administrators and coaches were conducted during the sport season whereas interviews with athletes and parents were conducted immediately following the sport season. The school's principal has held the position for more than three years and is an alumnus of the institution. Prior to being the school's principal, he was a history, English, and physical education teacher for more than seven years and an academic counselor for five years. The principal was also involved in the school's soccer program as a coach. The athletic director has more than 30 years of experience in sport administration and has been managing this particular school's sport program for 16 years. The coaches (12 males, 3 females) were on average 30 years of age, had an average of five years of experience in coaching and were involved in the four sports offered at the school. Although only three coaches were teachers at the school, the majority had close ties tothe institution as two thirds were alumni. Student-athletes (10 males, 10 females) were carefully selected in order to have participants of various backgrounds. Student-athletes were between 13 and 17 years of age (M = 15.05), had one to five years of experience in high school sports and were involved in all four sports offered at the school. Finally, efforts were also made to have parents (8 males, 12 females) of children of both genders, various ages, sports practiced, and sporting experience. Two of the parents interviewed were also teachers at the school. Ethical approval to conduct interviews with all participants was secured from the Research Ethics Board (REB) of the researchers' university.

INTERVIEW GUIDE

A structured interview guide was developedas part of a larger study on the values and life skills developed through high school sport participation. A version of the interview guide was developed for each type of participant. In the first section, demographic details and information onparticipants' experiences in sport were gathered. The second section focusedspecifically on the school's mission statement.

Administrators were asked to describe their level of knowledge of the mission statement, if they were involved in its elaboration, how knowledgeable they believed coaches were of the mission statement, and if initiatives were put in place to communicate the mission statement to practitioners. The coaches, athletes, and parents were simply asked if they knew the school's mission statement. Those who knew of the mission statement were asked to comment on the usefulness of the different elements as it relates to the practice of sport at the school. Those who did not know of the mission statement were presented a copy and were asked to read it and comment on it.

DATA ANALYSIS

All interviews were conducted in Frenchand were transcribed verbatim. The software NVivo (Qualitative Solution and Research, 2006) was used to assist in the coding and management of the data. A content analysis was performed as data was analyzed by breaking text and segmenting sentences into categories which were submitted to descriptive treatment (Creswell, 2003). Concerning the data gathered specifically on mission statements, categories were essentially developed based on the questions of the interview guide. For administrators, four categories were developed: a) knowledge level, b) involvement in the elaboration of the mission, c) perceived knowledge of coaches, and d) communication initiatives. For coaches, athletes, and parents, responses were categorized according to their reported knowledge level, (i.e., highly knowledgeable, moderately knowledgeable, no knowledge).

RESULTS

Results are presented in four sections. The first section examines administrators' knowledge of the mission statement, their involvement in its elaboration, their perceptions of coaches' knowledge of the mission, and their reported efforts to convey the mission to practitioners. The second, third, and fourth section each respectively explore coaches', parents', and athletes' knowledge of the school's mission statements. Participant identification codes are provided for each participant quote (Coaches = C; Athletes = A; Parents = P) along with a number determined by the order in which participants were interviewed.Careful consideration was taken when translating the participant quotes used in this section from French to English in order to accurately present the participants' ideas.

ADMINISTRATORS

The school principal reported being actively involved in numerous school-related activities during his time as a teacher at the school, in his capacity as a coach, and as a member of various committees such as the teachers' board. He reported being very knowledgeable of the school's mission statement given that his participation on committees allowed him to be involved in the elaboration of the original mission: "I was a teacher at that time, the school initiated consultations in order to establish, What is our educational mandate?, What is our school?, What do we want to be?". When asked if he believes coaches are knowledgeable of the school's mission statement, the school principal stated "I think they know about it, most of them are alumni, it's anchored in their value system". The principal reported minimal interactions with the coaches and did not believe he needed to personally communicate the mission to them: "We don't have meetings where we explain and remind them about it. The athletic director is there to ensure that they know it since he's in charge of sports here".

The athletic director mentioned being very knowledgeable of the school's mission statement, having also contributed to its elaboration: "Yes, I participated since I am an educator here at the school, creating the objectives of the educational project, so the mission, yes". The athletic director was then asked if he believes the coaches at the school are knowledgeable of the school's mission statement and his answer was similar to the principal: "The fact that most of our coaches are alumni, they see things the same way, I am aware of that, it's noticeable in the way they interact with youth, so yes I think they know it". Again, similar to the school principal, the athletic director reported being infrequently in contact with coaches and therefore did not have discussions with them concerning the mission statement: "Because of the large number of teams, we have a structure where each sport has a coordinator, so I am more in contact with coordinators given that my duties are mostly administrative".

COACHES

Over half of the coaches (n = 8) reported being fairly knowledgeable of the school's mission statement. For example, one of the coaches, who was also an alumnus, stated "At the start of the school year, I signed a contract on which it was written. In addition, I've been at this school for long enough to know it" (C1). Another coach said "I know the school's mission statement, you can find it on the school's website" (C12). Five coaches stated they were more or less familiar with the mission statement and where able to provide some of the fundamental principles. For example, this coach said "I have a bit of an idea but I couldn't tell you exactly what it is…I think the school wants to develop good citizens and have students be respectful in all types of situations" (C2). Two coaches reported not knowing what the mission statement was, perhaps because they were from the community at-large and were not familiar with the school's culture: "I have no idea what it is, I'm not from here and this is only the first year I've been coaching at this school" (C5).

PARENTS

The vast majority of parents (n = 16) did not know the school's mission statement. While acknowledging their lack of knowledge, a few of them still tried to describe what they believed to be the mission statement: "No, I don't know it but I think it's developing a healthy mind in a healthy body, I think it's related to that" (P8) and "No, not really, but I assume it's about having responsible students who love to learn" (P1). A few parents felt they were slightly knowledgeable, having been exposed to the mission statement in certain circumstances. For example, some parents stated "I heard people talking about it at a meeting once at the start of the school year, it states the school has certain objectives, but to know it by heart, no" (P3), "Ah, I read it once but I can't remember" (P9), and "I've read it, it's in the school guide, if you gave me a choice, I could recognize it" (P10). Only two parents indicated they were highly knowledgeable of the mission statement: "Ah yes, very familiar, the first section talks about the total development of students, it's part of the school's educational project" (P15). It is important to note that the two parents who knew the mission statement were also both teachers at the school.

ATHLETES

Not a single athlete interviewed knew what his/her school's mission statement was. Some, similar to the parents, tried to describe what they thought the mission was: "Well, I don't know, it must be about having students succeed in different aspects of life, something like that" (A6). In addition to not knowing the mission, some athletes were not even aware that the school had a mission statement: "The what? What is the mission statement? I didn't even know the school had that" (A12). It was also discovered that some athletes did not even grasp the concept of a mission statement. For example, when asked to state if he knew his school's mission statement, this athlete said "Not really, I don't really know what a mission statement is" (A5).

DISCUSSION

This study was a first step in understanding the complexity of how mission statements are communicated to and understood by stakeholders in the context of sport. Interestingly, the relatively small academic institution where the study took place did develop its mission statement in dialogue with individuals at different levels. Bart and Baetz (1998) demonstrated that the more individuals internal to an organization are involved in the development of the mission, the greater its effect will be on their behavior. However, the school's mission statement had not been reviewed or modified since its original inception over 15 years ago. Current school stakeholders might not feel a strong connection with the mission statement given that the most of them probably did not participate in its original development. Although the mission statement had not been reviewed over those years, a number of initiatives were put in place by school administrators to have it communicated to its members. The mission was posted on the school's website, on contracts, and in the annual school guide. Despite these efforts, findings suggest that the level of mission statement knowledge of different school stakeholders varied considerably. Administrators reported being very knowledgeable, having actively participated in the development of the original statement. As for the other stakeholders, the majority of the coaches said they were at least familiar with the mission and its principles whereas the majority of athletes and parents did not know the school's mission statement. It should be noted that the only two parents who knew the mission statement were also teachers at the school and that some athletes and parents reported not knowing the school had a mission. These findings parallel the results of Desmidt, Prinzie, and Heene (2008) who found that a large proportion of nurses in Flemish hospitals did not know their institution had a mission statement.

It appears that the different groups of individuals taking part in this study can be classified in three categories, depending on theirvarying levels of mission statement knowledge. First, there were the administrators responsible for communicating the mission statement who reported being very knowledgeable of their school's mission. The second category of individuals consisted of the coaches and teachers delivering the services who worked at the school. For the most part, this group of individuals reported knowing or being at least familiar with the mission statement, given that they were exposed to the school's culture and to the various initiatives in place to communicate the mission statement. The final category of individuals consisted of athletes who received the services and parents who were not physically present at the school on a regular basis. These individuals reported limited or no knowledge of the school's mission statement.

A number of factors appear to have contributed to the majority of second and third category of individuals only being familiar or having no knowledge of their school's mission statement. In the present study, the school administrators assumed that the coaches knew about the mission statement. The principal and athletic director both stated that because many of the coaches are alumni, they must already know the mission statement and understand the school's culture and values. As a result of their assumptions, the administrators were not as successful as they could have been in ensuring that the goals, values, and philosophy the mission conveys were effectively communicated, especially to the coaches who were not alumni and were new to the organization. There also appeared to be very little communication occurring between administrators and coaches. Both administrators reported having minimal interactions with coaches, spending most of their work time on administrative issues. Montreuil (2007) showed in a study with Canadian high school principals that exchanges between principals and high school coaches are nearly non-existent. All these factors appear to have contributed to coaches, parents, and athletes having limited or no mission statement knowledge at this particular school.

In order to increase members' mission statement knowledge, Bart (2004) asserted that multiple types of outlets, such as annual reports, posters, and manuals, must be employed. Although this particular school's mission statement was posted in a number of areas, such as on the school's website and in the annual school guide, very few second and third category individuals clearly knew about it. Therefore, it appears that organizations should be proactive and implement strategies to ensure that their mission statement is clearly understood by all involved, including internal and external stakeholders. Despite the documented time constraints faced by school principals (Montreuil, 2007), they could try to organize meetings with coaches, athletes, and parents and engage in a dialogue about the organization's mission, values, and philosophy. During these meetings, coaches could be made aware of the importance of transferring the mission statement into practice by behaving in an ethically responsible manner and by discussing the mission's values with their athletes. Organizing such meetings would be especially useful for athletes and coaches who are new to the institution and for parents who are not directly exposed to the school's mission statement. Research has shown that members knowledgeable of their organization's mission statement are more motivated towards achieving an organization's purpose and are more disposed to embrace an organization's values and goals as their own (Bart & Baetz, 1998). Without appropriate levels of knowledge, mission statements might just be a misuse of administrators' time and effort (Bart, 2004).

The results of this study have implications for sport psychology organizations. Although they serve a different type of membership and are faced with specific challenges, it is crucial that sport psychology organizations recognize the importance of establishing initiatives to ensure that their members, who are responsible for delivering a service to clients, are aware of the mission statement. One of the challenges faced bysport psychology organizations is that the consultants are not based in a specific physical setting. Rather, theyare spread across the country, making it more difficult to communicate and have members involved in the development of the mission statement. The present study showed how individuals not physically present at the institution on a regular basis were less likely to know the mission statement given that they were not exposed to the organization's culture and the initiatives implemented to communicate the mission. Therefore, it is up to the managing councils of organizations such as AASP and CSPA to take advantage of events where many members are present, such as conferences and workshops, to organize meetings and enter into a dialogue with members to discuss the organization's values and how the mission statement should translate to action. Having opportunities to internalize the mission statement is important for members, making it possible for them to understand the organizational values that form the basis of the principles found in codes of ethics. A study by Etzel, Watson, and Zizzi (2004) suggested that the topic of ethics remains of limited interest to AASP members and that they do not always follow, in a consistent manner, the ethical principles set out in the organization's codes of ethics. In addition to organizing meetings during conferences, Etzel et al., (2004) recommended that organizations make material on ethics part of continuing education and articles, books, and newsletters on the topic should be made available. Such initiatives would help create a climate in which mission statements and codes of ethics become an integral part of the organization's culture, increasing the likelihood that they would impact behavior (Chonko & Hunt, 1985).

CONCLUSION

Mission statements serve a valuable purpose given that they establish an organization's values and philosophy on which codes of ethics are based. However, the ultimate value of a mission statement is dependant on individuals' knowledge of it. By tracing the process of how mission statements are communicated to andunderstood by practitioners, this study highlighted the importance of not assuming that individuals are knowledgeable of their organization's mission. Efforts must be made by administrators to communicate the mission to those delivering as well as those receiving the services, the ultimate goal being that the philosophy of the organization be implemented practically. For a new organization such as the CSPA, whose member's are based throughout Canada, it is about creating opportunities to get together with members and to discuss and negotiate ethical principles and the ethical behaviors that should follow.

Although the findings of this study suggest potential issues in the communication of the mission statement at one academic institution, they must be interpreted with care and should not be generalized across all types of organizations, given that a case study approach was employed. This research was exploratory, the goal being to gain an understanding of how mission statements in sport and their ethical messages are communicated to and understood by different sport stakeholders. This study can serve as a starting point for future research with the next step consisting of documenting stakeholders' mission statement knowledge across different types of sport organizations in different contexts.

ACKNOWLEDGMENTS

This research was supported by a grant from the Social Sciences and Humanities Research Council of Canada.

REFERENCES

Bailey, R. (2008). Youth sport and social inclusion. In N. L. Holt (Ed.), *Positive youth development through sport* (pp. 85-96). New York: Routledge.

Bart, C. K. (1999). Mission statement content and hospital performance in Canadian not-for-profit health care sector. *Health Care Management Review, 24,* 18-29.

Bart, C. K. (2004). Innovation, mission statements, and learning. *International Journal of Technology Management, 27,* 544-561.

Bart, C. K., & Baetz, M. C. (1998). The relationship between mission statements and firm performance: An exploratory study. *The Journal of Management Studies, 36,* 823-853.

Bart, C. K., & Hupfer, M. (2004). Mission statements in Canadian hospitals. *Journal of Health Organization and Management, 18,* 92-110.

Bartkus, B., Glassman, M., & McAfee, B. (2005). Mission statement quality and financial performance. *European Management Journal, 24,* 86-94.

Canadian School Sport Federation (2004). *Constitution.* Retrieved September 17, 2008, from http://www.schoolsport.ca/pdfs/Constitution_2004_e.pdf

Canadian Sport Psychology Association. (2007). *About CSPA: Mission.* Retrieved October 6, 2008, from http://www.en.cspa-acps.ca/about/about.html

Chonko, L. B., & Hunt, S. D. (1985). Ethics and marketing management: An empirical examination. *Journal of Business Research, 13,* 339-359.

Creswell, J.W. (2003). *Research design: Qualitative & quantitative and mixed methods approaches.* Thousand Oaks, CA: Sage.

Desmidt, S., Prinzie, A., & Heene, A. (2008). The level and determinants of mission statement use: A questionnaire survey. *International Journal of Nursing Studies, 45,* 1433-1441.

Etzel, E. F., Watson, J. C., & Zizzi, S. (2004). A web-based survey of AAASP Members' ethical beliefs and behaviors in the new millennium. *Journal of Applied Sport Psychology, 16,* 236-250.

Hockey Canada. (2008). *About Hockey Canada: Mandate and mission*. Retrieved October 6, 2008 from http://www.hockeycanada.ca/6/8/3/6/index1.shtml

Kozhaya, N. & Cowley, P. *Bulletin des ecoles secondaires du Quebec: Edition 2006. [Quebec high school report: 2006 edition]* Retrieved March 7, 2008, fromhttp://www.iedm.org/uploaded/pdf/bulletin06_fr.pdf

International Olympic Committee. (2007). *Olympic charter.* Retrieved October 4, 2008, from http://multimedia.olympic.org/pdf/en_report_122.pdf

International Society of Sport Psychology (2005). *Mission: About ISSP.* Retrieved October 6, 2008, fromhttp://www.issponline.org/ab_mission.asp?ms=2

Mandigo, J., Corlett, J., & Anderson, A. (2008). Using quality physical education to promote positive youth development in a developing nation. In N. L. Holt (Ed.), *Positive youth development through sport* (pp. 110-121). New York: Routledge.

Montreuil, R. (2007). *High school sports: The perspectives of the school principals.* Unpublished master's thesis, University of Ottawa, Ottawa, Ontario, Canada.

National CapitalSecondary School Athletic Association. (2005). *Constitution.* Retrieved March 1, 2008, from http://64.26.159.233/features/administrative/ncssaa/2006-2007/ncssaaConstitution-2005-12-19.pdf

National Collegiate Athletic Association. (2007). *Our mission.* Retrieved September 25, 2008, from http://www2.ncaa.org/portal/about_ncaa/overview/mission.html

Patton, M. Q. (2002). *Qualitative research & evaluation methods*. Thousand Oaks: Sage.

Qualitative Solution and Research (2006). *NVivo* (Version 7.0) [Computer software]. Doncaster, Australia: Author.

United Nations (2004). *Our mandate:What does sport have to do with the UN?* Retrieved September 25, 2008, from http://www.un.org/themes/sport/intro.htm

Vandijck, D., Desmidt, S., & Buelens, M. (2007). Relevance of mission statements in Flemish not-for-profit healthcare organizations. *Journal of Nursing Management, 15,* 131-141.

Williams, J., Smythe, W., Hadjistavropoulos, T., Malloy, D. C., & Martin, R. (2005). A study of thematic content in hospital mission statements: A question of values. *Health Care Management Review, 30,* 304-314.

Yin, R. K. (1994). *Case study research: Design and methods* (2nd ed.)Thousand Oaks, CA: Sage.

In: Introduction to Sport Psychology
Editor: Robert Schinke

ISBN: 978-1-61761-973-1
© 2011 Nova Science Publishers, Inc.

DIFFERENT EFFECTS OF ACTIVITY- AND PURPOSE-RELATED INCENTIVES ON COMMITMENT AND WELL-BEING IN THE DOMAIN OF SPORTS

Julia Schüler[*], *Sibylle Brunner*[†] *and Marianne Steiner*[‡]
University of Zurich, Switzerland

ABSTRACT

Incentives play an important role in human motivation (see Beckmann & Heckhausen, 2008). In the present research we used Rheinberg's (2008) distinction of activity-related incentives (e.g., having fun) and purpose-related incentives (e.g., improved fitness) and investigated the influence of these two types of incentives on commitment and well-being in the domain of sport. Assuming that activity-related incentives have stronger rewarding effects on human behaviour than purpose-related incentives, we hypothesized activity-related incentives to be stronger predictors of sport-commitment and well-being than purpose-related incentives. Study 1 ($N = 129$) confirmed this hypothesis using a correlational design. In Study 2 ($N = 67$) we experimentally induced activity- and purpose-related incentives. We found stronger effects of activity-related incentives on sport-commitment and well-being compared to purpose-related incentives.

INTRODUCTION

There is no doubt that regular sport-activity has positive effects on physiological health (Biddle, Fox, & Boutcher, 2000; Pfaffenbarger, Hyde, Wing & Hsieh, 1986; Saltin, 1990), psychological and mental health (Biddle & Mutrie, 2001; Dishman & Buckworth, 1997; O'Connor, Raglin & Martinsen, 2000; Mutrie, 2000) and well-being (Biddle, Fox & Boutcher, 2000; Biddle & Mutrie, 2001). Despite the common knowledge of these positive effects, a high percentage of people fail to perform sports or drop out of sport-activity after a few weeks. For example, every second participant of sport-programs fails to complete the program (Marcus et al., 2000; Wing, 2000). Why do some people manage to

[*]Corresponding author: University of Zurich; Department of Psychology; Binzmühlestrasse 14/6; 8050 Zürich; Switzerland; Phone:+41 44 635 75 08; e-mail: +41 44 635 75 19; j.schueler@psychologie.uzh.ch
[†] sibyllebr@web.de
[‡] mariannesteiner@freesurf.ch

exerciseregularly whereas others do not? Theoretically driven approaches of motivation research might explain determinants of sport behaviour and its maintenance (e.g., Biddle et al., 2000; Dishman, 1990; Dishman & Sallis, 1994).

The present research focuses on the motivational concept of incentives. Incentives are believed to be important determinants of behaviour (e.g., Beckmann & Heckhausen, 2008).They are understood as situational stimuli that refer to affective goal-states and thereby stimulate goal-directed behaviour (Beckmann & Heckhausen, 2008; Schmalt, 1996). Incentives explain why individuals behave the way they do. For example, when asked for the reasons of exercising, individuals typically list health, winning a competition, reduction of body-weight, having fun, leisure time with sport-friends and relaxation (e.g., Gabler, 2002; Sit, Kerr, & Wong, 2008). Individuals are "incited" by those anticipated goal-states. These different reasons show that one and the same behaviour can be "incited" by different incentives. This broad variety of incentives needs systematization. But, although researchers on motivation agree that incentives are important determinants of behaviour (e.g., Atkinson, 1957; Beckmann & Heckhausen, 2008; Bolles, 1972; Lewin, 1931, 1951; Tolman, 1932; Vroom, 1964) they seldom used systematizations of incentives. An exception is Rheinberg (1989, 2008), who proposed two qualitatively different types of incentives, activity-related incentives and purpose-related incentives. While activity-related incentives are connected to the activity itself and are experienced whilst an activity is performed (e.g., having fun, enjoying movements), purpose-related incentives are connected to the result of the activity and occur after the actual activity (e.g., health as a result of exercising). Rheinberg (1989) could show in learning settings that the differentiation into activity- and purpose-related incentives enhances the power to predict learning activities.

One aim of the present research is to apply Rheinberg's (1989, 2008) differentiation into activity- and purpose-related incentives*to thedomain of sport behaviour* in order to predict sport commitment and well-being. Secondly we aim to underline the importance of differentiating activity- and purpose-related incentives by showing that the two incentive types have *different effects* on human behaviour. We hypothesized that activity-related incentives have a stronger influence on sport-commitment and well-being than purpose-related incentives due to a stronger rewarding effect (see below). The third aim of the present research is to test whether incentives can be experimentally induced and with this their positive outcomes. The following paragraphs embed our assumptions into their theoretical background.

THE CONCEPT OF INCENTIVES

Incentive approaches take into account that individuals are not only driven by drives, needs or motives that are currently experienced but that they also anticipate future affective states that guide their behaviour (e.g., Atkinson, 1957; Beckmann & Heckhausen, 2008; Lewin, 1951; McClelland, 1985; Schneider & Schmalt, 2000; Vroom, 1964). Situational stimuli that refer to a positive affective goal-state direct and energize human behaviour towards this desired end-state (Beckmann & Heckhausen, 2008; McClelland, 1985). For example after theannouncement of a sport course (stimulus) an individual might anticipate the feeling of pride after successfully taking part in the sport class (affective goal-state) and this will motivate him or her to actually take that class (motivated behaviour).

Incentives are a key concept in the broad family of traditional expectancy-value models (e.g., Rotter, 1954; Vroom, 1964; Edwards, 1954; Heckhausen & Rheinberg, 1980). These models suggest that activity is stimulated by an anticipated positive end-state of the activity and by the expectancy that this end state can be achieved. The most influential expectancy-value model within the achievement motive research is the risk taking model (Atkinson, 1957). In this model the *affect of pride* is the essential incentive to initiate certain behaviour (McClelland, Atkinson, Clark, & Lowell, 1953; Feather, 1961). When the affect of pride is high, so is the tendency of action.

Present research stresses the important role of incentives for sport behaviour while taking the variety of incentives into account. Schüler and Brunner(2006) asked athletes for the reason why they are doing sports. The answers revealed that sport behaviour is characterized by very different incentives such as social issues, control of body weight, body sensations or health aspects. Previous studies revealed that sport behaviour is affected by different incentives. For example, Fuchs (1997) and Coakley and White (1992) emphasized the influence of competence experience and trim on sport exercising. Burton and Martens (1986) described the perception of improved skills or merely having fun as crucial for committing to continue sport exercising. The reported studies show that incentives are not only influential predictors of sport activity (see also Gould & Petlichkoff, 1988; Biddle & Mutrie, 1991), they also demonstrate the broad variety of incentives for one and the same behaviour (exercising). Some individuals perform sports first and foremost because of the feeling of competence while others primarily do sports to have fun. Thus, sport behaviour is characterized by a variety of incentives and a high individuality. In order to consider such individual differences in the present study, we either asked for individual incentives (Study 2) or we used an incentive list that was gained by interviewing sport athletes about their personal incentives to perform their sports (Study 1). In order to systematize the variety of incentives we used the differentiation into activity- and purpose-related incentives provided by Rheinberg (1989, 2008).

THE DIFFERENTIATION BETWEEN ACTIVITY-RELATED INCENTIVES AND PURPOSE-RELATED INCENTIVES

Traditional research on motivation postulated that an action is only attractive and meaningful if the result of this action has a high positive value (Crespi, 1942, 1944; Vroom 1964; Hull, 1952). In this research tradition the source of the incentives was seen in the anticipated desired end-state. This is in line with the Extended Cognitive Model (Heckhausen & Rheinberg, 1980; see Figure 1, solid lines) in which incentives are conceptualized as the consequence of an action outcome. The model postulates that human action can be characterized by four components (see boxes in figure 1).

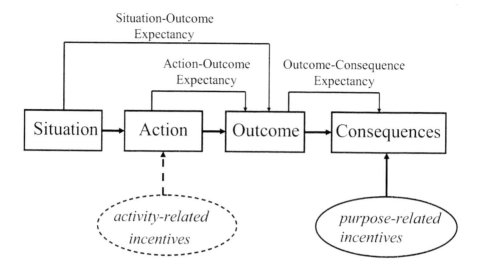

Figure 1. The Extended Cognitive Model (see solid lines, adapted from Heckhausen & Rheinberg, 1980) and its revision by Rheinberg (see dotted lines, adapted from Rheinberg, 1989).

The first component is the situation in which an action takes place. The second is the action itself which is followed by the outcome of the action. The outcome will have certain consequences (fourth component). For the present research it is important to note that the Extended Cognitive Model saw the consequences as critical to explain human motivation. For example in the domain of sports this model can explain exercise activity as resulting from the urge to experience the positive consequences of exercising, such as improved physical fitness, winning a competition or reducing body weight.

Rheinberg (1989) revised the Extended Cognitive Model because the original model could not explain behaviour that is performed without such purpose-related incentives. For example, a sports person may exercise without caring for one of the above mentioned purpose-related incentives. In the revised version Rheinberg (1989) postulated that human behaviour can also be driven by incentives that lie in the action itself (see dotted line in Figure 1; for activity inherent incentives see also Bühler, 1922; Koch, 1956; Woodworth, 1918). Individuals may exercise for the sake of the sport activity itself, for example because it is fun or because they enjoy the movements or other rewarding aspects of the activity itself. These incentives are called *activity-related incentives*, as opposed to incentives related to the outcome which are termed *purpose-related incentives* (Rheinberg, 2008).

Rheinberg's (1989, 2008) approach is conceptualized for different domains of human life. Activity-related incentives determine behaviour in the domain of sports (e.g., having fun and enjoying movements while performing a sport-activity), but also in other leisure activities (e.g., playing music for fun), learning situations (e.g., being highly interested) or work (e.g., feeling absorbed by action) (see also Csikszentmihalyi & LeFevre, 1989). Similarly, purpose-related incentives determine behaviour in various domains, such as improving health or impressing others by one's sport performance (sport), feeling proud after having played a piece of music flawlessly (leisure), getting a good grade (learning situation) or earning money (work).

The present research takes Rheinberg's (1989) approach one step further by testing whether activity- and purpose-related incentives differ in their predictive power. It is yet unclear which incentives can better predict sport-commitment and well-being, having fun (activity-related incentive) or improving health (purpose-related incentive). Research on the concept of intrinsic and extrinsic motivation suggests that activity-related incentives may have a stronger effect (e.g., Deci & Ryan, 1985; 2000). Intrinsic and extrinsic motivation is closely related to the concept of activity- and purpose-related incentives (see Rheinberg, 2008 for similarities and differences between these concepts). Compared to extrinsic motivation, intrinsic motivation could better predict sport-maintenance (Goudas, Biddle, & Underwood, 1995; Ingledew, Markland & Medley, 1998; Ryan, Frederick, Lepes, Rubio & Sheldon, 1997), investment of effort (Pelletier, Fortier, Vallerand, Tuson, Bière & Blais, 1995; Williams & Gill, 1995) and positive affect (e.g, McAuley & Tammen, 1989; Scanlan & Lewthwaite, 1986; Brière, Vallerand, Blais, & Pelletier, 1995; Li 1999; Pelletier et al., 1995). Despite the convincing demonstration of the superiority of intrinsic motivation, relatively little research has been conducted exploring the mechanisms that link intrinsic motivation with the positive outcome variables.

PRESENT RESEARCH

In the present research we provide an explanation why activity-related incentives are attributed stronger to commitment and well-being than purpose-related incentives. This assumption is due to a simple rationale. We assume activity-related incentives (having fun, enjoying movements) to be positive experience-qualities that immediately reward the activity they are associated with. In contrast, purpose-related incentives (improving health, loosing body-weight) are rewards that occur much later, long after the activity was performed. According to the principle of operant conditioning (Skinner, 1938), a close time association between the reward and the activity has stronger rewarding effects than less close time associations (e.g., Grice, 1948; Tarpy & Sawabini, 1974; Shanks & Dickinson, 1991) and therefore enhance the probability that the activity will be performed again. Due to its positive experiencequality activity-related incentives should also lead to better well-being. To sum up, we hypothesized that activity-related incentives have a stronger effect on sport-commitment and well-being than purpose-related incentives.

Another aim of the present research is the experimental induction of activity- and purpose-related incentives. For this, we referred to an experimental procedure Brandstätter (2003) used in order to analyze the role of incentives in human goal-striving and goal-disengagement. In her study, fitness athletes were randomly assigned to one of four experimental groups. To induce positive incentives of goal striving, one group was asked to focus on pleasant aspects and advantages of regular exercising and imagine them as vividly as possible. The second group focused on unpleasant aspects and disadvantages of regular exercising, thus inducing negative incentives of goal-striving. The third group was asked to imagine pleasant aspects and advantages of non-regular exercising (positive incentives of goal-disengagement) and the last group imagined unpleasant aspects and disadvantages of non-regular exercising (negative incentives of goal-disengagement). This simple experimental manipulation had a strong influence on the dependent variables. Participants who imagined positive incentives of goal-striving as well as athletes who imagined negative incentives of goal-disengagement reported higher values in motivational variables (motivation, activation and goal-commitment) and in sport maintenance (for example frequency of exercising) than the other groups. With this, Brandstätter (2003) showed that incentives can be experimentally induced and that these induced incentives can influence human sport behaviour. However, she did not differentiate between activity- and purpose-related incentives. In the present research we experimentally induced activity- as well as purpose-related incentives using an adaptation of Brandstätter's (2003) procedure and tested the hypotheses that activity-related incentives will affect sport-commitment and well-being more strongly than purpose-related incentives.

Two studies were conducted to test our assumptions. Study 1, a correlative field study, tested the assumption that incentives are important predictors of sport-commitment and of well-being and that activity-related incentives are stronger predictors than purpose-related incentives. Study 2 was conducted to further explore the effects of activity- and purpose-related incentives by using an experimental design in which activity- and purpose-related incentives were induced using an adaptation of Brandstätter's (2003) imagery task. Participants who focused on activity-related incentives and imagined them as vividly as possible were expected to report a higher sport-commitment and better well-being than participants who focused on and imagined purpose-related incentives.

In order to increase confidence in the validity of the findings, we varied the measurements and samples across our studies. Athletes of two different sport activities (badminton players and group-fitness athletes) served as participants and different indicators of sport-commitment and well-being were used.

Because incentives are the core-construct of our research, we hoped to obtain converging results with different measures of incentives. Although different kinds of sports will share some common incentives (e.g. fun, health, improving fitness), there are some incentives that seem to be sport-typical. In Study 1 we used a sport-specific incentive questionnaire which was developed on the basis of half-standardized interviews with badminton-players (Steiner, 2006). In Study 2 sport-unspecific incentives were induced using an experimental manipulation based on an imagination task.

STUDY 1

In Study 1 we assumed activity-related incentives to be stronger predictors of sport-commitment and of well-being than purpose-related incentives. We measured incentives by a questionnaire which was especially developed for badminton sports (Steiner, 2006). It is described in detail below.

In motivation research one important component of goal commitment is determination. It is measured by items such as "No matter what happens, I will never give up this goal" (e.g., Maier & Brunstein, 2001). In order to adapt the abstract goal commitment measure to the sport domain we asked participants how often they fail to attend the sport activity even if they had planned to (revised item).

METHOD OF STUDY 1

Participants and Procedure

We examined 129 non-professional badminton players (46 women and 83 men) of different performance levels from Swiss and German clubs. Nine athletes had to be excluded from the study due to missing data. The average age of the sample was 22 years ($SD = 10.3$). Most of the badminton players classified themselves as advanced players ($N = 118$), whereas others considered themselves as experts ($N = 11$). Because both groups were very similar (e.g. have been playing badminton for more than eight years and took part in competitions) and because the performance level did not influence the study's outcome, we pooled the groups for further analyses. Data were collected by administering a questionnaire at the beginning of a regular training session. The athletes filled in the badminton incentive questionnaire described below and answered questions concerning sport-commitment and well-being.

Measures

Measurement of Incentives

We developed a badminton-specific incentive questionnaire by conducting half-standardized interviews with experienced badminton-players. We modified the interview procedure used by Rheinberg (1993, 2004) and asked four female and five male badminton players of different performance levels for their incentives in badminton sports (average age = 37.4, $SD = 10.2$). All the players had competition experience and their average playing experience was 20.5 years ($SD = 10.9$). Using questions like "When you compare badminton with other activities – What are its special features?", "Can you remember a perfect day, when everything went well – what were the characteristics of this situation?", and "When you could not play badminton because you were ill or were on holiday, what did you miss the most?", athletes were asked to name incentives which are relevant for their sport. The interview lasted about twenty minutes and was recorded and transcribed. Two trained raters coded the incentives and ascribed them to activity-related or purpose-related incentives. Initially the co-ratings had an agreement of 83.3%. After discussing the disagreements by specifying the coding system, the percentage of agreement increased (97.9%). The badminton-players reported a mean of 10 purpose-related incentives ($SD = 3.6$) and a mean of 26.7 activity-related incentives ($SD = 8.2$). The athletes often mentioned the feeling of optimal challenge ($N = 37$), feeling of competence ($N = 24$) or having fun ($N = 22$) as activity-related incentives. Success ($N = 26$) or fitness ($N = 11$) were often mentioned as purpose-related incentives. In order to create a questionnaire, the statements of the interview were reformulated into items which represent a broad spectrum of activity-related and purpose-related incentives in badminton sport. Because athletes reported more activity-related incentives than purpose-related incentives, the questionnaire contained 44 items of activity-related incentives and 18 items of purpose-related incentives. Examples for badminton specific activity-related incentives are *"I like to train hard"* or *"while playing badminton I like the physical challenge"* or *"I like to feel my physical limits"*. Examples for purpose-related incentives are *"Badminton offers me the opportunity of success"* or *"Playing badminton makes me feel better in my everyday life"*. Each incentive had to be rated on a 7-

point scale (1 = *disagree completely* and 7 = *agree completely*). An index for activity-related incentives and purpose-related incentives were created by computing the mean of all activity-related incentive items and all purpose-related incentive items, respectively. The indexes had good internal consistencies (activity-related incentives: α= .89, purpose-related incentives: α= .81.

Measurement of the Dependent Variables

Positive well-being was assessed by positive affect items used by Brunstein (1993). The athletes were asked to indicate how they felt at that moment and they rated four adjectives (happy, pleased, content and glad) on a 7-point response scale (1 = *not at all* and 7 = *extremely*). The mean of all four items was computed. The reliability was adequately high (α= .79). *Sport-commitment* was assessed by the item *"How often do you not attend the sport activity even if you had planned to"*. The item had to be rated on a 5-point scale with endpoints labelled *not at all* (1) and *very often* (5). The item was recoded so that a high score on this item means a high commitment.

RESULTS OF STUDY 1

Preliminary analyses showed that neither age nor sex of athletes influenced the results reported below. Table 1 shows descriptive statistics, two-tailed correlations and internal consistencies among variables.

Table 1. Descriptive Statistics and Pearson-Correlations among Variables (Study 1)

	2	3	4	M	SD	A
1. Activity-related incentives	.66**	.33**	.31**	4.77	.57	.89
2. Purpose-related incentives		.27*	.20*	4.20	.74	.81
3. well-being			.06	5.01	.96	.79
4. sport-commitment[1]				3.33	.74	-

Note. [1] Correlation with non parametric variable calculated by Spearman
* *p*< .05.　** *p*< .01.

Activity-related incentives and to a lesser degree also purpose-related incentives were associated with commitment (activity: *r* =.31, *p* <.01; purpose: *r* = .20, *p* < .05).A significant positive correlation between activity-related incentives and purpose-related incentives (*r* = .66, *p* < .01) indicated a high amount of shared variance. In order to separate the common variance, a linear regression analysis was conducted in which both types of incentives were entered simultaneously into the regression equation. Activity-related incentives predicted sport-commitment (β = .24, *p* = .05), whereas purpose-related incentives did no longer predict commitment (β = .06, *n.s*). The total model was significant (R^2 = .08, $F(2,118)$ = 4.90, *p*< .01).

For positive well-being we found the same pattern of results. Activity- as well as purpose-related incentives were associated with well-being ($r = .33$, $p < .01$ and $r = .27$, $p < .05$). A linear regression analysis with both incentive types as predictors showed that activity-related incentives predicted well-being ($\beta = .26$, $p < .05$), whereas purpose-related incentives no longer predicted well-being ($\beta = .03$, *n.s.*, overall model: $R^2 = .10$, $F(2, 118) = 6.61$, $p < .01$).

BRIEF DISCUSSION OF STUDY 1

Study 1 confirmed our hypotheses showing that incentives were important predictors of sport-commitment and well-being. Additionally, we could show that in a (sport) situation several incentives simultaneously can be salient and meaningful: It was easy for badminton-players who were interviewed in order to generate badminton-specific incentives to list activity-related as well as purpose-related incentives of their sports. In our study sample, the results of linear regression analyses in which the common variance of both incentive types were controlled for showed that activity-related incentives were better predictors than purpose-related incentives.

In order to underline the causality of the relationship between incentives and commitment and well-being, Study 2 employed an experimental design.

STUDY 2

Although several incentives may be salient and meaningful in a single situation (e.g., Heckhausen & Gollwitzer, 1987) the same incentive may not necessarily be important for everyone. For example loosing body-weight might be a meaningful incentive for one person but not for another. In order to consider this individuality, Study 1 used a sport specific incentive questionnaire, in which the athletes could rate the degree to which each incentive applies to them. In Study 2 we considered the individuality of incentives in more detail. We directly asked athletes which incentive was most important for them. To activate the influence of these personal incentives on behaviour, we used an imagination task which was proposed by Brandstätter (2003). As already mentioned above she showed that athletes who were instructed to focus on incentives of regular sport exercising and to imagine them vividly reported a higher persistence and a higher activation than athletes who focused on incentives of non-regular sport exercising. We adapted this procedure and asked one group of athletes to focus on and imagine a meaningful and individual activity-related incentive while another group was told to focus on and imagine a salient and individual purpose-related incentive.

Assuming that activity-related incentives are stronger predictors of sport-commitment and well-being than purpose-related incentives, we hypothesized that the athletes who focused on and imagined an individual activity-related incentive would report higher sport-commitment and well-being than athletes who imagined and focussed on a purpose-related incentive.

In Study 2 we improved the commitment measure of Study 1 by additionally asking participants how often they think they will fail to go to the sport lesson in the future even though they had planned to. In order to consider the sport psychological understanding of sport commitment as "the desire and resolve to continue sport participation" (Scanlan, Carpenter, Schmidt, Simons, & Keeler, 1993 , p. 6), we added an item that better represents the mentioned desire of doing sports ("How much are you looking forward to the next training lesson?").

METHOD

Participants and Procedure

Sixty-seven group-fitness athletes (60 female, 7 male) participated in this study. All participants regularly exercised for more than six months, at least once a week in sport classes. The average age of the sample was 35.97 years (SD = 11.82). Data were collected in three phases. In the first phase athletes were recruited after a sport lesson (T1) by the experimenter who explained the procedure of data collection in detail. Athletes who agreed to participate received a take-home booklet which contained questionnaires assessing sport-commitment and well-being. This booklet was handed back to the experimenter in the following week's sport lesson. This is where the second phase of data collection started (T2). The athletes were randomly assigned to either an activity-related incentive group or a purpose-related incentive group. The athletes filled in a questionnaire which contained the experimental manipulation. After the induction the athletes performed their exercise as usual. Directly after the lesson sport-commitment and well-being were assessed again (T3).

Experimental Manipulation

For the experimental manipulation an imagination task was used. In a first step the concept of activity-related incentives was described to the activity-incentive group and the concept of purpose-related incentives was described to the purpose-incentive group. Participants of the activity-incentive group were informed that people usually like different aspects during sport activity (activity-related incentives) as for example having fun or body sensations. Participants of the purpose-incentive group were informed about different aspects after the sport activity as a result of exercise behaviour (purpose-related incentives) like improving health or building up muscles. The athletes were requested to imagine a typical sport lesson and to think about their personal and important aspects either during (activity-incentive group) or after exercising (purpose-incentive group).

Afterwards, participants of the activity-related group were asked to write down their personal aspects:

"Now, please focus on enjoyable aspects (incentives) you encounter during exercising. Imagine a typical sport lesson. Please, concentrate on the enjoyable and positive aspects, which are very important for you during exercising. It could be having fun or enjoyment of movements or the feeling of your body or something different. It is important that you mention aspects which are very important to YOU. Now, please list your personal aspects on the following blank lines. If you cannot think of more aspects you can leave the lines blank."

Participants of the purpose-incentive group received the following instruction:

> "Now, please focus on enjoyable aspects (incentives) you encounter after exercising. Imagine a typical sport lesson. Please, concentrate on the enjoyable and positive aspects, which are very important for you after exercising. It could be feeling relaxed or proud after exercising or something different. It is important that you mention aspects which are very important to YOU. Now, please list your personal aspects in the following blank lines. If you cannot think of more aspects you can leave the lines blank."

In a second step all athletes were asked to choose the most important aspect from their list and focus on it intensively. They were asked to imagine this aspect as vividly as possible and to describe their feelings and thoughts concerning this incentive.

> "Now, please choose the most important and most enjoyable aspect of your list. Imagine this aspect as clearly and vividly as you can".

To deepen the athletes' imagination of the incentives, additional questions were added. Participants answered these questions by making notes:

> "Why is this aspect meaningful for you? Try to feel how enjoyable this aspect is. Describe your feelings and thoughts connected to this aspect."

Measures

Measuring the Dependent Variables

The athletes' *positive well-being* was assessed by four activation items used by Schallberger (PANAVA; 2000), e.g., "wide awake", "shiftless", "enthusiastic" and "afraid". The athletes indicated how they felt at the moment by using a 7-point scale from for example 1 (tired) to 7 (high awake). After recoding the items "shiftless" and "afraid" a sum score was computed. The well-being score at T1 ($\alpha = .79$) and at T3 ($\alpha = .66$) matched sufficient internal consistencies. *Sport-commitment* was assessed at home (baseline T1) using the items *"How often do you not attend the sport activity even if you had planned to"* and *"How much are you looking forward to the next traininglesson."* Both items had to be rated on a 7-point scale with endpoints labelled *not at all* (1) and *extremely* (7). The first item was recoded and the mean of both items was computed. Commitment was again assessed after the exerciselesson (T3) by the item *"How much are you looking forward to the next training lesson"* and by the modified item *"How likely is it that you won't go to the sport lesson in the future even though you planned to"*. Both items were again rated on a 7-point scale with endpoints labelled *not at all* (1) and *extremely* (7). The second item was recoded and the mean of both items represent an index of commitment at T3.

Control Variable

To check how well the athletes could imagine the situation they were asked after the experimental manipulation *"How intensively did you experience the described thoughts and feelings"*. They rated the item on a 7-point scale with endpoints labelled *not at all* (1) and *extremely* (7). The mean score was adequately high ($M = 5.34$, $SD = 1.26$).

RESULTS

Preliminary analyses showed no difference between men and women in none of the assessed variables and no correlations between age and any of the assessed variables. The item assessing how well athletes could imagine the situation did not correlate with the dependent variables. Five athletes did not answer the question. Furthermore, athletes of either group did not differ in their ability to imagine the activity- and purpose-related incentive, F (1, 62) = .69, $p = .41$, $\eta^2 = .011$). Sport-commitment assessed at home (T1) correlated highly with commitment after the training lesson (T3) ($r = .64$, $p < .001$). Thus, commitment at T1 was controlled for in further analyses in which commitment at T3 was the dependent variable. Similarly, well-being at T1 correlated with well-being at T3 ($r = .46$, $p < .001$), so well-being at T1 was controlled for in further analyses with well-being at T3 as the dependent variable. Furthermore, well-being at T1 was related to commitment at T1 ($r = .27$, $p = .05$) and T3 ($r = .32$, $p < .01$). Finally well-being at T3 correlated with commitment at T1 ($r = .29$, $p < .05$) and commitment at T3 ($r = .38$, $p < .01$).

In order to test the effect of the experimental manipulation on sport-commitment, an analysis of variance with commitment at T1 as covariate, the two experimental groups as a between-subjects-factor and commitment at T3 as the dependent variable was conducted. Results showed a marginally significant effect for the experimental groups ($F(2, 66) = 3.55$, $p = .06$, $\eta^2 = .053$), indicating that focusing on activity-related incentives led to a higher sport-commitment ($M = 6.40$; $SD = 0.60$) than focusing on purpose-related incentives ($M = 6.01$; $SD = 1.03$) (see Figure 2). The covariate commitment at T1 reached significance ($F(2, 66) = 53.08$, $p < .001$, $\eta^2 = .45$).

A second analysis of variance was conducted to test whether the activity-related incentive group and the purpose-related incentive group differed in well-being. Well-being at T1 was controlled as a covariate. Results showed a significant group effect ($F(2, 66) = 6.95$, $p < .05$, $\eta^2 = .098$), indicating again that athletes who had focused on activity-related incentives reported better well-being after the training lesson ($M = 23.78$; $SD = 3.46$) than athletes who had focused on purpose-related incentives ($M = 22.15$; $SD = 3.77$) (see Figure 3). The covariate well-being at T1 also reached significance ($F(2, 66) = 22.24$, $p < .001$, $\eta^2 = .26$).

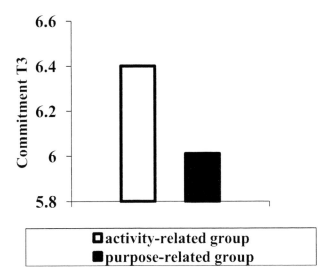

Figure 2. Differences in commitment at T3 between the activity-related incentive group and the purpose-related incentive group controlled for commitment at T1 (Study 2).

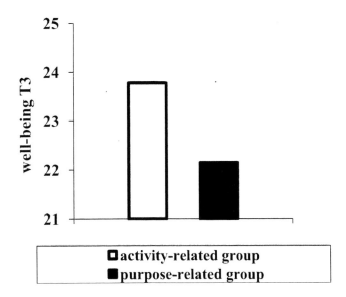

Figure 3. Differences in well-being at T3 between the activity-related incentive group and the purpose-related incentive group controlled for well-being at T1 (Study 2).

BRIEF DISCUSSION

Study 2 confirmed the results of Study 1 showing that activity-related incentives have a stronger effect on sport-commitment and well-being than purpose-related incentives. The study was an extension of the first study, because the stronger effect of activity-related incentives was demonstrated using an experimental design. When focusing on and imagining an individually important activity-related incentive, sport-commitment and well-being was higher than when focusing on an individually important purpose-related incentive. The results support our assumption that two qualitatively different incentive types exist. They encourage explaining sport behaviour by a systematic analysis of incentives.

Although male and female athletes did not differ in any of the assessed variables, it is important to note that far more women than men participated in the Study and therefore the generalizability of the study results might be limited. However, the fact that in Study 1 the hypothesis could be confirmed with far more men than women suggests that there are no obvious theoretical reasons why gender might influence the reported effects.

GENERAL DISCUSSION

Two studies with badminton-players and group-fitness athletes showed that within a single sport situation several different incentives such as having fun, competing with others, losing weight, making new friends, or feeling muscular power, can be simultaneously salient and meaningful. A closer look at these different incentives showed that they can be categorized into two types of incentives, activity-related incentives and purpose-related incentives (see Rheinberg, 1989, 2008). Both studies showed that this differentiation is worthwhile, because they affect sport-commitment and well-being differently. The differentiation into two incentive types extends classical approaches to incentives which focused mainly on single incentives associated with the result of an action (e.g., Crespi, 1942, Heckhausen, 1977; Atkinson, 1957).

Referring to the regularities of operant conditioning, the present research assumed that activity-related incentives are more closely time-associated with the sport activity than purpose-related incentives. These activity-related incentives were therefore hypothesized to have a stronger rewarding effect on the sport-commitment and well-being than purpose-related incentives. We found the stronger effect of activity-related incentives in both studies. The fact that we found similar results for different sport activities underlines the validity of our findings. In Study 1 activity-related incentives were stronger predictors of commitment and well-being than purpose-related incentives. Study 2 not only confirmed this result, but also took the research on incentives one step further by showing that incentives can be experimentally induced and with them their positive effects on commitment and well-being. As hypothesized, imagining activity-related incentives like enjoying the movements or feeling the muscles and body led to better well-being and a higher sport commitment than imagining positive purpose-related incentives such as health effects. To conclude, the present research contributes to research on incentives by showing that the differentiation in activity-related and purpose-related incentives is not only worthwhile to predict learning activity (see Rheinberg 1989), but also to predict sport behaviour. Second, our studies demonstrated that activity-related incentives have a higher potential to predict behaviour commitment and well-being than purpose-related incentives. Third, we showed that incentives and therefore their positive outcomes can be synthesized by a simple experimental manipulation. Present research suggests focusing on activity-related incentives rather than on purpose-related incentives. One explanation is that activity-related incentives have more positive effects than purpose-related incentives (e.g., on commitment). Another reason is that the positive experience quality of activity-related incentives can be seen as a goal by itself.

The fact that incentives and with them their positive effects can easily be induced by asking participants to vividly imagine an important incentive of their sport activity has important practical implications for health programs. This may also have implications for other domains of human life in which behaviour change and behaviour maintenance is required. For example, in order to prevent the high drop-out rates of leisure-and health-oriented sport courses and to support exercise adherence, the induction of incentives could be part of complex health programs or of therapeutic consulting. Maybe even sport advertisements of public health campaigns could include the induction of activity-related incentives by stressing the individual positive experiences while doing sports. Patients in rehabilitation could also be helped to implement their clinical training in everyday life by listing their purpose-related (e.g., health, pain-reduction) and activity-related incentives (e.g., enjoying moving to music; feeling of muscular power) of the stationary training lessons and use this material to remind themselves of the positive aspects associated with the training activity when they return home.

AUTHORS' NOTE

Dr. phil. Julia Schüler, University of Zurich, Switzerland.
Dr. phil. Sibylle Brunner, University of Zurich, Switzerland.

Lic.phil. Marianne Steiner, University of Zurich, Switzerland.

This work was supported by a grant of the Swiss Federal Council of Sports (Eidgenössische Sportkommission, ESK) and the Federal Office for Sport Magglingen (Bundesamt für Sport Magglingen, BASPO) dedicated to Julia Schüler.

Correspondence concerning this article should be addressed to Julia Schüler, Department of Psychology, University of Zurich, Binzmühlestrasse 14/6, 8050 Zürich, Switzerland. Email: j.schueler@psychologie.uzh.ch

REFERENCES

Atkinson, J.W. (1957). Motivational determinants of risk-taking behaviour. *Psychological Review, 64,* 359-372.

Beckman, J., & Heckhausen, H. (2008). Motivation as a function of expectancy and incentives. In H. Heckhausen & J. Heckhausen (Eds.), *Motivation and action* (pp. 99-136). Cambridge, UK: Cambridge University Press.

Biddle, S., & Mutrie, N. (1991). *Psychology of Physical Activity and Exercise.* London: Springer Verlag.

Biddle, S., & Mutrie, N. (2001). *Psychology of physical activity.* London, UK: Routledge.

Biddle, S., Fox, K.R., & Boutcher, S.H. (2000). *Physical activity and psychological well-being.* London, UK: Routledge.

Bolles, R.C. (1972). Reinforcement, expectancy, and learning. *Psychological Review, 79,* 394 – 409.

Brandstätter, V. (2003). *Persistenz und Zielablösung [Persistence and goal disengagement]*. Göttingen: Hogrefe.

Brière, N.M., Vallerand, R.J., Blais, M.R., & Pelletier, L.G. (1995). On the development and validation of the French form of the Sport Motivation Scale. *International Journal of Sport Psychology, 26,* 465-489.

Brunstein, J. C. (1993). Personal goals and subjective well-being: A longitudinal study. *Journal of Personality and Social Psychology, 65*(5), 1061-1070.

Bühler, K. (1922). *Die geistige Entwicklung des Kindes* [The cognitive development of a child]. Jena: Fischer.

Burton, B., & Martens, R. (1986). Pinned by their own goals: An exploratory investigation into why kids drop out of wrestling. *Journal of Sport Psychology, 8*(3), 183-197.

Coakley, J., & White, A. (1992). Making decisions: Gender and sport participation among british adolescents. *Sociology of Sport Journal, 9,* 20-35.

Crespi, L. P. (1942). Quantitative variation of incentive and performance in the white rat. *American Journal of Psychology, 55,* 467-517.

Crespi, L. P. (1944). Amount of reinforcement and level of performance. *Psychological Review, 51,* 341-357.

Csikszentmihalyi, M., & LeFevre, J. (1989). Optimal experience in work and leisure. *Journal of Personality and Social Psychology, 56,* 815-822.

Deci, E. L., & Ryan, R. M. (1985). *Intrinsic motivation and self-determination in human behaviour*. New York: Plenum.

Deci, E. L., & Ryan, R. M. (2000). The "what" and "why" of goal pursuits: Human needs and the self-determination of behavior. *Psychological Inquiry, 11,* 227-268.

Dishman, R. K. (1990). Determinants of participation in physical exercise. *Health Psychology, 1,* 237–267.

Dishman, R. K., & Buckworth, J. (1997). Adherence to physical activity. In W. P. Morgan (Ed.), *Physical activity and mental health* (pp. 63-80). Washington, DC: Taylor & Francis.

Dishman, R. K., & Sallis J. F. (1994). Determinants and interventions for physical activity and exercise. In C. Bouchard, R. J. Shephard, & T. Stephens (Eds.), *Physical activity, fitness, and health*(pp. 214–238). Champaign, IL: Human Kinetics Books.

Edwards, W. (1954). The theory of decision-making. *Psychological Bulletin, 51,* 380-417.

Feather, N. T. (1961). The relationship of persistence at a task to expectation of success and achievement related motives. *Journal of Abnormal and Social Psychology, 63,* 552-561.

Fuchs, R. (1997). *Psychologie und körperliche Bewegung* [Psychology and physical exercise]. Göttingen: Hogrefe.

Gabler, H. (2002). *Motive im Sport* [Motives in sport]. Schorndorf: Verlag Karl Hofmann.

Goudas, M., Biddle, S., & Underwood, M. (1995). A prospective study of the relationships between motivational orientations and perceived competence with intrinsic motivation and achievement in a teacher education course. *Educational Psychology, 15,* 89-96.

Gould, D., & Petlichkoff, L. (1988). Participation motivation and attrition in young athletes. In F. L. Smoll, R. A. Magill, & M. J. Ash (Eds.), *Children in sport* (3rd ed., pp. 161-178). Champaign, IL: Human Kinetics Books.

Grice, G. R. (1948). The relation of secondary reinforcement to delayed reward in visual discriminating learning. *Journal of Experimental Psychology, 38,* 1-16.

Heckhausen, H. (1977). Motivation: Kognitionspsychologische Aufspaltung eines summarischen Konstrukts [Motivation: Splitting of a summary concept within a cognitive process model]. *Psychologische Rundschau, 28*, 175-189.

Heckhausen, H., & Gollwitzer, P.M. (1987). Thought contents and cognitive functioning in motivational versus volitional states of mind. *Motivation and Emotion, 11*, 101-120.

Heckhausen, H., & Rheinberg, F. (1980). Lernmotivation im Unterricht, erneut betrachtet [Learning motivation – reconsidered]. *Unterrichtswissenschaft, 8*, 7-47.

Hull, C. L. (1952). *A behaviour system: An introduction to behaviour theory concerning the individual organism.* New Haven: Yale University Press.

Ingeledew, D. K., Markland, D., & Medley, A. R. (1998). Exercise motives and stages of change. *Journal of Health Psychology, 3*, 477-489.

Koch, S. (1956). Behaviour as „intrisically" regulated: Work notes towards a pre-theory of phenomena called „motivational". In M. R. Jones (Ed.), *Nebraska Symposium on Motivation* (pp. 42-87). Lincoln, NE: University of Nebraska Press.

Lewin, K. (1931). *Die psychologische Situation bei Lohn und Strafe* [The psychologicial situation in reward and punishment]. Leipzig: Hirzel.

Lewin, K. (1951). *Field theory in social science.* Chicago: University of Chicago Press.

Li, F. (1999). The Exercise Motivation Scale: Its multifaceted structure and construct validity. *Journal of Applied Sport Psychology, 11*, 97-115.

Maier, G. W., & Brunstein, J. C. (2001). The role of personal work goals of newcomer's job satisfaction and organizational commitment: A longitudinal study. *Journal of Applied Psychology, 86*(5), 1034 – 1042.

Marcus, B. H., Dubbert, P. M., Forsyth, L. H., McKenzie, T. L., Stone, E. J., Dunn, A. L., & Blair, S. N. (2000). Physical activity behaviour change: Issues in adoption and maintenance. *Health Psychology, 19* (1), 32-41.

McAuley, E., & Tammen, V.V. (1989). The effects of subjective and objective competitive outcomes on intrinsic motivation. *Journal of Sport & Exercise Psychology, 11*, 84-93.

McClelland, D. C. (1985). *Human motivation.* Glenview, IL: Scott, Foresman.

McClelland, D. C., Atkinson, J. W., Clark, R. A., & Lowell, E. L. (1953). *The achievementmotive.* New York: Appleton-Century-Crofts.

Mutrie, N. (2000). The relationship between physical activity and clinically defined depression. In S. J. H. Biddle, K. Fox, & S. H. Boutcher (Eds.), *Physical activity and psychological well-being*(pp. 46-62). London: Routledge.

O'Connor, P. J., Raglin, J. S., & Martinsen, E. W. (2000). Physical activity, anxiety and anxiety disorders. *International Journal of Sport Psychology, 2000*(31), 136-155.

Pelletier, L.G., Fortier, M. S., Vallerand, R. J., Tuson, K. M., Bière, N. M., & Blais, M. R. (1995). Toward a new measure of intrinsic motivation, extrinsic motivation, and amotivation in sports: The Sport Motivation Scale (SMS). *Journal of Sport & Exercise Psychology, 17*, 35-53.

Pfaffenbarger, R. S., Hyde, R. T., Wing, A., & Hsieh, C. C. (1986). Physical activity, all-cause mortality, and longevity of college alumni. *New England Journal of Medicine, 314*, 605-613.

Rheinberg, F. (1989). *Zweck und Tätigkeit* [Purpose and activity]. Göttingen: Hogrefe.

Rheinberg, F. (1993). *Anreize engagiert betriebener Freizeitaktivitäten – ein Systematisierungsversuch* [Incentives of dedicatedly pursued leisure activities – an attempt of systematization]. Manuskript, Potsdam: Psychologisches Institut der Universität Potsdam.

Rheinberg, F. (2004). *Motivationsdiagnostik* [Motivation diagnosis]. Göttingen: Hogrefe.

Rheinberg, F. (2008). Intrinsic motivation and flow-experience. In H. Heckhausen & J. Heckhausen (Eds.), *Motivation and action* (pp. 323-348). Cambridge, UK: Cambridge University Press.

Rotter, J. B. (1954). *Social learning and clinical psychology*. Englewood Cliffs, NJ: Prentice-Hall.

Ryan, R., Frederick, C. M., Lepes, D., Rubio, N., & Sheldon, K. M. (1997). Intrinsic motivation and exercise adherence. *International Journal of Sport Psychology, 28,* 335-354.

Saltin, B. (1990). Cardiovascular and pulmonary adaptation to physical activity. In C. Bouchard, R. J. Shepard, T. Stephens, J. R. Sutton, & B. D. McPherson (Eds.), *Exercise, fitness, and health*(pp. 187-204). Champaign, IL: Human Kinetics Books.

Scanlan, T. K., Carpenter, P. J., Schmidt, G. W., Simons, J. P., & Keeler, B. (1993). An introduction to the sport commitment model. *Journal of Sport & Exercise Psychology, 15,* 1 – 15.

Scanlan, T.K., & Lewthwaite, R. (1986). Social psychological aspects of competition for male youth sport participants: IV. Predictors of enjoyment. *Journal of Sport Psychology, 8,* 25-35.

Schallberger, U. (2000). Qualität des Erlebens in Arbeit und Freizeit: Eine Zwischenbilanz [Quality of experience in work and leisure time: An interim balance]. *Berichte aus der Abteilung Angewandte Psychologie* (31). Zürich: Psychologisches Institut der Universität Zürich.

Schmalt, H.- D. (1996). Zur Kohärenz von Motivation und Kognition [The coherence of motivation and cognition]. In J. Kuhl & H. Heckhausen (Eds.), *Enzyklopädie der Psychologie. Motivation, Volition und Handeln* (pp. 241-273). Göttingen: Hogrefe.

Schneider, K., & Schmalt, H. D. (2000). *Motivation* [Motivation].Stuttgart: Kohlhammer.

Schüler, J., & Brunner, S. (2006). Exercise – adherence: The role of incentives. *http://www.erasmus.gr/congresses/ICAP2006/*. Talk at the 26th International Congress of Applied Psychology, 2006-Athens, Greece.

Shanks, D. R., & Dickinson, A. (1991). Instrumental judgement and performance under variations in action-outcome contingency and contiguity. *Memory & Cognition, 19,* 353-360.

Sit, C. H. P., Kerr, J. H., & Wong, I. T. F. (2008). Motives for and barriers to physical activity participation in middle-aged Chinese women. *Psychology of Sport and Exercise, 9,* 266-283.

Skinner, B.F. (1938). *The behaviour of organisms.* New York: Appleton-Century-Crofts.

Steiner, M. (2006). Motivationale Kompetenz und Anreize im Badminton. [Motivational competence and incentives in badminton sports]. *Unpublished thesis at the University of Zurich, Department of Psychology.*

Tarpy, R. M., & Sawabini, F. L. (1974). Reinforcement delay: A selective review of the last decades. *Psychological Bulletin, 81,* 984-997.

Tolman, E. C. (1932). *Purposive behaviour in animals and men.* New York: Appleton Century.

Vroom, V. H. (1964). *Work and motivation.* New York: Wiley.

Williams, L., & Gill, D. L. (1995). The role of perceived competence in the motivation of physical activity. *Journal of Sport & Exercise Psychology, 17,* 363-378.

Wing, R. R. (2000). Cross-cutting themes in maintenance of behaviour change. *Health Psychology, 19*(1), 84-88.

Woodworth, R. S. (1918). *Dynamic psychology.* New York: Columbia University Press.

In: Introduction to Sport Psychology
Editor: Robert Schinke

ISBN: 978-1-61761-973-1
© 2011 Nova Science Publishers, Inc.

COACHES' AND ELITE TEAM PLAYERS' PERCEPTION AND EXPERIENCING OF COLLECTIVE COLLAPSE

Erwin Apitzsch[*]

Department of Psychology, LundUniversity, P.O. Box 213, SE-221 00 Sweden

ABSTRACT

The phenomenon of collective collapse in team sports, conceived in terms of negative psychological momentum when the players on a team suddenly perform below the expected level despite having had a good start, was investigated in two studies. One of them involved four male coaches of different sports, all at the elite level, and the other involved nine male players from a handball team, likewise at the elite level. Semi-structured interviews were employed in both cases. The major causes of collective collapse were found to be inappropriate behavior, failure of the role system to function properly, negative communication within the team, a change in the tactics of the opposing team, and goals being scored by that team. Factors seen as needing to be dealt with to prevent collective collapse included negative thinking, negative emotions, and negative emotional contagion. The studies provide a team perspective on negative psychological momentum as well as tentative proposals for avoiding collective collapse.

INTRODUCTION

In team sports, sudden and unexpected shifts in performance can sometimes be observed. A soccer team may be ahead 2-0 after 70 minutes of play, only to lose by 2-3 after the final 20 minutes have been played. This can be termed collective collapse when such an outcome is due to the sudden underperformance of the players of the team originally in the lead. Apitzsch (2006) has suggested that collective collapse occurs when, in a match of considerable or decisive importance, the majority of the players on a team suddenly perform below their expected level after the team has had a good or normal start, or when they underperform from the very start. What causes collective collapse?

Sport performance is heavily influenced by psychological factors such as an athlete's thoughts and emotions, and by the context at hand. It thus appears reasonable, in investigating the phenomenon of collective collapse within team sports, to examine not only the overt behavior but also the cognitions and affects associated with it. Apitzsch (2006) reported

---

[*]Phone number: + 46 46 222 9115; Fax number: + 46 46 222 4209; Email: Erwin. Apitzsch@psychology.lu.se

possible theoretical bases for a link between collective collapse and a cognitive approach (Janis, 1982), an affective approach (Kelly & Barsade, 2001), a behavioral approach (Bion, 1961), and connections between emotions and cognition (Cacioppo & Gardner, 1999; Tickle-Degnan & Puccinelli, 1999; Totterdell, 2000).

However, a number of terms in general use are related to collective collapse, such as psychological momentum (Taylor & Demick, 1994), critical moments (Carlstedt, 2004), choking (Baumeister, 1984; Coward, 2006), slumps (Goldberg, 1998), and mistakes (Halden-Brown, 2003). The literature on these terms deals with what happens at the individual level, whereas reports at the team level are missing.

Psychological momentum can be either positive or negative, in accordance with the definition suggested by Taylor and Demick (1994, p. 54) of its being "a positive or negative change in cognition, affect, physiology, and behavior caused by an event or series of events that will result in a commensurate shift in performance and competitive outcome." A multidimensional model proposed by Taylor and Demick (1994) is one of three different models that have been suggested as serving to explain psychological momentum, which refers to a chain of events that starts with a precipitating event which lead to changes in cognition, affect, and physiological arousal, and thus to changes in behavior, performance and outcome that can be either positive or negative. In terms of that model, both opponent factors and what the team members experience can moderate the strength and the effects of psychological momentum. The precipitating events leading up to it can be of crucial importance. The negative momentum of the one team can also precipitate positive momentum on the part of the other. Thus, a goal in soccer scored by the trailing team can result in negative momentum for the team in the lead. The other two models proposed to explain psychological momentum are the Antecedents-Consequences Model (Vallerand, Colavecchio, & Pelletier, 1988), which only deals with positive psychological momentum, and the Projected Performance Model (Cornelius, Silva, Conroy, & Peterson, 1997), which considers psychological momentum as a way of describing performance shifts.

The unique contribution of the following studies is to provide data on negative psychological momentum at the team level, thus extending the Multidimensional Model of Taylor and Demick (1994). In the present investigation, two studies were conducted aimed at shedding more light on the team phenomenon of collective collapse, concerned in one case with the perspective of coaches regarding this phenomenon and in the other with that of players.

STUDY 1 – INTERVIEWS WITH COACHES OF
TEAM SPORTS AT THE ELITE LEVEL

Since collective collapse in team sports has received little attention in the scientific literature, obtaining a better understanding of the phenomenon was the primary outcome of this investigation. The intention in Study 1 was to explore how coaches at the elite level experience collective collapse and how they deal with it.

METHOD

Participants

Four male coaches working at the top national or international level (all of them of Swedish nationality, the one at the international level coaching the national team of another Scandinavian country) – one of them in handball, two in ice hockey, and one in soccer - were interviewed. They were selected on the basis of availability and of their having experienced collective collapse in their respective teams. Their mean age was 51.0 years (range 41-57 years) and each had more than five years of experience as head coach of either a first-division team or a national team. They were informed of the aims of the study, each of them giving his informed consent. The four interviews of this sort carried out were deemed sufficient for the present purposes, in view of the explorative aims of the study.

Procedure

Because knowledge of collective collapse at the team level is very limited, an exploratory interview was employed, involving use of semi-structured questions based in part on theoretical considerations (pertaining to affective, cognitive or behavioral factors) and in part on newspaper reports of collective collapse. In particular, it was seen as important to obtain detailed information on how a collective collapse is perceived (Item sample: "Describe what happens when a collective collapse occurs. Give an example from a match where it has happened"), what indicators of a sudden decrease in performance there may be prior to a match or at the beginning of it ("Are there any indications that a collective collapse is about to happen?"), whether a triggering factor can be identified ("Why does it happen?"), what external influences there are ("Are there any external factors such as reactions of spectators or calls of the referee that may cause a collective collapse?"), the actions a coach undertakes when collapse occurs ("What do you as a coach do when the team suddenly underperforms?"), and what preventive measures had been taken or should be taken to avoid collective collapse in matches thereafter ("How can a collective collapse be avoided?"). Prior to the study, three pilot interviews with experienced team coaches were conducted, resulting in minor changes to the interview guide.

The interviews took place during the period of September 2005 to November 2006 and were conducted by the author in the hometowns of the coaches, or in one case in connection with a conference. The interviews were 45-80 minutes in length. They began with presentation of background information and of the definition of collective collapse. Theinterviewer noted subjects' responses as exactly as possible. Coding was done separately by the author and an experienced member of the research team. The three categories involved were the origin of a factor (one's own team, the opposing team or external circumstances), the factors in question(cognitions, emotions or behaviors of various types), and their valence (positive, neutral or negative). The inter-rater agreement, measured using Cohen's kappa, gave correlations of1.00, .91, and .95 respectively. Disagreements were discussed until the examiners reached consensus (Côté, Salmela, Baria, & Russell, 1993).Interviewees were given feedback upon request.

Quotation marks are used in presenting statements by the participants, though the approximate character of recording their statements, as well as the fact that the interviews themselves were conducted in Swedish and that when appropriate slight changes in formulation were madeaimed at making the intent of the participant as clear as possible, should be borne in mind.

RESULTS

Nature and Antecedents of Collective Collapse

The overlap of the responses the coaches gave to the themes contained in the interview guide led to the results being subsumed under three major headings: 1) the nature and the antecedents of collective collapse, including indicators, triggering causes, external influences, reactions of individual players, and actions of the opponents, 2) actions of the coach, and 3) prevention of collective collapse.

Regarding the nature of collective collapse, the reactions of individual players that were reported concerned mainly inappropriate behavior on their part. The following, for example, was said: "When the team has a substantial lead, the players focus on defending the lead, which results in passivity" (Coach 1: designated as C1). "If one player makes a mistake, mistakes by other players follow. It's like a chain reaction" (C4). Negative thoughts and negative emotions were also mentioned, though to a lesser extent, one of the coaches stating, "If the players think that the match is already won, there's the risk that they'll act recklessly and do things they wouldn't normally do" (C3). Statements of the following sort were made regarding the actions of the opponents: "A goal by the opposing team results in a sense of frustration in the players of one's own team" (C1).

Each of the indicators of an approaching collective collapse that were taken up concerned matters pertaining to one's own team. Emotions and the effects these had were involved primarily. The most frequent observation was of recklessness, manifested by feelings of the type "We've already won the match" (C2 and C3). Recklessness at the individual level involved doing something unusual or spectacular, and at the team level failing to adhere to the tactics of the team. Fear was an element in other observations that were made:"Fear, cowardliness, and laying responsibility for things that go wrong on your teammates are all indicators of bad performance" (C1). Fear was seen as being expressed by negative body language or by a person's playing without making a genuine effort, trying simply to avoid making mistakes. Negative thoughts and inappropriate behavior were also mentioned, but to a lesser extent. It was felt that, prior to a match, indicators that a collective collapse was in the making were difficult to detect. Remarks of the following sort were made: "It's likely that the mood of the players before a match affects their performance, but it's difficult to predict how things will develop" (C1).

The main categories of response seen as triggering collective collapse were those of errors made by members of one's own team (players failing to carry out their tasks properly or mistakes made by one or more individuals) and actions of the opposing team. Each of the coaches spoke of the importance of roles. "Some players don't do what's expected of them" (C1). References made to individual mistakes included "Players make mistakes when they're overconfident" (C1). Actions by the opposing team mentioned as triggering collective collapse were expressed the following way: "When the opposing team scores, their game improves" (C1 and C2).

Remarks concerning external influences had to do in part with influences prior to the match, and in part with those present during the match. Expectations expressed beforehand regarding results of the match that were seen as putting pressure on the team and possibly contributing to collective collapse which were expressed in the media, by interested individuals or by sponsors were reported by two of the coaches (C3 and C4). Coach 2 noted, "During the world championships neither the coaches nor the players were to read any newspapers." During a match, the only external sources of influence present are the referee and the spectators. None of the coaches mentioned either of these as being decisive for the outcome of a match.

Actions of the Coach

The situation at hand, the behavior of the coach in response to it, and the emotions involved emerged as categories pertaining to the actions of the coach. Possible actions of a coach to try to avert or overcome a collective collapse that were mentioned included taking a time-out (in those sports in which time-outs can be taken), talking with the players at half-time (C2, C3, and C4), and substituting players (C1 and C4). Time-outs were described as providing a chance to reconsider tactics and individual roles (C2). One of the coaches said, "You have to do something definite. Drastic measures are needed sometimes to alert the players to what needs to be done" (C3). The coaches referred to the importance of enhancing the players' self-confidence by emphasizing the fun of playing, and also of conveying a sense of trust in the players, and emphasizing what had gone well. There was the general view, nevertheless, that it is very difficult to produce change under such conditions. This was expressed by the statement, "There's a feeling of powerlessness. You know what to do and what to tell the players, but it's like speaking to the deaf" (C4).

Prevention of Collective Collapse

Thoughts regarding the prevention of collective collapse fell into two major categories: developing appropriate behavior and adopting a cognitive mindset. It was felt that one should endeavor to be prepared for different short-term scenarios that could occur (C1 and C2) and that mental training geared to more long-term readiness should be carried out (C2). A variety of further ideas were expressed: "The players need to accept the tactics that have been agreed upon and stick to their roles" (C1). "It's essential to gain an understanding of mistakes that have been made, rely on team spirit, and focus on what needs to be achieved" (C3).

DISCUSSION

The discussion will deal primarily with the first form of collective collapse mentioned in the definition that was given earlier, that of a majority of the players on a team suddenly performing below their expected level in a match of considerable or decisive importance, despite a normal or a good start to the match having been made. Most of what the participants discussed concerned collective collapse of this sort.

Factors related to the occurrence of collective collapse that were reported could be classified as being either internal (in principle in control of the team that collapses) or external (not controllable by the team). Most of the factors considered are internal ones. These can be present either at the individual or at the team level. At the individual level there are mental factors such as feeling the pressure to win, or experiencing insecurity regarding the role one is to perform, as well as behavioral factors such as those of making mistakes, or of playing without making adequate effort. Factors at the team level referred to included negligence in sticking to the tactics decided upon, a sense of irritation developing which negatively affects team spirit, and the failure of players to perform the roles expected of them. Role performance is defined by Beauchamp, Bray, Eys, and Carron (2002) in terms of the extent to which the behavior of individual players is consistent with the roles they are assigned or are expected to fulfill. If a player fails to measure up to a given role, there may be no other players ready or able to take over the role in question. The feelings associated with a collective collapse may be either negative (such as a sense of fear or insecurity) or anywhere from positive to indifferent (such as a sense of recklessness), though feelings of both sorts readily result in mistakes, which in turn can affect relationships between the players (such as leading to irritation or to players shouting at each other). Individual mistakes and negative feelings can affect the entire team. The negative emotional contagion that develops can make the already precarious situation of a collapsing team still worse. Regarding external factors, the actions of the opposing team appear to generally create greater problems than the media, the spectators or the referee do. A goal by the opposing team can negatively affect a collapsing team in two quite differing ways. For one thing, it can increase the confidence of the opposing team and the energy that members of that team invest in the game. In addition, it can lower the self-confidence of the collapsing team, and produce both a decrement in the team's performance and negative social interactions between members of the team. The effect of a goal by the opposing team is probably more pronounced in those team sports in which relatively few goals are scored (such as ice hockey and soccer) than in team sports in which many goals are scored or point scorings are made (handball or basketball). The media, spectators, and sponsors can all exert pressure on a team prior to a match, yet this pressure appears to be, in most cases, much less than that exerted by the opposing team. None of the coaches reported the referee to contribute to a collapse coming about, though in newspaper accounts this is often purported to be the case.

In most team sports the coach can call a time-out if a team seems about to collapse. The break in the match may disrupt the play and also the performance (cf. Eisler & Spink, 1998) of the opposing team, and it also gives the coach a chance to talk to the players. The extent to which the coach's instructions to the players or talking with them can turn the negative developments around is far from certain, and surely varies with the situation. The case of a coach who noticed that his instructions did not get through to the players has already been mentioned. Kroll (1982) noted that more than 20% of the stress that coaches experience is due to their inability to reach through to the players adequately. Obviously, greater attention should be directed at how a coach can best communicate with players who are in an aroused state, and often in a negative mood as well. In addition to the communication style of the coach, the attentional style of individual players should be taken into account. The coach can also remove players who are not performing well or are momentarily in difficulties, sending in substitutes, yet this may fail to have the desired effect, since the entire team can be affected by substitutions.

On the basis of the obtained results, it seems highly important for preventing collective collapse that the team and the coach be mentally and behaviorally as well prepared as possible for problematical situations that may turn up and, unless immediate changes appear called for, to basically adhere to the game plan. Maintaining the role structure that has been worked out, i.e. continuing to play as a team, should generally be followed, since individual actions decided upon on the spot are usually easier for the opposing team to handle and to deal with effectively. Mental training may be useful for purposes of preventing collective collapse, although there appears to be little information available regarding its frequency of use. Analyzing a match afterwards and learning from mistakes can obviously be very useful for later training and for future matches, a matter which the coaches emphasized.

STUDY 2 – A CASE STUDY OF A COLLAPSING TEAM HANDBALL TEAM

In the qualification series for the top division in handball, Team A (the away team) was leading against Team B (the home team) by five goals with only 14 minutes left to play. Team A was unbeaten in the series and appeared to clearly be on its way to victory, after having dominated the match from the start. Team B called for a time-out then, after which it went over to guarding two of Team A's top scorers man-to-man. Team B made seven goals in a row, whereas Team A collapsed and, with 30 seconds left, missed a penalty shot that would have tied the match. Team B ended up winning by one goal. The aim of Study 2 was to investigate the thoughts, emotions, and behaviors of the players involved in the collective collapse of Team A.

METHOD

Participants

Nine handball players 18-33 years of age (mean age 23.1 years) from Team A, all of whom had played in the match just described, participated. These players, and the team to which they belonged, represented a convenience sample. Two of the players, who had left the team at the time of the interviews, were not included in the study.

Procedure

An interview guide consisting of 15 questions was constructed by the author for the purpose of gaining in-depth knowledge of factors connected with the occurrence of collective collapse. The questions were based on the results of Study 1 and on the newspaper report of this particular match. In addition to personal background questions, there were questions concerning how the players had experienced the collective collapse that had occurred ("When did you notice that it was about to happen?", "Describe what happened"), how they had reacted to it ("What were your thoughts, emotions and what did you do?"), the role of the key players and how they were affected by the reactions of the teammates. The coach and the key players were also asked how they reacted to the expression of emotions at the time by the coach and by their teammates. Due to time limitations and other practical considerations, it was not possible to test the interview guide prior to its use.

The interviews took place in the team's home town in May of 2006, four months after the collective collapse had occurred, a time chosen in part so as to not interfere with what was going on during the handball season. The participants were informed beforehand of the purpose of the study and agreed to participate. The interviews, lasting 40-60 minutes, were conducted by the author and a graduate student involved in research on collective collapse. The interviews began with a brief oral account of the match. The interviewers wrote down the participants' answers to questions as exactly as possible. The coding of the answers was done as in Study 1. The inter-rater agreement, measured using Cohen's kappa, gave correlations of .79, .70, and .78, respectively. Disagreements were discussed until the examiners reached consensus (Côté, Salmela, Baria, & Russell, 1993). Feedback to the interviewees was given upon request.

RESULTS

The discrepancy between the results of the inter-rater agreement between Study 1 and Study 2 was mainly found in factor two, the interpretation of cognitions, emotions and behavior. The responses of the coaches were straight-forward and thus easier to classify, whereas the responses of the players were characterized by overlapping of the factors. One examiner classified according to the factor which was first mentioned, whereas the other examiner classified according to the dominant factor in the response.

Thoughts and Emotions when the Team Had a Five-Goal Lead

With 14 minutes left to play, Team A was leading by five goals. At this point, the thoughts and emotions of the players were obviously very positive. Eight of the players reported having only positive thoughts, and one player to have both positive and negative thoughts. The positive thoughts were expressed in such ways as the following: "Things looked good.", "It was an important match and we felt we were approaching victory, definitely not defeat." The only player who appeared to have been doubtful said, "I felt the victory wasn't quite safe yet, but that it was very close." The emotions expressed were also largely positive, though less so than the thoughts that were reported. Expressions of positive emotions included the following: "It felt really good. We were the better team and were in control of the match. The opposing team seemed to have given up." Negative feelings were expressed by two of the players: "There were negative feelings. The pressure the fans were putting us under made us feel anxious". Mixed feelings were expressed by one of the players: "We were excited, but also worried. We were in the lead, but it didn't feel safe. The goals we'd scored had been easy ones, whereas the goals of the opponents were made after good combinations and shots that were well-taken."

Perceived Causes of the Collective Collapse

The reasons participants gave for collective collapse fell into two major categories: the behavior of one's own team, and the actions of the opposing team. The behavior of one's own team was seen as involving underperformance in the offensive play of nearly all of the players, fatigue, anxiety, and lack of experience. The underperformance, particularly of key players, was regarded as affecting the team as a whole. The remarks made included the following: "Our play was characterized by the contagious effects of playing badly and each of us expecting someone else to take the initiative." The sense of lacking experience was expressed, for example, as follows: "A young team is not as consistent in its performance as a team in which the players are older." Anxiety found expression in the statement, "We became anxious and began thinking about failure." It was felt that the team was very much under stress through the opposing team being able to read off the offensive moves undertaken against them and to adjust their defensive tactics accordingly. One player remarked, "The stress we were under and our difficulties in anticipating the actions of the opponents resulted in our losing possession of the ball repeatedly and it being easy for them to score goals."

Reactions of the Players

The reactions of the players to the collective collapse that occurred involved the feeling of losing control of things. This was accompanied by largely negative thoughts, as well as negative emotions and negative behavior, i.e. behavior that failed to contribute properly to success of the team (see figure 1).

Although most of the thoughts that were cited were negative, two of the players mentioned positive thoughts: "We can still win the rest of our matches and end up ahead." For the most part, however, the thoughts of the players were negative: "We've been close to victory before but failed. Is this what's about to happen again?" Positive, task-oriented thoughts included the following: "I have to act on my own and do the best I can to challenge the opponents." The emotions that were expressed were all negative. "Frustration" and "stress" were the words most frequently employed. Anger was expressed in one case: "I got angry at myself when I discovered how close the opponents' score had gotten to ours." Loneliness was expressed as well: "I felt completely deserted on the court and became paralyzed." Lack of motivation was likewise expressed: "I had no inspiration to play." A sense of powerlessness was expressed too: "I knew I wouldn't get any time on the court." The behavior participants reported was classified as being task-related, communicative, or irrelevant. The task-related behavior was of a sort that affected the play negatively, such as careless passes ("Balls were being thrown away"), playing without making any real effort ("No one took responsibility"), playing only as individuals ("The offensive combinations collapsed"), being regressive in one's style of play ("We played like juniors"), and making wrong decisions ("The shots were taken too quickly and from unfamiliar positions"). Communication within the team was mainly negative, both in verbal terms ("We started to shout at each other") and in terms of body language (giving expression to anger). There were reports of attempts to communicate constructively, but of these being unsuccessful ("I tried to encourage my teammates, but it didn't work. They were all so down."). Irrelevant behavior was manifested by focusing on the referee instead of on what one was to do ("We got some calls against us and started to argue with the referee, although we knew it was pointless").

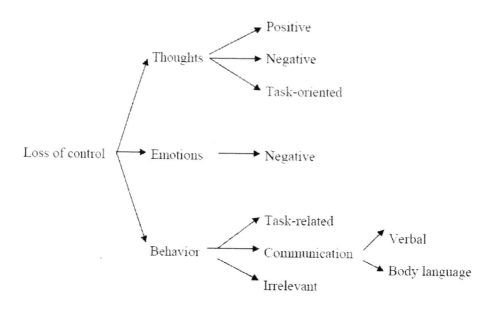

Figure 1. Reactions in the case of collective collapse.

Reactions of the Coach and of the Key Players

According to the players, the coach was also taken by surprise by the opposing team's change in tactics and reacted emotionally ("He was stressed, worried, and frustrated", "He raised his voice and shouted." Answers to the question "What did he do?" gave a divided picture of things. Some players could not remember what the coach had done, whereas others remembered but were very critical ("He had no ideas. He seemed lacking in competence"). The coach called a time-out after two goals by the opposing team, which had reduced the team's lead to three goals. The atmosphere during the time-out could be described as chaotic ("Everybody talked at the same time. It led to nothing. No encouragement was given"). Some of the players questioned the decision to call a time-out ("A time-out in such a situation could result in anxiety and doubting one's own ability"). Two of the key offensive players were marked man-to man, after which they became basically stationary in their actions. One key player had two yellow cards against him and had to play carefully to avoid being suspended. The general view of matters was that the team was taken by surprise and did not play well, and also that the offensive play failed when two of the players became marked. Shots were taken from odd positions because of stress. The key players failed to fulfill their roles, and the man-to-man marking of two of the players clearly showed that, in the new situation that had come about, there was a lack of clarity regarding individual roles. The formal role of the team captain is that of his being the voice of the coach on the court and encouraging his teammates. He is usually an experienced player and is expected to be a good role model. The team captain in this particular match was described as trying to do his job, but failing at this ("He tried to coach us defensively, but he wasn't alert"). His communications were seen as being mainly negative ("He shouted and bawled, which is negative in a match like this"), and his behavior was regarded as being directed at himself ("He focused on himself and on negative things. He became frustrated with the other players").

Reactions to the Expression of Emotions by the Coach and by Teammates

Most of the players indicated that they were affected by the emotions of others on the team ("Yes, consciously or unconsciously. It's contagious", "Unconsciously, I'm affected by body language"). All of the players reported that negative emotions of the others had a clear influence on their own emotions and behavior. The reactions of the players varied from partial agreement with the idea that negative emotions are contagious ("It depends on how long it goes on. I try to focus on the next ball") to complete agreement ("Of course I'm affected by any sort of negative atmosphere within the team"). There were also players who tried to do something about the negative emotions that were evident ("I tried to calm down the players who were upset, but it isn't easy to change a whole team"). One player reacted with anger ("Why can't they pull themselves together?").

DISCUSSION

It is scarcely surprising that, with a five-goal lead and only a short time left to play, most of the thoughts and emotions of the team members were positive. The players could readily interpret the match, both in cognitive and in emotional terms, as though they had already won it. A turning point in the match came when the opposing team changed its tactics. Although most of the players reported that the collective collapse that occurred then was due mainly to factors within their own team, some of their statements – such as "We didn't succeed in changing the way in which we played" or "No one turned out to be able to lead the team" – indicate that certain of the reactions they showed could be interpreted as responses to actions by the opponents. Fatigue, inexperience and the feeling of many of the players that it was someone else who should take the initiative resulted in their exerting less effort than otherwise.

The team's offensive play, negatively affected as it was by what the opponents were doing, collapsed, whereas the defensive play appeared to not have changed considerably. Failure of the offensive play to function as it should resulted in an almost complete change in their thinking, emotions and behavior, which suddenly changed from being primarily positive to primarily negative in character. Their negative thoughts ("What's going to happen if we lose?"), distracted them from the ongoing match and placed limitations on their behavior. Their negative emotions appeared to have a highly detrimental effect on their performance. The team was carried away emotionally instead of acting in a rational way.

Noteworthy is that the few attempts to act rationally that they made, such as efforts to communicate constructively, failed. The players were not receptive. This could reflect their having too high an arousal level. The findings provide support for the views of Baumeister (1984) and of Coward (2006) regarding negative or irrelevant thoughts readily disrupting performance, and of Goldberg's (1998) indicating performance slumps to start in the head of the athlete. They are also in line with Halden-Brown's (2003) assertion that both frustrationand anger need to be handled properly in order for top performance to be achieved. In the present case, role performance broke down – neither the coach, the captain of the team nor other key players performing in accordance with the roles they were to carry out. The coach called a time-out but failed then to show effective leadership. Since he could not calm the players down and he gave them no apparent instructions, no change in tactics was brought about. The key players underperformed and the team captain was likewise unable to effect a change in the team's performance. The lack of leadership was obvious. According to Carron, Hausenblas, and Eys (2005), the role of the team captain is not an easy one and the leadership demands placed on him often appearing overwhelming. In this particular match, the team captain failed to live up to the expectations placed on him, or to demonstrate a person-task compatibility. This suggests it could be a good idea, in some cases at least, to let two or more players share responsibility for the team captain role. The few constructive initiatives taken were by players whose status appeared to be too low, and their teammates did not listen.

Adequate role performance is highly important in team sports. Hagger and Chatzisarantis (2005) emphasize the necessity, for team success, of players fulfilling their roles. Carron, Hausenblas, and Eys (2005) underline the important role the coach has in the communication process. Team members tend readily, if the information provided them is unclear, to experience frustration and dissatisfaction and to act inappropriately. In the present case, the social function of creating a positive atmosphere failed. It is not clear whether the team had appointed anyone as a kind of socio-emotional leader, but in any case no one was performing such a role adequately. One can note that in several of the interviews negative emotions were reported to be contagious and to affect the entire team, both players on the court and those on the bench. This is a phenomenon that has also been reported by Totterdell (2000), who found the mood and performance of teammates on a cricket team to be contagious, the mood or performance of the one affecting that of the others. Since positive emotions readily lead to feelings of performing better and to an increase in self-confidence (Heath & Jourden, 1997), the present team could have profited from having a player who could take on a socio-emotional role for the team as a whole.

To conclude, it appears to be important to be prepared for at least those tactical changes by one's opponents that are readily foreseeable, to withstand distracting thoughts and thus be able to focus adequately on the ongoing match, to have players who can take over important roles if theplayers designated to perform them fail to fulfill them properly, to always play as a team, to avoid being beset by negative emotions, and if possible to give someone the role oftransferring positive emotions to the others.

GENERAL DISCUSSION

Initially, three theoretical approaches seen as able to contribute to an understanding of collective collapse were presented. Janis' (1982) theory of groupthink appears to be applicable to the decision making involved. In the match taken up in Study 2 the coach shouted at the players but failed to provide them constructive advice during the time-out. He seemed unable to adjust to the needs of the situation and, after the time-out, the passive play of the team continued. The results of the investigation as a whole support Kelly and Barsade's (2001) findings of strong negative emotions (players' shouting at each other) seemingly having a detrimental effect on group cohesion, as well as on commitment (loss in motivation), and performance (failing to play as a team), and of such effects being contagious, affecting the team as a whole. Support was also obtained for Totterdell's (2000) finding of an increase in positive mood in the one team resulting in the mood of the opposing team becoming more negative.The present findings are also in line with Bion's (1961) conceptions of assumption-group dependency (none of the other players taking over the roles of players who were performing unsatisfactorily) and of flight group (play having become passive).

The most firmly established model for the study of team sports would appear to be that of Carron, Hausenblas, and Eys (2005). This model suggests, in brief, that attributes both of the environment and of the team members form the basis for the physical and psychological structure of a team, which in turn affects those team processes that lead to the individual and team outcomes that are achieved. Team cohesion is the variable seen as mediating between team structure and the processes involved.

Applying results of the present investigation to the conceptual framework of the model enables collective collapse be described as follows: Despite the attributes of a team, as far as the abilities of its individual members is concerned, tending to be stable during a given season and the physical condition of most of the players usually not changing much from one match to the next, the motivation of the players can change quickly, also during a single match. There can be a drop in motivation in the team which is in the lead, for example, if winning the match looks easy and this results in the team's underestimating the abilities of the opposing team. This can possibly set the stage for collective collapse of the team which is in the lead if certain additional factors are present, in part factors specific to the situation, such as the actions of the opposing team, of the referee, and of the crowd, and the venue of the match. What the players of the opposing team do clearly has a stronger impact on whether collective collapse occurs than any of the other factors specific to the situation. If the opposing team scores a goal, this gives that team a boost, and if the team also changes its tactics, this can confuse players on the team that had looked forward to winning easily and possibly even put them into a state of panic. The other factors just mentioned that are specific to the situation appear to be of lesser effect, although some of the participants did direct attention at the need of dealing adequately with pressures produced by the spectators.

What follows then in the case of a collective collapse of the team which is or has been in the lead is a momentary disintegration of its team structure, the communicative processes normally found, and with this the usual team environment. The psychological structure of a team is a function of the position, the status and the roles of the various players and of norms that have been established. In a collective collapse, the structure of the team breaks down. Key players fail to do what is expected of them and the role system ceases to function properly. Team processes – in particular those of interaction, cooperation, communication, and decision making – also fail to function as they should.Constructive interactions become less frequent, and team members begin to play primarily as individuals, while also disregarding the tactics. Communications become negative, players become irritated, beginning to shout at each other, and negatively affecting each others' play. Decision making becomes poor, wrong decisions being made both by the players regarding such matters as when to shoot, and by the coach concerning questions such as when to substitute players. The achievement of the individual players declines radically due to recklessness, stress, and failure of the players to act as a team, the ultimate result being one of chaos and defeat.

In both of the studies carried out, the changes most frequently noted in connection with the collective collapse of a team were changes in the actions of the opponents and changes both in role performance (team structure) andcommunication (team processes) within the team stricken by collective collapse.The actions of the opponents represent the only one of the three factors just mentioned that the collapsing team cannot directly control. Matters of the opposing team playing better than its ranking indicated, of its changing its tactics, and of its scoring an easy or unexpected goal were regarded by each of the two groups that were interviewed (coaches and players, respectively) as contributing to the collective collapse of a team. Effects which collective collapse had on the team that was afflicted, and which were mentioned frequently included those of irritation, insecurity, fear of losing, shouting at each other, and chaos. The collapsing team can be seen as being faced with an increasingly difficult and discouraging situation, at the same time as the opposing team is encouraged by the events taking place, a situation described earlier by Totterdell (2000).

One can suggest that a team,in order to minimize the negative influence on its play that the opposing team can have, should prepare itself tactically and mentally for those problematical actions by its opponents that are most foreseeable, and that it should train itself to react insofar as possible with positive rather than negative · emotions under such circumstances. Halden-Brown's (2003) advice is to express emotions that are genuinely appropriate to the situation, especially when the going gets tough. Negative emotions such as shouting at teammates or disputing the calls of the referee distract from what needs to be done. The task at hand in many difficult situations is to refocus on the match, take position on the court and play in accordance with the tactics. Since negative emotions are usually not constructive, they should be avoided in a practical situation, both at an individual and at a group level. Remaining "cool" in the sense of not giving up, even when faced with a highly threatening situation, can be seen as the mark of a great athlete or a great athletic team.

The failure of players to perform the roles expected of them when collective collapse occurs could be noted in Study 2 in the underperformance of the key players in particular, together with the inability of the team captain to encourage his teammates, and the failure of the coach to provide clear instructions. In Study 1, each of the coaches who were interviewed emphasized the importance of roles. The failure of players, under conditions of impending collapse, to do what is expected of them may be due to a lack of clarity of roles (players not understanding what behavior is expected of them, or the instructions provided them by the coach being too diffuse), to role conflicts (players lacking either the ability or the motivation needed), and/or to lack of role efficacy (players being insecure regarding their capacity to perform the role assigned them). Reasonable measures that could be taken to counteract such difficulties include the development of alternative role systems that can be employed in case of the underperformance of various players, such as players who are momentarily performing under par or who are temporarily restricted in the tasks they are to perform (such as marked players), the appointing of a team captain who is highly expressive emotionally andis particularly adept in influencing his teammates in a positive way (Hatfield, Cacioppo, & Rapson, 1994), and the adopting of a communication pattern that facilitates the achievement of mutual understanding.

The maintaining of adequate communication between team members on the court can be seen as particularly important and to be very much lacking in situations characterized by a high level of stress, by negative thinking, and by organizational disorder. In a situation such as that described above, in which the team is faced with a genuine crisis, constructive communication can readily decrease, communication both verbal and in terms of body language becoming negative in character. Despite its obvious importance, communication within sport teams during matches is an under-researched area within sport psychology (LaVoi, 2007; Sullivan & Feltz, 2003). It is important that someone present on the court assumes a leadership role for the team, helping the other players focus on the job at hand. It is also important that negative emotions and negative communication be avoided. The contagious effect of negative emotions readily results in negative communication, which can have a detrimental effect not only on those who are playing, but also on players on the bench. According to Barsade (2002), emotional contagion is largely an unconscious phenomenon. This suggests that an initial step to take to avoid it would be to make players aware of the phenomenon. The next step could be to endeavor to find ways of helping players, both those on the court and those on the bench, avoid negative emotions and avoid being affected by negative emotional contagion. A rational communication pattern needs to be established. LaVoi (2007) notes that certain interventions targeting communication have been successful and suggests the implementation of programs of this sort in order to improvecommunication patterns between the players on a team.

The non-constructive behavior that characterizes collective collapse is obviously preceded by cognitions and negative affects that stem from these. Taylor and Demick's (1994) model for explaining positive or negative momentum, is regarded as a highly useful model in this area (Mack & Stephens, 2000).However, it does not predict what the direction of causal relationships is between cognitions, affects, and physiological changes. One can assume, on the basis of the present findings, there to be differences between how cognition, emotion and behavior are related to each other. As suggested in figure 2, it can be assumed that, prior to a match, two possible causal chains that both are of problematical character exist, one of them of the sort negative thoughts leading to negative emotions, this resulting in a passive playing style, and the other of the sort positive thoughts leading to overconfidence, this resulting in mistakes and being followed by negative communication.

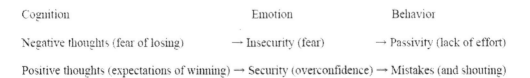

Cognition	Emotion	Behavior
Negative thoughts (fear of losing)	→ Insecurity (fear)	→ Passivity (lack of effort)
Positive thoughts (expectations of winning)	→ Security (overconfidence)	→ Mistakes (and shouting)

Figure 2. The tentative relation between cognition, emotion, and behavior in collective collapse before the start of a match.

In contrast, as suggested in Figure 3, by the end of the match, various critical events can have occurred, such as mistakes by individual players or goals scored by the opponents, that lead to negative emotional reactions followed by negative thoughts and result either in passivity and thus lack of effort, or further mistakes, followed by negative communications. Physiological changes can be the result of thoughts, of emotions or of actions that are carried out. Whether it is thoughts or emotions that appear first is more of academic than of practical interest. They appear to occur within close temporal proximity and can be assumed to influence each other.

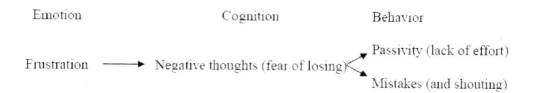

Figure 3. The tentative relation between cognition, emotion, and behavior in collective collapse after critical moments during a match.

The discrepancy between the results of the inter-rater agreement between Study 1 and Study 2 was mainly found in factor two, the interpretation of cognitions, emotions and behavior. The responses of the coaches were straight-forward, and typically mentioned only one of these factors and were thus easier to classify. In contrast, the responses of the players were characterized by a blend of cognitions, emotions and behavior and were more difficult to categorize. One examiner classified according to the factor that was first mentioned, whereas the other examiner classified according to the dominant factor in the response.

In conclusion, the major causes of a collective collapse are to be found partly in factors within the collapsing team. Such factors include those of inappropriate behavior, failure of the role system to function as it should, and negative communication. The causes are also to be found in the actions of the opposing team. These include their changing their tactics and their scoring of goals. Such external influences as false calls by the referee appear to be negligible in their effect. Collective collapse is characterized by a loss of control, accompanied by negative thoughts and negative emotions, all of which have a detrimental affect on performance. The expression of negative emotions is also contagious, affecting the other players on the court and those on the bench.

LIMITATIONS OF THE INVESTIGATION

In Study 1 only four coaches were involved. Although they came from different parts of Sweden and represented three different team sports, their responses can scarcely be regarded as representative of coaches who have experienced a collective collapse generally. The differences between the three team sports that are represented here in the playing conditions involved constitute a further limitation. In soccer, for example, neither the calling of time-outs nor the substituting of players back and forth is allowed, as they are in handball and in ice hockey. The actions of the coach are thus limited by the rules of the game involved. In Study 2, the team selected constituted a convenience sample, the responses to collective collapse found to have occurred only reflecting with certainty the reactions to it of that particular handball team on the occasion in question. All the data in that study are also retrospective and may be subject to response bias. This is evidenced by the inability of some of the participants to recall what happened during the time-out that was taken. These various factors represent clear limitations of the two studies.

FUTURE STUDIES

In order that more adequate knowledge of collective collapse can be obtained, it is important that the occurrence and the perceptions of collective collapse be studied in a wide variety of different team sports and that intervention projects be carried out examining ways of counteracting or averting collective collapse and reducing its effects. Gender differences in this area are also very much in need of investigation. It can also be asked what men can possibly learn from women and women from men in this respect.

ACKNOWLEDGMENTS

This study was supported by the Swedish Sport Research Council.

REFERENCES

Apitzsch, E. (2006). Collective collapse in team sports: A theoretical approach. In F. Boen, B. De Cuyper, & J. Opdenacker (Eds.). *Current research topics in exercise and sport psychology in Europe*(pp. 35-46).Leuven: LannooCampus Publishers.

Barsade, S.G. (2002). The ripple effect: Emotional contagion and its influence on group behavior. *Administrative Science Quarterly, 47*, 644-675.

Baumeister, R.F. (1984). Choking under pressure; Self-consciousness andparadoxical effects of incentives on skillful performance. *Journal ofPersonality and Social Psychology, 46*, 610-620.

Beauchamp, M.R., Bray, S.R., Eys, M.A., & Carron, A.V. (2002). Role ambiguity, role efficacy, and the role performance: multidimensional and mediational relationships within interdependent sport teams. *Group Dynamics; Theory, Research and Practice, 6*, 229-242.

Bion, W. R. (1961). *Experiences in groups*. London: Tavistock/Routledge.

Cacioppo, J.T., & Gardner, W.L. (1999). Emotion. *Annual Review of Psychology, 50*, 191-214.

Carlstedt, R.A. (2004). *Critical moments during competition. A mind-body model of sport performance when it counts the most*. New York: Psychological Press.

Carron, A.V., Hausenblas, H.A., & Eys, M.A. (2005). *Group dynamics in sport (third edition)*. Morgantown: Fitness Information Technology.

Cornelius, A., Silva, J.M., Conroy, D.E., & Peterson, G. (1997). The projected performance model: Relating cognitive and performance antecedents of psychological momentum. *Perceptual and Motor Skills, 84*, 475-485.

Côté,J., Salmela, J.H., Baria, A., & Russell, S.J. (1993). Organizing and interpreting unstructured qualitative data. *The Sport Psychologist, 7*, 127-137.

Coward, S. (2006). Choking under pressure: The effects of auditory subliminal psychodynamic activation on male competitive performance. Unpublished doctoral dissertation, University of Western Sydney.

Eisler, L., & Spink, K.S. (1998). Effects of scoring configuration and task cohesion on the perception of psychological momentum. *Journal of Sport & Exercise Psychology, 20*, 311-320.

Goldberg, A.S. (1998). *Sports slump busting. 10 steps to mental toughness and peak performance.* Champaign, IL: Human Kinetics.

Hagger, M., & Chatzisarantis, N. (2005). *The social psychology of exercise and sport.* Glasgow: Open University Press.

Halden-Brown, S. (2003). *Mistakes worth making. How to turn sports errors into athletic excellence.* Champaign, IL: Human Kinetics.

Hatfield, E., Cacioppo, J., & Rapson, R.L. (1994). *Emotional contagion.* New York: Cambridge University Press.

Heath, C., & Jourden, F.J. (1997). Illusion, disillusion, and the buffering effect of groups. *Organizational Behavior and Human Decision Processes*, 69, 103-116.

Janis, I.L. (1982). *Victims of Group Think.* Boston: Houghton Mifflin.

Kelly, J.R., & Barsade, S.G, (2001). Moods and emotions in small groups and work teams. *Organizational Behavior and Human Decision Processes, 86,* 99-130.

Kroll, W. (1982). Competitive athletic stress factors in athletes and coaches. In L.P. Zaichkowski & W.E. Sime (Eds.). *Stress management for sport* (pp 1-10).Reston, VA: American Alliance for Health, Physical Education, Recreation and Dance.

LaVoi, N.M. (2007). Interpersonal communication and conflict in the coach-athlete relationship. In S. Jowett & D. Lavallee (Eds.) *Social psychology in sport* (pp. 29-40). Champaign, IL: Human Kinetics.

Mack, M.G., & Stephens, D.E. (2000). An empirical test of Taylor and Demick's multidimensional model of momentum in sport. *Journal of Sport Behavior, 23,* 349-363.

Sullivan, P., & Feltz, D.L. (2003). The preliminary development of the scale for effective communication in team sports (SECTS). *Journal of Applied Social Psychology, 33,* 1693-1715.

Taylor, A.J., & Demick, A. (1994). A multidimensional model of momentum in sports. *Journal of Applied Sport Psychology, 6,* 51-60.

Tickle-Degnan, L., & Puccinelli, N.M. (1999). The nonverbal expression of negative emotions: Peer and supervisor responses to occupational therapy students' emotional attributes. *The Occupational Therapy Journal of Research, 19,* 18-39.

Totterdell, P. (2000). Catching moods and hitting runs: Mood linkage and subjective performance in professional sport teams. *Journal of Applied Psychology*, 85, 848-859.

Vallerand, R.J., Colavecchio, P.G., & Pelletier, L.G. (1988). Psychological momentum and performance: A preliminary test of the antecedents-consequences psychological momentum model. *Journal of Sport and Exercise Psychology, 10,* 92-108.

In: Introduction to Sport Psychology
Editor: Robert Schinke

ISBN: 978-1-61761-973-1
© 2011 Nova Science Publishers, Inc.

Establishing a Hierarchy of Psychological Skills: Coaches', Athletic Trainers', and Psychologists' Uses and Perceptions of Psychological Skills Training

Samuel J. Zizzi[1], Lindsey C. Blom[2],
Jack C. Watson II[1], V. Paul Downey[1] and John Geer[3]
[1]West Virginia University, Morgantown, WV., U.S.A.
[2]Ball State University, Muncie, Indiana, U.S.A.
[3]University of North Carolina, Greensboro, U.S.A.

Abstract

As applied sport psychology continues to grow, a variety of professionals may attempt to teach athletes mental skills; however, there is little research to suggest which skills professionals may be qualified to use with their clients. This research examined sport professionals' use of psychological skills training (PST) and their previous training, self-efficacy, and perceptions of each skill. After a national survey, the final sample included 54 athletic trainers, 64 coaches, and 50 licensed psychologists ($n = 168$). Psychologists reported using hypnosis and self-talk more frequently than ATCs and coaches, while coaches reported using team building and time management most often. Participants perceived hypnosis, energy management, imagery, and cognitive restructuring to require the most training out of the nine skills. These results are discussed within the context of developing a hierarchy of psychological skill used to guide professionals in their future work.

Introduction

Competitive athletes and coaches are continuously looking for methods to enhance their training and performance. Advanced training methods are beginning to include applied areas of sport science, such as exercise physiology and biomechanics, to help athletes achieve an ideal volume and intensity of training (Balague, 2000). Optimal performance also requires the proper application of psychological skills, but these skills have not been systematically adopted and integrated into practice settings like other sport science training methods. Coaches and athletes typically only turn to learning and practicing psychological skills when there is a crisis or a specific problem, even though a preventative approach is considerably more effective (Weinberg & Gould, 1999). By establishing a psychological skills training (PST) program early, it may be possible for athletes to reach their potential more quickly by learning how to perform consistently through increased behavioral control (Balague, 2000).

Various professionals have attempted to define and categorize psychological skills in their own ways, with a common emphasis on the importance of utilizing them regularly. O'Donohoe and Krasner (1995) explain psychological skills training by breaking down the different terms. *Skills* are defined as the "ability to perform in a certain manner" (p. 3) not whether the individual actually performs in relevant situations. *Performance* involves the actual display of a behavior by an individual. *Competency* refers to the "effects of the performance of skills on the individual's environment" (p.3). In time, and with successful performances, competence with psychological skills will develop.

Psychological Skills and Sport Performance

Athletes have been shown to perform best when their psychological skills are developed to a point where consistent performance is displayed across a variety of competitive situations. Mahoney, Gabriel, and Perkins (1987) assessed psychological skills relevant to exceptional athletic performance and found the topics of concentration, anxiety management, self-confidence, mental preparation, and motivation having potential importance in skill-level differentiation. Gould and Dieffenbach (2002) examined the psychological characteristics of 10 United States Olympic champions and how they developed these characteristics. Triangulated results from interviews and psychological assessments indicated that these outstanding performers had strong psychological skills. These Olympians scored high in confidence, goal setting, mental preparation, concentration, readiness for competition, relaxation, emotional control, freedom from worry, and attentional focus. Greenleaf, Gould, and Dieffenbach (2001) discussed Olympians' perceptions of major positive and negative factors affecting performance. They reported that negative influencing factors included departing from normal routine, distractions, overtraining, injury, and team issues, while positive factors included mental skills and preparation, support services, multifaceted preparation, and coaching.

Psychological skill training programs have been shown to positively affect performance across various sports and levels of competition. For example psychological skills training programs have been shown to be effective for improving elite athletes' performances in golf putting (Cohen, Tenenbaum, & English, 2006; Thomas & Fogarty, 1997), tennis (Mamassis & Doganis, 2004), lacrosse (Brewer & Shillinglaw, 1992), cycling (Kress, Schroeder, Potteiger, & Haub, 1999), football (Holm, Beckwith, Ehde, & Tinius, 1996), swimming (Holm et al., 1996; Sheard & Golby, 2006), basketball shooting (Pates, Maynard, & Westbury, 2001; Meyers, Schleser, & Okwumabua, 1982), running (Patrick & Hrycaiko, 1998), equestrian (Blakeslee & Goff, 2007), karate (Seabourne, Weinberg, Jackson, & Suinn, 1985), scuba diving (Terry & Mayer, 1998), and triathlon performance (Thelwell & Greenlees, 2001). Overall, PST programs have evidence of effectiveness across a variety of sport settings for highly-skilled athletes. Elite athletes have also been shown to use psychological skills and strategies in practice and training sessions, not just competition (Taylor, Gould, & Rolo, 2008). However, the benefits of using PST can extend to non-elite populations. As an example, a study by Terry and Mayer (1998) provides evidence that novice divers may benefit from learning skills that can help reduce anxiety, improve attentional control, and increase self-affirmations as part of their pre-dive instruction. In a different study, researchers taught novice golfers psychological skills and found the skills helped improve performance compared to control groups (Beauchamp, Wayne, Fournier, & Koestner, 1996).

Examining patterns of use among elite-level consultants provides some insight into the frequency with which specific skills are taught. Gould, Tammen, Murphy, and May (1989) surveyed 44 sport psychology consultants who had worked with more than 25 U.S. Olympic sports during the 1984 and 1988 Olympics. Through group seminars, professionals used arousal regulation skills most frequently with imagery, relaxation training, motivation, goal setting, and concentration close behind. Individual consultations revealed similar results with imagery-visualization and arousal regulation as the first and second most commonly practiced skills, and relaxation, goal setting, concentration also frequently taught. Kirschenbaum, Parham, and Murphy (1993) assessed types of services provided to athletes at the 1991 Olympic Festival and reported that consultations primarily pertained to reducing pre-performance anxiety, improving concentration skills, setting goals, and working on mental plans for competition. Sullivan and Nashman (1998) examined interventions utilized by Olympic sport psychologists who had a history of working with Olympians anywhere from the 1960 to 1994 games. Interventions used by at least 80% of the sport psychologists included breathing techniques, focusing, behavior modification, cognitive restructuring, positive self-talk, imagery, goal setting, and arousal regulation.

Ethical Issues with Psychological Skills Training

With an increase in research and applied interest in PST (Weinberg & Gould, 1999), professionals have begun to debate the training requirements for individuals teaching psychological skills to athletes. The discussion often stalemates when examining specific skills (e.g. goal setting, hypnosis, relaxation) and who is qualified to teach them to whom, particularly since there are currently no guidelines for practice. Furthermore, individuals and sporting organizations who want to hire consultants to conduct psychological skills training with their athletes often have difficulty determining the competency of available consultants. The United States Olympic Committee (USOC) emphasizes the importance of having objective measures for assessing the qualifications of individuals at least on a minimal competence basis (Gross, 1993). As a positive step forward, the USOC established the Sport Psychology Registry and The Association of Applied Sport Psychology (AASP) certification for consultants continues to grow (Zizzi, Zaichkowsky, & Perna, 2002). In regards to other sport professionals, The Commission on Accreditation of Athletic Training Education (CAATE) requires certified athletic trainers (ATCs) to be educated on the psychological aspects of injury and the use of psychological skills within that setting, while The Commission on Accreditation in Physical Therapy Education (CAPTE) does not specify psychology course work for physical therapists (PTs; Hamson-Utley, Martin, & Walters, 2008).

The establishment of sport psychology-specific consultant credentials by the USOC and AASP have been steps forward in defining competence for PST, but neither organization provides specific boundaries of practice in this area aside from using the American

Psychological Association's (APA) ethical principles as guidance (APA, 2002). The Canadian Society of Psychomotor Learning and Sport Psychology (CSPLSP) points out that competence is hard to ensure even with specific certifications or titles as those providing sport psychology services may come from diverse backgrounds (Gross, 1993). Furthermore, the accrediting bodies for coaching education, athletic training education, and physical therapy are vague in their description of training requirements regarding psychological skills (National Association for Sport and Physical Education, 2006). These organizations may identify the skills that should be learned (i.e. relaxation, visualization, and desensitization techniques; National Athletic Trainers Association [NATA], 2006) without requiring trained professionals to teach the skills, or an organization may not require any training in psychological skills (CAPTE, 2006). Some argue that only licensed psychology professionals (e.g., counselors, psychologists) can help, but as Danish and Hale (1981) pointed out, there are not nearly enough to help all athletes and teams. This requirement would also eliminate coaches and athletic trainers from providing services (Danish & Hale, 1981), and they are the professionals who are most frequently involved with athletes.

For example, can Certified Consultants (CCs) from AASP conduct the same interventions with athletes as licensed psychologists (LPs) even though many CCs are not licensed? Can certified athletic trainers ethically teach injured athletes relaxation training and healing imagery even though they have not had formal training? Are coaches qualified to mentally train their athletes by using cognitive restructuring and focusing techniques? While these questions may be currently unanswered, understanding current usage patterns and perceptions of competence across the broad range of psychological skills may begin to provide direction.

Coaches, ATCs, and other professionals who work with athletes are asked to assist athletes in performing to the best of their ability, and with this job description, they may attempt to teach psychological skills. Without proper training in teaching these skills, these attempts may lead to negative experiences or conclusions that PST does not work. Either of these adverse outcomes may produce frustration with sport psychology and decrease intentions to use performance enhancement services in the future. Potential problems for untrained professionals teaching psychological skills include missing or ignoring important information about an athlete's experience, lacking the range of intervention skills necessary for the athlete's concern, not adjusting for individuality and using a "canned" approach, lacking the ability to communicate how to use skills, and lacking the knowledge about how and when to appropriately use skills (Danish, Petitpas, & Hale, 1993). The outcomes of poorly conducted PST programs can include lack of improvement, frustration, and negative stigmatization of sport psychology interventions.

Another training concern is that given the small number of certified or registered sport psychology consultants (Zizzi et al., 2002) and the growing demand for PST (Weinberg & Gould, 1999), it may be unrealistic to assume that "qualified sport psychology professionals" can provide all the necessary services (Danish & Hale, 1981). With a clarification of the boundaries of practice, other professionals such as coaches and athletic trainers could be involved in teaching psychological skills in limited capacities. Psychological skills training can be used effectively with athletes of all ages and skill levels, but many high school and community programs do not have access to or the finances to fund comprehensive services from a sport psychology consultant. Educating and involving other sport-related professionals in the PST process may help alleviate this problem and grow public awareness of the benefits of applied sport psychology. There is research suggesting athletes have reported coaches often help them with psychological skills (Gould & Dieffenbach, 2002); however there is no research evaluating the effectiveness of coaches' efforts. Weinberg and Gould (1999) recommend a model where sport psychology professionals would provide advanced training to coaches, with the goal of increasing coaches' teaching competence. More research is needed in assessing whether instructional techniques may be designed so that positive results can be obtained by non-sport psychology professionals.

The purpose of this study was threefold. First, we examined sport professionals' use of psychological skills (e.g., teaching of skills to others) as well as their levels of previous training and self-efficacy for teaching these skills. We hypothesized that licensed psychologists (LPs) would report the highest scores in each of these three areas with coaches and certified athletic trainers (ATCs) reporting lower but similar scores. The second purpose was to examine perceptions of what skills specific professions are qualified to teach. It was hypothesized that LPs would be rated highest overall (averaging across all skills), followed by performance enhancement consultants (PECs) and then the group of non-psychology professionals (i.e., ATCs, physical therapists (PTs), and coaches). Additionally, it was hypothesized that the professionals (i.e., ATCs, coaches, and LPs) surveyed would rate their own professions as more qualified than others would rate them objectively. Finally, the third research question explored boundaries of practice as perceptions of the amount of training needed to teach each psychological skill were assessed. Specific hypotheses were not generated for the order of psychological skills aside from an expectation that hypnosis would be rated as needing the most training by all groups.

METHODS

The survey research project received Institutional Review Board approval and consent was obtained prior to survey administration. Internal grant funds from the School of Physical Education provided partial support for the project.

Survey Development

During the initial phase of item development for the survey, an extensive literature search was conducted to identify the most common terms used under the umbrella of psychological skills training. This literature review involved consulting commonly used sport psychology texts (VanRaalte & Brewer, 2002; Weinberg & Gould, 1999; Williams, 2001) and included using the terms "mental skills training" and "psychological skills training" in search engines such as PsycInfo and SportDiscus. Based on this search process, the following nine skills were included in the survey instrument: attention/concentration, communication, energy management, goal setting, hypnosis, imagery/visualization, self-talk, team building, and time management. A handout with brief definitions was included in the survey packet to avoid misinterpretation of terminology (see Appendix A). Brief job descriptions of the professions were also provided to familiarize participants with the professional titles.

Measures

Experiences with PST

Established survey design protocols were followed during initial item development (e.g., Dillman, 2000; Fink & Kosecoff, 1998; Fowler, 1993). The first section of the survey included items on personal experiences with PST such as frequency of use, previous training, self-efficacy, and perceptions of effectiveness for each of the nine selected psychological skills. To prompt them to review the definition sheet, a warm-up question started the survey asking participants to rate their familiarity with the psychological skills listed on the sheet. The next four questions asked participants to rate their current use, previous training, self-efficacy, and perceptions of effectiveness (in improving athletic performance) for each of the nine skills. The following specific questions and seven-point scales were used to collect this data, with each question followed by a list of the nine psychological skills:

- *Frequency of use.* How often do you use and demonstrate each of the following skills to your athletes? "Never" (1) to "Always" (7)
- *Previous training.* To what extent did your training prepare you with knowledge of each of the following skills? "Not at all" (1) to "A great deal" (7)
- *Self-efficacy.* How confident are you that you could effectively use and demonstrate each of the following skills? "Not at all confident" (1) to "Very confident" (7)
- *Effectiveness.* How effective do you think the following interventions are for improving an athlete's performance? "Not at all effective" (1) to "Very effective" (7)

Qualifications to Teach Psychological Skills

The second section of the survey assessed participant perceptions of qualifications of various professionals in their ability to teach psychological skills. Individual items included asking participants to rate the perceived qualifications of ATCs, PTs, coaches, PECs, and LPs to teach each of the nine skills on a seven-point scale from "Not at all qualified" (1) to "Very qualified" (7). A sample question from this section read "How qualified do you perceive certified athletic trainers to be able to demonstrate each of the following skills?" Other questions were worded identically with the professional title changed in each case.

Perceived Training Requirements and Demographics

The final section of the survey assessed perceived training requirements for each specific skill. This question asked "How much training do you feel is required for a person to effectively use and demonstrate each of the following skills?" with each skill rated from "Little or no training" (1) to "Extensive training" (7). Following this question, items were included measuring demographic variables, work-related experience, and previous exposure to sport psychology. The initial draft of the survey included 25 items.

Pilot Testing

Extensive pilot testing of the survey was conducted prior to the study, as suggested by Fink and Kosecoff (1998). First, a small group of experts ($n = 3$) in sport psychology provided qualitative feedback on the content and structure of the survey. Second, a group of master's degree-seeking coaches and athletic trainers ($n = 33$) participated in pilot testing the survey instrument to provide feedback on the clarity, completeness, and ease of responding to all items. This pilot procedure resulted in a refined format, including the omission of four items and changes to the structure of several questions to improve ease of completion. Pilot testing also revealed that the survey took approximately 10-15 minutes to complete. After adjustments from pilot testing, the final version of the survey included 21 items.

Sampling

The present study used a stratified-randomized sampling design to generate lists of mailing addresses for 300 ATCs, 300 coaches, and 300 LPs. A randomly generated list of mailing labels for ATCs in clinical settings was obtained from the National Athletic Training Association (NATA). Similar mailing lists for coaches and LPs were obtained from the National Collegiate Athletic Association (NCAA) and the American Psychological Association (APA) respectively. Psychologists were randomly selected from Divisions 17 (Counseling Psychology) and 47 (Sport and Exercise Psychology). As a provision for obtaining these labels, though, none of the three sources allowed follow-up labels to be generated, which is a common strategy for increasing response rate (Dillman, 2000). As a small incentive to complete the survey, free access to a website dedicated to applied sport psychology was provided for a period of three months. This temporary webpage, which was housed within a university department website, provided information describing each of the psychological skills and links to news articles featuring examples of athletes or coaches using sport psychology. The sampling methods resulted in the following response rates per group: 18% for athletic trainers (n = 54); 21.3% for coaches (n = 64); and 17% for psychologists (n = 50).

RESULTS

The final sample included 54 certified athletic trainers, 64 college coaches, and 50 licensed psychologists ($n = 168$). The sample was 60% male (range = 59.2-63.5%) with an average age of 42 years ($SD = 10.75$). Athletic trainers were the youngest group on average ($M = 34.6$), followed by coaches ($M = 40.42$), then psychologists ($M = 52.4$). Average years of work experience for the overall sample was 14.74 years ($SD = 8.33$), including sub-group scores of 9.5 years of experience for ATCs, 15.3 years for coaches, and 19.6 years for psychologists. Thirty-seven and fifty-eight percent of ATCs and coaches respectively held a master's degree, while 100% of the psychologists held a doctoral degree. On a seven point scale with anchors of "no training" and "considerable training," previous training in sport psychology averaged 3.07 ($SD = 1.6$) with psychologists reporting the lowest average scores ($M = 2.67$), followed by coaches ($M = 3.17$), then ATCs ($M = 3.3$). Means and standard deviations for previous training, frequency of use, and self-efficacy for individual psychological skills are listed in table 1.

Table 1. Previous training, frequency of use, and self-efficacy for psychological skills across professions

	Athletic Trainers (n = 54)		Coaches (n = 64)		Psychologists (n = 50)		
	Mean	SD	Mean	SD	Mean	SD	Effect Size
Attention / Concentration							
Previous training	3.79	1.39	4.03	1.62	4.06	2.00	NS
Frequency of use	4.15	1.57	4.64	1.77	4.66	1.56	NS
Self-efficacy for use	4.70	1.51	5.00	1.46	5.95	1.48	.11
Communication Skills							
Previous training 1	5.40	1.31	5.67	1.30	5.60	1.30	NS
Frequency of use	5.68	1.36	5.95	1.09	5.77	1.52	NS
Self-efficacy for use	5.67	1.05	5.89	1.14	6.70	.63	.16
Energy Management							
Previous training	3.23	1.58	3.52	1.76	3.43	1.99	NS
Frequency of use	3.06	1.49	3.48	1.64	4.00	1.94	.05
Self-efficacy for use	4.28	1.32	4.17	1.74	4.98	1.77	.04
Goal Setting							
Previous training	5.31	1.43	5.88	1.16	5.34	1.26	.04
Frequency of use	5.74	1.25	6.31	.92	5.40	1.33	.10
Self-efficacy for use	5.98	1.11	6.32	.84	6.48	.76	.05
Hypnosis							
Previous training	1.26	.76	1.55	1.34	2.72	2.27	.14
Frequency of use	1.03	.19	1.15	.57	2.47	1.74	.28
Self-efficacy for use	1.31	1.04	1.44	1.00	3.48	2.38	.28
Imagery / Visualization							
Previous training	3.67	1.60	4.14	1.84	4.85	1.76	.07
Frequency of use	3.89	1.80	4.52	1.53	4.53	1.55	NS
Self-efficacy for use	4.50	1.42	4.64	1.72	6.02	1.28	.16
Self-talk (modification of)							
Previous training	3.38	1.53	4.05	1.64	5.49	1.47	.23
Frequency of use	3.42	1.68	4.34	1.55	5.72	1.33	.20
Self-efficacy for use	4.04	1.58	4.86	1.61	6.61	.69	.35
TeamBuilding							
Previous training	4.30	1.64	5.07	1.47	2.98	1.76	.22
Frequency of use	4.17	2.04	5.80	1.21	2.94	1.57	.35
Self-efficacy for use	4.80	1.62	6.00	1.06	4.70	1.85	.14
Time Management							
Previous training	4.92	1.58	5.48	1.25	3.74	1.63	.19
Frequency of use	4.77	1.55	5.55	1.28	4.38	1.45	.11
Self-efficacy for use	5.39	1.09	5.89	1.21	6.05	1.03	.06

[a] Univariate effect size (Eta-squared; interpreted as percentage of variance explained).

Frequency of Use, Previous Training, and Self-Efficacy for Psychological Skills

To assess differences across the three professions in their frequency of use, previous training, and self-efficacy for the various psychological skills, three one-way multivariate analyses of variance (MANOVA) were conducted. Each of these MANOVAs used profession as the independent variable (three levels: ATC, Coach, Psychologist) and the nine skills as the multiple dependent variables. Preliminary checks of the assumptions of multivariate and univariate normality were conducted prior to analyses. In cases where assumptions were violated, adjusted F and degree of freedom values are reported. Significant multivariate main effects were followed up with univariate analysis of variance (ANOVA) and Tukey post-hoc testing where appropriate. In the within-subjects models (i.e., repeated measures ANOVAs), appropriate contrast analyses were used to determine pairwise differences. All effect size estimates for MANOVA and ANOVA designs are reported as eta-squared (η^2)which can be interpreted as the proportion of variance in the outcome variable due to the independent factor (George & Mallory, 2001). Eta-squared estimates of less than .09 are considered small, .10-.25 are moderate, and estimates greater than .25 are considered large.

With respect to differences in frequency of use across the three professional groups, the multivariate main effect was significant, Wilk's lambda = .347, $F(18, 306) = 10.30$, $p < .001$, $\eta^2 = .41$. Univariate follow-up analyses revealed that LPs reported using hypnosis ($\eta^2 = .28$) and self-talk ($\eta^2 = .26$) more frequently than ATCs and coaches, while coaches reported using team building ($\eta^2 = .35$) and time management ($\eta^2 = .11$) more often than the other professionals.

A large multivariate effect for previous training was also found, Wilk's lambda = .392, $F(18, 306) = 10.14$, $p < .001$, $\eta^2 = .37$. With respect to univariate results, LPsreported significantly more previous training on the skills of self-talk ($\eta^2 = .23$), imagery ($\eta^2 = .07$), and hypnosis ($\eta^2 = .14$) compared to the other two groups. Coaches reported significantly more previous training related to team building ($\eta^2 = .22$) and time management ($\eta^2 = .19$) when compared to ATCs and LPs (see Table 1).

For the third model using self-efficacy scores as the dependent variables, multivariate analyses suggested that LPs had the highest self-efficacy scores overall (5.66), followed by coaches (4.91) then ATCs (4.52); Wilk's lambda = .375, $F(18, 300) = 10.55$, $p < .001$, $\eta^2 = .39$. Univariate analyses revealed that coaches were more efficacious than LPsand ATCs in using team building ($\eta^2 = .14$). Psychologists reported higher self-efficacy values on attention and concentration ($\eta^2 = .11$), imagery ($\eta^2 = .16$), self-talk ($\eta^2 = .35$), communication skills ($\eta^2 = .16$), and hypnosis ($\eta^2 = .28$) than coaches and ATCs (see table 1).

Perceived Qualifications to Practice

In the second section of the survey, participants rated the perceived competence of ATCs, PTs, coaches, LPs, and PECs to use and demonstrate (i.e., teach) psychological skills with their clients. To help answer the research question "how are the five professional groups ranked in their perceived qualifications to teach psychological skills," scores across the nine psychological skills were averaged to create a mean qualification score for each professional category. This research question did not target perceived competence to use one particular skill but rather the overall set of skills. A 3x5 repeated measures ANOVA (profession x professional category) using average qualification scores revealed two significant main effects (eta-square values of .54 and .09 respectively) and a significant interaction ($\eta^2 = .19$). Post-hoc testing was subsequently used to create a ranked hierarchy of perceived professional competence across the five listed categories, while the interaction effect provided information on where self-perceptions of competence (e.g., coaches rating coaches' competence) differed from external ratings of competence (e.g., ATC/LP ratings of coaches' competence). Overall, post-hoc testing suggested a three-tiered pattern among the five professional groups where ATCs and PTs were perceived as least qualified, coaches as moderately qualified, and PECs and LPs as most highly qualified (see table 2). Notably, there were no significant differences found in the perceived qualifications between ATCs and PTs or between PECs and LPs. Additionally, when interpreting the interaction effect, as hypothesized, ATCs and coaches perceived themselves to be significantly more qualified than other respondents perceived them to be. However, LPs' self-perceptions of competence were not higher than the independent ratings of other respondents.

Table 2. Perceived average qualifications[a] for using PST across five professional categories

	ATCs (n = 54)		Coaches (n = 64)		Psychologists (n = 50)		Overall (n = 168)		Effect Size[b]
	Mean	SD	Mean	SD	Mean	SD	Mean	SD	
Athletic Trainer	4.62	1.00	3.09	1.31	3.60	1.20	3.74	1.36	.23
Physical Therapist	4.25	1.17	3.43	1.38	3.37	.96	3.71	1.28	N/A
Coach	4.48	.87	4.83	.89	3.75	.89	4.46	.97	.17
Licensed Psychologist	5.58	.83	5.52	1.02	5.61	.84	5.56	.91	.002
Performance Enhancement Consultant	5.56	.98	5.87	.91	5.03	1.27	5.57	1.07	N/A

[a] Perceived qualification was assessed using a seven point scale with anchors of "Not at all qualified" (1) to "Very qualified" (7)
[b] eta-squared estimates for differences between self and independent ratings of competence
N/A - since physical therapists and PECs were not a part of the sample, self-perceptions could not be compared to independent ratings.

Perceived Training Necessary to Use Specific Skills

To address the third research question related to which skills require the highest levels of training to teach, perceptions of training scores were analyzed using a 3 x 9 (profession x skill) repeated measures ANOVA. On average, skills were rated as needing between moderate and extensive levels of training ($M = 5.22$; $SD = .79$), with values ranging from a low of 4.77 (time management) to a high of 6.51 (hypnosis). Contrary to hypotheses, perceptions of training across professions did not differ, $F (2, 157) = .82, p > .05$, and the interaction effect was very small and not interpretable ($\eta^2 = .03$). However, a main effect for skill supported the hypothesis that professionals perceive that some skills do require relatively more or less training, $F (5.55, 871.4) = 50.6$, $p<.001$, $\eta^2 = .24$. Hypnosis was rated as needing the highest level of training, with the group of attention/concentration, goal setting, and time management rated as needing the lowest level of training out of the nine skills. Repeated measures post-hoc testing was used to establish the groupings displayed in table 3. The skill groupings within the hierarchy indicate reasonably different groups, as skills in each group were not statistically different from each other but were rated differently from skills in other groups.

Table 3. Hierarchy of training necessary to use various psychological skills (as rated by athletic trainers, coaches, and psychologists)

Skill	Mean [a]	SD
Hypnosis	6.51	1.19
Imagery and visualization	5.49	1.09
Modifying self-talk	5.27	1.17
Energy management	5.14	1.06
Communication skills	5.12	1.23
Team building	5.06	1.37
Attention / concentration	4.83	1.14
Goal setting	4.81	1.26
Time management	4.77	1.23

[a] Means on a scale with anchors of 1 (little or no training needed to use this skill) and 7 (extensive training needed to use this skill).

DISCUSSION

This project sought to add clarity to the literature base by describing the self-reported uses and perceptions of psychological skills of coaches, ATCs and LPs. We initially hypothesized that LPs would report the highest levels of previous training, current use, and self-efficacy of the three groups sampled; however this hypothesis was only partially supported. LPs did report higher previous training and use of self-talk, imagery, and hypnosis, but coaches reported higher previous training and use of team building and communication skills. The patterns of use reported by LPs in the present study were similar to those of elite level consultants in the Gould et al. (1989) and Sullivan and Nashman (1998) studies, suggesting commonalities may exist in the use of PST across athletic and clinical populations. One caveat, though, is that LPs did not commonly report using attentional focusing or energy management techniques suggesting they may not use these skills as frequently in their clinical work as some of the other skills. The coaching data on previous training and frequency of use supports the assertion by Ravizza (1988) that coaches may play a key role in teaching some psychological skills to their athletes, particularly those related to team processes that have been shown to impact performance (Carron, Spink, & Prapavessis, 1997).

The self-efficacy findings supported our hypotheses more closely in that LPs reported the highest self-efficacy on all skills with the exception of team building. When comparing self-efficacy scores within professions, ATCs were most confident with goal setting, while coaches were most confident in using team building and goal setting, and LPs reported the highest self-efficacy for communication skills and cognitive restructuring (self-talk). These efficacy perceptions corresponded directly with skills that were used most frequently by each group (see Table 1).

Psychologists may have been conservative when reporting their own previous training and competence given the emphasis placed on ethics in their professional training and licensure (APA, 2002). At the same time, ATCs and coaches may have over-reported competence in some areas with less of a focus on ethical practice. However, both of the accrediting bodies for athletic training education and coaching education do require minimal course work in psychology, with specific mention of psychological skills. Psychologists, however, consistently reported high self-efficacy values on skills where they also reported low to moderate training and frequency of use. Thus, the self-reported values may not be entirely accurate, and each professional group may be over-estimating their confidence in teaching psychological skills.

Perceived Qualifications to Teach Psychological Skills

In support of our hypotheses, coaches and ATCs rated their qualifications to teach psychological techniques significantly higher than they were rated by the other groups. Psychologists, however, rated themselves similarly to their objective ratings. This data may suggest that coaches and ATCs perceive themselves to have a potential role in the application of PST within their respective work environments while other professionals may fail to recognize this possibility. It may be that coaches and trainers feel they are qualified to use psychological skills because they have had informal experience "counseling" athletes or because they see this as an area where they could expand their professional skills. However, the data may simply reflect over-confidence on the part of ATCs and coaches in their ability to teach these skills to athletes. Research has already shown that both of these populations value the importance of psychological skills in performance and injury rehabilitation (Larson, Starkey, & Zaichkowsky, 1996; Partington & Orlick, 1987; Sullivan & Hodge, 1991; Thelwell, Weston, Greenless, & Hutchings, 2008). Coaches and ATCs may be open to taking part in PST programs conducted by other more qualified professionals, or they could continue teaching psychological skills without further training. ATCs with formal training in teaching psychological skills have been shown to be more confident in the effectiveness of the skills and express a more positive attitude regarding use of the skills than those without formal training (Thelwell et al., 2008).

The qualification data provided more interesting insight into the perceptions of coaches and ATCs in that both LPs and PECs were rated as equally qualified to apply PST programs. This result may demonstrate recognition by coaches and ATCs of the unique role of PECs or a higher degree of familiarity with sport psychology than expected. Conversely, this similarity in ratings could suggest that participants read the definition sheet included with the survey and were impacted by the descriptions. Additionally, this result may provide some evidence that sport psychology specific credentialing such as Certified Consultant status from AASP is worthwhile and recognized. Psychologists' perceptions of professional qualifications directly supported our hypothesis as they rated LPs and PECs first and second respectively with the group of non-psychology professionals rated equally lower. Those LPs who are unfamiliar with the sporting environment or the roles of coaches and ATCs may have disregarded the potential for these groups to be involved with PST due to ethical concerns over lack of competence to use psychological interventions. Finally, physical therapists and athletic trainers were rated similarly and the lowest of the five professional groups offered despite the fact that athletic trainers are likely to have significantly more experience with athletes. Thus, coaches and LPs may not have accurate understanding of differences in the training paths of these two professionals or they regard them as equally lacking in training in psychology.

Moving towards a Hierarchy of Training for Psychological Skills

There was very little deviation in the hierarchy of training for the psychological skills as rated by coaches, ATCs and LPs. This pattern may suggest that those ATCs and coaches that chose to respond were more familiar with sport psychology than the overall population, which could be an artifact of the lower than desired response rate. Despite this, those who did respond may have had a strong interest in sport psychology, thus leading their perceptions to be similar to those from psychology backgrounds. All skills were rated as needing more than a moderate level of training, which could suggest that participants felt a reasonable amount of training is needed to gain competence in each of the individual skills. Despite this finding, it is unclear why introductory skills such as time management and goal setting were rated above the scale's midpoint, even though they were the lowest rated of the nine skills listed. This lack of variability in ratings may suggest that some professionals had difficulty differentiating the training requirements across the skills.

Developing a hierarchy of psychological skills indicating what training level is required for each skill may clarify some of these issues and act as a first step towards establishing boundaries of practice. With an increased understanding of the professional issues related to the application of PST, many parties may benefit. Sport psychology professionals would be able to increase awareness of the use of psychological skills and train other sport-related professionals to properly administer PST programs. These benefits may also lead to increased employment opportunities in training and direct service within coaching and sports medicine environments. Increased training among coaches and ATCs may also serve to reduce the stigma of sport psychology services, which often prevents service use and referral (Maniar, Curry, Sommers-Flanagan, & Walsh, 2001). Coaches and athletes have been found to more favorably respond to psychological skills training programs when they have an understanding of psychological skills and have input in the development and management of the training program (Hardy & Parfitt, 1994). Ultimately, by training more professionals to properly teach psychological skills, a greater number of athletes could be reached with more effective programming to promote life skills and consistent performance.

A hierarchy of skills was established based on the empirical data generated from the survey (see Table 3). Four reasonably independent groups emerged with goal setting, time management, and attention/concentration in the first group (e.g., lowest level of training needed). This first group of skills would seem useful to both coaches and ATCs in their work with athletes, and have been shown to be the most frequently utilized skills by Olympic athletes during practice sessions (Taylor et al., 2008). Additionally, none of these skills currently require a credential to legally practice, so with proper guidance, ATCs and coaches may already be prepared to teach the first group of skills to athletes. In support, Cramer-Roh and Perna (2000) suggest that ATCs can be trained to effectively use systematic goal setting and pain management techniques, the latter of which could include the use of association and dissociation strategies. The only exception among these skills that may require additional training is the attention and concentration area. Some researchers have argued that these focusing skills are often misunderstood, and comprehensive training programs are necessary to achieve mastery (Nideffer, 1978).

The second group of skills, which our data showed that coaches frequently use, included team building and communication skills. These skills are common components of coaching education programs (Martens, 1987) and are considered critical to team success (Cox, 2002; Ebbeck & Gibson, 1998). Coaches seem the most appropriate audience for using these skills, and some coaches may have already received training in this area. ATCs, however, may rarely need to conduct team building interventions but many of their individual interactions with clients could be improved with increased communication skills.

The next group of skills included imagery, cognitive restructuring (self-talk), and energy management. In previous research, these skills were all reported by coaches and athletes as key components of sport psychology interventions (Gould et al., 1989; Kirschenbaum et al., 1993), but were the least frequently used by athletes in competitive situations (Tayler et al., 2008). Olympic athletes may not be using imagery and relaxation techniques frequently because the individuals who are working with them do not have the competency to teach these skills (Tayler et al., 2008). Furthermore, these findings were to a study of professional coaching in the United Kingdom that reported coaches used self-talk and imagery more often than relaxation and goal setting because of the perceived usefulness and familiarity of the skills (Thelwell et al., 2008).

Applied psychology graduate programs typically offer specialized training in cognitive restructuring, relaxation and imagery, thus most LPs and PECs would have this training. It is unlikely that many ATCs and coaches would have formal training in these areas, but some may seek out additional training to gain competence in these skills. Without additional educational degrees and proper training, it would not seem appropriate that ATCs or coaches use these skills with athletes due to the possibility of adverse reactions to poorly designed interventions (Cramer-Roh & Perna, 2000). As hypothesized, hypnosis was considered to require the most training of all the skills listed. This result suggests that hypnosis requires even more specialized training than imagery, cognitive restructuring, and energy management. In support, the American Society for Clinical Hypnosis (ASCH, 2003) offers voluntary certification programs in hypnosis for psychology professionals. ASCH certification is available only to those professionals who are already registered (Canada) or licensed (US) to practice psychology in their home province or state. Other organizations do offer training programs in hypnosis but many are not recognized by the American Psychological Association. Thus, ATCs and coaches would not have access, and many PECs without counseling degrees would not be appropriate audiences for this type of training either.

Limitations and Future Directions

Although the responding group sizes were reasonably equal and provided more than enough power for the statistical analyses, the overall response rate of 19% is considered lower than desired for this type of research and limits generalizability of the results. This limitation in response rate may have increased the bias due to voluntary participation in survey research as the respondents may have been more familiar with sport psychology than non-responders. Also, the wording of some items ("use and demonstrate with your clients") may have led to participants to think of their personal use instead of their ability to teach the skills to others. However, pilot testing did not result in any negative feedback on these items so initial wording was kept. Finally, the survey did not focus on the application of psychological skills to injury rehabilitation but instead took a general approach to "working with clients" across a variety of professional settings. This omission of specific scenarios or descriptions of how PST could be applied in injury rehabilitation may have made the survey less applicable or interpretable by ATCs in the sample.

In conclusion, many types of professionals may be "qualified" to teach psychological skillswith athletes given the proper training and circumstances. From the current study, it appears that ATCs, coaches, and LPs perceive hypnosis, energy management, imagery, and cognitive restructuring to require the most training out of these skills. The next step appears to be surveying sport psychology professionals on the same issues and comparing their hierarchy of skills to those of coaches, ATCs, and LPs. This continued line of research is warranted to establish firm standards of practice and help accrediting bodies determine what psychological skills are appropriate for their group of sport professionals. Furthermore, it is hopeful that the current data provide a step in the right direction in clarifying issues of competence with PST, while helping spread the positive effects of sport psychology techniques to a wider audience.

REFERENCES

American Psychological Association. (2002, December). Ethical principles of psychologists and code of conduct. *American Psychologist, 57(12),* 1060-1073.

American Society for Clinical Hypnosis. (2003). Certification in clinical hypnosis (online). Retrieved July 30, 2003 at http://www.asch.net/certification.htm.

Balague, G. (2000). Periodization of psychological skills training. *Journal of Science and Medicine in Sport, 3*(3), 230-237.

Beauchamp, P.H., Wayne, R.H., Fournier, J.F., & Koestner, R. (1996). Effects of cognitive-behavioral psychological skills training on the motivation, preparation, and putting performance of novice golfers. *The Sport Psychologist, 10,* 157-170.

Blakeslee, M.L. & Goff, D.M. (2007). The effects of a mental skill training package on equestrians. *The Sport Psychologist, 21,* 288-310.

Brewer, B.W., & Shillinglaw, R. (1992). Evaluation of a psychological skills training workshop for male intercollegiate lacrosse players. *The Sport Psychologist, 6,* 139-147.

Carron, A.V., Spink, K.S., & Prapavessis, H. (1997). Team building and cohesiveness in the sport and exercise setting: Uses of interventions. *Journal of Applied Sport Psychology, 9,* 61-72.

Cohen, A.B., Tenenbaum, G., & English, R.W. (2006). An IZOF-based applied sport psychology case study. *Behavior Modification, 30,* 259-280.

Cox, R.H. (2002). *Sport psychology: Concepts and applications.* (5th ed.) New York: McGraw-Hill.

Commission on Accreditation in Physical Therapy Education. (2006). *Accreditation handbook.* Retrieved September 17, 2008 from

http://www.apta.org/AM/Template.cfm?Section=CAPTE3&Template=/TaggedPage/Tag
    gedPageDisplay.cfm&TPLID=65&ContentID=49490

Cramer-Roh, J.L., & Perna, F.P. (2000). Psychology / counseling: A universal competency in
    athletic training. *Journal of Athletic Training, 35*, 458-465.

Danish, S.J., & Hale, B.D. (1981). Toward an understanding of the practice of sport
    psychology. *Journal of Sport Psychology, 3*, 90-99.

Danish, S.J., Petitpas, A.J., & Hale, B.D. (1993). Life development intervention for athletes:
    Life skills through sports. *The Counseling Psychologist, 21*(3), 352-385.

Dillman, D.A. (2000). *Mail and internet surveys: The tailored design method* (2nd ed.). New
    York: Wiley & Sons.

Ebbeck, V., & Gibson, S.L. (1998). The effect of a team building program on the self-
    conceptions of grade 6 and grade 7 physical education students. *Journal of Sport &
    Exercise Psychology, 20*, 300-310.

Fink, A., & Kosecoff, J. (1998). *How to conduct surveys: A step-by-step guide* (2nd ed.).
    Thousand Oaks, CA: Sage Publications, Inc.

Fowler, F.J., Jr. (1993). *Survey research methods* (2nd ed.). Thousand Oaks, CA: Sage
    Publications, Inc.

George, D., & Mallery, P. (2001). *SPSS windows step by step: A simple guide and reference.*
    New York, NY: Allyn and Bacon.

Gould, D., & Dieffenbach, K. (2002). Psychological characteristics and their development in
    Olympic champions. *Journal of Applied Sport Psychology, 14*, 172-204.

Gould, D., Tammen, V., Murphy, S., & May, J. (1989). An examination of U.S. Olympic
    sport psychology consultants and the services they provide. *The Sport Psychologist, 3*,
    300-312.

Greenleaf, C., Gould, D., & Dieffenbach, K. (2001). Factors influencing Olympic
    performance: Interviews with Atlanta and Nagano U.S. Olympians. *Journal of Applied
    Sport Psychology, 13*, 154-184.

Gross, J.B. (1993). Training sport psychologists for a community role. *New Zealand Journal
    ofHealth, Physical Education, and Perception, 18(3)*, 15-18.

Hamson-Utley, J.J., Martin, S., & Walters, J. (2008). Athletic trainers' and physical
    therapists' perceptions of the effectiveness of psychological skills within sport injury
    rehabilitation programs.*Journal of Athletic Training, 43*, 258-264.

Hardy, L. &. Parfitt, G. (1994). The development of a model for the provision of psychologial
    support to a national squad. *The Sport Psychologist, 8*, 126-142.

Holm, J.E., Beckwith, B.E., Ehde, D.M., & Tinius, T.P. (1996). Cognitive-behavioral
    interventions for improving performance in competitive athletes: A controlled treatment
    outcome study. *International Journal of Sport Psychology, 27*, 463-475.

Kirschenbaum, D.S., Parham, W.D., & Murphy, S.M. (1993). Provision of sport psychology
    services at Olympic Events: The 1991 U.S. Olympic festival and beyond. *The Sport
    Psychologist, 7*, 419-440.

Kress, J., Schroeder, J., Potteiger, J.A., & Haub, M. (1999). The use of psychological skills
    training to increase 10KM cycling performance: An exploratory investigation.
    International Sports Journal, 3(2), 44-54.

Larson, G. A., Starkey, C., & Zaichkowsky, L. (1996). Psychological aspects of athletic
    injuries as perceived by athletic trainers. *The Sport Psychologist, 10*, 37-47.

Mahoney, M.J., Gabriel, T.J., & Perkins, T.S. (1987). Psychological skills and exceptional athletic performance. *The Sport Psychologist, 1*, 181-199.

Mamassis, G., & Doganis, G. (2004). The effects of a mental training program on juniors pre-competitive anxiety, self-confidence and tennis performance. *Journal of Applied Sport Psychology, 16*, 118-137.

Maniar, S.D., Curry, L.A., Sommers-Flanagan, J., & Walsh, J.A. (2001). Student-athlete preferences in seeking help when confronted with sport performance problems. *The Sport Psychologist, 15*, 205-223.

Martens, R. (1987). *Coaches guide to sport psychology: A publication for the American coaching effectiveness program level 2 sport science curriculum.* Champaign, IL: Human Kinetics.

Meyers, A.W., Schleser, R., & Okwumabua, T.M. (1982). A cognitive behavioral intervention for improving basketball performance. *Research Quarterly for Exercise and Sport, 53*, 344-347.

National Athletic Trainers' Association. (2006). *Athletic training educational competencies* (4th ed). Dallas: Author.

National Association for Sport and Physical Eduation. (2006). *Quality coaches, quality sports: National standards for sport coaches* (2nd ed). Reston, VA: Author.

Nideffer, R. M. (1978). *Attention control training: How to get control of your mind through total concentration.* New York: Harper Collins.

O'Donohoe, W., & Krasner, L. (1995). Psychological skills training. In W. Donohoe and L. Krasner (Eds.), *Handbook of psychological skills training: Clinical techniques and applications.* (pp. 1-19). Boston: Allyn & Bacon.

Partington, J., & Orlink, T. (1987). The sport psychology consultant: Olympic coaches' views. *The Sport Psychologist, 1*, 95-102.

Pates, J., Maynard, I., & Westbury, T. (2001). An investigation into the effects of hypnosis on basketball performance. *Journal of Applied Sport Psychology, 13*, 84-102.

Patrick, T.D., & Hrycaiko, D.W. (1998). Effects of a mental training package on endurance performance. *The Sport Psychologist, 12*, 283-299.

Ravizza, K. (1988). Gaining entry with athletic personnel for season-long consulting. *The Sport Psychologist, 2*, 243-254.

Seabourne, T.G., Weinberg, R.S., Jackson, A., & Suinn, R.A. (1985). Effect of individualized, nonindividualized, and package intervention strategies on karate performance. *Journal of Sport Psychology, 7*, 40-50.

Sheard, M, & Golby, J. (2006). Effects of a psychological skills training program on swimming performance and positive psychological development. *International Journal of Sport and Exercise Psychology, 4*, 149-169.

Sullivan, J., & Hodge, K. P. (1991). A survey of coaches and athletes about sport psychology in New Zealand. *The Sport Psychologist, 5*, 140-151.

Sullivan, P.A., & Nashman, H.W. (1998). Self-perceptions of the role of USOC sport psychologists in working with Olympic athletes. *The Sport Psychologist, 12*, 95-103.

Taylor, M.K., Gould, D., & Rolo, C. (2008). Performance strategies of US Olympians in practice and competition. *High Ability Studies, 19*, 19-36.

Terry, P.C., & Mayer, J.L. (1998). Effectiveness of a mental training program for novice scuba divers. *Journal of Applied Sport Psychology, 110*, 251-267.

Thelwell, R.C., & Greenlees, I.A. (2001). The effects of a mental skills training package on gymnasium triathlon performance. *The Sport Psychologist, 15*, 127-141.

Thelwell, R.C., Weston, N.J.V., Greenlees, I.A., & Hutchings, N.V. (2008). A qualitative exploration of psychological-skills use in coaches. *The Sport Psychologist, 22*, 38-53.

Thomas, P.R., & Fogarty, G.J. (1997). Psychological skills training in golf: The role of individual differences in cognitive preferences. *The Sport Psychologist, 11*, 86-106.

Van Raalte, J. L., & Brewer, B. W. (2002). Exploring sport and exercise psychology. (2nd Ed). American Psychological Association: Washington, DC.

Weinberg, R. S., & Gould, D. (1999). *Foundations of sport and exercise psychology.* (3rd Edition). Champaign, IL: Human Kinetics.

Williams, J.M. (Ed.) (2001). *Applied sport psychology.* (4th Edition). Palo Alto, CA: Mayfield.

Zizzi, S.J., Zaichkowsky, L., & Perna, F.M. (2002). Certification in sport and exercise psychology. In Van Raalte, J. and Brewer, B. (Eds.), *Exploring sport and exercise psychology* (2nd ed.)(pp. 459-477).Washington, DC: American Psychological Association.

APPENDIX A: HANDOUT ON PST DEFINITIONS

Attention and Concentration Control (focusing) - commonly used to help individuals identify their current situation and the relevant stimuli within that situation. These skills help them maintain their mental intensity within a situation. Common techniques include: 1) attention control training and 2) techniques to expand awareness (e.g:, focused breathing, attending to sounds and bodily sensations).

Communication - used to help improve group cohesion and individual interactions in a sport setting (e.g., athlete-athlete, athlete-coach, coach-parent). Techniques used with this skill include: 1) teaching active listening and communicating skills (reflecting, clarifying, encouraging, paraphrasing), 2) helping individuals create a free and open environment, and 3) assertiveness training.

Energy Management - most commonly used to help individuals who experience arousal at a level that is not effective (i.e., too high or too low) for optimal performance. These techniques have also been used for anxiety, stress, and anger management. Common treatments include: 1) breathing exercises (e.g., diaphragmatic breathing, sighing with exhalation, and rhythmic breathing), 2) progressive relaxation, 3) meditation, 4) visualization, 5) autogenic training, and 6) cognitive techniques (e.g., thought stopping and cognitive restructuring).

Goal Setting - commonly used for enhancing motivation and for focusing attention upon the aspects of performance that are most in need of improvement. The establishment of a goal setting program often includes several common components, including identifying target dates for attaining goals, identifying goal achievement strategies, and providing regular goal evaluation.

Hypnosis – used to help individuals achieve a state of deep relaxation, altered consciousness or focused attention and heightened suggestibility. Participants typically experience changes in sensations, perceptions, thoughts, or behavior. Used most commonly in the treatment of anxiety, attentional problems, and phobias.

Imagery, Visualization, Mental Practice - using all of the mind's senses to re-create or create an experience in the mind. Uses include: 1) mental preparation, 2) arousal control, 3) attention, 4) building self-confidence, 5) learning new skills, and 6) injury recovery. Common components include the evaluation of imagery ability, the establishment of the proper physical and mental setting (i.e., relaxed and quiet), and practice creating vivid and controllable images.

Self-talk - what you say or think to yourself. Self-talk patterns are related to how people feel and act. Changing self-talk is commonly used for 1) prompting a specific behavior, 2) improving self-confidence, 3) attention control, 4) motivation, and 5) arousal control. Common components include the identification of negative or irrelevant thoughts, challenging these thoughts, the creation of positive thoughts, and the substitution of positive thoughts for the negative thoughts.

TeamBuilding - the process of helping the members of a group enhance their ability to work cohesively through the improvement of communication, group objectives, trust, and respect. Team building strategies are often used at the beginning of a season to help group members become more familiar and trusting of each other. Common techniques include group introductions of each other, ropes courses, and individual and team goal setting.

Time management/Organization - the ability to plan and maintain one's regular schedule in a way that avoids confusion, conflict and undue stress. Common techniques in this area include: 1) teaching how to use a planner, 2) learning about the demands of a task, 3) setting legitimate goals for tasks, 4) understanding the demands of one's life, and 4) developing pre-performance routines.

Professional Role Definitions

Athletic Trainer – typically works with a specific sports team to provide acute and long-term care for athletic injuries. Designs and monitors rehabilitation programs.

Physical Therapist – typically works in a sports medicine or hospital clinic to provide acute and long-term care for a variety of sport and work-related injuries. Designs and monitors rehabilitation programs.

Coach – the organizational leader of a specific sports team. Often manages team affairs (travel, recruiting, scheduling) in addition to having a primary role as a teacher of sport-specific skills and strategy.

Psychologist – trained in clinical or counseling psychology to provide individual or group therapy relative to a broad range of behavioral and emotional issues. Typically work in a public clinic or private practice.

Performance Enhancement Consultants – professionals trained in sport psychology but are not licensed psychologists or counselors. Also known as sport psychology consultants or mental coaches. Provide individual or group consultations geared towards performance-related issues.

In: Introduction to Sport Psychology
Editor: Robert Schinke

ISBN: 978-1-61761-973-1
© 2011 Nova Science Publishers, Inc.

CULTURE IN SPORT PSYCHOLOGY: WHOSE CULTURE IS IT ANYWAY?

*Tatiana V. Ryba**

University of Jyväskylä, Finland

> Just as you cannot fully understand human action without taking account of its biological evolutionary roots and, at the same time, understand how it is construed in the meaning making of the actors involved in it, so you cannot understand it fully without knowing how and where it is situated. For, to paraphrase Clifford Geertz, knowledge and action are always local, always situated in a network of particulars.
>
> *Jerome Bruner, 1996, p. 167*

INTRODUCTION

In spring 2008, I was shortlisted for a Senior Lecturer post in the European Master's in Sport and Exercise PsychologyProgramme at the University of Jyväskylä. Thesubsequentstage in the competition was to deliver a 20-minute lecture entitled "Current Issues in Sport and Exercise Psychology." As I was perusing the latest issues of international journals in the field in an attempt to get a better grasp of "hot" topics, my list of "current issues" was growing. There were plenty of topics I could raisein my lecture.Yet, I was feeling uneasy—contemporary issues seemed but the recurrentold ones. Take for example, present anxieties about growing rates of child obesity and urgency of instigating physically active lifestyle in the developed countries; or models of sport psychology practice and delivery; or using sport as a tool for peace and international collaborations.These issues continuously makenational and international news, peer-reviewed journals, and scientific conferences. Yet they are certainly not new. In the late 19th century, Russian biologist, anatomist and educator Piotr Lesgaft (1901) stressed the importance of physical activity for healthy physical and psychological development of children. The scientifically inspired model of physical education developed by Lesgaft was later incorporated into the school system by the soviet state. At the turn of the 20th century, we see medical doctors and physical educators across Europe and North America pointing to physiological, psychological and social benefits of regular engagement in physical activity (Welch and Lerch, 1981). Recent empirical research provides convincing support to previous theoretical and descriptive essays produced by

---

* Forward all correspondence to: Tatiana V. Ryba, PhD, Faculty of Sport and Health Sciences, P.O.Box 35 (Viveca). FI-40014 University of Jyväskylä.Finland. Email: tatiana.ryba@jyu.fi

scholars around the world. Similarly, debates about the best provision of psychological services for athletes and coaches have been ongoing since the late 1960s, if not earlier. In addition, sport as an important sociocultural practice has been historically utilized for social integration, nationbuilding, and peace diplomacy. I began to realize that it is not the issue per se that makes news but the meaning it is given at a particular historical conjuncture. The meaning, of course, is based on what our best explanatory theories can provide.

THE TURN TO CULTURE IN SPORT PSYCHOLOGY: THE DOUBLE MEANING

Since the publication of the often cited paper "Cross-cultural Analysis in Exercise and Sport Psychology: A Void in the Field" by Duda and Allison (1990), in which the authors challenged scholars of sport and exercise psychology to give serious consideration to the role of race and ethnicity in producing human behavior, there has been an increase in cross-cultural research activity in the field. Much of the work was devoted to cultural validation of psychological instruments and identification of cultural similarities/variations in psychological constructs across cultures. In that sense, we can talk about scholars turning their gaze to culture while maintaining their epistemological anchors in positivism. Another reading of the shift to culture in sport psychology is linked to the "cultural turn" which swept through social sciences in the 1960s and which is a permutation of the postmodernist critique of the production of knowledge. The cultural turn gave rise to such discourses as cultural studies and cultural/indigenous psychology that are firmly positioned in social constructionism. While cross-cultural and cultural researchers, arguably, are interested in understanding of the role of culture in psychological processes, they approach the study of culture from different perspectives.

The conceptualization of culture within psychology tends to take either "etic" or "emic" perspective. According to Ponterotto (2005), the etic view refers to universal laws and behaviors that transcend nations and cultures to apply to all humans while the emic view refers to constructs and behaviors that are unique to the individual or the group in a particular sociocultural context. Etic studies are typically taken within cross-cultural psychology where psychological aspects of performance are compared across cultures. Culture is used to indicate some type of belonging to a group, usually based on a geographical location or linguistic identification. Hence for cross-cultural researchers culture is a coherent given, "theorized as an independent variable and assumed to influence the psychological functioning of individuals" (O'Dell, de Abreu, and O'Toole, 2004, p. 138). Emic studies are commonly found within cultural and indigenous psychology where psychological processes are assumed to be mediated through different cultural contexts. Cultural psychology places emphasis on the study of meaning from the point of view of cultural members and the understanding of how identity, belonging, and culture are produced in and through everyday practices. Hence, for cultural researchers, there is no separation between subject and context as they "live together, require each other, and dynamically, dialectically, and jointly make each other up" (Shweder, 1990, p. 1).

If we consider the repercussions of Duda and Allison's (1990) article, in light of the aforementioned brief tutorial, I would argue that the authors' call to begin to incorporate culture at a conceptual level (i.e., contextualizing results obtained within cultural specificity of a sociocultural group) was not answered, for the most part, by cross-cultural researchers. As Ram, Starek,and Johnson, (2004) concluded after conducting a content analysis of articles published in *Journal of Sport and Exercise Psychology* (1988-2000), *Journal of Applied Sport Psychology* (1989-2000), and *The Sport Psychologist* (1987-2000), only 15 and 4 papers out of all articles published looked at race/ethnicity and sexuality respectively in a conceptual way. The failure of cross-cultural sport psychologists to work with conceptual difficulties of culture observed by Ram et al. is hardly surprising if we consider the philosophical assumptions underpinning cross-cultural research. Indeed, methodological issues are inseparable from ontological and epistemological assumptions that underpin our inquiry. Scientific method(modeled on the natural sciences) presupposes realist ontology, making it problematic for cross-cultural researchers to incorporate a social constructionist understanding of culture since such arrangement would lead to the study's epistemological antinomy. If, for example, we subscribe to the objective, independent, and single version of reality, conceptualizing culture as a coherent entity that exists outside of us, then our inevitable methodological choice is to study the effect of culture on psychological processes and behaviors of sport and exercise participants. Using culture as an explanatory variable (i.e., X is due to culture), however, does not shed light on how culture is accounted in psychological processes and human movement. Indeed, as Reichenbach (1938, 1951) contended scientific method is not concerned with the question of generating theoretical ideas but of theory and/or hypothesis testing.

If these lines of reasoning make sense, then we have an uncomfortable realization on our hands: scientific method tends to normalize "us" and neglect "them." Moreover, resting our knowledge claims on procedure-driven inquiry leads to the "construction of epistemological 'blind spots'—the method begins to determine the general ways in which researchers think" (Valsiner, 2004, p. 11).

SPORT PSYCHOLOGY IN GLOBAL TIMES

The globalization processes accompanied by mobile technologies, nomadic professionals, athletic migration, and the random flow of cultures have brought the need for understanding cultural difference to the fore of civic and academic discourses.Appadurai (1990) highlighted five aspects of social change in a globalised society. These changes are "ethnoscapes" or landscapes of people on the move, such as migrant and immigrant athletes and exercisers, sporting tourists, guest coaches, and nomadic scholars; "technoscapes" and "financescapes" that are produced by the rapid flow of money, technology, national and trans-national corporations and governments; the "mediascapes" produced by the flow of images and information, creating a hyper-real mediated experience of being in multiple locations of the world at the same time; and finally "ideascapes" that are linked to the exchange and battle of ideas and ideologies. These politicized processes have profoundly affected the way we experience the world. Indeed, economic globalization, consumerism, technology, media and migration situate local issues in a global context, affecting and shaping the psychic organization of human experience. Hermans and Dimaggio (2007) have argued that the major impact of globalization on self and identity stems from the experience of ambiguity and uncertainty in so far as the homogenizing tendencies inherent in globalization clash with the local consciousness of a distinct cultural identity. Paradoxically, a power-blind metaphor of the "global village" is full of contentious heterogeneity that stresses cultural difference and engenders new oppositions.

The growing rate of athletic migrationis an essential aspect in current patterns of sports development (Bale and Maguire, 1994; Magee and Sugden, 2002), pointing yet again that the globalised social context in which sporting behaviour occurs has profoundly changed.In this sense, cultural sport psychology is not concerned simply with what might be seen as a sub-topic within social sport psychology but represents a particularly significant development for the entire discipline. Cultural psychology views human psyche as culturally constituted and rearticulates the most foundational object of psychological study—the self—as an effect of power relations of specific cultural, social and linguistic discourses at a particular historical conjuncture. In other words, motivations, experiences and aspirations of sport and exercise participants are dynamic and change not only across lifespan but also in relation to the contextual matrix of social, political, economic and technological articulations of sport occurring at the specific historical conjuncture.

As we face challenging questions pertinent to the human condition in unchartered waters of the shifting ethnoscapes, what concepts, theories and models do we draw upon? A recent special issue of the *International Journal of Sport and Exercise Psychology* (2009, issue 3) has attempted to answer this question while simultaneously examining the implications of over-reliance on universal sport psychological models in different cultural contexts. Stambulova and Alfermann (2009), for example, provided a reflexive analysis of career development and transition research conducted in different parts of the world. The authors illuminated numerous ways in which research practices (from the questions we consider important to investigate to the way we interpret findings) are inextricably linked to different sociocultural forces at play in a particular historical context. Excavating their vast research experience against the backdrop of dramatic political changes in their respective countries, Russia and Germany, Stambulova and Alfermann shared insightful observations of how research problems acquire scientific significance within sifting systems of meaning that underlie academic discourses.The authors further argued that using "universal" (mostly North American) theoretical frameworks in different cultural context often results in a total neglect of culture and its constitutive role in career development processes.

Concerns raised by the authors of the Special Issue echo arguments put forward byindigenous psychologists, postcolonial scholars, and recently cultural sport psychologists. Representing the indigenous view, Yang (1997) asserted that doing traditional psychological research with Chinese subjects results in "an Americanized Chinese psychology without a Chinese 'soul'" (p. 65). In a similar vein, Smith (1999) argued that imposing Western male-centered worldview that presupposes mainstream research practices disconnects cultural members from "their histories… and their own ways of thinking, feeling and interacting with the world" (p. 28). These ontological tensionsstem from our attempts to apply ethnocentric Western theories, models and concepts to the human psyche which is "inter-penetrated by intentional worlds that are culturally and historically variable" (Shi-xu, 2002, p. 6).

Without slipping into unreflective, and indeed reckless, radical relativism, I invite readers to ponder on what Thomas Kuhn observed in 1962—namely, that there is no theory-neutral observation against which theories/hypothesis can be tested; that knowledge claims of the world are mediated by paradigmatic assumptions. Thus, if theories we employ to make sense of empirical data are "cultural and linguistic artifact[s]" (Kincheloe, 2005, p. 324), can we claim their universal applicability? Furthermore, hegemonic research practices in sport psychology grew out of the European intellectual traditions. In that sense, scientific method is implicated in the way we understand the world and, therefore, its universal knowledge claims mask the underlying philosophical assumptions of Eurocentric scientific discourses. Truth then is "always already" from a perspective of the West.

I finish this section with a quote from *Discipline and Punish: The Birth of the Prison* whichI apply to our globalised scholarship. As we witness a heavy traffic of knowledge production around the world, multiple, diverse sport psychologies "of different origin and scattered location...overlap, repeat, or imitate one another, support one another, distinguish themselves from one another according to their domain of application, converge and gradually produce the *blueprint* of a general method" (Foucault, 1995, p. 38). In the context of this paper, the blueprint is certainly a Westernized sport psychology.

CONCLUDING THOUGHTS

Cultural sport psychology aims at a culturally sensitive research and practice of sport psychology. Central to the debates of what constitutes a culturally sensitive approach is an understanding of culture itself. To attempt to answer the deceptively simple question "What is culture?" opens a Pandora boxof interpretation and takes one on a journey of discovery. I've been on this journey since I was first introduced to cultural studies in 2000. My research foci have been shifting over time from exploration of how sociocultural difference is an effect of power relations to genealogical analysis of the production of knowledge in sport psychology. My current concern is that "culture"increasingly becomes a commodity in our globalised scholarship—something that is packaged, marketed, and consumed by at times unreflective application of research based knowledge. In this paper, I raise the urgency of critical engagement with the most basic but perhaps most challenging epistemological questions: How do we generate knowledge that is culturally relevant? What are the criteria we use to evaluate knowledge as "scientific" and "cultural"?*Inwhose cultural voice does the sport psychology speak?*

REFERENCES

Appadurai, A. (1990). Disjuncture and difference in the global culture economy. *Theory, Culture, and Society, 7,* 295-310.

Bale, J., and Maguire, J. (Eds.). (1994). *The global sports arena: Athletic talent migration in an interdependent world.* London, UK: Frank Cass and Co. Ltd.

Bruner, J. (1996). *The culture of education.*Cambridge, Mass.: Harvard University Press.

Duda, J. L., and Allison, M. T. (1990). Cross-cultural analysis in exercise and sport psychology: A void in the field.*Journal of Sport and Exercise Psychology, 12,* 114-131.

Foucault, M. (1995). *Discipline and punish: The birth of the prison* (A. Sheridan, Trans. 2 ed.). New York: Vintage Books.

Kincheloe, J. L. (2005). On to the next level: Continuing the conceptualization of the bricolage. *Qualitative Inquiry, 11,* 323-350.

Kuhn, T. S. (1962).*The structure of scientific revolutions.*Chicago, IL: University of Chicago Press.

Lesgaft, P. F. (1901). *Rukovodstvo k fiziceskomu obrazovaniju detej shkolnogo vozrasta [A guide to physical education of school age children]*. St. Petersburg.

Magee, J., and Sugden, J. (2002). "The world at their feet": Professional football and international labor migration.*Journal of Sport and Social Issues, 26*, 421-437.

O'Dell, L., de Abreu, G., and O'Toole, S. (2004). The turn to culture.*The Psychologist, 17*, 138-141.

Ponterotto, J. G. (2005). Qualitative research in counseling psychology: A primer on research paradigms and philosophy of science. *Journal of Counseling Psychology, 52*, 126-136.

Ram, N., Starek, J., and Johnson, J. (2004). Race, ethnicity, and sexual orientation: Still a void in sport and exercise psychology.*Journal of Sport and Exercise Psychology, 26*, 250-268.

Reichenbach, H. (1938). *Experience and prediction: An analysis of the foundations and the structure of knowledge.*Chicago, IL: University of Chicago Press.

Reichenbach, H. (1951). *The rise of scientific philosophy.*Berkeley, CA: University of California Press.

Shi-xu. (2002). The discourse of cultural psychology.*Culture and Psychology, 8*, 65-78.

Shweder, R. A. (1990). Cultural psychology—what is it? In J. W. Stigler, R. A. Shweder, and G.Herdt (Eds.), *Cultural psychology: Essays on comparative human development*(pp. 1 - 43).Cambridge: Cambridge University Press.

Smith, L. T. (1999). *Decolonizing methodologies: Research and indigenous peoples.* Dunedin: University of Otago Press.

Stambulova, N., and Alfermann, D. (2009). Putting culture into context: Cultural and cross-cultural perspectives in career development and transition research and practice.*International Journal ofSport and Exercise Psychology, 7*, 292-308.

Valsiner, J. (2004). Three years later: Culture in psychology - between social positioning and producing new knowledge.*Culture and Psychology, 10*(5), 5-27.

Welch, P. D., and Lerch, H. A. (1981). *History of American physical education and sport.* Springfield, IL: Charles C Thomas.

Yang, Kuo-Shu (1997). Indigenizing westernized Chinese psychology. In M. H. Bond (Ed.), *Working at the interface of culture: Eighteen lives in social science.* London: Routledge.

In: Introduction to Sport Psychology
Editor: Robert Schinke

ISBN: 978-1-61761-973-1
© 2011 Nova Science Publishers, Inc.

Sport Psychology Consultations for Professional Soccer Players – Working with Diverse Teams

Ronnie Lidor[*1] andBoris Blumenstein[2]

[1]The ZinmanCollege of Physical Education and Sport Sciences,
Wingate Institute, and Faculty of Education, University of Haifa, Israel
[2]RibsteinCenter for Sport Medicine Sciences and Research,
Wingate Institute for Physical Education and Sport, Israel

Since the 1950s soccer has established itself as one of the most popular team sports in Israel (Ben-Porat, 1998, 2001).Professional and amateur soccer is played around the country, in both large and small cities. Although soccer is played by females as well, the sport has been exclusively dominated by males. There is only one amateur league for adult females (composed of 8 teams). However, there are two professional and three semi-professional *divisions* for male players, and there are many amateur leagues for male players comprising teams from all over the country. All the games played in the two male professional divisions are regularly televised, while games played in the female league can seldom be seen on television.

This article focuses on the provision of sport psychology consultations to three professional soccer clubs by one sport psychology consultant (SPC). Over the past 10 years, the SPC worked with three different professional soccer clubs in Israel, each during a separate season. This article presents the experiences of the SPC based on his work with these three clubs. Typically, the team of experts that works for a professional soccer club in Israel is composed of a head coach, assistant coach/s (one or two), a strength and conditioning coach, an athletic trainer, a physiotherapist, and a physician specializing in sports medicine. Few clubs hire a SPC in order to regularly provide their players and coaches with the required psychological preparation for practices and games. The reason for this is that most of the owners of the clubs believe that soccer is a physical game and not a mental game. They insist that a good coach should, with the help of his or her regular assistants, be able to prepare the players to overcome any psychological barriers they may face during the season. Furthermore, they believe that if a coach demands to work with a SPC on a regular basis, he or she may lack strong leadership, and in turn, this may have a negative influence on the relationships with his or her players. This belief is not a cultural perspective but rather a

* Correspondence to: Dr. Ronnie Lidor, Associate Professor. The Zinman College of Physical Education and Sport Sciences.Wingate Institute. Netanya 42902. Israel. Fax: +972-9-8650960. E-mail: lidor@wincol.ac.il

sport-specific perspective, since in other ball games such as basketball, team-handball, and volleyball, club owners are more open to hiring SPCs to help the coaches better deal with the psychological preparation of their players.

However, a small number of professional soccer clubs in Israel do hire a SPC to work with their players and coaches on a regular basis during the yearly training program. An attempt was made in this article to demonstrate how a sport psychology program operated in three professional soccer clubs in Israel. Since a typical professional soccer club in Israel is composed of players coming from different backgrounds and cultures (e.g., Jewish players, Arab players, and foreign players who are typically recruited from different countries in Africa, Europe, or South America), emphasis was made on describing how the SPC dealt with these diverse teams, and what actions he took to improve his consultation process when working with the main clients of the clubs – the players.

The purpose of this article was threefold: (a) to describe how one SPC worked with the players, coaches, and representatives of the club's management of three professional clubs; (b) to discuss three consultation cases demonstrating how the SPC took advantage of the diversity existing in these professional soccer clubs; and (c) to provide a number of practical recommendations for SPCs working with professional soccer clubs.

THE SPORT PSYCHOLOGY PROGRAM

Information on the operational principles of the sport psychologyprogram, the background of theSPC who worked with the professional soccer clubs, the composition of the soccer clubs, and the groups of the provision of sport psychology consultations within the soccer clubs follows.

Operational Principles of the Sport Psychology Program

The sport psychology program provided to the soccer players is based on five operational principles, which have already been described in the literature (see Blumenstein, Lidor, and Tenenbaum, 2005; Lidor, Blumenstein, and Tenenbaum, 2007a, 2007b). These principles were used by the SPC when working with athletes from both individual (e.g., judo, track and field, and tennis) and team (e.g., basketball, soccer, and rhythmic gymnastics) sports. The five principles are as follows:

(a) The SPC should discuss his or her psychological program with the coaches of the athlete/team. He or she should explain the objectives and procedures of the interventions he or she plans to use. After receiving agreement from the coaches, the SPC can begin the sport psychology program;

(b) The SPC should be one of the members of the team of experts that works with the individual athlete or the team, along with the head coach, assistant coaches, strength and conditioning coach, athletic trainer, physiotherapist, and physician specializing in sports medicine. The SPC should attend practices, competitions, or games, as well as all other professional activities of the athlete/team;

(c) The SPC should meet regularly with the coaches and other members of the team of experts that works with the athlete/team. Ideas and experiences of all the experts involved in the training program should be shared, in order to provide the coaches with the most relevant information for effectively planning the training program;

(d) Three types of sessions can be used by the SPC while working with the individual athlete or the team – laboratory, practice, and home assignments. The objective of the laboratory sessions is to enable the athlete or athletes to practice the interventional techniques under controlled and sterile conditions. The objective of the practice sessions is to enable the athletes to perform the interventional techniques under real life conditions such as those existing in practices, competitions, and games. The objective of the home assignments is to enable the athlete to practice the interventional techniques at home in a quiet and relaxed setting;

(e) The SPC should maintain an open-door approach when working with the individual athlete, the team, or the coaching staff, in order to build a solid and trustful relationship with all experts who work with the individual athlete or the team as a whole.

The SPC – Background Information

The operational principles of the sport psychology program used with the soccer players were developed by the two authors of this article, as was the specific psychological training program (which is presented in this article in the section on the provision of sport psychology consultations to the soccer clubs). However, the second author was the SPC who worked with the soccer clubs. The consultant (male, PhD in sport psychology, 32 years of experience working with elite and Olympic athletes in individual [judo, kayaking, rhythmic gymnastics, tennis] and team [basketball, soccer] sports) signed a yearly contract with each club. The SPC was approached by the coaches of the soccer teams. The first soccer coach to approach the SPC told him that he had heard about his work with elite judokas and kayakers, and based on this information he wanted him to provide consultations to his soccer players. The other two coaches who approached the SPC had already heard about his experience working with one professional soccer club, and therefore approached him. All three coaches stressed to the SPC that their request to work with him had been approved by the club's management..

When working with one soccer club, no sport psychology consultations were provided to the players, coaches, or individuals from the club's managements of any other club. That is to say, the SPC worked with only one soccer club at a time during the entire season. When providing psychological consultations to the soccer club, the consultant did not work with any other team sports; however, he did give consultations to a number of athletes from different individual sports. In addition, he taught one undergraduate class in sport psychology at a college of physical education and sport sciences, and was involved in a number of research projects in applied sport psychology. According to his request, it was not revealed in public that he served as the SPC of the clubs.

The Soccer Clubs – Background Information

The sport psychology interventions presented in this article were provided to professional male soccer players who played for three different clubs which were part of Division 1, the highest professional soccer division in Israel. At the time the SPC worked for the clubs, Division 1 was composed of 12 professional clubs. The clubs were located in medium- and large-size cities around the country, and consisted of about 22 players each: about 15 Jewish players (the majority of the team), 3 to 4foreign players (players who were not born in Israel and did not carry Israeli citizenship), and 2-3 Arab players (typically Muslims who are Israeli citizens). Among the clubs, two were ranked among the five best teams in the league at the time the psychological consultations were given. One club was ranked among the five weakest teams in the league; only during the last month of the season did this club succeed in keeping its status in Division 1, and not dropping down to a lower division, which was also composed of 12 professional clubs.

The Provision of Sport Psychology Consultations to the Soccer Clubs – Three Groups

The SPC provided his consultations to three groups of individuals within the soccer clubs – the players, the coaches, and a number of representatives of the club's management. All meetings with these individuals were conducted during the preparation and competition phases of the training program. The preparation phase lasted about seven weeks (four weeks in July and three weeks in August) of daily practices, a training camp, and unofficial games with other teams who played in either Division 1 or Division 2. The competition phase lasted about nine months (the last week of August until the third week of May). During this period the teams played one league game each week (in most cases on Saturdays but a number of times on Mondays), and a number of cup games. In the league games the teams played against teams only from Division 1, on a home-away system). In the cup games, the teams played not only against teams from Division 1 but also against teams from Division 2 and Divisions 3 and 4 (which were composed of semi-professional clubs). No psychological consultations were provided during the transition phase.

Group 1: The players. The players were the primary clients of the SPC when working with the soccer clubs. The SPC attended at least three practices each week during the preparation and competition phases of the season. He typically observed the players practicing while he sat on a bench at the side of the field. During the practice, no interactions took place between the SPC and the players. They saw him sitting on the bench, but he as well as the head coach requested that they not approach him during practice time. Only the head coach and his assistant/s could interact with him during practice. In fact, this time was used by the SPC to provide the coaches with short reports on the psychological state of a number of the players. During this time, the coaches also made their own recommendations (e.g., that he meet with a single player or a number of players at the same time) to the SPC.

The SPC watched most of the team's games (home and away) while sitting in the stands, however he was close enough to observe some of the reactions (e.g., kicking the field after missing a pass, encouraging another player who failed to pass, or shouting at another player after he inaccurately passed the ball) of the players demonstrated during the games. This information was used by the SPC when meeting with the players.

The meetings with the players were conducted in the laboratory/office of the SPC at a scheduled time or after practices and games. The SPC preferred meeting with the players individually or in small groups, namely two to three players at the same time. At the beginning of the consultation process, the SPC met with those players that the coach had chosen to meet with him, among them the foreign players and those that the coaches thought would lead the team during the up-coming season. The SPC met with most of the 22 players on the team during the season; only two or three players were not provided with the sport psychology interventions, among them the young players who also played for the youth team in the club and therefore did not attend all the practice sessions of the adult professional team, and players who were traded to another club by the management during the first part of the competition phase. Group sessions with the whole team (i.e., the twenty-two players who were on the roster) were seldom undertaken.

Group meetings. Only three group sessions were conducted with all the players of the team, for each of the three clubs. All meetings took place during the first month of the season, namely during the preparation phase, one week apart. In the first group meeting between the SPC and the players, the head coach and his assistants attended as well. The coaching staff did not attend the second and third group meetings, in order to enable the SPC to start building a confidential relationship with the players.

In the first group meeting, the SPC provided the players with an overview of the sport psychology program he would apply during the season. He explained to the players the objectives of his program, the various ways that he would interact with them (e.g., individual meetings in his office/laboratory, phone calls, e-mails), what techniques he was going to use (a general description of techniques such as imagery and self talk), and the main topics they would deal with (e.g., mental preparation for practices and games, focusing attention, and setting goals). He delivered a 60-minute lecture, during which he used a number of video clips demonstrating a high level of team effort exhibited by players playing for well-known European clubs, such as Arsenal and Manchester United from England and Barcelona and Real Madrid from Spain. He emphasized that appropriate psychological preparation throughout the training program is one of the factors that contributes to a high level of proficiency in soccer.

In each of the second and third group meetings, the SPC focused on one specific topic related to the program. He lectured on Group Cohesion in the second meeting and on Mental Preparation in the third meeting. Since a number of new players had joined the team, among them a number of players (two to four) who were playing for the first time for an Israeli club, the SPC decided to introduce first the topic of Group Cohesion. He wanted to present this topic in the first meeting that he conducted by himself with the team.

The second and third group meetings were divided into two parts. In the first part the SPC defined the selected topic and explained its contribution to the achievement of success in soccer. Video clips of good and poor performances of elite soccer players were shown to emphasize the importance of group cohesion and mental preparation in soccer. In the second part of the meetings, the SPC discussed with the players how he was going to approach these topics in his future meetings with them. For example, in order to facilitate group cohesion, meetings with small groups would be conducted. Each group would be composed of two or three players, according to the objective of the specific meeting. The SPC aimed at taking advantage of the diversity existing in the soccer teams. In the meetings with a number of players, he tried to create an atmosphere in which the players on the teams would be aware of the different backgrounds of their counterparts, respect their cultures, and accept the situation that in such a diverse group different players would demonstrate different patterns of behaviors, on and off the field. For example, he emphasized that not all the players wanted to adopt a similar code of dressing, listen to the same style of music, or spend time after practices at the same places. He delivered the message that it was a unique opportunity for the players to learn from others who grew up in different environments, and therefore were exposed to different experiences. He pointed out that these experiences could be shared and used to build a positive professional and social climate among the players (see Case 1 in the following section of this article). For the purpose of developing effective mental preparation in the soccer players, one-on-one meetings would be conducted. Each player would be provided with the specific interventional techniques that most fit his psychological state and individual needs (see Case 2 in the following section of this article).

Individual meetings. Individual meetings took place in several venues: in the laboratory of the SPC, in his office, in a separate room in the stadium of the club (after practices), or on the soccer field. These meetings were held either with one player or with a small number of players (two to three at the same time). The main objective of the individual meetings was to enable the players to practice the interventional techniques which were selected for them by the consultant to help them to be mentally prepared for practices and games.

Two main interventional techniques were used by the SPC when meeting individual players: The Five-Step Approach (5-SA; Blumenstein and Bar-Eli, 2005) and the specific psychological training program (Blumenstein and Lidor, 2007). The 5-SA is a self-regulation technique incorporating biofeedback (BFB) training. This technique enables athletes to transfer the psycho-regulative skills performed in sterile laboratory settings to real practice and competition settings, utilizing testing and various simulative materials (Blumenstein and Bar-Eli). The 5-SA is composed of five stages: (a) introduction – learning various self-regulation techniques (e.g., imagery, focusing attention, and self talk), (b) identification(identifying and strengthening the most efficient BFB response modality), (c) simulation (BFB training with simulated competitive stress), (d) transformation (bringing mental preparation from the laboratory to the field), and (e) realization (achieving optimal regulation in competition).

The specific psychological training program is composed of mental skill techniques – focusing attention, imagery, self talk, and relaxation – that were developed by the SPC throughout many years of professional practice. These techniques have also been used by other SPCs who work with athletes at the elite level (Henschen, 2005; Moran, 2005), and they have been provided with empirical support (e.g., Short et al., 2002). When the consultant decides on which of these techniques to work on with the athlete/s, the current physical and psychological states of the players as well as the specific phase of the training program (i.e., preparation or competition) are taken into account.

The psychological interventions – the 5-SA and the specific psychological training program – were identically applied to all the players on the teams, regardless of their background and culture. The SPC did develop different programs for players who played different positions; he considered the specific professional needs of each player and the progress he made during the individual meetings. For example, different emphases were made for the goalkeepers compared with those of the strikers, since they played different positions and therefore had to cope with the demands of different tasks.

Typically, the first meetings with the individual player took place in the office of the SPC. The player was asked to complete two questionnaires. One questionnaire provided background information on the player, such as age, family status, the number of years he played competitive soccer, and the number of clubs that he had played for. The second questionnaire collected information on the experiences of the player with SPCs and the interventions techniques he had been exposed to. The objective of the second questionnaire was to determine how many players had worked with SPCs in the past, and how many players had not. Both questionnaires were written in Hebrew and given only to the Jewish and Arab players playing for the clubs. Since the foreign players came from different countries in Africa, Europe, and South America, they could not speak Hebrew, and therefore the SPC translated the questions of both questionnaires into English, and collected the relevant information through an oral conversation with the foreign player.

Although all the players completed the two questionnaires, or verbally provided the required information, not all of them were enthusiastic about doing it. Some of them thought that the SPC would share the information obtained from the questionnaires/conversations with the coaches, particularly the information on their lack of experience working with a SPC. However, the SPC expected these reactions from the players, and therefore did not force them to provide all the information at the first meeting. He did not make a big deal when a number of the players hesitated to provide the information, and told them that he could wait a few more meetings for it. While some of the players did provide the information at the first meeting, others did it at the third or fourth meetings, probably because their trust in the SPC had increased.

After the first meeting, the SPC began to teach each player the foundations of the 5-SA. After a series of meetings focusing on the five steps of the strategy, the SPC introduced the specific psychological training program to the player. A specific technique (e.g., focusing attention, imagery) was selected for each player according to his requirements. For example, if one player complained that he had difficulties in focusing attention when performing kicking drills in practices, the SPC taught him a focusing-attention technique. If another player needed to learn how to relax because he lost his temper too often during practices or scrimmages, the SPC taught him imagery and relaxation techniques.

After some experience was gained with the learned interventional techniques under sterile laboratory/office conditions, the individual sessions would then take place under practice conditions. The SPC met with the player on the field; the player performed the specific psychological training program in situations that reflected more real-world soccer situations. For example, the player was asked to perform imagery while executing a series of stretching drills. In another situation, the player performed a focusing-attention technique while carrying out kicking drills from the corner of the field. In practice settings, the SPC did not provide the player with any feedback related to his soccer performances, and only worked with him on the selected psychological technique.

The SPC also met with a number of players together in his laboratory/office or after practices. These meetings were held after the SPC had already conducted a series of individual meetings with the players, particularly those who were considered to be starters. The SPC had several considerations when grouping the players in these meetings, among them (a) the need to work with players sharing dissimilar background and culture (see Case 1 discussed later in this article), (b) the need to consult players playing in a similar position (e.g., goalkeepers, defenders, or strikers), (c) the need to work with players requesting similar interventional techniques (e.g., setting goals for injured players returning to practices, focusing attention for the bench players, relaxation and setting goals for players who were going to be starters for the first time). When meeting with a number of players at the same time, the SPC explained to the players the reason for grouping them, outlined what they were going to do, and asked them to perform the interventional techniques. At the end of the meeting, he spent time discussing with the players their feelings about using the techniques.

Home assignments. Home assignments were given to the players following six weeks of practice. After the player met with the SPC – in both individual and group meetings (with the entire team, but particularly with a small number of players) – the SPC asked the players to practice their learned psychological techniques at home, in a quiet and relaxed atmosphere. There were two objectives of the use of home assignments: (a) to develop awareness among the players of the importance of the psychological program by asking them to spend a few more minutes each day, or every other day, working on their learned techniques on their own; (b) to enable the players to become familiar with the learned techniques and feel comfortable using them before practices and games.

Group 2: The head coach and his assistant/s. A formal monthly meeting between the SPC and the head coach and his assistant/s was conducted. The term *formal* is used to describe only the monthly meetings between the coaches and the SPC that were scheduled in advance, since several informal meetings regularly took place between them when the SPC attended practices. On several occasions, the other experts who worked with the players, such as the strength and conditioning coach, the athletic trainer, or the physiotherapist, attended these monthly meetings as well.

The objective of the meetings between the SPC and the coaches was threefold: (a) to provide the coaches with detailed reports on the psychological state of the players with whom the SPC had met; (b) to describe the psychological interventions that would be used during the next month of the consultation program; and (c) to listen to the coaches' requests for the SPC to meet with specific players, individually or with other players at the same time. All the coaches of the teams had a number of years' experience working in Division 1 (one of the coaches had 7 years of experience, the second 5 years, and the third 2 years). They realized that it would take a considerable amount of time to group the individual players into one cohesive team. Therefore, they asked the SPC to help them "break down" the psychological and social walls among the Jewish, Arab, and foreign players. They insisted that the sooner the players felt they were part of one big family, the better they would perform on the field.

Group 3: Representatives of the club's management. Only two meetings were held between the SPC and representatives of the club's management throughout the annual training program: one during the first week of practice and the second toward the end of the season. The objective of the first meeting was to give the members of the club's management the opportunity to meet the SPC and listen to his "philosophy of consultation." The SPC used a PowerPoint presentation which demonstrated the five operational principles of the sport psychology program that he would provide to the players and coaches throughout the season. He described his experience working with elite athletes in Israel and implementing the five principles of the program, demonstrated BFB technology using a 7-min video presentation, and stressed his intention to create a professional dialogue with the other experts working with the players, in order to advance the understanding of the psychological and physical states of the individual player and the whole team.

The objective of the second meeting of the SPC and the representatives of the club's management was to summarize the work done by the SPC during the season. Itwas not an official evaluative meeting in which the actual contribution of the sport psychology program to the individual player and the team was assessed. Instead, the representatives asked the SPC to share his experiences throughout the season working with the players and coaches. For them, it was the first time they hired a SPC, and they wanted to understand his contributions to the team. The SPC outlined the main issues he had dealt with during the season, for example working with a diverse team, injured players, and players who developed a "bad attitude" toward other players, the coaches, or the club. No names of players who had consulted with the SPC were revealed during the meeting.

THREE CASES OF CONSULTATIONS

Three cases of consultations reflecting the work of the SPC with the diverse teams are discussed. Case 1 describes the attempts of the SPC to prevent divisions and cliques in the soccer teams. Case 2 illustrates how the consultant managed to work with players who had different approaches toward mental preparation, and Case 3 explains how the SPC convinced the foreign players to disregard threats of terror attacks.

Case 1: Preventing Divisions and Cliques

Since the soccer teams were composed of Jewish players, Arab players, and foreign players, it was one of the primary objectives of the SPC to prevent the formation of divisions and cliques among the players. Also, the coaches of the teams had requested that he help them prevent divisions and cliques. Throughout the preparation phase, the players from each club typically preferred to interact with those players who spoke their language and shared a common cultural background. For example, the Arab players spent time together on and off the court; they not only preferred to work out together during practices, but also to go out together after practices. The foreign players did the same, since some of them came from the same European country (e.g., Croatia), or from different countries in which the same language was spoken (e.g., players who came from France and Belgium and spoke French).

Two steps were taken by the SPC to prevent divisions and cliques. First, the SPC conducted a series of meetings in which a number of players sharing a similar cultural background, such as the foreign players or the Arab players, were grouped together. In these meetings, he mainly discussed with the players the similarities and dissimilarities of their own culture and the Israeli culture. Among the issues discussed were the dress codes adopted in daily life (e.g., formal in Europe vs. informal in Israel), the different ways people approach each other on the street (e.g., formal in Europe vs. informal in Israel), and the significance of Saturday (typically a regular day for Muslims and Christians, however the Sabbath for the Jews).

The second step was to conduct an additional series of meetings in which players from different cultures, namely one Jewish player, one Arab player, and one foreign player, were invited. The objective of these meetings was to enable each player to tell "his story," from both a personal and professional perspective. The players talked about their experiences in soccer, their families which usually remained in their native countries, their motives for playing for the club, and their professional expectations from the upcoming season. When listening to one player, the other players could interrupt either by asking questions or by adding pieces of information that were connected to the story of the player. For example, while talking about leaving their families behind in their native countries, the foreign players told how much they missed their children. However, the Jewish and the Arab players expressed similar feelings, by saying that they did not have much time to play with their kids during the season due to the busy schedule of practices and games. The players all felt that although they came from different backgrounds, they shared common perspectives on daily life matters.

In order to achieve an open approach in these meetings, the SPC intentionally created an informal atmosphere, so that each player could express himself comfortably. For example, the consultant and the players sat around a table. Cold drinks and fruits were provided in advance by the SPC, and the players could serve themselves during the meeting. English was used in these meetings to overcome the language barrier among the players. Although not all the players felt comfortable communicating in English, the informal atmosphere of the meetings, as well as the intimacy achieved by having groups of only two to three players at the same time, helped the players to interact with each other. The aim of these meetings with players sharing a similar cultural background and those coming from different cultural background, was to enable the players to get to know each other, and therefore to adopt an open approach to one another. For example, the players enjoyed talking about their future plans. For the local players – Jewish and Arab – it was their dream to play for a big European club. For the foreign players, it was the objective to make more money than they had earned in the previous seasons. Therefore, the Jewish and Arab players were enthusiastic to hear about the experience of some of the foreign players who had played in famous European clubs. They wanted to know what it was like to play in the "big leagues" (e.g., the professional leagues in England, Italy, or Spain). The foreign players wanted to hear about the economic strengths of the professional clubs in Israel, so that they could consider playing for the ones that would pay them more money in the future. By talking together about the abovementioned topics, the players started to feel more comfortable with each other. Most of these meetings were conducted only during the preparation phase.

During the competition phase, the SPC did conduct meetings in which players from different cultures were grouped together; however, the objective of these meetings was to convince as well as motivate those players who had not practiced sport psychology interventions in the years before they joined their current club (e.g., the Arab players) that the sport psychology program could help them to perform better (see Case 2).

Case 2: Coping with Different Approaches to Mental Preparation

Not all the players on the teams had regularly practiced sport psychology interventions.Some of them had not worked with a SPC when playing for other clubs. For example, in their previous clubs, the Arab players did not have the chance to work with an SPC because their clubs did not hire one. As a result, they adopted an approach that only physical preparation is the key factor to achieving success. They worked very hard in practices, particularly in the conditioning sessions. They assumed that being in a good physical shape would impress the coaches, and therefore they would be provided with more playing time. When the SPC asked them to join the interventional meetings, either by themselves or with other players, they did it only because they felt they had to. Their motivation to interact with the SPC and the other players was extremely low. For example, when they attended the first meetings, the Arab players sat quietly and only listened to the conversations between the SPC and the foreign players without adding any input. Sometimes they looked at the screen of their cellular phone, without actually using it. Although they did not ignore the other players, they did not have any verbal interactions with them. The SPC discerned that it was indeed hard for them to be involved in the conversation.

In order to convince the Arab players that they could benefit from the sport psychology program, the SPC conducted a series of meetings composed of the Arab players and foreign players. The foreign players had attended special soccer academies in Europe in their youth. They had practiced in well-equipped training facilities, worked with top-level coaches, and received medical and psychological support. From an early age, they worked with a SPC and practiced psychological techniques such as focusing attention, goal setting, imagery, and self talk. In his first meetings with the foreign players, the SPC realized that they were already familiar with some of the psychological techniques that he was presenting to them, and therefore he developed an advanced consultation program for them, taking into account their previous experiences. Consequently, he used their knowledge and positive attitude toward sport psychology intervention by setting up meetings between the foreign players and the Arab players. His intention was to expose the Arab players to other players who truly believed that they could benefit from the psychological interventions. As indicated before, at the beginning of the consultation meetings the Arab players did not interact with either the SPC or with the foreign players. However, after the foreign players began practicing the interventions, particularly the first steps of the 5-SA using the biofeedback apparatus, the Arab players showed more interest in the sport psychology program. At this stage of the consultation, the SPC was pleased that these players increased their motivation to practice the interventions.

In the meetings with the foreign and Arab players, the SPC first presented the 5-SA and then the specific psychological training program. Each step of the 5-SA was performed individually by each player, while the rest of the players stayed in the room and observed him performing the step. The players were asked to share their experiences after performing the step. The objective of this procedure was to enable the Arab players to listen to the reactions and remarks of the foreign players. The SPC wanted the Arab players to learn the foundations of the 5-SA in a positive and reinforcing setting.

A similar procedure used with the 5-SA was also used when elements of the specific psychological training program were performed, namely that after performing a technique (e.g., imagery), the players were asked to share their perspectives with each other. While each step of the 5-SA was performed individually, all players performed the specific psychological training program at the same time. After the players experienced the 5-SA and the specific psychological program in the meetings with the other players, they began their own individual program. Therefore, the subsequent meetings with the SPC that focused on mental preparation were conducted with one player at a time.

All the players on the teams – Jewish, Arab, and foreign – practiced the same interventions. The basic steps of the 5-SA were presented to all the players, however the transition from one step to another took place according to the individual progress of each player. Among the most common practiced techniques of the specific psychological training program were imagery, focusing attention, and relaxation. Most of the players asked the SPC to practice imagery. This technique enabled the players to see themselves performing actions related to their role in actual game situations. Each player was individually instructed to imagine what he had to do during the game, and what he should be doing in order to improve his on-field performances.

Case 3: Dealing with Terror Attacks

Unfortunately, athletes in Israel, as part of the population at large, are exposed on a regular basis to threats of terror, terror attacks, or military attacks (Lidor and Blumenstein, 2009). Although the threat of terror and particularly the actual terror attacks themselves interfere with the daily life of the people who live in the country, it is their goal to continue with their lives, regardless of the uncertainty. The slogan *"life must goon"* accurately reflects the motto of Israeli citizens.

While the Jewish and the Arab soccer players were used to this precarious situation, and had the experience to cope with it, for most of the foreign players it was a new and very unsettling experience. All the foreign players who were recruited to play for the clubs had heard about the political situation in Israel before coming to the country. They knew about the extended conflict between the Israelis and the Palestinians. Despite the unique political situation, the foreign players accepted the offers from the clubs and came to the country.

It was the objective of the SPC to prepare the foreign players to deal with threats of terror and terror attacks. From the very beginning of the orientation meetings with the foreign players (see Case 1), when the SPC discussed the characteristics of the Israeli culture, the issue of terror was mentioned. The SPC provided the foreign players with a general overview of the political situation in Israel, spending a considerable amount of time explaining the complex relationships between the Israelis and the Palestinians. No political discussions were generated by the SPC during these meetings; the security issue was not the *main* issue but instead used as a background for the need of psychological preparation. In order to help the foreign players cope with the uncertain situation of threats of terror, relaxation techniques were practiced, not only during the individual meetings, but also as home assignments. The SPC did not overestimate the effects of the relaxation technique on reducing stress and fear of terror attacks. However, by teaching these techniques, he wanted to deliver a clear message to the foreign players that he was aware of their fears, and was there to help them cope with their concerns.

Another action that was taken by the SPC to help the foreign players cope with threats of terror was to conduct meetings with them and the Jewish players, or between them and the Arab players, to discuss how the Jewish and Arab players dealt with a terror event which had occurred in the past. The foreign players listened to the Jewish or Arab players, asked them some questions, and then all players practiced imagery or relaxation. When terror was discussed, the SPC did not invite the Jewish and Arab players to participate together in the same meetings, in order to prevent political discussions that might lead to emotional debates.

The SPC, as well as the other professionals who worked with the soccer teams, realized that terror events could diminish the cohesion among the players, particularly the relationships between the Jewish and Arab players. They were also aware that the Arab players could be verbally abused during games by the crowd after terror events occur. Therefore, they asked all the players, particularly the leading Jewish players, to support the Arab players during practices and games. For example, they asked the Jewish players to stand next to the Arab players during games when the Arab players were booed by the fans, or to encourage them to ignore the hostile behavior of the crowd and concentrate on the game. They stressed that the team should stay united, and show the crowd that they were professional players who were there to do their job, namely to play hard and win the game.

PRACTICAL RECOMMENDATIONS FOR THE SPC

Based on the experience of the SPC working in three different professional soccer clubs in which the players came from different backgrounds and had different approaches to the sport psychology program, six practical recommendations are given to SPCs who work with professional soccer clubs:

(a) The SPC should work as closely as possible not only with the players, but also with the coaches. In addition, we suggest that he or she initiate a number of meetings with the representatives of the club's management during the season;

(b) All players, in our case Jewish, Arab, and foreign, should be treated equally. The nationality, culture, or political preference of the players should not play any role when providing them with psychological interventions. In addition, no political discussion should be encouraged by the SPC during meetings;

(c) Although he or she works with soccer teams, the SPC should conduct individual meetings and meetings with a small number of players in order to effectively administer his or her interventional techniques;

(d) The SPC should use the diversity among the soccer players to enhance his or her psychological program. Grouping together players from different backgrounds and cultures can help the consultant overcome cultural barriers and facilitate mutual understanding among players;

(e) The SPC should cooperate with all experts working with the club in order to increase his or her understanding of the physical and psychological states of the soccer players;

(f) Although various interventional techniques have been reported in the literature, the SPC should use those techniques that he or she is familiar with, and which have empirical support. In our case, the 5-SA and our specific psychological training program served as the major consultation techniques. Both interventions were developed and empirically examined by the SPC after many years of providing psychological consultation to elite and Olympic athletes.

REFERENCES

Ben-Porat, A. (1998). The commodification of football in Israel. *International Review of the Sociology of Sport, 33,* 296-276.

Ben-Porat, A. (2001). 'Biladi, Biladi': Ethnic and nationalistic conflict in the soccer stadium in Israel. *Soccer and Society, 2,* 19-38.

Blumenstein, B., and Bar-Eli, M. (2005). Biofeedback applications in sport. In D. Hackfort, J. L. Duda, and R. Lidor (Eds.), *Handbook of research in applied sport and exercise psychology: International perspectives* (pp. 185-197). Morgantown, WV: Fitness Information Technology.

Blumenstein, B., and Lidor, R. (2007). The road to the Olympic Games: A four-year psychological preparation program. *Athletic Insight – The Online Journal of Sport Psychology,9(4).*

Blumenstein, B., Lidor, R., and Tenenbaum, G. (2005). Periodization and planning of psychological preparation in elite combat sport programs. *International Journal of Sport and Exercise Psychology, 3,* 7-25.

Henschen, K. (2005). Mental practice – skill oriented. In D. Hackfort, J. L. Duda, and R. Lidor (Eds.), *Handbook of research in applied sport and exercise psychology: International perspectives* (pp. 19-34). Morgantown, WV: Fitness Information Technology.

Lidor, R., and Blumenstein, B. (2009). Psychological services for elite athletes in Israel: Regional challenges and solutions for effective practice. In R. J. Schinke and S. J. Hanrahan (Eds.), *Cultural sport psychology*(pp. 141-152).Champaign, IL: Human Kinetics.

Lidor, R., Blumenstein, B., and Tenenbaum, G. (2007a). Psychological aspects of training in European basketball: Conceptualization, periodization, and planning. *The Sport Psychologist, 21,* 353-367.

Lidor, R., Blumenstein, B., and Tenenbaum, G. (2007b). Periodization and planning of psychological preparation in individual and team sports. In B. Blumenstein, R. Lidor, and G. Tenenbaum (Eds.), *Psychology of sport training* (pp. 137-161). London, UK: Meyer and Meyer Sports.

Moran, A. (2005). Training attention and concentration skills in athletes. In D. Hackfort, J. L. Duda, and R. Lidor (Eds.), *Handbook of research in applied sport and exercisepsychology: International perspectives* (pp. 61-73). Morgantown, WV: Fitness Information Technology.

Short, S. E., Bruggeman, J. M., Engel, S. G., Marback, T. L. Wang, L. J., Willadsen, A., et al. (2002). The effect of imagery function and imagery direction on self-efficacy and performance on a golf-putting task. *The Sport Psychologist, 16,*48-67.

In: Introduction to Sport Psychology
Editor: Robert Schinke

ISBN: 978-1-61761-973-1
© 2011 Nova Science Publishers, Inc.

MENTAL TRAINING IN MOTOR SPORTS: PSYCHOLOGICAL CONSULTING FOR RACECAR DRIVERS IN JAPAN

*Yoichi Kozuma**

Applied Sport Psychology and Mental Training Lab
TokaiUniversity, 1117 Kitakaname
Hiratsuka City, Kanagawa 259-1292 JAPAN

The Japanese sports world has a longstanding tradition of using a mentoring style of coaching where the coaches train their athletes in the same manner in which they were trained. This coaching style is a reflection of traditional Japanese cultural disciplines such as martial arts, religious practices, music, fine arts and crafts as well as tea and flower ceremonies where the master would teach the apprentice the skills and techniques that were imparted to them from previous masters who lived ages ago. In sports, this coaching legacy cycle repeats over and over again through the years as the athlete becomes the coach and the time-honored training practices are passed down to a new generation of athletes. These training practices are so culturally ingrained into the sport that the use of any other method is often considered to be a show of disrespect towards the tradition of the sport. This attitude towards implementing new ideas and methods hold true for both traditional Japanese sports as well as for sports introduced from the West. With such strong traditional and cultural beliefs firmly in place, it is often difficult to introduce innovative sports science methods to Japanese coaches and athletes.

In addition to the cultural barriers mentioned above, there are also personal obstacles. With easy access to rapid global information, Japanese athletes and coaches now have the ability to study and gather information of successful training practices from around the world. Even with this information, those involved in the Japanese sports world are still divided on whether or not new scientific methods or ideas should be implemented or even be tried. There are times when some athletes are willing to utilize new methods that may lead them to performance enhancement, but their coaches may be wary of introducing an unfamiliar new training method because it goes against tradition. By the same token, it is also possible for the coaches to be willing to seek new practical solutions for improving athletic performances, while the athletes themselves are unwilling to cooperate in a new training method that defies the tradition of the sport. Facilitating new training methods based on science becomes a

* E-mail: kozuma@keyaki.cc.u-tokai.ac.jp

daunting task because both the coaches and the athletes have preconceived notions of the types of training that are necessary or important. Unfortunately, these set ideas often hinder their ability to look beyond tradition and culture. Once in a while, however, there comes a time when both the coaches and the athletes are willing to seek new training methods that is considered to be completely outside of the realm of that particular sport. This transformative moment happened in Japan for the sport of motor racing.

In 2005, the major Japanese automobile manufacturing companies of Honda, Nissan and Toyota banded together to establish a project called Formula Challenge Japan (FCJ). The purpose of this project is to cultivate talented young racecar drivers to eventually compete at the world level through a progression of different racing categories starting with a newly initiated junior formula race circuit category. Promising young drivers from ages 16-26 who are Japanese kart-racing champions are tested and selected to participate in this innovative program. Once in the program, the young drivers are mentored and coached by racing advisers. The role of the racing adviser is to help support and train the young drivers to become world-class racers. Even though the goal is to have the racecar drivers compete at an international level, the motor sport field in Japan also fosters the same pattern of the traditional Japanese training approach in order to train their young drivers. Namely, the racing advisers use the techniques and psychological factors from their own experiences as racecar drivers to train and teach the new crop of drivers.

Shortly after the start of this young driver's program, I was contacted by one of the FCJ racing advisers. Upon reading a book that I wrote called "Mental Training Program for Athletes" (Kozuma, 2002), which introduces a step-by-step mental training program for performance enhancement to athletes, the racing adviser called to let me know that he was opened to the idea of using mental training as a component of the young driver's training program. The adviser was a past champion of the 24 hour Le Mans race in France and felt that mental training could be an effective tool in Formula 1 (F1) racing. I was asked to be the sport psychology consultant for his team of young drivers.

AN INTRODUCTION OF MENTAL TRAINING TO THE RACE FIELD

In 2006, I conducted a 3-hour mental training seminar specifically tailored to young racecar drivers of Formula Challenge Japan (FCJ). 27 racecar drivers from Honda, Toyota, and Nissan as well as over 10 racing advisers and other racing affiliated people participated in the seminar. This was the first time in Japanese racing history that an event was held with the sole purpose of educating racecar drivers, racing advisers, and others about sport psychology and mental training. The seminar was designed to introduce a mental training program for performance enhancement specifically for the racecar drivers. The introduction consisted of an explanation to the young racecar drivers of basic psychological skills such as goal setting, relaxation, psyching-up, visualization, concentration, positive thinking, self-talk, communication and mental preparation for the race. Each of the 27 racecar drivers were administered a sport psychology test in order to analyze their psychological aptitude. All of the seminar participants were also assigned my mental training textbook (Kozuma, 2008a), the companion workbook (Kozuma, 2008b) and a mental training log (Kozuma, 2008c).

For the next two days, I was able to observe the racing situations as well as the racecar drivers at the racetrack. As a result, I found that mental preparation for the races was an area of great concern for many of the drivers. Many racecar drivers communicated with me that they felt a lot of pressure before the actual race. The pressure was especially heavy at the start of the race and for many drivers this was a very serious psychological concern for them. The majority of the drivers were still in their mid-teens, and they really did not know how to control their emotions when faced with pressure. They had to learn about self-control without having any knowledge of any psychological methods that might have been effective for them. The racing advisers were also not familiar with sport psychology, much less any self-control skills or techniques, therefore they could not offer any guidance to the young drivers. Because of this lack of information, both drivers and advisers admitted that drivers were on their own when it came to self-control and facing pressure.

APPLIED MENTAL TRAINING PROGRAM TO THE RACE FIELD

After the initial introduction of mental training at the seminar held for FCJ drivers and associates, I was approached by Toyota to continue my mental training program for a new project Toyota was supporting called the Toyota Young Drivers Program (TDP). The TDP is a formula racing training school with a targeted age group of 16-26 year old racecar drivers. Candidates to enter TDP are selected from those who have been identified to have outstanding potential as racecar drivers based on their experience in the kart-racing category. TDP supports the young drivers by providing a wide range of opportunities for these drivers to gain race experience and to hone their skills so they can eventually compete both domestically and internationally. TDP was interested in starting a mental training program for performance enhancement for the 2007 race season. I was initially contracted as a sport psychology consultant for racecar drivers in the FCJ and the Formula 3 (F3) categories. My work for TDP started in March before the start of the 2007 race season and the participating members were three F3 drivers, nine FCJ drivers and one Formula Nippon (F Nippon) driver. The F Nippon category is the highest race circuit in Japan and one stage away from Formula One. All three categories of racing are considered to be the mandatory steppingstones that propel a driver into a career in F1 racing.

An all day introductory seminar was conducted for the participating drivers. The purpose of this seminar was to introduce a beginner's level of mental training to all the drivers as well as to evaluate their psychological aptitude. The participants were administered a Japanese sport psychological test called DIPCA.3 (Diagnostic Inventory of Psychological Competitive Ability for Athletes) in order to analyze the racecar driver's psychological aptitude. DIPCA.3 (Tokunaga, 2001) is designed to analyze 12 different psychological scales associated with sports, such as patience, fighting spirit, achievement motivation, motivation to win, self-control, relaxation, concentration, self-confidence, decision-making, prediction, judgment, and cooperation. In addition, DIPCA.3 also measures five factors of competitive motivation, self-confidence, cooperation, psychological stability& focus and strategy& imagery. DIPCA.3 was administered three times throughout the race season: preseason, mid-season, and before the last race of the season. The results of all of the factors involved from DIPCA.3 are consolidated into a web chart. The total score for DIPCA.3 is 240 points. To give an overview of what we are looking for with DIPCA.3, we use the score of 200 points as the baseline for any athlete from any sport. Athletes who score above 220 have the aptitude or potential to become national champions. For younger athletes, a score of 180 points is national championship potential. On the whole, the average score for a middle school athlete is about 140 points and a high school athlete averages about 160 points.

An example of the combined racecar drivers' DIPCA.3 results is provided in Figure 1 (See Figure 1). The mean score plotted on the web chart makes it easy for us to see areas that may need attention. A web chart of a psychologically balanced athlete would look like a round ball. Areas that the athlete may show weakness in or have concerns about will be dents made into the round ball. In Figure 1, two thirds of the graph is well rounded. These particular drivers had an unusual result that showed a strong positive mental aptitude even before the race season and the mental training seminar. This result could stem from the fact that many of the young racecar drivers who participated in this seminar were already champions in the kart-racing category at a young age, therefore they started the mental training program with a slightly elevated level of mental toughness.

There is one third of the graph where dents in the round ball can easily be seen. The psychological factors of concentration, relaxation, self-control and motivation to win make the round ball look more like a jagged rock. These factors show that the drivers were not mentally strong when faced with pressure. Based on these results, we are able to design a mental training program to help improve problematic areas.

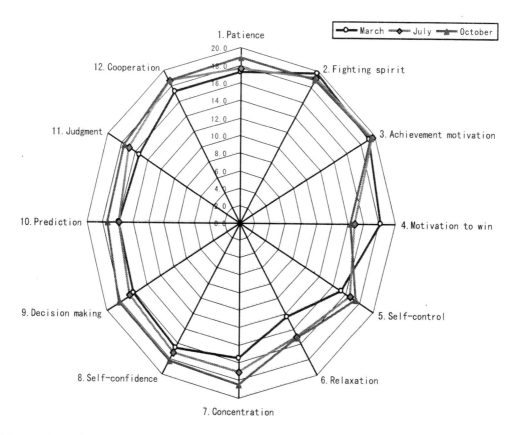

Figure 1. Mean Score Diagnostic Inventory of Psychological Competative Ability for Athletes (DIPCA 3) for TDP Team for March, July and October.

As part of their preseason training schedule, all of the racecar drivers participated in an all day mental training workshop to help jumpstart the 2007 race season. The introductory lecture presented the drivers with psychological skills such as goal setting, relaxation, psyching-up, visualization, concentration, positive thinking, self-talk, communication and mental preparation for the race. A textbook (Kozuma, 2008a), workbook (Kozuma, 2008b) and a mental training logbook (Kozuma, 2008c) were provided to all participants. The 8-hour session was conducted as follows:

Collected and analyzed data through DIPCA.3. An explanation about a driver's data analysis based on their DIPCA.3 results was provided individually to the drivers. The analysis is made on site at the seminar and is only used as a baseline to design a training plan for the individual driver. Recommendations of what kind of training is necessary for the drivers to help them enhance their performance in future competitions were advised and suggested.

Self-analysis. In order to evaluate the driver's knowledge of mental training and their awareness of their own psychological factors, the participants had to provide short answers that reflected their race experience in their workbooks. The drivers had to fill out questions in the workbook that dealt with pressure, balance for mental/technical/physical training, or best race compared to worst race.

Background information. An explanation was provided to the drivers on why psychological skills are important to their sport. An overview of the history of mental training in other countries and in Japan was presented. Video recordings of specific examples from my past consulting experiences were also used to illustrate the advantages of mental training and to justify why mental preparation is important for competition.

Goal setting. The racecar drivers were instructed to write down their goals on a goal-setting sheet provided in the workbook. The drivers had to write specific goals such as goal setting for the race's outcome or goal setting for the race season. In addition a yearly plan, a monthly plan, a weekly plan and a daily plan were compiled. Each driver received a logbook, which is a training diary, as part of the reading material for the workshop and was asked to start writing in the diary specifically for mental training.

Relaxation and psyching-up. A packaged relaxation program was introduced utilizing a variety of relaxation techniques that I created and developed in 1995 (Kozuma, 1995) for various sports teams in Japan. The relaxation exercises include relaxation music, smiling, self-massaging, breathing control, stretching with breathing control, progressive relaxation techniques, simplified autogenic training, meditation for three minutes and imagery. Specific video examples from other athletes in different sports demonstrating relaxation, psyching-up and self-conditioning were shown to the drivers. After the relaxation exercises, a psyching-program was initiated. The psyching-up program consists of dance music, several dancing exercises, shadow boxing, fun partner games (e.g., rock, paper, scissors) and a team workout routine. Furthermore, as part of their self-conditioning program, a 30-minute daily morning exercise routine was launched and scheduled.

Visualization training. A video introduction of a step-by-step systematic visualization program was shown. Using imagery for visualization was conducted right after the relaxation exercises. I told the drivers to create mentally an image of their best driving experience. Then I told them to try to add physical movements (e.g. shifting gears) to that best driving image that they had just created. Next, I instructed them to try to recreate their best driving image with the same physical movement but this time to do it in slow motion. First, the visualization was in half the normal speed and then it was revert back to full normal speed. The purpose of this exercise is to transform their imagery rehearsal into a physical rehearsal. I would ask them to visualize in slow motion so that they can create a clearer image. I want them to be aware of their physical movement: to check which muscles they are using and/or to be conscious of the coordination of their hands and feet. Every detail needs to be part of their visualization.

As homework, the drivers were assigned to do the visualization exercises every day after the relaxation exercises. I also asked them to write down their visualizations in the logbook. Examples include 1. Visualize the Past (recall today's or your last race); 2. Visualize the Present (recall missed or failures and then change them to a positive image with the physical activity); 3. Visualize the Future (repeat the positive image multiple times and merge it with an image of the next race).

Concentration training. This portion of the seminar dealt with concentration training and refocusing exercises through breathing control, vocalization, and focusing activities.

The main techniques taught to increase concentration were:

1. Breathing control techniques such as deep breathing; breathing with body action; breathing with stretching; and breathing with progressive relaxation techniques.
2. Vocal shouting techniques such as using a strong voice, ascending one's voice from normal to loud, positive self-talk in a loud voice; counting numbers out loud in a big voice; exhaling loudly; and a sharp and strong exhalation routine.
3. Focal point techniques such as focusing on a certain point (e.g. the palm of your hand) with deep breathing, focusing on a certain point with positive self-talk, focusing on a certain point with a positive image.
4. Imagery techniques such as counting the numbers in an image (e.g. multiplication table).
5. Playing fun game such as the children's hand-slapping game, shadow boxing with a partner or a martial art training exercise of preventing your partner from touching your shoulder by only using an open hand.

Positive thinking. A lot of time was spent on positive thinking techniques for self-talk, positive communication skills and building self-confidence because these are areas that Japanese athletes truly lack. Japanese society as a whole can be described as very taciturn and impassive in nature. Emotions are generally not shown or expressed in public and compliments are rarely given. Instead, negative and disparaging remarks are often used to degrade a person into submission or compliancy. This is especially evident when you look at the coach and athlete's relationship. The volatile relationship between the coaches and the athletes has created a landscape filled with self-doubt and negative thinking. Because positive thinking is a foreign concept for many coaches and athletes, the importance and efficacy of positive thinking is strongly emphasized throughout my teachings.

Psychological preparation for competition. Throughout the day, the drivers received instructions and training on different types of psychological skills, but they then need to be guided to see how these skills can be applicable for the racecar drivers' situation. The drivers were provided with examples and demonstrations on how to consolidate the mental skills that they had just learned and to apply these skills to their individual racing situations.

2007 RACE SEASON

After the initial introductory seminar, my work with the racecar drivers continued on site at the racetracks. Since the races occur on Saturdays and Sundays, my consultation session covered a whole weekend and included the qualifying rounds in addition to the one main race per day. During the 2007 race season, I had six consultation sessions and was on site for 12 races for the 9 FCJ racecar drivers and three of the F3 drivers. The mental training program continued for the 2008 season and I was able to have eight consultation sessions over the season and was on site for 16 races for 9 FCJ drivers and four of the F3 drivers. The following section discusses the agenda of my consultations with the racecar drivers as well as some case examples that arose from my work.

At the Race Track: Before the Race

With the assistance of one of my graduate students, we would be at the race venue early in the morning around 6:00 am before any of the racecar drivers arrived at the racetrack. Since the races are held at different racetracks throughout the season, our first job was to locate an area where we could conduct our relaxation and psyching-up program. Once the racecar drivers arrive, we would start our relaxation program using relaxation music, positive communication, attitude training, smiling at each other, breathing control, breathing control with stretching, progressive relaxation techniques in a standing position, shouting techniques with visualization, simplified autogenic training, progressive relaxation techniques in a supine position, mediation, visualization for best start and visualization for best start of the race with body action.

The music is switched to an upbeat dancing music to indicate the start of a 20-25 minute psyching-up program. The dance music and other physical activities such as shadow boxing with a partner or fun hand games are incorporated into the exercise in order to increase the heart rate and breathing rate. The drivers also performed a team workout routine. The team workout routine is designed to create and foster an atmosphere of teamwork and to give the drivers their psychological warm-up as a team.

To start their physical warm-up, the next segment of the pre-race workout included a 40-minute session with a strength training coach. After this session, the drivers had about an hour to do the necessary preparations for the actual race. During this time, I am able to give psychological advice and consultation when needed to the drivers around the garage area. The talk is conducted in a casual manner in order to maintain a relax atmosphere before the race. Often times, drivers will request advice to help them refocus after a qualifying heat that made them eligible for the main race of the day. They are usually worried about refocusing after a car spin due to a driving mistake or by being hit by another car. For many drivers, the major refocusing concern was the starting segment of the race, especially after they made a mistake in the previous race due to anxiety and pressure. In motor racing, the position placement in the starting grid is very crucial for the outcome of the race. Starting errors are penalized and as a result they may change the driver's position in the starting grid, which may negatively affect the results of the race.

An example of making errors at the start of the race can be illustrated with a case of one of the drivers I was consulting. This particular driver had the unfortunate experience of committing a false start twice in two races in two consecutive days. On that particular weekend, he had the best race time during the qualifying heat and was given the pole position (first car) for the starting grid of both races. It was his big chance to place first in the two main races and boost his overall standing. After the first false start in the first main race, many of the racing advisers and friends gathered around him and gave him advice and comments about his mistake. This was a rare occurrence for this driver in his racing career, so he quickly understood and recognized the reason for his error. Putting his mental training knowledge to use, he immediately tried to visualize many positive race starting images that he had successfully completed in the past and tried to increase his self-confidence through mental preparation. He thought that he was aware of the psychological skills he would need for the next race and tried to apply his mental training skills towards the next race, however, during the start of the main race on the following day, he committed the same false start blunder again.

What was the reason for this? Well after the race, the driver and I analyzed video recordings of both of his false starts together. In the first race, the driver explained that he felt pressured for being the first car in the line up and that he was also obsessed about the possible winning outcomes of the races. When he was cited for his false start, he received a lot of random advice from many different people. His racing adviser scolded him and he apologized to his adviser for not being more careful. This small verbal exchange further reinforced his negative attention toward his error, thus raising his anxiety level and creating even more pressure for him for the following race. After consulting with me, the driver realized that he was weak in his positive thinking and refocusing skills. He thought he knew how to perform the psychological skills that he used at the time of the incident, but the problem was that he did not use these skills appropriately. He was not mentally prepared because he thought that mental training was something that was used only when needed. He then realized that he needed training in applying his mental skills to his every day practices and in his daily life. In my seminars, I would often tell the participants that mental training is a psychological training program that should be practiced every day just like any segment or component of their physical training program. This is the most important point to remember in order to improve your psychological skills. However, may athletes in Japan miss this point and simply think that mental training can be utilized after reading a book or attending a seminar once. In the case of the false start driver, he realized that psychological training was equally important to him as his physical training. After the second false start incident, the driver changed his attitude about mental training and started to practice his mental training every day. He never repeated the same false start blunder again. At the end of the season, he placed third in the overall ranking standing for the F3 category, a precursor category of races for F1 drivers.

There was another racer who was only able to perform a good clean start at a dismal rate of less than 10% of the time. At the beginning of each race, he was constantly making errors through false starts, delayed starts or simply was not be able to perform a nice smooth start. He realized his problem was psychological and decided to integrate mental training as part of his practice routine. As a result, he was finally able to overcome the anxiety he felt at the start of each race and eventually became the F3 category National Class Series Champion.

After all the mechanical and logistical inspections have been completed by the crew, the racecar driver settles into a pre-performance routine which includes self-talk while putting on their helmet and getting inside the car. They also reset their emotions by using the steering wheel as the focal point and looking up at me to give me a smile. During this pre-performance routine, there is a little bit of time for me to check the expressions of their faces and eyes as well as their behavior, attitudes and body language. My assistant records a video footage of this moment before the race for post-race analyses. As the driver is recorded, audio comments are made about the driver's facial expressions, their communication towards others, the manner in which they talk to the crew and the way they carry themselves as they walk towards their racecar. The driver is not aware of any of the comments made at this time. DVD copies of all the drivers' pre-race recordings are given to all of the racecar drivers and to the racing advisers for team-analysis. For self-analysis, the drivers are told to focus on their facial expressions, behavior, attitudes and body language. This is helpful because some drivers may tell me that they are relaxed and are ready for the race, but their stiffness in their walk or their tensed face is telling a totally different story. For homework, they are assigned to do an activity in the workbook by writing down what was going on in their minds or what they were thinking about at that particular time on the video footage. As a teaching tool, copies of the video footage of the F2 and F Nippon drivers were also given to the lower race category drivers so that they can have an opportunity to observe the more experience driver's mental preparation routine. Being able to observe the pre-race routines of drivers from higher level racing categories is very helpful because the video can be used as a good example and a good role model for the younger less experienced drivers.

Before an actual race, the racecar drivers are allowed to drive around the track once before lining up in the starting grid. Once the racecar is in position at the starting line, there is still 10 minutes before the race when the crew and staff are allowed to still enter the track. This is the last opportunity for the mechanics and the racing advisor to communicate with the driver and to double-check the racecar. This is also a chance for me to check the driver's mental condition. Once again, the drivers are videotaped, but this time due to their helmets their facial expressions are limited to their eyes. Even with this limitation, the eyes can easily express the emotional state of a person. Calmness, concentration or focusing can be revealed through the eyes of a person. If I notice anything, I make comments on the video recording for the driver to review later. Even though the engines are not running, hand gestures are used for communication because the driver is not only wearing a helmet but is also wearing earplugs too. Once the driver is mentally prepared for the race, the driver will look up at me and give me a thumbs-up gesture.

There are some drivers, however, who require a few words of advice from me before the race. Of course as a sport psychology consultant, I am fully aware that is not preferable to give any advice or talk just before a competition because it may interfere with the athlete's concentration. However, in the case of the racecar drivers, some are still very young and are not really mature enough to control and settle themselves emotionally before the race. In situations like these, I would work with them and give them simple advice or words of encouragement as part of their mental preparation for the race. After the race, I would talk with the driver and ask him how my advice affected him before the race. I would ask him whether or not my advice was useful to him at that time and if not, then what did the driver considered to be the best advice I have ever given him. The underlying objective of this conversation is to keep it positive for the driver and to also build a foundation that would enhance my communication with him so that I can help the driver further improve his mental preparation before the next race.

Once I receive the thumbs-up gesture, I pan the video camera to record the view of the racetrack from the viewpoint of the driver. For example, if the driver is in the pole position of the race, then as the first car in the grid he does not have any other cars blocking his view. But if the driver were the 3rd car in the grid, then his view would have both the pole position car and the second position car to the left and right of his field of vision. The views from the drivers' perspective of the race are recorded in order to help create a vivid starting image for the visualization exercises for the next race. When the all-clear signal is issued, I leave the track and the race officially starts after the formation lap has been completed.

After the race, I would interview each of the drivers and ask them about their state of mind during certain segments of the race, such as at the start of the race, during the race, after any kind of mistake or accident and at the outcome of the race. My assistant makes a video recording of these interviews and I review these post-race interviews with the drivers after every race. DVD copies of the interviews are also given to the racecar drivers and to their racing advisers. This allows the drivers to check their post-race reaction for self-analysis.

Seminars before and after the Races

My assistant and I continued to provide psychological support throughout the entire race season. Racecar drivers usually practice at the racetrack on Thursdays and Fridays. They are allowed to practice for only two hours a day for a total of four hours. The qualifying rounds are 15 minutes long and are held twice a day on Saturdays and Sundays. There is only a 10-minute break in between the two qualifying heat. The results of the qualifying heat determine the position in the starting grid for the main races, which are held only once a day on Saturday and Sunday afternoons. After the main race on Saturday, whenever I was on site at the racetrack I would hold a two-hour seminar. This time period was selected because it would be the day before the second qualifying races and it was also a good time for reflection, refocusing and preparation for the Sunday's main race. As the race season progressed, I would tailor the seminars to meet the needs of the racecar drivers' situations and age group. The following examples are approaches that I used to teach certain psychological skills to racecar drivers when they were beginners in the mental training program.

Cultural Approach

To approach the racecar drivers about mental training, I relied on many techniques gleaned from traditional Japanese martial arts. In junior high school and senior high school, all boys must learn either judo or kendo as part of their physical education requirement. Thus, it can be said that most Japanese males are familiar the techniques and practices that are associated with martial arts. They may not be aware of the various purposes behind the techniques and practices, but they have at least experienced some martial arts training, therefore the concept is not foreign to them. Because the racecar drivers were teens with a background in martial arts, it was easy for me to adapt the skills and techniques used in martial arts as a foundation for my mental training program. Also, it made it easier for the racecar drivers to understand the mental training program when they could see a correlation between mental training and martial arts.

I came upon this idea a long time ago when I was a graduate student. When I was learning about sport psychology and mental training, I realized that I already knew the skillsand techniques that were being described from my own martial arts training. I started to think that techniques such as *ibuki* (breathing control for concentration), *kata* (arranged fighting forms) or *ma* (refocusing techniques) from karate could be adapted and used in other sports. My conviction grew stronger years later when I was talking to a friend and colleague Richard M. Suinn, who is now professor emeritus of counseling psychology at ColoradoStateUniversity. He asked me why was I looking to the west for information when research from the United States was looking into eastern practices. He suggested that I should look closer to home, and that is exactly what I started to do as I created mental training programs for various athletes.

For motor sports, I saw similarities with the training practices of racecar drivers and martial artists. Although the main objective for Formula Challenge Japan (FCJ) is to train Japanese racecar drivers so they can compete in an international arena, the training environment in Japan is really not conducive to achieve this goal. One limitation found in the Japanese training program is the amount hours a driver can practice in order to compete for a race season. In Europe, the training program affords the drivers to log in nearly 20,000 hours of practice on the track. Due to financial constraints, the racecar drivers in Japan receive about 6,000 hours of practice. So the Japanese racecar drivers are expected to compete internationally, yet when compared to other countries they have less practice hours to prepare for competition--a clear disadvantage.

Training in martial arts is very similar. Contrary to images created and seen in many movies, martial artists do not constantly fight all the time. The traditional idea behind martial arts is to protect and defend oneself. For the martial artist, their contact time with an opponent is limited, but when the warriors do meet they are fighting for their lives. In order to maximize their training, martial artists practice *kata*, which is a sequence of arranged fighting forms and techniques that is performed against an imaginary opponent. To those who are not familiar with *kata*, it may look as if the martial artist is performing choreographed dance movements, but in actuality the martial artist is using visualization and image training to defeat his or her opponent. *Kata*, especially for karate, utilizes autogenic training and progressive relaxation techniques. This is because *kata* involves both striking attack techniques as well as defensive movements. Sandwiched in between these movements, is a pause called *ma*. This pause is not for the martial artist to rest, but to refocus on the task at hand. This pause is very similar to the pause that can be seen between pitches in a baseball game: a time to refocus and concentrate on the next pitch. In addition, breathing control techniques is used for concentration and self-control. The outcome of each *kata* movement is a successful completion of the skill or technique to incapacitate the opponent in an actual combat situation. The martial artists always defeat his or her *kata* opponent.

Kata has been a part of karate training since the very beginning. Karate was developed on the island of Okinawa at a time when the Shimazu Clan from Satsuma, Kyushu invaded the Ryukyu Islands around the early 17th century (Yan, 2004). During the occupation of Okinawa, weapons were prohibited to ensure that the people of Okinawa would not revolt against the Satsuma rule. According to folklore, this banishment of weapons did not discourage the people of Okinawa from planning a rebellion. With a covert plan to defend their land and drive out the occupying forces, the people of Okinawa started to developed a style of martial arts that did not rely on traditional Japanese sword fighting. In order to keep their training a secret from their enemies, their training time was limited because they could only train at night in the woods and since it was a grassroots movement, they would use farm tools and anything in the environment such as the stones, the trees and the rivers to improve their skills. It was a matter of life or death for them; therefore, it was essential to train as much as they could before they confronted their enemy. *Kata* was a way for them to maximize their training in a dangerous situation.

In a similar manner, Japanese racecar drivers are involved in a very dangerous sport with limited amount of training. A wrong move on the track could be fatal to the drivers, the crew or even the fans watching from the stands. Therefore, it is also essential for the racecar drivers to practice and train as much as they can before each race. With limitation placed on the actual practice time on the racetrack, a visualization program would be crucial in order to maximize their training time, to create a positive image for their racing and to be mentally prepared for any obstacles that they may encounter.

Visualization

Visualization is an important mental training skill, yet many of the racecar drivers were not familiar with this skill. This was a difficult task for several of the drivers, so I decided that I would guide them through this process so that they could fully understand the importance and effectiveness of visualization. To start, I asked the drivers to visualize an image of an Australian football team. I selected this particular sport because most Japanese are simply not familiar with Australian football and without any knowledge of the sport, it would be very difficult for anyone to create any image associated with the Australian sport. Next, I asked them to demonstrate some moves that are used in Australian football or to visualize how many members are on a team. As a group, I then asked them if anyone was able to create an image of the sport. Since no one was familiar at all with the sport, no one was able to create an image.

This is a simple demonstration that I often used for beginners in mental training to introduce visualization techniques. I want the athletes to realize that it is difficult to create a positive image if they do not have any foundation or building blocks to help them to develop the image. I want the athletes to become aware that once they have created a positive image, then it is possible to achieve what they see in that image because they have the necessary information and knowledge needed to build it into a successful image.

In order to adapt the visualization process specifically to the racecar drivers, I asked the drivers to visualize a successful image that represents their best smooth start of a race. I felt that this would be an ideal situation to use because all of the drivers have experience a successful start in a race thereby making it easier for them to create a positive image. I then asked the drivers to recall every physical detail about their best start of the race and to visualize this successful start in slow motion at 50% of the normal speed. Once they were able to visualize in a slow manner, I asked them to once again visualize their best start of the race back to the normal speed of 100%. This helps create a clear vivid picture in their minds as well as convert their imagery rehearsal into a physical rehearsal.

Because accidents are detrimental physically and psychologically to the racecar drivers, visualization techniques need to also include images of what the drivers would do in the event of an accident. Generally, the time when most accidents occur is during the first segment of the race. At the start of the race, there are 27 racing cars careening towards the first corner of the track. With drivers handing powerful machines at a high speed, often times it really does not take much for the race cars to be involved in a multi-vehicle crash. It could be a racecar driver who over compensated in taking the curb or just simply racecars slightly bumping into one another and sending the vehicles into a tailspin. Other times it can be a mechanical problem or sometimes a racecar starts to spin around on its own accord without any interference whatsoever. Accidents happen and in any situations like these, visualization skills can be an effective tool. Whether or not the driver is involved in the mishap, the driver can visualize what to do when an accident occurs. The drivers can practice self-control by visually mapping out how he would gain control of his vehicle as he maneuvers over the track to avoid any of the racecars that might become a deterrent or an obstruction in his path.

Daily practice is the key to the success of using visualization. Just as the martial artist practice their *kata* over and over again in order to be prepared for any happenstance that might occur, such as knowing what to do when they see a weapon, a kick or a punch coming towards them, the racecar drivers were also instructed to practice visualization every day.

Seminar for Concentration

In order to introduce techniques for concentration, I would often use a traditional breathing technique that is used in Japanese martial arts. First, I asked the drivers to inhale and exhale through their nose. After several attempts, I asked them how they felt when they did this type of breathing control. Next, I asked them to inhale and exhale by their month and once again, I inquired about how they felt after breathing in the manner. I continue to ask them to inhale through their mouths and exhale through their nose and then reverse it by inhaling through their nose and exhaling through their mouths. Finally, I asked the drivers to decide on which breathing manner they felt more comfortable with if they had to concentrate and focus on their driving. For most athletes, inhaling through the nose and exhaling through the mouth is the most common manner of breathing control. Just as it is difficult to swing a bat or golf club as you inhale, it is the forced air through your mouth that gives you power and speed to do what needs to be accomplished. Breathing through your nose and exhaling through your mouth is an efficient and quick manner to increase your focus and concentration.

As I take them through several variations of breathing control techniques, I asked the drivers to pay attention to their body's reaction as they go through the deep breathing exercises while stretching or performing progressive relaxation techniques or vocalization techniques. The reason is that this type of breathing control works best when the inhalation and exhalation is matched with a physical activity. When the drivers add physical movement to their breathing exercise, they are becoming more cognizant of when they need to inhale and when they need to exhale.

In addition to these breathing techniques for concentration and refocusing, Japanese martial artists use these vocal techniques to create power, speed and a rhythm for the drive behind a particular movement. In Japanese, it is called, "*ibuki*" and this is the breathing control technique used just before you break a wooden board or a slab of ice with a karate chop. The sound that is expressed by the martial artist is a type of psyching-up and concentration techniques to channel one's power and speed into a focal point of energy powerful enough to break a solid object.

Racecar drivers especially need concentration and refocusing skills when they are hit or have mechanical problems on the track. If a driver is hit during a race or if a driver has mechanical problem, then the driver is automatically disqualified from continuing the race for that particular day. If the accident should happen on a Saturday, then the racecar is repaired and ready to race again the following day. During the repair time, different issues can easily arise that may distract the driver so the goal is to use this time in a positive manner. For some, distractions can come from the mechanics as they give the drivers a report on their racecar or from the racing adviser who is unhappy about the accident. For others, financial concerns may cloud their minds because drivers who are not on scholarship are financially responsible for the expensive repairs of their vehicle. With such a short turn around time and with endless possibilities for negative thinking to increase, the racecar drivers need to be able to quickly and efficiently refocus and concentrate on racing again.

Positive Thinking

I am a big fan of the psychological skill of self-talk. I am also a firm believer that self-talk can be used to improve one's positive thinking. The use of positive self-talk during a race is a quick and efficient tool to keep a driver in a more positive frame of mind. If a racecar driver has the ability to use positive self-talk, then he will also have the ability to maintain a positive state of mind throughout different segments of the actual race such as the start of the race, when taking a corner, after committing error or when the car is in an uncontrollable spin.I also consider self-talk as a type of breathing control and self-suggestion technique. When we use positive words, it is usually accompanied with a strong breath and a big exhalation or air. For example, try to say words like "Nice! OK! Very Good! Great! " or "Awesome Job!". These words are usually expressed with a strong breath and a big exhalation of air, not to mention the fact that you are usually smiling as you say these words. These positive expressions and breathing techniques will enhance your self-confidence and give you an overall positive state of mind.

In Japanese martial arts, breathing control along with the vocal shouting techniques that were previously discussed earlier are important skills for positive thinking. Going back to the example of a martial artist trying to break a board or a large slab of ice, you may have probably noticed that a martial artist will use a combination of breathing control and vocal shouting techniques to increase their concentration just before the performance. This is a type of psyching-up routine that incorporates positive thinking, self-confidence and concentration skills for the martial artist. The function of vocalization is similar to self-talk because it is used to enhance the performance of the task by increasing the power and the speed of the martial artist. This is the reason why you will often hear loud voices from many Japanese martial artists during their practices and competitions. These traditional ideas were taken from the past, modified and adapted for the purpose of making them applicable for a non-martial art sport in order to improve the performance of an athlete.

I also consider communication to be a type of self-control technique that can be used for positive thinking. When we use positive communication, we are generally in a positive state of mind. When we are in a negative state of mind; then it is reflected in our speech and it makes it very difficult for us to use any positive words in our speech. Of course, communication is used to exchange information with other people, but it can also be used to influence oneself. Just as the breathing control example given previously of expressing positive words with a strong breath and a big exhalation of air, expressing negative words has the direct opposite effect. Negative words are usually expressed with a weak breath, a shallow exhalation of air, and without a smile. The bottom line is that nothing deflates your self-confidence quicker than negative thinking. The good news is that negative thinking can be reversed through breathing control, positive self-talk and positive thinking.

Additional Sport Psychology Consulting Work

After every race, the racecar drivers will send me an email containing their post-race report. I would reply to each of their emails with advice or suggestions for any of the psychological concerns the drivers may have experienced. Table 1 is a sample of a racecar driver's post-race report that was submitted to me electronically.

Table 1. A Sample of Post-race Report

Circuit	Fuji Speed Way		Driver	Toyota
Date	2007 Jun 6 ~ 7		Car	FCJ
Team	I have good open communications with the mechanic, driver and adviser.			
Car	Having no problems with my machine. I can adjust the air pressure of the tires.			
Engine	I had an engine oil problem, but no other problem surfaced.			
Transmission	I had trouble with the transmission in the previous race, but I experienced no problems for this race.			
Tires	They were too strong at the start of the last race. I controlled the pressure of the tires for this race.			
Brakes	I changed the master cylinder after the last race. The brakes felt better in this race.			
Driver's Impression	In the qualifying heat, I was not attuned to the pace of the race. I could not control my mind. I want to control myself and my machine.			
Mental Conditioning	I tried visualization for the qualifying race and the race before the practice session. I had good concentration before the race, but I could not control my mind during the race after I experienced a spin. A sport psychology consultant held a seminar after the race, and he talked about the flow of the race. I could not feel the flow in this race. I need more mental preparation such as relaxation and psyching-up before the next race.			
Physical Conditioning	A training coach had us warming-up before the race. I was well prepared physically.			
Achievement	My purpose for this race was for me to find my self-confidence. But I could not find any reason to boost my self-confidence in this race.			
Problems to be solved	I have to change my mind about racing. I need more mental, physical and technical preparations and I need to use it in my daily life. Especially, I need more self-confidence for racing. I would like to find a reason for my low self-esteem.			

In addition to the on site consultations, some of the racecar drivers would also visit Tokai University, which is located just outside of Tokyo, in order to attend a weekly mental training meeting that I conduct. This meeting is open to anyone who is interested in mental training and many athletes, coaches, students, training coaches, athletic trainers, and other sport related people have actively participated in these weekly meetings. The agenda of these meetings include lectures symposium, discussions, workshops conducted either by me or by selected sport psychology graduate students in my department. Some of the racecar drivers who have participated in this weekly mental training meeting were able to gather additional information on how they could further improve their psychological skills and knowledge and apply it to their racing.

2009 RACE SEASON

I am still continuing my work as a sport psychology consultant for the TDP racecar drivers. The drivers that I work with now are from the FCJ, F3 and F Nippon categories. From 2006-2009, I have had an opportunity to work with over 50 young racecar drivers in Japan. Through this opportunity, my staff and I have been able to make an impact on the racing advisers and sponsors of motor sports about the importance and effectiveness of mental training in auto racing. This has been a vital step in educating those who are involved in motor sport about sport psychology. We have been able to dismantle the myth and uncertaintyof psychological support offered to the athletes and coachesby presenting a correlation of psychological skills training with similar skills used in traditional Japanese martial arts. This cultural familiarity helped strengthen the racecar drivers' comprehension of mental training and also helped diminish the notion that it is a foreign concept that is not suited for the Japanese. I have also noticed that more racing advisers are attending our monthly mental training meetings to further improve their coaching style. It has been reported from the racetrack that the racing advisers are using a more positive approach when instructing the new drivers. In addition, the drivers are more positive about racing and are even using positive words when they speak to each other or give each other encouragement.

Due to the current global economic uncertainties, the budget of TDP has been affected and the financial support to continue the program has decreased. So far in 2009, I have only been able to attend six races, instead of the usual dozen or so I have worked at in the years past. Even with the budget restraint, TDP has expressed that it would like to continue to provide mental training and psychological consultations for its young driver's program. This gesture tells me that TDP is visibly aware of the importance of psychological training and is sincerely committed to support the use of mental training in motor sports.

REFERENCES

Diagnostic inventory of psychological competitive ability for athletes: DIPCA.3. Fukuoka, Japan: Toyo Physical.

Kozuma, Y. (1995). *Asukara tsukaeru mentarutore-ningu* [Mental training you can use from tomorrow]. Tokyo, Japan: Baseball Magazine Sha.

Kozuma, Y. (2002). *Ima sugu tsukaeru mentarutore-ningu: A mental training program for athletes.* Tokyo, Japan: Baseball Magazine Sha.

Kozuma Y. (2003). *Ima sugu tsukaeru mentarutore-ningu: A mental training program for coaching.* Tokyo, Japan: Baseball Magazine Sha.

Kozuma, Y. (2008a). *Kiso kara manabu mentarutore-ningu* [Learning the fundamentals of mental training]. Tokyo, Japan: Baseball Magazine Sha.

Kozuma, Y. (2008b). *Kiso kara manabu mentarutore-ningu waakubukku* [Learning the fundamentals of mental training workbook]. Kanagawa, Japan: TokaiUniversity Press.

Kozuma, Y. (2008c). *Le-sa no mentarutore-ningu waakubukku* [Mental training workbook for racers]. Kanagawa, Japan: TokaiUniversity Applied Sport Psychology and Mental Training Lab.

Kozuma, Y. (2008d). *Yakyusenshu no mentarutoreningu* [Mental training for baseball players]. Tokyo, Japan: Baseball Magazine Sha.

Tan, K. S. Y. (2004). Constructing a martial tradition: Rethinking a popular history of karate-dou. *Journal of Sport and Social Issues, 28,* 169-194.

Tokunaga, M. (2001). Evaluation scales for athletes' psychological competitive ability: Development and systematization of the scales. *Journal of Health Science, 23,* 91-102.

In: Introduction to Sport Psychology
Editor: Robert Schinke

ISBN: 978-1-61761-973-1

TRANSITIONING INTO THE AFL:
INDIGENOUS FOOTBALL PLAYERS' PERSPECTIVES

Emma E. Campbell[*1] and *Christopher C. Sonn*[2#]
[1]Dubai Women's College, Dubai
[2]VictoriaUniversity
Melbourne, Australia

Transitioning into the AFL: Indigenous Football Players' Perspectives Sport plays an important part in Indigenous culture, politics is an important part, sport's important, and it brings the community together. On some communities it is a matter of life and death. It's what our programs bring, being part, participating in football, community being involved, raising awareness on alcohol and drugs, health issues, very important part in how we can make an impact on Australia. Football is such a powerful tool, it's one thing Indigenous people love, that's football, not saying it's going to change our world, but geez we've got something there that can attract the kids, families and can change an ecosystem, make an impact on all different levels. We've got players, Indigenous players that are powerful tools; they are seen as heroes, role models. They can have an impact through a leather ball. (Michael Long, AFL Ambassador, cited in Roberts, 2005).

The quotation above highlights the important and powerful role of sport in Indigenous communities in Australia. Participation in sports can be a way of integrating Indigenous people to the larger society and providing opportunities for social participation and social identity construction, as well as opportunities for engaging in meaningful and rewarding roles. Since the mid 90's, there has been a steady increase in the number of Indigenous Australian footballers joining the Australian Football League (AFL). In 1990, the number of Indigenous footballers was 16 and, twenty years later, in 2009, the number has risen to 82 (AFLPA, 2009). The numbers exceeded 50 for the first time in 2006 and, in 2009, Indigenous footballers make up more than 14% of the AFL lists. In comparison, Indigenous Australians make up 2.2% of the Australian population (ABS, 2006). There are various views about the popularity of Australian Rules football within Indigenous communities, in particular with young Indigenous men. Some of these views include that the AFL is a prospect for social mobility and opportunity, suggesting limited options in other workforce areas. The popularity of AFL may be due to the increasing visibility of Indigenous men experiencing successful

---

*Dr Emma Campbell, Higher Colleges of Technology, Dubai Women's College, PO Box 16062.Dubai, United Arab Emirates, E-mail: emma.campbell@hct.ac.ae

The authors would like to acknowledge the participants and also Robert Schinke and Lutfiye Ali for their comments on an earlier draft of this article.

AFL careers. The heightened status of AFL may have been influenced by the promotion of AFL programmes in rural remote Indigenous communities (Godwell, 2000; Hallinan, Bruce, and Burke, 2005).

Researchers who have considered challenges associated with transition and relocation include a growing body of work that focuses on the study of culture and wider economic, social, political issues, and transition in sport psychology (e.g., Gutierrez, 1999; Parham, 2005, Schinke et al., 2006). These authors have highlighted the importance of culture and social location in shaping the transition experiences of ethnic minority groups. Gill (2002) pointed out that sport in general has been developed and viewed from the dominant Western perspective (male, white, heterosexual) and overlooks other social identities such as those based on race, gender, and class. Over the last 30 years several sport psychologists have started to examine the void in sport psychology that has resulted because of minimal attention to race, ethnicity, gender, and culture (Butryn, 2002; Duda and Allison, 1990; Kontos and Arguello, 2005; Martens, Mobley, and Zizzi, 2000; Parham, 2005; Schinke et al, 2006).

In the year 2000 in Australia, past and present AFL players from both Indigenous and non-Indigenous backgrounds attended a meeting with the primary goal of addressing issues faced by Indigenous AFL footballers. Subsequent to the meeting, Dr. Robert Kerr, Executive Officer of the AFLPA Players' Association (AFLPA) at that time, addressed the press about the current issues affecting Indigenous footballers in AFL clubs. These issues included; isolation, lack of family support, racial abuse, inadequate financial management, the need to promote education and training, attention to issues of numeracy and literacy and relocation (Australian Associated Press, 2000). Dr Kerr highlighted that almost all of the AFL clubs had insufficiently provided for new Indigenous recruits giving little recognition to the aforementioned issues. The increase in participation and the issues raised in the committee provided the impetus for the present research project, where the authors set out to explore AFL players' experiences and perceptions of relocation and settling into AFL clubs. Specifically, we intended to examine the processes of negotiating relocation and the nature and function of the support mechanisms in the relocation process for the players.

Although there has been a significant increase in participation in the AFL, some have raised concerns about the settlement and other experiences of Indigenous players joining AFL clubs. Leaving family and community ties can make relocation a difficult experience for any athlete and it is accentuated when an individual's identity and culture are tied to a specific geographical area or region (Dudgeon, Garvey and Pickett, 2000). People moving within their own country are not shielded from challenging experiences when moving into a new environment (Bhugra and Ayonrinde, 2004). Relocating away from home appears to be more challenging for an individual from a minoritized group because of social and cultural disparities and differences between dominant and nondominant ethnic groups as well as experiences of racism (Glover, Dudgeon and Huygens, 2005; Sellers, 1993; Sonn, Bishop and Humphreys, 2000). The way an individual from a non dominant ethnic group experiences relocation may be directly influenced by the degree of incongruence between his/her and the dominant group's value systems (Berry, 1999). Berry's research was further enhanced by his work with Indigenous Australians during the 1967 referendum. He expanded his existing theory of acculturation by including Indigenous Australians and the way in which they negotiated intergroup contact in their own country. He conducted a series of studies with Indigenous, immigrant and ethnocultural groups in Australia, Canada, and India and suggested two strategies for negotiating intergroup contact -- cultural maintenance and contact-participation. Cultural maintenance refers to the extent to which people maintained their cultural identity and behaviours such as continuing to wear traditional dress, attending social venues or clubs for people of the same culture, or celebrating cultural days or religious holidays. Contact-participation refers to the extent to which people valued and sought out contact with others outside their own group and their wish to participate in the daily life of the larger society.

Some researchers have focused on culture shock to illustrate the challenges of moving from one culture to another (Furham and Bochner, 1986; Sonn and Fisher, 2005; Zapf, 1993). Oberg (1960) defined culture shock as "precipitated by the anxiety that results from losing all our familiar signs and symbols of social intercourse" (p.177). A feeling of impotence may prevail when all of the familiar signs and symbols of social interaction an individual has taken for granted in one's own culture, have no place in the new culture he/she is moving into (Haskins, 1999). Circumstances leading to cultural shock depend upon previous experiences with other cultures, the degree of difference in one's own and the host culture, the degree of preparation, social support networks, and individual psychological characteristics (Furnham and Bochner, 1986).

Sonn et al. (2000) investigated the relocation and settlement experiences of Aboriginal students at a higher education institution in Western Australia. They reported that Indigenous students had to negotiate ways to deal with the relocation process and challenges associated with settlement (Furnham and Bochner, 1986). For one student moving away from a context characterised by separation between groups to a main city that is more integrated resulted in a heightened awareness of her racial and cultural identity. The experience of interacting with most 'white' people who she was previously separated from resulted in challenges for settlement and intergroup relations (Sonn et al.). The differences in social and community structures because of the disparities between metropolitan and rural remote areas may also challenge relocation and settlement. As one Indigenous student remarked, "We have all those barriers to overcome which are probably similar to overseas students, but it is different in a way because we are in our own country" (Sonn et al., p.9).

Michael Long who is recognised for his work in challenging racism entrenched in the football culture stated in a media story on the Indigenous Footballers camp of 2004 that:

> The issues they face are, homesickness, being away from family, living a different lifestyle, basically being in a different culture, being in a city like Melbourne or Perth and you come from such a remote community you've got to embrace it and vice versa they learn a lot about you, the club (Roberts, 2005)

Relocation is not as simple as moving from one place to the next; it involves re-defining oneself in a new environment and negotiating how to maintain a sense of self in that new environment. The way an individual negotiates settlement in a new sociocultural environment requires the ability to manage daily life and the difficulties associated with the new environment (Berry, 2003). To adapt to the new environment depends on an individual's psychological and physical wellbeing. At an intrapersonal level, this is enhanced by personality characteristics such as a strong identity and self worth (Berry, 1997). At an interpersonal level, social support is believed to enhance adaptation, and at an organisational level, adaptation is facilitated by cultural awareness from both the receiving environment and the individual making the relocation and the intergroup attitudes. At a deeper ontological level cultural embeddedness can also serve a protective function and is reflected in the notion kindredness. Dudgeon and Oxenham (1989) described kindredness as "an implicit depth of feeling/spirituality which transcends our cultural diversity and contributes to the continuing unification of other Aboriginal people." (p. 37) Kindredness connects a person to both country and other Indigenous Australians. Goodes (2008) described kindredness and Indigenous identity in the following way;

> It's not about a map, not a town or a community you can stick a pin into and say "that's home" because it's not about a place. We all come from different places and different experiences, yet we come from the same place inside. What we have is a knowledge. A culture. And an understanding borne of being different in skin colour, which in Australia means far more off the football field, but that's where people like my teammate Micky O'Laughlin and I get to express our Aboriginality. (p.19)

Understanding relocation as a transactional process broadens the definition to include the interplay between person, environment, and society. According to Cronson and Mitchell (1997), moving to a new city is a major life event. Being drafted to play football in the AFL may involve two major life events – relocation to join a club in a different area or city and major career shift (progressing from one level of football to the highest echelon). These two major transitions involve adaptation, which refers to how people from a given culture "understand their surroundings [and within these learn to] function competently (Fiske, 2004, p. 25). "Humans are adapted to fit into face-to-face groups; groups are important to survival. People are not adapted to survive as isolated individuals (Fiske, p.12). If there is a degree of consistency in norms and expectations between the existing and new cultures, adaptation may materialise quickly (Marks and Jones, 2004). Adjusting to the new environment may depend on other considerations including; an individual's ability to deal with expectations of the receiving environment; establishing whether the individual is familiar with the future destination; ensuring the individual has the opportunity to access family and social supports; and investigating how an individual perceives the new move. The parallel processes of identity formation or resynthesis may also challenge adaptation to the new environment. Juggling the move, new career, settlement and answering the coinciding identity questions such as "Who am I?" illustrate some of the complexities of relocation.

To date there has been inadequate consideration of the relocation experiences of Indigenous Australians into the AFL. Within the current study, we aim to examine relocation and adaptation experiences and specifically; 1) describe and clarify the challenges faced by Indigenous footballers joining interstate AFL clubs, 2) identify the social, cultural and psychological resources that facilitate transition and adaptation.

METHODOLOGY

Limited research has been conducted investigating the relocation experiences of Indigenous Australian football players in the AFL. Through the current study the researchers sought to identify and describe the relocation processes from the vantage point of a group of Indigenous footballers. However, researchers have warned about the exploitative nature of social and scientific research in relation to Indigenous peoples (e.g., L. T. Smith, 1999). There have been extensive advances in developing research approaches that are sensitive to the realities and needs of Indigenous people and other minorities involved in research programmes (e.g. Schinke et al. 2006; Smith, 1999). The current study was informed by the principles suggested by the National Health and Medical Research Council (NHMRC) for engaging in responsive research. The NHMRC emphasise collaboration, competence and reflexivity. In this research we engaged in a collaborative process that centred on the establishment of an advisory group. The advisory group played a central role in promoting relationships within the Indigenous community, mentoring the first author about Indigenous cultural processes, and fostering a bridge role between different groups (Brodsky, O'Campo and Aronson, 1999; Dudgeon, Garvey and Pickett, 2000; Kim, Kim and Kelly, 2006; Sue, 2006; Westerman, 2004). The advisory group also fostered critical reflexivity. Following Parker (2003), we define critical reflexivity as a process in which we examine our own assumptions, motivations, and professional and personal identities in the context of relating across cultural boundaries. Critical reflexivity also requires that we understand the political and ideological nature of research and knowledge production and the implications research and knowledge production for those we seek to work with. In this research, the advisory group fostered critical reflection by supporting the first author in examining issues of colonialism and racism as well as exploring her anxiety about addressing unfamiliar issues or topics and accountability for the research process.

Within this collaborative model, a qualitative research design was adopted because it has the potential to empower a person when the researcher provides a space for the participants to voice their own subjective experiences. More specifically, qualitative research is naturalistic and through it, the researcher seeks to understand the subjective experiences of individuals and the meanings that they attribute to events (Patton, 2004; J. A. Smith, 1999, 2004).

Ethical Considerations

Given this research process involved Indigenous football players, a primary ethical responsibility was to seek the advice from cultural advisors. The cultural advisors recommended that a Strength, Weakness, Opportunity and Threat (S.W.O.T) analysis be used to identify the strengths, weaknesses, opportunities, and threats involved in the research, and to identify the internal and external factors that are favourable and unfavourable for individuals participating in the research. The S.W.O.T. analysis was recommended and driven by members of the Advisory group for the purpose of minimising harmful effects on participants and providing a basis for preventative support measures for participants if required. The main threats were; topics of harm, misinterpretation of information by community, poorly communicated relaying of information to participants, and breach of confidentiality.

Participants

The first author worked with the AFLPA and this facilitated an invitation to the first author to attend the 2006 AFLPA Indigenous camp to recruit participants. Two trusted people who were already known to the footballers, the AFLPA Indigenous Programme Coordinator and AFL Sports Ready Project Manager, facilitated the relationships with the participants

(Fielder et al., 2000). A total of 10 Indigenous Australian football players representing seven Victorian AFL clubs, belonging to eight different Indigenous nations spanning four Australian states and territories participated. Five participants were interviewed within 12 months of relocating to Victoria and ages ranged from 18 to 22 years (new draftees) and five participants who had relocated prior to 2002 (established players) whose ages ranged from 23 to 27 years. Selection of participants required that they first identify as Indigenous Australian and second be listed as an AFL player.

Recruiting Participants

After the first stage of recruitment at the AFLPA Indigenous camp, participants were contacted by telephone and during each conversation the following five steps ensued. First, each participant was offered the option of having an advisory group member present during the interview and reminded about the role of the advisory group. Second, participants were offered the opportunity to view the letters of disclosure containing information regarding traditional tribal origins, family ties, and professional status from the advisory group. Similarly, letters of disclosure containing information pertaining to professional status, family background, education, and knowledge of Indigenous culture from the researcher was available for the prospective participant. Third, each participant was asked to nominate a venue suitable for the interviews to take place. Fourth, during this phone call the first author checked in with participant that they had understood the content of the information for participants. Fifth, participants were asked if the interviews could be audio taped.

Interview Guide and Process

Guiding questions were developed in consultation with advisory group members based on the issues they anticipated may emerge for participants and based on research conducted with Indigenous participants who have relocated for study and career purposes (see Sonn et al., 2000). Some of the topics and questions included: the role of social supports and networks (Who would you say supported you most during this time?), settlement experiences (What did you do to get through a season being away from home, partner, children?), and family and community reactions to participant leaving home (How did the family respond to the news of you being selected by a Victorian club?).

Prior to interviewing, each participant was reminded of the strict confidentiality of responses and that there were no correct or incorrect responses. Participants were also reminded that participation in the research was voluntary and they could withdraw at any time without the need for any reason or explanation and without penalty. Participants had the opportunity to ask questions throughout the interview. Participants were debriefed after completion of the interview allowing the opportunity for additional conversation and questions. For example, at the end of the meeting with one of the participants, we were walking back to the clubrooms discussing the interview and how he felt about the procedure. The participant began talking about the difficulties he experienced being away from his family. Each participant was informed that once the audiotapes were transcribed, they would be contacted via post, telephone, or email to let them know that the transcript had been completed and was ready for review. Each participant chose a method of contact (email or post) and agreed to review the transcript. The aim of reviewing the transcript was to add any missing information the participant felt was relevant or necessary, and change any information in the transcript that was inaccurate in their view. Interviews were semi-structured (interviewer had a list of guide questions to keep conversation flowing) and conversational, allowing participants to speak about issues that matter to them. Semi-structured interviews invite a conversational format and provide a method conducive to building rapport with each participant (Glesne and Peskin, 1992; Patton, 2004).

Data Analysis

Data was analysed for unique and recurring themes following the procedures outlined by J. A. Smith (1999) and Patton (2004). Sections of the text were highlighted and short descriptive headings (e.g. family's reaction to player leaving home) written in the right hand margin. This resulted in a list of major themes and sub themes that was constructed to capture the issues discussed in the interviews. Microsoft Excel was used to produce a table with each of the themes and the participants' corresponding statements. Each participant's information was colour coded. Participants, advisory group, and authors' reviewed the data thereby providing analyst triangulation and enhancing the trustworthiness of the analysis of the data.

FINDINGS

Following data analysis we constructed several themes that can be conceptualised as facilitative and barrier factors.

Table 1. Themes in The Relocation Experiences

Function	Theme	Category
Barriers	Culture Shock	Indigenous Visibility
		Isolation
		Professional Training
		Homesickness
	Racism	Homogenisation
		Stereotyping
Facilitative	Social Support	Family
		Mentoring
		Kindredness

Barrier factors are those that hinder the relocation and adaptation processes and included challenges related to the lack of familiarity with the new physical, social and cultural environment as well as dynamics related to intergroup relations. Facilitative factors are those that enable the relocation and adaptation processes by buffering or protecting individuals from adverse events. These factors include social and cultural resources that provide supportive functions to individuals. Both Barriers and Facilitative factors are listed in Table 1. Pseudonyms are used in reporting the findings.

Culture Shock

Most transition experiences can involve barriers that can affect relocation and settlement. In the current study participants mentioned experiences that resemble culture shock. Culture shock occurred when participants were faced with the lack of indigenous visibility, isolation, and professional training regimes. James, a new draftee, said: "You don't see many Indigenous people down here and when you do it's sort of special because you have that comradeship, you learn to adapt though. There's more (Indigenous) people coming through now."He continuedstating that: "Traffic is a big one. I still haven't adapted to the traffic. Just the culture down here, you have to change everything. Like (hometown) is easy going, do whatever you want whereas in Melbourne you've got to watch your step and everything you do". Chris, another new draftee, said: "Getting used to training. I remember I used to come home from training about 1:30pm, 2:00pm and wouldn't even get to my room, I'd fall asleep on the couch" and, another new draftee, Max, commented that: "There is so much paperwork; I am not too good with that. They should warn you about the paperwork". (Max, New Draftee)

Homesickness is part of the culture shock experience and was also evident in the transcripts. Chris described his experience in the following way: "I do think about homesickness a fair bit, that's probably the biggest thing. I grew up probably looking after my brothers and sisters 'cos I was the eldest. You can't just get up and go around the corner and see family. I used to ring home about 4 or 5 times a week when I first got here and I went home at least 7 or 8 times". William, an established player, who had been in the AFL system for over five years, described his ongoing feelings of homesickness:

> I think you experience a lot of lonely times, a lot of down times, but there's always light at the end of the tunnel you know, nothing is ever smooth sailing so you have to roll with the punches but um it takes a while to get used to a place. It probably took me three or four years to get comfortable here and I just stuck it out and was pretty lucky I was playing games early on and that sort of made it easier. Not having the family there is always the hard bit and not working a lot and not having enough money is hard on them too but thankfully, I can pay my own way now. The hardest thing was not having family there to fall back on.

Racism

Another barrier experienced by some participants was racism, which was reflected in practices that homogenised Indigenous players. Racism operates as a form of stereotyping that undermines the individuality and agency of each person because they are judged according to a set of predetermined expectations. Paul, a new draftee, described his experiences in the following way:

If you've got some issues (coach) will pull you aside and tell you...it doesn't mean just because you're Indigenous you will experience what Michael Long experienced. There are very different cultures and different languages with Aboriginals so everything is different to what they say. They say all Aboriginals are the same but they're not. That's the one thing everyone has got to get straight, we're not all the same.

Alexander, an established player, made a similar comment:

When I got drafted they had just had the (Indigenous player) era, 'cous' was probably one of the best Indigenous players going around. The only thing that pissed me off a little bit was that I think that a couple of things that he used to do away from the club with his night life, I think a lot of it reflected back on me when I was there. Therefore, they, a lot of the club thought his behaviours were going to be my behaviours and that sort of ticked me off a little bit. Dad got that sort of drift and didn't appreciate it either.

Here the diversity of Indigenous Australians is denied and players are categorised according to scripts produced by mainstream Australia. The scripts, in turn, inform expectations about how Indigenous players will behave. This is what Hall (1990) referred to as inferential racism.

Social Support

A key theme that we identified can be understood using the notion social support. Social support includes those *family* members who relocate with the player and provides a range of supportive functions such as someone to talk with and that helps put the struggle of relocation into perspective. Campbell, a new draftee, described the importance of relocating with a family member in the following way:

It would have been pretty hard without my mum. I remember speaking to a lot of boys last year, the other Indigenous boys that got drafted and found it hard 'cos they were missing their families. Me having mum here they said "You're lucky, I wish I had my parents here". That opened my eyes up and I saw I was lucky to have my mum here and have her help me out. Takes my mind off other things being with my mum and just being able to talk about something else other than footy.

Support can also include mentors such as a family friend or an existing Indigenous player in the new context. *Mentoring* can take on many forms including validating players' experiences. Chris felt that a family friend was crucial for his relocation and settlement;

My dad had friends here and I met Greg through one of my dad's friends. It was really good having him here because we are so similar, brought up the same, he understands. It's been real hard but having said that, Greg has been really good and helped me out a lot. Sometimes I have experienced times when I am trying to explain something and people don't seem to understand what I am saying. I think to myself "What the hell's wrong with this fricken idiot". I don't know how to explain it, but sometimes when you are different you feel as though others don't understand you. It was hard but I had Greg, he understood me. I was lucky to have him.

Max relied on the knowledge, familiarity, and open door from an established Indigenous footballer at his club. He stated that: "There is another older Aboriginal player at the club and he has helped me heaps…. Just because he was Aboriginal, I just felt comfortable with him from the start. I didn't know him before I moved to Melbourne and we just clicked. He treated me like a brother. If I didn't have him I don't know what I would have done." A third way in which support is derived is tied with the notion of kindredness (Dudgeon and Oxenham, 1989). The term kindredness is used to denote a shared tacit experience between Indigenous footballers and was noted by many participants as an important relationship that facilitated relocation, settlement, and adaptation in a new environment. William described it in the following way;

> It is just having people around you, you can trust, it is probably the same with anyone, whenever another Aboriginal or Indigenous person comes to the club you just always immediately feel comfortable with them, because they know what it's like and it is so much easier to relate to them. They know and you know what they are going through because you have been in that boat at some stage.

Although Oliver, an established player, did not use the term kindredness, he spoke about the values and characteristics he and other Indigenous players shared that illustrate the features of kindredness. He commented that:

> It's one of those things having older Aboriginal players at the club, there are (number) of us, they kind of look up to us. You look after them, that's just the way we are, we just sense that we got to make them feel welcome, I mean we all get on well. We don't even realise it but they are probably going home and think they are looking up to us, and we just treat them on the same level. That's our job to make them feel welcome, it's nothing different, that's just the way we are.

These three factors do not operate in isolation, but must be understood within a broader historical, social and cultural context as well as the history of race relations in Australia. Each player emphasises different aspects of support. For some players family is central and, for others, Indigenous players or friends are important supports. But for all players there is kindredness that informs their sense of self. This is not an essentialist notion, rather it is a dynamic notion that speaks to the historical, lived and situated experiences that informs Indigenous realities (Dudgeon and Oxenham, 1989).

DISCUSSION

From the findings there is indication that relocation and adaptation is a complex process that can be facilitated and hindered by a host of factors. In this research we identified social support as facilitative while culture shock and forms of racism worked as barriers to the relocation and adjustment processes. In this section we will discuss the themes (i.e., culture shock, racism, and social support) that we identified in relation to the relevant literature.

Culture Shock

Many of the initial challenges experienced by Indigenous players in the current study can be understood as culture shock. These challenges included Indigenous invisibility, isolation, and professional training regimes. Those players who experienced a degree of consistency between their home and new environment tended to settle quickly as has been indicated in other research on relocation (Farrington et al., 2001; Furnham and Bochner, 1986; Kutieleh, Egege and Morgan, 2002; Sonn and Fisher, 2005; Sonn et al, 2000; Zapf, 1993). Indigenous AFL players moving away from smaller towns with fewer non-Indigenous Australians were faced with a heightened awareness of their own racial and cultural identity. Some players felt as though the differences between new and home environments were too drastic to adjust to in their first year of football. The lack of Indigenous visibility in AFL clubs and in the general community was also considered a barrier for adaptation. Limited access to Indigenous Australians can contribute to feelings of loneliness and sometimes a sense of "standing out" and being on show. Enhancing Indigenous visibility in the AFL is a way of combating culture shock. Yet, currently Indigenous visibility in coaching and administrative roles is rare and does send a misleading message about opportunities for Indigenous footballers after their football careers have ended. This is a problematic situation because the lack of representation may be interpreted as Indigenous players being locked into roles that do not extend to the administration and governing of football.

Similar to McCubbin's (1998) findings, it can be argued that the host AFL club has the responsibility of creating an environment that is supportive and will foster a sense of community. It is important for receiving AFL environments to create a welcoming environment for the new players. Such an environment may include having space for family members to visit, access to a mentor or like-minded person offering an open door, and education and information sharing between all parties about the home and receiving environment. Many things can be done to promote coherence, which relies on the mutual understanding of each player's needs. Communication is essential in the planning processes, not just between the player and manager, but also between the club, player, and family. As McCubbin et al. (1998) have stated, a stronger sense of coherence is created when the individual relocating feels that they fit, belong, have some say in their future, and have some degree of predictability in a new place.

Racism

The findings highlight the complex way in which racism manifests. In the present study racism was reflected in tendencies that homogenise Indigenous players in the AFL. These processes of treating all Indigenous players as the same is akin to inferential racism (Hall, 1990), which means treating players on the basis of unexamined assumptions and expectations. Hallinan et al., (2005; Glover et al., 2005) also discussed the role of this stereotyping in reproducing new racisms. Some participants experienced first hand the fall-out from previous Indigenous players behaving badly at their AFL clubs. They were "warned" about what not to do, and felt there was an expectation that they too would make those mistakes. There were many stories pertaining to modern racism, whereby an individual from a minority group is judged by dominant mainstream values. Players who were warned about "how not to act" were singled out based on their Indigeneity and appearance. One participant noticed a new draftee was warned about a previous Indigenous player's indiscretions but a higher drafted Indigenous player with a fairer complexion did not receive a caution. Engaging with people based on the assumptions of homogeneity can lead to 'sensitive' stereotyping (Andersen, 1993). A sensitive stereotyper may have good intentions, but has an unclear understanding of his or her own assumptions and stereotypes and may overlook or minimise contextual cultural information or overgeneralise from a limited level of cultural awareness (Gridley, 2005). Players were very clear about what "worked" during their transitions. Several times they mentioned people in positions of coach, PDM, and player agent, who respected each new recruit's individuality. Taking this approach was considered supportive and culturally aware in comparison with those that adopted an "expert" position. Consultation with and listening to players about their needs was described by players as more helpful than taking a position of expert knower, which more often than not reproduces racism and exclusion (Green and Sonn, 2006). Although racism occurs at every level of society, many Indigenous players are resisting and challenging stereotypes through community work and by expressing their 'voice' and telling their own story. Engaging in community is an excellent tool for mentoring and helping younger Indigenous Australians to have self-belief and a willingness to dream and to maintain contact with one's own culture. At another level, being a role model to both Indigenous and non-Indigenous Australians was considered a way of breaking down negative stereotypes, showing others what is achieved with determination, self-belief, and dedication.

In this study the researchers investigated the relocation and settlement experiences of Indigenous Australian footballers in the AFL. Following qualitative analyses of interview data it was evident that the factors that influence Indigenous AFL footballer's experiences are diverse and operate at various levels of the social ecology. Based on the analysis, the researchers showed that players who identified with their old and new environments tended to integrate into their role as AFL footballer easier than those who did not. A greater awareness and insight into the new environment and the possible hurdles to overcome assisted with settlement and adaptation. A combination of cultural maintenance and contact-participation appeared to enhance the likelihood of adaptation and settlement (McCubbin, 1998).

Social Support

Players who relocated with family tended to settle and adjust because of their additional support. These findings are consistent with previous research (Berry, 1997; Cutrona, 1990; Gullan, 2000; Petch, 2006; Robinson, 2005; Sarason and Duck, 2001; Trickett and Buchannan, 2001) showing the beneficial role of social support in buffering stressful experiences. It was also found that social support was important during the transition process because it provides continuity in terms of identity, culture, and sense of belonging. Although relocating with family can strengthen the support base for the Indigenous footballer, it can also add to the stress of transition and adjustment. It often means the entire family is separated from their own sources of support including extended family and country. A common observation was that each Indigenous player joining an AFL club has 45 new friends immediately; but the family are not so fortunate. This research suggests that footballers who relocated with parents had a smoother transition experience compared with footballers that relocated with partners (and children). These findings are consistent with McCubbin's (1998) research with migrant families in the armed forces. Players struggled with their relocation and settlement when their partners experienced difficulties adapting and finding their own autonomy and independence through new communal supports. With the strict demands of AFL as an elite sport time spent with family is dictated by training and game schedules, club appearances, charity work and, in some cases, the footballer may also have a part time job which ultimately limits the quality time spent with family, a key ingredient for successful adaptation (see McCubbin 1998).

Having access to a person who is culturally aware and provides an 'open door' type of support was seen as important. Similar to the findings of Sartour (1992) and Sonn et al. (2000), having somewhere to go to that resembles home, where a person feels they belong and can be themselves, was crucial for settlement and adaptation. Players chose to be with like-minded people (mentors) where they could express and strongly identify with their own Indigenous culture. Some players felt their AFL clubs minimised the importance of culture and felt pressured to withhold from asserting or expressing their cultural identity. One player went as far as saying he believed there was a strong expectation for him to assimilate into the mainstream culture at the club, but instead chose to seek out others that were similar to him for consensual validation.

A common theme emerging in the data was the familiarity shared among Indigenous footballers, knowledge about each other's culture even if they have lived miles apart. We used the notion of *kindredness*, a term coined by Dudgeon and Oxenham (1989) to reflect this shared emotional connection. Although their 'country' was sometimes 1200 kilometres apart, players talked of sharing a bond. The players reported the importance of extended family, ancestry, and heritage (kinship), and referred to the mutual understanding Indigenous Australians share. It is during these interactions that players spoke of being able to make sense of their new environment, when they were with similar others and sharing experiences. Whether the player was mentoring or being mentored, each discussed the importance of being with others from a similar cultural background.

Almost all players engaged more with other Indigenous Australians (teammates, friends, family) and this facilitates cultural maintenance (Berry, 1999).As time progressed, some players engaged more with others outside of their group – a strategy known as contact-participation (Berry). Players who combined cultural maintenance and contact participation adapted to their new environments (home and AFL club) and settled into their new routines quicker than the players who preferred contact with only Indigenous Australians. Over-reliance on social supports was sometimes described as disadvantageous to adaptation and settlement it can prolong the transition process thereby undermining adaptation. Sonn and Fisher (2005) called this an insular escape mechanism – a survival strategy in an ostensibly hostile environment. There appeared to be several reasons for players choosing to socialise with only Indigenous people, including a lack of Indigenous visibility at the club, uncertainty about how to integrate their culture into their new environment, feeling uncomfortable in a predominantly white environment, and feeling lost.

CONCLUSION

The current project responded to the call for research that is inclusive and respectful. To achieve culturally inclusive and competent research, an advisory group was established and several processes implemented to ensure Indigenous voices are involved in formulation and execution of the research. To ensure and sustain engagement was difficult and often not possible. However, there is much more that needs to be done to promote culturally inclusive research. For example, we can extend processes for participation and inclusion by using "talking circles" and "community meetings" or similar grounded techniques for information gathering and sharing. Having greater community involvement would have enriched the current study and strengthened collaboration. Nevertheless, the current study provides a glimpse into the experiences of 10 Indigenous Australian footballers and how they have negotiated their relocation experiences away from their home and into mainstream cultural settings. Although social and economic indicators continue to point to disparities between Indigenous and non-Indigenous Australian wellbeing, this study provide examples of stories of strength, perseverance, and patience. Importantly, from the research there is indication that the footballers must negotiate multiple transitions as they become professional footballers. Recognising and understanding these dynamic transitions is important because at the heart of the transition and settlement process is the ongoing struggle to protect and strengthen Indigenous cultural identities within a broader context of race relations -- Australian Football League clubs provide the setting for these negotiations.

REFERENCES

Andersen, M. (1993). Questionable sensitivity: A comment on Lee and Rotella. *The Sport Psychologist, 7,* 1-3.

Australian Associated Press (2000, November 20). AFL clubs fail Koori recruits. *Herald Sun,* p. 26.

Australian Bureau of Statistics (2006). *Year Book of Australia,* Retrieved March, 20, 2007, from URL: http//www.abs.gov.au.

Australian Football League Players' Association (2009). 82 Indigenous players on AFL lists 2009. [URL:http://aflpa.com.au/articleimage/82-indigenous-players-afl-lists-2009].

Berry, J. (1997). Immigration, acculturation and adaptation. *Applied Psychology: An International Review, 46,* 5-68.

Berry, J. (1999). Aboriginal cultural identity. *Canadian Journal of Native Studies, 19,* 1-36.

Berry, J. (2003). Conceptual approaches to acculturation. In K. M. Chun, P. B. Organista, and G. Marin (Eds.), *Acculturation: Advances in theory, measurement and applied research*(pp. 17-37). Washington, D.C.: American Psychological Assoc.

Bhugra, D., and Ayonrinde, O. (2004). Depression in migrant and ethnic minorities. *Advances in Psychiatric Treatment, 10,* 13-17.

Brodsky, A., O'Campo, P. J., and Aronson, R. E. (1999). PSOC in community context: Multilevel correlates of a measure of psychological sense of community in low-income, urban neighbourhoods. *Journal of Community Psychology, 27,* 659-679.

Butryn, T. M. (2002). Critically examining white racial identity and privilege in sport psychology consulting. *The Sport Psychologist, 16,* 316-336.

Cronson, H., and Mitchell, G. (1987). Athletes and their families: Adapting to the stresses of professional sports. *The Physician and Sportsmedicine, 15,* 121-127.

Cutrona, C. E. (1990). Stress and social support: In search of optimal matching. *Journal of Social and Clinical Psychology, 9,* 3-14.

Duda, J. L., and Allison, M. T. (1990). Cross-cultural analysis in exercise and sport psychology: A void in the field. *Journal of Sport and Exercise Psychology, 12,* 114-131.

Dudgeon, P., Garvey, D., and Pickett, H. (Eds.). (2000). *Working with Indigenous Australians: A handbook for psychologists.* Perth, Australia: Gunada Press.

Dudgeon, P., and Oxenham, D. (1989). The complexity of Aboriginal diversity: Identity and kindredness. *Black Voices, 5(1),* 22-39.

Farrington, S., Page, S., and DiGregorio, K. (2001). The things that matter: Understanding the factors that affect the participation and retention of Indigenous students in the Cadigal program at the Faculty of Health Sciences, University of Sydney. *Journal of the Australian and New Zealand Student Services Association, 18,* 40- 55.

Fielder, J., Roberts, J., and Abdullah, J. (2000). Research with Indigenous communities. In P. Dudgeon, D. Garvey, and H. Pickett, (Eds.), *Working with Indigenous Australians: A handbook for psychologists* (pp. 349-356). Perth, Australia: Gunada Press.

Fiske, S. T. (2004). *Social beings: A core motives approach to social psychology.* NJ: Wiley.

Fontana, A., and Frey, J. H. (2000). The interview: From structured questions to negotiated text. In N. K. Denzin and Y. S. Lincoln (Eds.), *Handbook of qualitative research*(2nd ed) (pp. 1845- 672). Thousand Oaks, CA: Sage Publications.

Furnham, A., and Bochner, S. (1986). *Culture Shock: Psychological responses to unfamiliar environments.* London, UK: Methuen.

Gill, D.L. (2002). Gender and sport behaviour. In T. Horn (Ed.), *Advances in sport psychology (2nd ed.).* (pp. 355-376). South Australia, Australia: Human Kinetics.

Glesne, C., and Peshkin, A. (1992). *Becoming qualitative researchers: An introduction.* White Plains, NY: Longman.

Glover, M., Dudgeon, P., and Huygens, I. (2005). Colonization and racism. G. Nelson and I. Prilleltensky (Eds.), *Community psychology: In pursuit of liberation and wellbeing* (pp. 330-347). New York, NY: Palgrave.

Green, M.J. and Sonn, C.C. (2006). Problematising the discourses of the dominant: Whiteness and reconciliation. *Journal of Community and Applied Social Psychology, 16,* 379-395.

Gridley, H. (2005). Commentary on Chapter 11. In M. Andersen (Ed.), *Sport psychology in Practice* (pp. 217-222). Chapaigne, IL: Human Kinetics.

Godwell, D. (2000). Playing the game: is sport as good for race relations as we'd like to think? *Australian Aboriginal Studies, 1and2,* 12-19.

Goodes, A. (2008). AFL Record: Celebration. Vol 97, Round 9 May 23-25. *Australian Football League.*Docklands, Australia: AFL Publishing.

Gullan, S. (2000, April 22). Eagle spreads his wings. *Herald Sun,* Weekend Sport, pp.42-44.

Gutierrez, P. (1999). Links in the chain. *Sports Illustrated, 90,* 78-80.

Hall, S. (1990). "The Whites of Their Eyes: Racist Ideologies and the Media." In M. Alvarado and J. O. Thompson (Eds.), *The Media Reader.* (pp.7-23).London, UK: BFI Publishing.

Hallinan, C.J., Bruce, T., and Burke, M. (2005). Fresh Prince of colonial dome: Indigenous logic in the AFL. *Journal of the Football Studies Group, 8(1),* 68-78.

Haskins, D. (1999). Culture Shock. *College Teaching, 47,* 122-124.

Kim, I. J., Kim, L. I. C., and Kelly, J. G. (2006). Developing cultural competence in working with Korean immigrant families. *Journal of Community Psychology, 34*, 149-165.

Kontos, A. P., and Arguello, E. (2005). Sport psychology consulting with Latin American athletes. *Athletic Insight: The Online Journal of Sport Psychology, 7, Issue 3.* www.athletic insight.com.

Kutieleh, S., Egege, S., and Morgan, D. (2002). *To stay or not to stay: Factors affecting international and Indigenous students' decisions to persist with university study and the implications for support services.* Student Learning Centre: FlindersUniversity, Adelaide, South Australia.

McCubbin, H. I. (1998). Resiliency in African-American Families: Military families in foreign environments. In H. I. McCubbin, E. A . Thompson, A. I. Thompson and J. A. Futrell (Eds.), *Resiliency in ethnic minority families: African American families.* (Vol 2, pp. 179-205). Madison, WI: University of Wisconsin System.

McCubbin, H. I., Futrell, J. A., Thompson, E. A., and Thompson, A. I. (1998). Resilient Families in an ethnic and cultural context. In H. I. McCubbin, E. A. Thompson, A. I. Thompson and J. A. Futrell (Eds.), *Resiliency in ethnic minority families: African American families* (pp. 329- 351).Madison, WI: University of Wisconsin System.

Marks, H. M., and Jones, S. R. (2004). Community service in the transition: Shifts and continuities in participation from high school to college. *The Journal of Higher Education, 75*, 307-339.

Martens, M. P., Mobley, M., and Zizzi , S. J. (2000). Multicultural training in applied sport psychology. *The Sport Psychologist, 14*, 81-97.

National Health and Medical Research Council [NHMRC]. (1991). *Guidelines on ethical matters in Aboriginal and Torres Strait Islander research.* .[URL:http://www. health.gov.au/nhmrc/publicat/pdf/e11.pdf].

Oberg, K. (1960). Culture shock: Adjustment to new cultural environments. *Practical Anthropology, 7*, 177-182.

Parham, W. (2005). Raising the bar: Developing an understanding of athletes from racially, culturally, and ethnically diverse backgrounds. In M. Andersen (Ed.), *Sport psychology in practice,* (pp. 201-215). Champaigne, IL: Human Kinetics.

Parker, I. (2005). *Qualitative psychology: Introducing radical psychology.* Maidenhead, UK: Open University Press.

Patton, M: Q. (2002). *Qualitative research and evaluation methods.* (3rd ed.). Thousand Oaks, CA: Sage Publications.

Petch, C. (2006, May 5). Young tiger picks right day to make his debut, dream come true, *Herald Sun,* Sport, 76.

Roberts, B. (Producer) (2005). Australian Football League Players' Association Indigenous Camp 2004. Fox Footy, A Foxtel Production.

Robinson, M. (2005, June 8). So Long. *Herald Sun.* p. 88.

Sarason, B., and Duck, S. (2001). *Personal relationships: Implications for clinical and community Psychology.* Chichester, England: John Wiley and Sons.

Sartour, T. (1992). Reply to Bourke. *Jumbunna News,* 1 (4), University of Technology; Sydney, Australia.

Schinke, R. J., Michel, G., Gauthier, A. P., Pickard, P., Danielson, R., Peltier, D., et al. (2006). The adaptation to the mainstream in elite sport: A Canadian Aboriginal perspective. *The Sport Psychologist, 20*, 435-448.

Sellers, R. (1993). Black student-athletes: Reaping the benefits or recovering from the exploitation. In D. Brooks, and R. Althouse. (Eds.), *Racism in college athletics: The African-American athlete's experience.* Morgantown, WV: Fitness Information Technology, Inc.

Smith, J. A. (1999). Part I: The search for meanings. In J. A. Smith, R. Harre, and L. Van Lagenhove (Eds.), *Rethinking methods in psychology,* (pp. 8- 26). London, UK: Sage Publications.

Smith, L. T. (1999). *Decolonising Methodologies: Researching and Indigenous Peoples.* Dunedin, NZ: University of Otago Press.

Smith, J. A. (2004). Reflecting on the development of interpretive phenomenological analysis and its contribution to qualitative research in psychology. *Qualitative research in psychology, 1,* 39-54.

Sonn, C. C., Bishop, B. J., and Humphries, R. (2000). Encounters with the dominant culture: Indigenous student's experiences in mainstream education. *Australian Psychologist, 35,* 128-135.

Sonn, C. C, and Fisher, A. T. (2005). Immigration and Adaptation: Confronting the Challenges of cultural diversity.In G. Nelson and I. Prilleltensky (Eds.), *Community psychology: In pursuit of liberation and wellbeing* (pp.348-363). New York: Palgrave Macmillan.

Sue, S. (2006). Cultural Competency: From philosophy to research and practice. *Journal of Community Psychology, 34,* 237-245.

Trickett, E., and Buchanan, R. (2001). The role of personal relationships in transitions: Contributions of an ecological perspective. In B. Sarason and S. Duck (Eds.), *Personal relationships: Implications for clinical and community psychology* (pp. 141-157). Chichester, UK: John Wiley and Sons.

Westerman, T. (2004). Guest Editorial. Engagement of Indigenous clients in mental health services: What role do cultural differences play? *Australian e-journal for the Advancement of Mental Health, 3,(3).* www.auseinet.com/journal/vol3iss3/westermaneditorial.pdf

Zapf, M. K. (1993). Remote Practice and Culture Shock: Social Workers moving to Isolated Northern Regions. *Social Work, 38(6),* 694-705.

INDEX

C

F

G

H

I

N

O

P

Q